GUN AND SOCIETY

The Social and Existential Roots of the American Attachment to Firearms

William R. Tonso
University of Evansville

UNIVERSITY
PRESS OF
AMERICA

Copyright © 1982 by

University Press of America, Inc.

P.O. Box 19101, Washington, D.C. 20036

Printed in the United States of America

Library of Congress Cataloging in Publication Data

Tonso, William R.
  Gun and society.

  Revision of thesis (Ph. D.)--Southern Illinois
University, 1976.
  Bibliography: p.
  Includes index.
  1. Firearms--Social aspects--United States.
I. Title.
TS533.2.T66 1982   306'.46   81-40261
ISBN 0-8191-2378-1   AACR2
ISBN 0-8191-2379-X (pbk.)

To Eva and Joe Tonso, my mother and father.

ACKNOWLEDGEMENTS

The author gratefully acknowledges permission to reprint from the following sources:

The Firearms Division of Colt Industries Operating
Corp for permission to utilize the quotes from several
Colt's advertisements.

Harper & Row, Publishers, Inc. for permission to quote
specified material from The Age of Firearms, by Robert
Held, copyright 1957 by Robert Held and Nancy Jenkins,
reprinted by permission of Harper & Row, Publishers,
Inc.

Random House, Inc., Alfred A. Knopf, Inc., for permission to reprint excerpts totaling approximately 465
words from "America as a Gun Culture", by Richard
Hofstadter, of American Violence: A Documentary History, edited by Richard Hofstadter and Michael Wallace.

TABLE OF CONTENTS

PREFACE

The idea for Gun and Society occurred to me sometime in the late 1960's as I began thinking seriously about a topic for my doctoral dissertation in sociology. I was determined that if I was going to expend all the time and effort that I suspected such a project would require that I was going to explore something that intrigued me, and that would be of interest to an audience far broader than my dissertation committee. Though several other interesting topics occurred to me, none of which had anything to do with firearms, I finally decided to explore the social and existential roots of the American attachment to firearms, and this book is an updated slightly revised version of the dissertation that resulted from my decision. For various reasons that I hope will become clear in the next few pages, I would like to share reflexively with the reader the sociological and other concerns that prompted me to explore this phenomenon and to write this book.

Since beginning my work toward a doctorate in sociology, I have been interested in those extremely relativistic sociological perspectives that focus on man's construction of reality through symbolic interaction--phenomenological and existential sociologies; the sociologies of knowledge, science, and sociology; and symbolic interactionism, etc.--as well as the non-moralistic varieties of conflict theory. My appreciation for these perspectives is not difficult to explain, since by the time I started my sociological studies in 1966 at the ripe old age of thirty-three, I had already been relativized through various life experiences. I was born in Herrin, Williamson County, Illinois, a small coal-mining town near the southern tip of the state; a town with a large Italian-American minority and an early 20th century history of Ku Klux Klan activity and labor and gang wars that has long fascinated me. I come from a close-knit, free-thinking, Italian (Piedmontese)-American family--a non-religious minority within an ethnic minority. While I have a Ph.D. in sociology (Southern Illinois University, Carbondale, 1976), I have an M.S. in business administration with a specialization in personnel management (S.I.U., 1966), and a B.S. in industrial education (S.I.U., 1955), a course of study that included machine design, mechanical and architectural drawing, and wood and metal shops. Between degrees, I served as an Air Force officer (an interceptor director at isolated Air Defense Command radar sta-

ix

tions), and worked as a purchasing expeditor in a washing machine plant, a cost accounting clerk in a rug cushion plant, and a supervisor of the handicapped in a closed workshop. While in graduate school, most of my friends were foreign students, and among them all of the major skin color variations, many nationalities, most of the worlds major religious perspectives, and several different political orientations were represented.

In other words, by the time that I started to get involved with sociology my ethnocentric complacency had already been disrupted by my first-hand exposure to the lifestyles and world views of many different class, ethnic, occupational, and academic groups. Consequently, I was prepared for and absorbed by those sociological perspectives that focus on the social construction of meaning, the meaningful basis of social action, and conflicting world views once I was exposed to them. And that exposure came early in my sociological studies through Reinhard Bendix's Work and Authority in Industry: Ideologies of Management in the Course of Industrialization and Arthur J. Vidich and Joseph Bensman's Small Town in Mass Society: Class, Power and Religion in a Rural Community, and continued through two courses from the late dramaturgical sociologist, Hugh D. Duncan, and a three-term theory sequence from the late sociologist of sociology, Alvin W. Gouldner, who from the fall of 1967 through the spring of 1968 commuted from St. Louis to Carbondale one day a week to teach that sequence.

There was never any doubt concerning the orientation that I would take to my study, therefore, but selecting a phenomenon to explore was complicated by the fact that there were several that I was interested in exploring. I considered doing a study of the coal-mining counties of my native Southern Illinois, focusing on the lifestyle and world view differences that helped to generate the ethnic conflicts that the area had experienced. The basis of my interest in this phenomenon, of course, was my own ethnic background and the stories that I had been told by various family members and friends about the Klan activities of the 1920's and related matters. I considered constructing an essentially symbolic interactionist theory of racial and ethnic discrimination and conflict. Again my interest in this broader ethnic project was related to my own experiences with ethnicity, but it was also prompted by my conviction that most social scientific explanations of race and ethnic relations that I had encountered were moralistic and ideologically contaminated. I considered studying the moralizing, editorializing, and propagandizing carried on through American newspaper comic strips. As an avid comic strip buff, I felt that the comics deserved more serious attention than they were receiving from social scientists. I even considered studying the unidentified flying object phenomenon. I no longer recall how I intended to approach that phenomenon, but the project still interests me and I now see it as a study in the sociology of science examining the paradigm clash between the sceptical scientific establishment on the one hand and those scientists who have begun to take UFOs seriously on the other hand. Though I personally am sceptical about UFOs, I have been interested in them since the big "flap" of 1947, and various experiences during my Air Force days and since have increased my interests in the social aspects of the phenomenon. Finally, I considered exploring the social and existential roots of the American attachment to firearms.

As was the case with the various other social phenomena that I considered examining, my fascination with the gun issue had personal as well as sociological roots. I had grown up with guns and with people who appreciated guns. Close and respected relatives and friends as well as many acquaintances of mine were collectors, target shooters, and/or hunters, and a few of these individuals, as civilians or as members of military or police forces, had regularly carried firearms. I had long owned firearms myself, and I had used them for target shooting, formal as well as informal. I was not a hunter, however. Though I had tried my hand at it, I had long been ambivalent about hunting due to my sympathetic feelings toward wild creatures. I had belonged to gun clubs in Illinois and Montana, and over the years I had fired nearly one hundred varieties of firearms ranging from a tiny .22 caliber derringer to a German 20mm anti-tank gun. And I had read a great deal about guns, their evolution and use, past and present, in the United States and elsewhere.

In other words, I had something that few other American social scientists of the time appeared to possess--a first-hand familiarity with the world of firearms and firearms users. And I also subscribed to a sociological frame of reference that allowed me to take

advantage of my access to a world that scholars of the
time had shown no interest in penetrating for the purpose of appreciative understanding, even though some of
their number were becoming quite critical of that world
due to its opposition to gun controls. I was even in a
position that allowed me to reverse the standard sociological approach to social phenomena. Instead of an
outsider sociologist attempting to gain entry into someone else's world in order to view that world from the
standpoint of an insider, I could as an insider step
outside and attempt to examine a previously taken-for-
granted world in relativistic sociological terms. The
project seemed made to order for me, but I doubt that I
would have even thought of it if those scholars who had
commented on the widespread civilian possession of firearms in the United States in the late 1960's and early
1970's had shown more concern for understanding the phenomenon than they had for making a case for gun controls.

To me, relativism is not a principle for any private citizen to live by; it is an analytical tool that
facilitates a social scientist's non-judgemental penetration of lifestyles, world views, and behavior that
he or she may or may not personally approve of but feels
called upon to examine, understand, and explain. Though
I have been fascinated by sociology since I started to
get seriously involved with the discipline, it did not
take me long to reach the conclusion that a large part
of what passes for sociology, and social and behavioral
science in general, is in one way or another blinded by
ethnocentrism and/or ideologically contaminated. Having
become very familiar with the social scientific literature on deviance and ethnic/race relations since I began
teaching in these areas at the University of Evansville
in 1969, I have become even more convinced of the existence of this contamination and dedicated to the losing
cause of combating it.

The reader should know that as a private citizen I
oppose gun controls on civil libertarian and what I consider to be practical grounds. But the reader should
also know that I am quite aware of my own ethnocentric
preferences and ideological commitments, and that as a
sociologist my appreciation for the socially-constructed
nature of my own preferences and commitments makes me
work very hard to keep to an absolute minimum my impo-
sition of them on the social phenomena I examine. Though
a number of the "scholarly" supports relied upon by ad-

xii

vocates of gun controls will be undermined in the following chapters, the goal of this book is scholarly, not political. What is being called into question, in other words, is ethnocentric, ideological "scholarship" that has taken too much for granted, not the political position--in this case gun control support--that has looked to that "scholarship" for legitimation. If I had chosen to do one of the ethnic relations studies mentioned above, I would have used it to make essentially the same critical points concerning the blind spots of biased social science.

I have had the experience of having former students of mine come up to me years after they had taken one of my courses and quote to me some profundity that they were convinced that I had uttered in that class; a profundity that was so out of keeping with anything that I have ever believed that I know that I could never have uttered it. I hope that I am not making the same mistake, but I recall Professor Gouldner saying something to the effect that one had to state one's scholarly conclusions dogmatically or they would not be taken seriously in the market place of ideas. If in fact, he did say something to that effect, he may have been correct, but I personally feel that the scholarly world could use much less dogmatism. What is presented in the following chapters is an honest attempt to penetrate a social phenomenon that has fascinated some Americans, including me, while it has infuriated some others, including a large part of the intellectual establishment. Through this study I have attempted to make a contribution to the sociological understanding of man as a social being, and even the study's underlying criticism of much that passes for social scientific scholarship is motivated by a sincere interest in promoting social science worthy of the name.

This book is not intended to be the final word on the gun phenomenon, and since it is not intended to serve as a scholarly support for a dogmatic opposition to gun controls, though I personally oppose such controls, I am free to admit that I am well aware of some of the study's limitations. The dissertation version of Chapter III, in fact, included a discussion of some of the epistemological problems associated with looking to history to support an argument based on the assumption that reality, historical and otherwise, is a social construct. All scholarly works have limitations, and criticism (supposedly other than ideologically based) is, after all, the name of the scholarly-scientific game.

Since the gun phenomenon is controversial in the United States, I have tried through this reflexive preface to let the reader know where I stand, personally as well as sociologically, in an attempt to reduce the possibility of misunderstanding. Now for a few words about the book itself. Chapter I of Gun and Society criticizes the "gun culture" view of the widespread civilian possession of firearms in the United States, and points out that the most publicized commentaries on the gun phenomenon take much too much for granted about firearms use, past and present, in the United States and elsewhere. After a summary and critique of the two most prominent explanations for the widespread civilian possession of firearms in the United States--the more publicized "cultural lag-vested interest" explanation subscribed to by those who advocate stricter gun controls, and the "utilitarian" explanation accepted by those who oppose such controls--Chapter II offers a "phenomenologically-oriented" explanation for the phenomenon. The chapter ends with a thesis statement composed of six propositions which attempt to explain how in theory patterns of firearms use in the United States and elsewhere can be accounted for by man's ability to create and use symbols as well as tools. Chapter III offers a means of testing--perhaps supporting would be more accurate-- these six propositions by "reading" firearms and placing them in historical and cross-cultural context. And this method is put to work in the next seven chapters of Gun and Society to support the six propositions of the study's thesis statement.

A brief discussion of the features and history of the basic types of firearms likely to be found in civilian hands down through the centuries in those parts of the world now considered to be modern, urban, and industrial is provided in Chapter IV. This chapter was written with those prospective readers in mind who know little about guns; consequently, technicalities have been kept to a minimum--"flintlock," for example, has been used to cover the snaphaunce and miquelet locks as well as the "true" flintlock. Chapter V describes the lifestyles and world views associated with various levels of society, as well as general social conditions, in western Europe and Japan since the introduction of firearms into these areas, and Chapter VI ties the evolution and use of shotguns, rifles, and handguns into

these worlds. Chapter VII describes social conditions
in what are now Australia, Canada, and the United States
since the introduction of firearms into these areas, and
Chapter VIII ties the evolution and use of shotguns,
rifles, and handguns into these worlds. Various recreational and symbolic aspects of firearms use that are
important to this study but that could not be incorporated readily into the preceding chapters are treated in
Chapter IX. And Chapter X pulls the material that has
been presented in Chapters IV through IX together and
relates it to the six propositions of the thesis statement that were presented at the end of Chapter II.

As noted previously, Gun and Society originated as
a doctoral dissertation, but I wrote it with a much
broader audience than my dissertation committee in mind.
Therefore, I owe a great debt of gratitude to the members of my committee (Professors Ernest Alix, Ned Mc-
Glynn, and Robert Rossel, all then of the S.I.U. sociology department, and Donald Detwiler of the history department); and particularly to my committee chairman and
dissertation advisor, Professor Peter A. Munch (now retired), for allowing me to do the study that I wanted
to do just as I wanted to do it. Their understanding
and cooperation made not only my dissertation but this
book possible. There are others whose assistance I
would also like to acknowledge.

Through a serendipitous chain of events, I became
acquainted with Don B. Kates, Jr., civil liberties at-
torney and prominent liberal opponent of gun controls,
during the spring of 1981. Since that time, Don has
sent me quite a bit of literature, including some information on gun ownership and control in Australia and
Canada that arrived just in time to be incorporated in
the revision of Chapter VIII. That material is much
appreciated and constitutes the only data used in this
study that I did not search out myself. Incidentally,
though I have been a member of the National Rifle Association since 1955, before gun control resurfaced as a
controversial issue after having faded during World War
II, to reduce the suspicion of ideological contamination
as much as possible, I did not ask for or receive any
assistance from the NRA, though in some areas this study would probably have benefited from such assistance.
As far as I know, no one at the NRA knew anything about
my book until the mid-spring of 1981.

The typist's work is hidden when most books are published, but this is not the case with those published by University Press of America. Consequently, Regina Racine has made a very visible contribution to this book, and I thank her for a job well done.

One of the members of my dissertation committee once accused me of being an anti-commaist, and I am afraid that grammatical perfection is still beyond my reach. However, several people helped me begin to bring some semblance of order to the chaos of the dissertation drafts upon which this book is based, with Barbara Halbrook making the greatest contribution toward that end.

Lone grammar editor for this final version of my study has been my wife, Beverley, however, and the least I can do is to give her a paragraph of her own to acknowledge her efforts, which were considerable. For the first two and a half years of our marriage, Beverley had to share me with my dissertation, and since then she has edited practically everything that I have written, including several papers and short articles dealing with gun ownership and controls. Consequently, I suspect that she is only half joking when she requests that I start writing about something besides guns. I may do just that. Thanks to her for the time taken from her busy student nursing to help me with such things. Since I have been the proof reader for this final copy, uncorrected errors reflect my shortcomings, not hers.

My gratitude to my parents, Eva and Joe Tonso, defies expression. I was introduced to the world of guns at a very early age by my father, as he and my mother took me on those memorable shooting expeditions to No. 7 mine pond, Dale Crossing, the wooden and iron bridges, and points in between out there in what to me was that wilderness past Herrin's eastern city limits. Without the insights into things symbolic that grew out of a childhood built around such events, I could not have considered this project. My parents also provided me with moral support through those years of shifting career interests that eventually brought me an all-consuming interest in sociology, and their direct contributions to this study have been considerable--my mother, for instance, did the first typewritten draft of what turned out to be this rather lengthy work. Thanks to them for all of these things, and much more. To them I dedicate this book.

CHAPTER I

AN AMERICAN GUN CULTURE?

INTRODUCTION

> The United States is the only modern
> industrial urban nation that persists in
> maintaining a gun culture. It is the
> only nation in which the possession of
> rifles, shotguns and handguns is lawfully
> prevalent among large numbers of its
> population.[1]

So said one of America's most prominent historians, the
late Richard Hofstadter, in an essay dealing with an
extremely controversial phenomenon that has been left
virtually untouched, in a non-aligned scholarly fashion
at least, by American social historians and behavioral
scientists.[2] In his essay Hofstadter discussed the
widespread civilian ownership of firearms in the United
States, and mentioned some possible reasons for the
existence of this undesirable (to him) state of affairs.
According to Hofstadter, those who have a vested interest in the domestic firearms industry have been able to
take advantage of the weaknesses of the American federal system of government to prevent the passage of
legislation of the sort he assumed other modern nations
have used to reduce the number of firearms in the hands
of their citizens.[3] This explanation of the so-called
American "gun culture" is based on some rather
questionable assumptions concerning the place of firearms past and present in other parts of what by Western
standards would be considered the modern world, and it
hardly takes seriously the grass-roots interest in firearms as it exists in the United States. To this extent
Hofstadter's explanation is typical of the anti-
firearms polemics that have been so common since the
early 1960s. But to the extent that the intent of his
essay was to explain the popular attachment to firearms
as it exists in the United States, and to the extent
that he did <u>touch</u> on some of the more basic social,
cultural, and historical roots of this phenomenon,
Hofstadter's work is rather different from other such
polemics. His essay, therefore, will serve as a convenient pad from which to launch this exploration of
the social and existential roots of the American firearms phenomenon.

While this book focuses on the firearms phenomenon, it is essentially a phenomenologically-informed case study, historical and cross-cultural in scope, aimed at demonstrating how interests evolve and are maintained as men interact with each other and attempt to cope with their "objective" environments. These environments, "the world out there" as experienced by men, include other people, of course, but they are not restricted to people. Here lies the books main justification. If what is said in the following pages about the evolution and maintenance of the interest in firearms is valid, the evolution and maintenance of other popular interests centering on various cultural artifacts such as automobiles, motorcycles, boats, power tools, cameras and even coins, stamps, and antiques can be explained in similar terms, as can be interests centering on various activities from work through leisure to the apparently frivolous.

However, by focusing on a phenomenon of the specific sort to be considered here, it is hoped that still another purpose will be served. When exploring phenomena they and others consider to be troublesome--"crime," "delinquency," "poverty," "violence," etc.--social scientists seem all too ready to assume that these phenomena are in fact troublesome in some objective sense. Such phenomena, therefore, are assumed to be essentially different from phenomena which seem to have social approval. Only a partial treatment of that which is to be explored is possible when such an assumption is made, since the value judgments involved in labeling a phenomenon troublesome are either overlooked or assumed to be rationally based and therefore unquestionable. In either case, explanations of the troublesome are likely to be inadequate and misleading. Once phenomena are considered to be objectively troublesome, and thereby essentially different from the non-troublesome, the troublesome are no longer explainable in the same terms as the non-troublesome. The troublesome must then be explained in terms of "irrationality" or "cultural lag."[4]

The phenomenon to be considered here is a case in point. To the extent that social scientists have dealt at all with the widespread civilian ownership of firearms in the United States, their research has been almost exclusively of the "applied" rather than of the "pure" science variety. The aim of such research has been to seek out the sources of criminal and political

2

violence in order that ways might be found to eradicate these "problems." Firearms, therefore, have been treated as contributors to social problems, and the troublesome aspects of the widespread civilian possession of firearms have thereby obscured the possession phenomenon by being taken as somehow representative of it. In short, research and anti-firearms polemics have tended to merge at the expense of non-aligned analyses of a complex social and historical development.[5] Hofstadter's essay, which was based on material taken from his introduction to his anthology entitled American Violence: A Documentary History, is a case in point.[6] The essay's title, "America as a Gun Culture," implies that he will be treating the phenomenon as a whole, and indeed he did so to a certain extent. Hofstadter pointed out that many of our popular heroes carry guns, that our children play with toy guns, and that millions of Americans own guns. But the troublesomeness of firearms is central to his essay, and when he tried to explain the American attachment to firearms he barely touched on social and psychological factors. Hofstadter concentrated instead on explaining why the United States government has been unable to regulate firearms as he took for granted other governments of modern nations have been able to do. "Gun culture," then, refers to the whole phenomenon, but the whole is seen in terms of its troublesome aspects and is compared to what Hofstadter believed to be the more satisfactory state of affairs he assumed exists in other parts of the modern world. Much was thereby taken for granted about the place of firearms in American life past and present as well as their place past and present in other parts of the modern world. Hence, much was also overlooked, with the result that vital dimensions of the phenomenon were not defined, let alone analyzed. Questions that Hofstadter did not raise and assumptions that he did not examine must be explored before relevant literature can be reviewed, a thesis statement can be formulated, and the methods to be utilized in this study can be elaborated upon. While necessary to the accomplishment of the objectives of this phenomenological study, what follows serves also to call into question the orthodox treatment of the troublesome.

FIREARMS AND THE "MODERN WORLD"

According to Hofstadter, the United States has a

3

"gun culture" while other nations considered to be
modern by Western standards do not. Is the United
States actually so unique with respect to the civilian
possession of firearms? Does the concept "culture" fit
the phenomenon to which it has been applied here? Considering the second question first, it should be noted
that the concept "culture" varies in its usage even
among social scientists, but most could probably agree
with the following definitions offered by two noted
social scientists. Clyde Kluckhon once wrote that "by
'culture' anthropology means the total life way of a
people, the social legacy the individual acquires from
his group. Or culture can be regarded as that part of
the environment that is the creation of man."[7] Similarly, Robert Bierstedt has written: "Culture is the
complex whole that consists of all the ways we think
and do and everything we have as members of society."[8]
If these definitions are accepted and "culture" is
taken to cover everything--material as well as non-ma-
terial--that goes into a lifestyle shared, created, and
maintained through time through the interaction of the
members of groups, to identify a particular culture as
a "gun culture" would seem to imply that guns are somehow central to the lifestyles of the people concerned.
It seems doubtful that Hofstadter or any other careful
scholar would be willing to argue that this is the case
in the United States, though some might be tempted to
do so. After all, in 1969 a federal commission estimated that some 90 million firearms--35 million rifles,
31 million shotguns, and 24 million handguns--were dis-
tributed among half or more of America's 60 million
households, and there are indications that these numbers, which were probably very conservative to begin
with, have increased considerably.[9] A 1981 National
Rifle Association estimate had 60 million Americans
owning 180 to 200 million guns, 55 to 60 million of
which were handguns.[10] Yet while the number of firearms in civilian hands in the United States might seem
awesome, particularly to those who doubt the wisdom of
allowing any civilians to possess them, it can hardly
be shown that firearms are central to the lifestyles of
the majority of Americans or even to the majority of
those Americans who own them. People who own guns but
cannot readily recall where they have stored them are
not uncommon at all. And given the ecological and
economic realities of modern industrial existence, one
would suspect that most of the 29 million or so hunters
who go into the field annually in the United States go
only when they can slip out of the city and away from

4

family and job responsibilities.[11]

In short, while firearms are rather easily obtained in the United States, while many Americans own and use them (for the most part in socially approved ways), and while many more Americans buy their children cap pistols and avidly follow the adventures of their gun-carrying TV, movie, paperback, or comic strip heroes, to claim that firearms are somehow central to the American way of life would seem to be a bit of an exaggeration. This is certainly not to deny that firearms come close to being central to the lifestyles of a large number of Americans. The National Rifle Association, after all, is approaching 2,000,000 members in 1981. But while one could argue that subcultures of dedicated target shooters, hunters, and collectors exist in the United States, their existence neither supports Hofstadter's "gun culture" thesis nor the centrality of firearms to the American way of life that it seems to imply.

Of course it could be argued that relative to other modern urban industrial nations the United States has a "gun culture." That is, while guns may not be central to styles of life common to the United States, they figure more prominently in American lifestyles than they do in lifestyles common to other parts of the modern world. Possibly so, but if this has ever been substantiated through research--historical, sociological, or otherwise--the results have not been widely publicized.

It seems generally to have been assumed that civilian possession of firearms in other modern nations has been so strictly regulated that nothing approaching a "gun culture" could ever have evolved in them. Yet regulations do not automatically enforce themselves, and even where and when a great deal of effort is put into attempts to enforce them, interest in and use of firearms sometimes thrives within the limits imposed by the enforced regulations. And there is evidence to the effect that this is the case in at least some other modern nations. In Switzerland, for instance, all able-bodied male citizens between the ages of 20 and 50 (55 for officers) are required to belong to the militia, since there is no standing army, and all reservists are required to keep not only their uniforms but their personal weapons-- submachine guns, automatic rifles, carbines, and pistols--along with a specified amount of

5

ammunition for them in their homes.[12] This means that
the government has placed some 650,000 military weapons
into the homes of 11% of Switzerland's nearly 6 million
citizens.[13] The 48 rounds of ammunition issued each
reservist to take home with him are contained in sealed
packs and are for emergency use only, but reservists
are encouraged to buy ammunition, which they can obtain
at cost, for target practice with their military rifles.[14] These weapons, however, are not to be used for
hunting. When a Swiss citizen completes his military
obligation at age 50 or 55, he is permitted to keep his
weapon--rifle or pistol--for personal use.[15] And when
the Swiss Army adopts a new infantry rifle, the obsolete rifles are sold to the public.[16] Permits are not
needed to buy military bolt action rifles, sporting
arms and ammunition. Permits, however, are required
for handgun acquisition and possession.[17] It would seem
then, that firearms figure prominently into lifestyles
common to Switzerland with the full blessing of the
government, and that the United States, even when pro-
minence of gun use rather than centrality is considered,
is not the only modern nation that persists in maintaining a "gun culture."

It could be argued, however, that Switzerland,
though modern by Western standards, is not nearly as
urban or industrial as the United States. Germany has
been both urban and industrial for some time, however,
and certainly is comparable to the United States. Yet
before World War II, according to historian William
Allen, "shooting societies" were important social life
features of many old German cities. In describing one
of these cities, Allen states that in medieval times
"all burghers had been mustered through the guilds to
man the city walls. An annual shooting festival kept
these part-time soldiers effective. When the old
guilds dissolved five shooting societies took their
place."[18] These shooting societies, each catering to
a different social strata of the community, still "held
regular practice sessions" in 1930, "and their three-
day shooting festival with parties, dances, prizes, and
parades was the social event of the year."[19]

France also is urban and industrial, but hunting is
so popular there that several million dollars' worth of
game has to be imported each year.[20] Some 2,000,000 of
France's approximately 50,000,000 citizens are licensed
to shoot, but this tells us little, for in parts of
France hunters seldom bother to get a license.[21] More

will be said about civilian firearms possession in France shortly, but while on the subject of the place of firearms in lifestyles common to modern nations, it should be noted that in Australia shooting is so popular "that Australians have their own ironic comment: If it moves, shoot it; if it doesn't, chop it down."[22]

It would appear, therefore, that firearms do figure prominently in lifestyles common to at least some other modern nations, even some that are urban and industrial. So how is the United States unique? Why are we said to have the only "gun culture" left in the modern world? Judging by his statement, as quoted above, Hofstadter seems to have felt that the sheer numbers of firearms in civilian hands and the fact that they are lawfully possessed in such large numbers did much to set the United States off from other modern nations. With respect to numbers, it has generally been taken for granted that there are more firearms per person in civilian hands in the United States than there are in other modern nations. And even if the 1969 90-million figure cited above was conservative, its very magnitude indicates that there may well be more firearms in civilian hands in the United States than there are elsewhere. Yet no one seems to have taken the time to make comparable figures for other modern nations available; therefore, for the time being we are still dealing with an assumption. While the number of firearms per person in Switzerland may not be as high as it is in the United States, between government issue and privately owned weapons, as noted above, it would seem that quite a large number of firearms are in civilian hands there.

Since most other modern nations require registration of firearms, it might seem that accurate figures could be rather easily obtained for purposes of comparison. There are at least two reasons why this is not the case. First, shotgun ownership has not been strictly regulated in a number of countries, with even England making an attempt to regulate shotguns only since 1968.[23] And second, after two world wars have spread military small arms all over Europe, there is no assurance that most firearms in civilian hands there have been registered. France, for instance, has strict firearms regulations which include registration; yet one observer wrote in 1964 that

> conditions brought about by the German oc-
> cupation in World War II have moderated the

7

enforcement of these laws considerably.
Almost every surviving member of the Resistance has kept his personal arms, unregistered. Even younger men follow the
example of their elders and frequently
keep unregistered pistols and sometimes
even submachine guns in their homes. The
French criminal is about as likely as the
American to be armed. Some villagers in
the foothills of the Pyrenees actually
hunt the chamois with full automatic weapons. Rifles for the .30-06 cartridge
/the regulation American military rifle
cartridge of the two world wars/ are numerous, even though technically illegal.[24]

And French firearms authority Michel Josserand noted in
1968 that police officials "estimate that only about 10
percent of the handguns in the region of Paris are registered."[25] He stated further that

> shotguns aside, the number of "illegal"
> weapons in private hands must number sev-
> eral hundreds of thousands and if all
> these citizens who live in endemic infrac-
> tion of the law decided simultaneously to
> put their firearms to ill use, it would
> take an armored column to get through
> from Paris to Dijon.[26]

Even in Britain, with its very strict gun controls,
there are indications, according to Chief Inspector of
Police Colin Greenwood, that thousands of firearms are
illegally in civilian hands.[27] Certainly the troubles
in Ulster would indicate that firearms can be obtained
in Great Britain, legally or otherwise. And there is
reason to believe that in Norway many World War II
weapons are still in circulation and unregistered.[28]

Of course, illegal possession of firearms in other
parts of the modern world is one thing, but Hofstadter's
claim was that large numbers of firearms are legally in
civilian hands in the United States and that this state
of affairs helps to set us apart from other nations.
But even here American uniqueness may be more imagined
than real, for while they are considered by some to be
less than adequate, federal, state, and local laws cov-
ering some aspect or other of firearms acquisition or
possession are numerous in the United States.[29] As

anyone familiar with the American firearms scene can verify, however, it is no rarity for otherwise "responsible citizens" to give little thought to violating these laws when they are perceived to be simple nuisances devoid of worth. Hence it would not be surprising to find that a considerable part of the millions of firearms in civilian hands in the United States are possessed in violation of some legal restriction or other.

From the above it should be clear that Hofstadter and others have taken much too much for granted concerning the place of firearms in lifestyles common to the United States and other parts of the world. There may well be more firearms per person in civilian hands in the United States than there are in other parts of the urban industrial world, and differences in firearms usage must surely also exist from area to area. But the distinction between gun cultures and non-gun cultures has certainly been blurred by the preceding discussion, and indeed the whole notion of a gun culture has been called into question.

With respect to differences between the phenomenon as it exists in the United States and elsewhere, at least two are worthy of note at this point, since they will figure significantly in this study. First, there is reason to believe that handgun ownership is much more prevalent in the United States than it is elsewhere. According to the commission estimates cited earlier, in 1969 there were 13,500 handguns per 100,000 persons in the United States.[30] According to estimates supplied to this same commission by diplomatic representatives of the following countries, handgun ownership in them runs as follows: Ireland, Finland, the Netherlands, Greece and Great Britain--500 per 100,000 population; Switzerland--insignificant; Yugoslavia-- 500 to 1,000; Israel--1,000; and Austria and Canada-- 3,000.[31] While estimates for such modern "free world" nations as France, Germany, and Japan were not provided and while the accuracy of the estimates cited might well be questionable, in the United States handguns are quite popular, with more than a quarter of the firearms in private hands here being of this type. Much has been made over the widespread civilian possession of handguns in the United States, since this possession relates to another state of affairs that has quite probably been primarily responsible for the belief on the part of some that firearms figure more pro-

9

minently in the American way of life than they do in
the lifestyles of other modern nations.

While there would seem to be no good reason to believe that firearms are central in any way to American
culture, and there is good reason to believe that firearms do figure rather prominently in lifestyles common
to some parts of the modern world outside of the United
States, there would seem to be no denying that guns
figure more prominently on the crime scene in the United
States than they do elsewhere. While it might behoove
one not to take statistics at face value, especially
when they are used to make cross-cultural comparisons,
there is statistical support to the effect that firearms do figure more prominently in American crime than
they do in crime elsewhere. According to the commission cited several times previously, of the four homi-
cides per 100,000 persons recorded in England and Wales
in 1967, only one of each four involved the use of a
firearm. In the United States during the same period,
61 crimes of this sort were recorded per 100,000 persons, with 38 of each 61 involving the use of firearms,
and with 76 percent of the firearms involved being
handguns. In England and Wales 97 robberies per
100,000 persons were recorded, but only 6 of each 97
involved the use of firearms. In the United States
during the same period, 1020 robberies per 100,000
persons were recorded. Of these 1020 robberies, 372
involved the use of firearms of which 96 percent were
handguns.[32]

While statistical support leaves much to be desired,
it is generally assumed that other modern nations re-
semble England and Wales rather than the United States
with respect to the criminal use of firearms. The link
is thereby made between the large number of handguns in
civilian hands in the United States and the large
number of firearms-related crimes committed in this
country. As noted previously, this link is the aspect
of the overall American gun possession phenomenon that
has been dealt with by reform-oriented social scientists to the exclusion of the rest of the phenomenon.
As acknowledged previously, there may be more firearms
in civilian hands in the United States than there are
in civilian hands in other parts of the modern world,
and firearms may fit into American lifestyles differently than they do into lifestyles common to other parts
of the world. But the differences in the criminal use
of firearms between the United States and other modern

10

nations and the great amount of attention given those differences by the media and various reformers seem to have caused differences in general firearms usage between the United States and some other nations to appear to be far greater than they actually are. This being the case, a considerable obstacle is put in the path of those trying to understand modern man's attachment to firearms here or wherever it may be found.

SUMMARY

From what has been said so far, it should be obvious that the phenomenon to be explored during the course of this study is not a distinctively American one; therefore, it must be understood in more universalistic terms. It should also be clear that those aspects of the phenomenon considered to be troublesome by law enforcement agencies, reformers, some applied social scientists, and some citizens are only a small and peripheral part of the whole. We can hardly understand the whole, therefore, by focusing on its minor and peripheral parts. Once the full implications of these two points have been realized, the American firearms phenomenon loses much of its mystery and lends itself to explanation in terms of basic sociological and social-psychological concepts.

FOOTNOTES

1. Richard Hofstadter, "America as a Gun Culture," *American Heritage* XXI (October, 1970), 4.

2. Virtually everything that has been written concerning the widespread civilian possession of firearms in the United States has not only focused on the issue of gun control, but taken a stand for or against controls. Prior to *Gun and Society*, the only exception to this rule seems to have been Lee Kennett and James LaVerne Anderson's *The Gun in America: The Origins of a National Dilemma* (Westport, Connecticut: Greenwood Press, 1975). *The Gun in America* also focuses on gun control, but rather than take a stand on the issue, the book presents a history of the controversy. And in presenting this history, *The Gun in America* examines some of the social historical roots of the American attachment to firearms.

3. Hofstadter, 85.

4. For other comments concerning the shortcomings of the orthodox social scientific handling of "troublesome" phenomena see David Matza, *Becoming Deviant* (Englewood Cliffs, New Jersey: Prentice-Hall, Inc. 1969), pp. 15-16; Stanislaw Andrzejewski, *Military Organization and Society* (London: Routledge & Kegan Paul Ltd., 1954), pp. 7-19, but particularly p. 12; William R. Burch, Jr., *Daydreams and Nightmares: A Sociological Essay on the American Environment* (New York, Evanston, San Francisco, London: Harper & Row, Publishers, 1971), pp. 7-29; and Tamotsu Shibutani and Kian M. Kwan, *Ethnic Stratification: A Comparative Approach* (New York: The Macmillan Company and London: Collier-Macmillan Limited, 1965), p. 15.

5. A prime example is provided by George D. Newton, Jr., Director and Franklin E. Zimring, Director of Research, *Firearms & Violence in American Life* (Washington, D.C.: U.S. Government Printing Office, 1969). Another example is provided by Hofstadter.

6. Richard Hofstadter and Michael Wallace (ed.), *American Violence: A Documentary History*, Vintage Books (New York: Random House, 1970), pp. 3-43.

7. Clyde Kluckhon, *Mirror for Man* (Greenwich, Connecticut: Fawcett Publications, A Premier Book, 1963), p. 24.

8. Robert Bierstedt, *The Social Order*, 3rd ed. (New York: McGraw-Hill Book Company, 1970), p. 123.

9. Newton and Zimring, xi & 9.

10. *NRA Firearms Fact Card*, Circulated by the National Rifle Association, 1981.

11. Ibid. This figure is "based on 1978 Decision Making Information Surveys."

12. "Switzerland," *The New Encyclopaedia Britannica* 15 edition Vol. 17; and Frank G. McGuire, "How Swiss Gun Laws Work," *The American Rifleman*, Vol. 114 (December, 1966), 44.

13. McGuire.

14. Ibid.

15. Ibid., 45.

16. Ibid.

17. Ibid., 44.

18. William Allen, *The Nazis Seizure of Power* (Chicago: Quadrangle Books, 1965), pp. 18-19.

19. Ibid., 19.

20. Joseph T. Carroll, *The French: How They Live and Work* (Newton Abbot: David & Charles, 1968), p. 172.

21. Jack Weller, "Hunting in France," *The American Rifleman*, Vol. 112 (February, 1964), 24-27.

22. Craig McGregor, *Profile of Australia* (London: Hodder and Stoughton, 1966), p. 139.

23. Newton and Zimring, 119. For much more detail see Colin Greenwood, Firearms Control: A Study of Armed Crime and Firearms Control in England and Wales (London: Routledge & Kegan Paul, 1972), pp. 183 & 234. According to Chief Inspector of Police Greenwood, even though firearms and shotgun certificates are required of all Englishmen who desire to possess such arms legally, shotguns themselves do not have to be individually registered. Therefore, the number of shotguns legally possessed by Englishmen is not known.

24. Weller, 26.

25. Michel H. Josserand and Jan Stevenson, Pistol, Revolvers, and Ammunition (New York: Crown Publishers, Inc., 1972), p. 285.

26. Ibid., 288.

27. Greenwood, 235-239.

28. Nils Kvale, "Gun Laws in Scandinavia," The American Rifleman, Vol. 114 (July, 1966), 19-20.

29. Josserand and Stevenson, 297.

30. Newton and Zimring, 121.

31. Ibid.

32. Ibid., 124 & 49 in that order.

14

CHAPTER II

THEORETICAL CONSIDERATIONS

THE SCOPE OF THE PHENOMENON

Even though it should be clear by now that Hofstadter's "gun culture" treatment of the phenomenon to be explored through this study is extremely misleading, it is tempting to retain "gun culture" as a convenient label. After all, to continue to speak of "the American firearms phenomenon," or "the widespread civilian possession of firearms in the United States," would be cumbersome. Because "gun culture" is so misleading, however, the temptation to use this label will be resisted and the phenomenon under consideration generally will be referred to as "the popular attachment to firearms" from this point on. "Attachment," as used here, refers simply to the relationship between people and artifacts manifested through the very fact of the widespread civilian possession of firearms. Since it is the very nature of this attachment that is to be explored through this study, it is hoped that this definition will suffice.

By the end of the previous chapter, it could be seen that the phenomenon under consideration in this study is not distinctively American, but simply an American manifestation--different in degree and with respect to specifics--of a popular attachment to firearms that, while not universal, is far from unknown in other parts of the modern world. Therefore, while the American popular attachment to firearms will remain the focal point of the study, if this attachment is to be examined in terms of basic sociological and sociopsychological concepts, the scope of the study will have to be broadened to the point where the popular attachment to firearms wherever it is to be found in the modern world will also be considered. Actually, the scope of the study could just as well be broadened to the point where the popular attachment to firearms wherever it is to be found, whether in non-modern or modern parts of the world, could be considered. However, the reasons for excluding non-modern parts of the world from the study should become apparent as current perspectives on the phenomenon under consideration are gleaned from the literature dealing with its various aspects. Nevertheless, even though the popular attach-

15

ment to firearms as it may exist in non-modern areas
will be touched upon only in passing, it is felt that
the conclusions arrived at in the following pages apply
to non-moderns as well as to moderns.

THE LITERATURE: RESPECTABLE AND
NOT-SO-RESPECTABLE EXPLANATIONS

Through his essay Hofstadter was trying to explain
a state of affairs--the widespread possession of firearms by civilians--that he felt no longer had any place
in the modern world and in fact still existed only in
the United States among modern nations. While he acknowledged that "responsible" citizens once had use for
firearms in the United States, he felt that this was no
longer the case. His reasoning seemed to be based on
the following premises: men need food if they are to
survive physically, and firearms enable men to utilize
other animals as sources of food; firearms also enable
men to cope offensively as well as defensively with
threats of various sorts posed by their own kind as well
as by other creatures; it follows, then, that since they
had to provide themselves with food and provide themselves and their property with protection from wild
creatures, Indians, and renegade whites, Americans
needed firearms during the early days of settlement.[1]
In the past, therefore, a firearmed response to objective environmental conditions was a "rational" response,
according to Hofstadter. Since citizens of modern nations no longer have to hunt their own food, and since
these citizens can be protected more effectively by the
police if firearms are not easily obtainable, firearms
possession no longer constitutes a "rational" response
to objective conditions.

Far from denying that crime poses a threat to the
American citizen, Hofstadter implied that attempts
should be made to reduce the amount of crime and that
fewer firearms in circulation among the general populace would be a step in this direction.[2] Hofstadter
felt, as the following statement indicates, that the
practicality of such a move had been demonstrated by
other modern nations.

> When the frontier and its ramifications
> are given their due they fall short of ex-
> plaining the persistence of the American
> gun culture. Why is the gun still so pre-

valent in a culture in which only about 4 percent of the country's workers now make a living from farming, a culture that for the last century and a half has had only a tiny fragment of its population actually in contact with a frontier, that, in fact, has not known a true frontier for three generations? Why did the United States alone among industrial societies cling to the idea that a substantially unregulated supply of guns among its city populations is a safe and acceptable thing? This is, after all, not the only nation with a frontier history. Canada and Australia have had theirs, and yet their gun control measures are far more satisfactory than ours. Their own gun homicide rates, as compared with our 2.7, range around .56 and their suicide and accident rates are also much lower. Again, Japan, with no frontier but with an ancient tradition of feudal and military violence, has adopted, along with its modernization, such rigorous gun laws that its gun homicide rate at .04 is one of the world's lowest. (The land of harakiri also has one of the lowest gun suicide rates-- about one-fiftieth of ours.) In sum, other societies, in the course of industrial and urban development have succeeded in modifying their old gun habits, and we have not.[3]

Hofstadter acknowledged the existence of activities involving the use of firearms in other than utilitarian ways--sports hunting, target shooting, and collecting, for example. But he implied that since civilians no longer need firearms for practical purposes, and since firearms now help to create more problems than they help to solve, activities that foster interest in firearms or facilitate the acquisition of skills in their use should not be encouraged.[4] According to Hofstadter, therefore, an armed citizenry makes no sense; it is out of place in the modern world--an anachronism, a cultural lag.

Hofstadter can hardly be credited with formulating the view of the popular attachment to firearms in the United States to which he subscribed. This view has

17

enjoyed almost complete acceptance in intellectual and politically "liberal" circles for quite some time, and it has prompted the little scholarly investigation of the civilian possession of firearms in the United States that has been done. As previously noted, and as Hofstadter's essay bears out, however, this view has permeated such investigation to the extent that the differences between supposedly scholarly research and anti-firearms polemics are not discernable. From such popular magazines as Time, and Newsweek, through Saturday Review, The Nation, The New Yorker, the New Republic, and books such as Carl Bakal's The Right to Bear Arms, to historian Hofstadter's essay, and Newton and Zimring's staff report to the National Commission on the Causes and Prevention of Violence, entitled Firearms & Violence in American Life, the prevailing treatment of the popular attachment to firearms in the United States is in terms of cultural lag.[5] Given this perspective, of course, the phenomenon under consideration can no longer be taken for granted or accepted as "natural" or "normal." Rather the popular attachment to firearms becomes something out of the ordinary in need of explanation, but at the same time it can no longer be explained in ordinary terms. And since the popular attachment to firearms is extraordinary because it has been taken for granted that it should not exist, not only explanation but practical action aimed at putting things back in order is called for. Therefore, explanations of the phenomenon must point out the props that enable the anachronism to survive.

Imbued with a touch of the reformer's belief in man's rationality and in progress through science, education, and legislation, reinforced by the belief that other modern nations have rationally done away with "gun cultures," and encouraged by poll results that can be interpreted as indicating that a majority of Americans wish to rid themselves of their own "gun culture," researchers--scholarly or journalistic--can hardly escape the conclusions arrived at by Hofstadter. The anachronism exists because irresponsible vested interests have been able to take advantage of weaknesses in the federal system of government in order to block the passage of the legislation that would do away with the anachronism.[6] Grass roots support for the "gun lobby" is taken to be minimal, and to the extent that it does exist, such support is taken to be unenlightened or psychiatrically suspect.[7] This explanation of the popular attachment to firearms in the United States will

18

be referred to as the <u>cultural lag-vested</u> interest explanation from this point on.

Of course, the cultural lag-vested interest explanation has not gone unchallenged. In fact, it has met formidable and increasing opposition from another explanation based on the same premises upon which it is based. Men need food if they are to survive physically, and firearms enable men to utilize other animals as sources of food. Firearms also enable men to cope offensively as well as defensively with threats of various sorts posed by their own kind as well as by other creatures. But according to this opposing explanation, the civilian need for firearms did not fade away with the passing of the frontier. While few modern Americans must hunt their own food in order to survive, the number of crimes committed each year indicates that Americans still have use for the protection a firearm affords. And there is also the need to protect the nation and the democratic way of life. Since it seems that crime and international aggression are not likely to fade from the human scene in the near future, and indeed may never do so, even modern men need firearms. If moderns in other parts of the world are not armed, they have probably already been enslaved by a totalitarian regime or they are vulnerable to such enslavement. Given this perspective, then, an armed citizenry makes sense even in the modern world. The reason for the popular attachment to firearms, therefore, is so obvious that encouragement rather than indepth analysis of it is needed. The relationship between the non-practical recreational uses to which firearms are put and the practical uses to which they are put do not have to be explored. Since non-practical uses of firearms either foster an interest in firearms or help develop skill in their use, these non-practical uses are simply regarded as obviously desirable wholesome forms of recreation.

This latter explanation, which will be referred to as the <u>utilitarian explanation</u> from this point on, can be found stated in part or in its entirety, with different degrees of sophistication, in practically every issue of such special-interest periodicals as <u>The American Rifleman</u>, the official journal of the <u>National Rifle Association</u>, <u>Guns</u>, <u>Guns and Ammo</u>, and other gun magazines. Articles in one way or another supportive of the utilitarian explanation can be found on occasion in "outdoor" magazines such as <u>Sports Afield</u>, <u>Outdoor Life</u>,

19

and Field and Stream, politically "conservative" magazines such as National Review and politically "libertarian" magazines such as Inquiry.[8] In intellectual and
scholarly circles, however, the utilitarian hypothesis
has been considered less than respectable until recently. Support for the utilitarian explanation is still
rarely to be found in periodicals and books catering to
those who consider themselves to be of the educated
elite, or even in those periodicals and books catering
to the general public.[9]

From the standpoint of the sociology of knowledge,
or at least Karl Mannheim's version thereof, the utilitarian explanation obviously provides ideological support for the maintenance of the status quo with respect
to the widespread civilian possession of firearms while
the cultural lag-vested interest explanation just as
obviously provides utopian justification for change.[10]
Therefore, it might behoove scholars exploring the
phenomenon under consideration to resist the temptation
to take either of the above explanations at face value.
This is not to say, however, that neither of these opposing explanations of the American popular attachment
to firearms are of any use whatsoever to those interested in getting at the social and existential roots of
the phenomenon. Before discussing that which either
explanation may have to offer, however, two other possible explanations for the popular attachment to firearms, wherever it may be found, should at least be
mentioned.

To those ethologists such as Konrad Lorenz and his
popularizers, who see man as basically an instinctively
aggressive, weapons - using ape, the roots of the popular attachment to firearms would hardly be mysterious.[11]
Weapons--using to the ethologists is simply considered
to be part of man's nature. Nor is the phenomenon ·
likely to puzzle those members of the intellectual community who subscribe to a Freudian interpretation of
human behavior. The Freudians are likely to see firearms as phallic symbols, fetishistic manifestations of
thwarted instinctive sex drives. Both perspectives
have been rather widely propagated through various pseu-
do-scientific works and even through fiction.[12] Consequently, each perspective has its own adherents within
the lay reading public as well as in "higher" intellectual circles.

Neither the ethological nor the Freudian perspec—

tive has been applied systematically in an in depth
study of the popular attachment to firearms, but each
can be used to supplement one or the other of the explanations summarized above. As noted previously, the
tendency of those who subscribe to the cultural lag explanation is to assume that popular support for the
civilian possession of firearms is minimal and that
such support as exists is unenlightened or psychiatrically suspect. To the more extreme anti-firearms
polemicist, weapons are at best necessary evils still
of use to the military, and possibly to the police, in
a world not yet free of violence. From the anti-firearms side, therefore, a private citizen's interest in
firearms is often assumed to be a sign of maladjust-
ment.[13] On the other hand, if man is what some ethologists say he is, those individuals who have an interest in weapons of various sorts, including firearms, do
not need explaining since they are much closer to
"natural man" than those who do not acknowledge such
interests. In a world which will never be free from
conflict, those persons interested in weapons are also
more likely to survive than are those who are not so
interested. Pro-gun ideologists, as might be expected,
have been known to invoke this ethological support by
way of justifying their stand.[14] Of course, neither
the Lorenzian nor the Freudian positions have gone unchallenged. It will not be necessary to criticize these
positions here, however, since the following pages
should make it apparent that neither instincts nor
frustrated instincts have to be resorted to in order to
explain the popular attachment to firearms.[15]

A PHENOMENOLOGICAL APPROACH

Implicit in both the cultural lag-vested interest
and utilitarian explanations for the popular attachment
to firearms seems to be a view of man as a problem sol-
ver possessed of a quality called intelligence, and of
some degree of a related quality commonly referred to
as rationality.[16] Other creatures are taken for granted
to possess little intelligence, relative to man at
least, and even less reasoning ability. These qualities
taken together supposedly enable man to create and use
the tools that allow him to cope with the objective conditions he faces. Tools, anthropologists tell us,
"considered functionally . . . are essentially exten-
sions of the forelimb."[17] Whereas other animals supposedly react to the world around them in a pre-pro-

21

grammed, fixed, instinctive fashion, man is considered
to be more flexible. Having no fixed or pre-programmed
responses to see him through, man must consciously sort
through those responses to which he has become sensi-
tized by past experience. He then must evaluate those
responses that seem appropriate to the situations he
faces, select from the responses, and apply them in
more or less modified form. If those responses from
which he has to select seem inappropriate, he may have
to come up with something essentially new. Thus he
fashions the tools he needs and it is assumed that he
also rids himself of tools in this way once they are no
longer useful or have become troublesome to him. As
noted above, this view of man as a rational being seems
implicit in explanations for the popular attachment to
firearms that are otherwise diametrically opposed. If
this is so, both explanations are based on a view of
man and his relationship to the world around him that
would be considered quite simplistic by those social
scientists who see reality as a social construct.

As noted earlier, some individuals who possess
firearms probably cannot recall where they have stored
them. But where firearms possession is as common as it
is in the United States, it would seem safe to assume
that most people have acquired firearms and continued
to possess them because they have felt that they had
some use for them or that they might have some use for
them. To take for granted that such feelings are mis-
guided, unenlightened, or irrational, as those who subscribe to the more uncompromising versions of the cultural lag-vested interest explanation do, does not help
us to understand why millions of citizens of other modern urban industrial nations as well as the United
States evidently feel the need to possess firearms. At
least the utilitarian explanation keeps our attention
focused on man's conscious problem-solving efforts and
the tool quality of firearms. Of course, in its ideological capacity the utilitarian explanation also may
foster the phenomenon it purports to explain.

Firearms must function in some way in the lives of
those who have put some effort into their acquisition,
for it is difficult to believe that the effort, however
minimal, would have been made if this were not the case.
And it is difficult to believe, in the light of the
widespread publicity given the troublesomeness of firearms, that millions of moderns would continue to possess
them if they did not function in some minimally impor-

22

tant way in the lives of the majority of their possessors. This is not to say, of course, that firearms should fit into people's lives as they do. It is rather to point out that they obviously do fit into people's lives. The basic questions to be answered through this exploration of the social and existential roots of the popular attachment to firearms, therefore, have to do with how and why firearms function as they do in the lives of those moderns who possess them.

PRACTICAL FUNCTION

In the following rather brief statement Hofstadter touched upon what may be the three basic ways in which firearms function in the lives of those who possess them:

> What began as a necessity of agriculture and the frontier took hold as a sport and as an ingredient in the American imagination. Before the days of spectator sports, when competitive athletics became a basic part of popular culture, hunting and fishing probably were the chief American sports. . . But for millions of American boys, learning to shoot and above all graduating from toy guns and receiving the first real rifle of their own were milestones of life, veritable rites of passage that certified their arrival at manhood.[18]

In the first sentence Hofstadter alluded to the practical uses to which firearms were first put in response to frontier conditions. But with his references to sport and imagination, Hofstadter also implied in this sentence that two other functions derived somehow from the practical. These derivative functions will be referred to from this point on as the recreational and symbolic functions, respectively. For the time being, however, the practical function will remain the center of attention, for it is this function that has faded away with the passing of the frontier, according to those who subscribe to the cultural lag-vested interest explanation for the popular attachment to firearms. Obviously, if the practical function has faded it can no longer help to account for the firearms phenomenon. According to the utilitarian explanation, of course, the popular attachment to firearms in the United States is still rooted in a practical function which has not faded away.

In their staff report to the National Commission on the Causes and Prevention of Violence, Newton and Zimring note that

> many Americans keep loaded firearms in homes, businesses and on their persons for the purpose of protection. Evidence of this practice is found in a 1966 poll in which about 66 percent of householders with guns list "protection" as one reason for having them and in a 1968 poll which revealed that guns were kept for protection in 26 percent of retail business establishments. Times and dangers have changed from frontier days when a gun was often necessary for survival. The extent to which guns are actually useful for defensive purposes must be reappraised.[19]

Then, in summarizing the results of their reappraisal, Newton and Zimring state that

> in our urbanized society, the gun is rarely an effective means of protecting the home against either the burglar or the robber; the former avoids confrontation, the latter confronts too swiftly. Possession of a gun undoubtedly provides a measure of comfort to a great many Americans. But the data suggest that this comfort is largely an illusion bought at the price of increased accidents, homicides, and more widespread illegal use of guns.[20]

In other words, firearms no longer function practically in the lives of modern Americans. Statistics concerning accidents are cited to demonstrate that firearms are in fact dysfunctional.[21]

For a number of years now, however, every issue of the American Rifleman, the official journal of the National Rifle Association, has carried a column entitled "The Armed Citizen," each installment of which month after month summarizes ten or so newspaper accounts of cases where housewives, storekeepers, and other ordinary citizens have actually successfully defended themselves, others, and their property from criminal acts.[22]

From the above it is obvious that Newton and Zimring account for the popular attachment to firearms in terms of cultural lag, and the tenor of their report also makes it clear that they accept the vested interest explanation for the lag.[23] It is just as obvious from the above that the National Rifle Association subscribes to the utilitarian explanation for the phenomenon under consideration. Both sides apparently take it for granted that firearms function practically in the lives of their possessors if they enable them to cope with objective conditions--conditions as they exist "out there" in the "real world." Those subscribing to both explanations apparently also take it for granted that men are directly in touch with reality, and that when men act rationally, certain responses follow almost automatically from their direct apprehension of reality. For instance, the reality reflected by Newton and Zimring's statistical study is that firearms not only seldom enable their possessors to defend themselves, but that firearms often help bring on accidents. Hence, given the troublesomeness of firearms, it follows that people should rid themselves of them or at least not acquire them for purposes of self defense. The reality reflected by the newspaper accounts summarized in The American Rifleman, however, is that in specific instances people have actually defended themselves successfully with firearms. Hence firearms can function practically in the lives of their possessors, and it follows that people might be well-advised to acquire firearms and skill in their use for purposes of self defense.

But the notion that men are directly in touch with reality, and that, to the extent that men act rationally, certain responses are called out almost automatically from their direct contact with the real world, would be considered naive in the extreme to phenomenologically-oriented sociologists--sociologists of knowledge, phenomenologists, symbolic interactionists and existentialists. According to those who subscribe to these perspectives, the real world may well exist "out there" unto itself in an objective form that cannot be wished away, but that world can be experienced only through a subjective frame of reference that is continually being constructed and reconstructed--maintained, modified or transformed--through symbolic interaction with others.[24]

25

Changes in this subjective frame of reference may be so gradual as to go unnoticed, but it is always changing, and while no two people can ever share a frame of reference completely, it is shared to a certain extent by all those who have had a hand in its construction.

If this phenomenological perspective is accepted, and it is the perspective upon which this study is based, it is hardly surprising that what are taken to be objective conditions are often perceived differently by those who come into contact with them. Neither is it surprising that even where there is apparent agreement as to the configuration of the object world at a given time, there may be sincere, heartfelt, and even "informed" disagreement as to how to respond to that world. Given this phenomenological perspective, therefore, the practical function of firearms in people's lives must be considered as part of a response to objective conditions as these conditions have been filtered through a subjective frame of reference rather than as an automatic response to a world that can be shown to exist, or not to exist, in some objective sense. Such little research as has been done on the firearms phenomenon has failed to take this point into consideration, because it has been oriented toward the cultural lag-vested interest explanation.

Evidence to the effect that firearms do function practically in the lives of many of their possessors in the subjective sense discussed above, is provided by the poll results cited by Newton and Zimring. Many firearms owners evidently feel that they need guns, or might need them, if they are to be able to cope with conditions in the "real world out there." To the extent that this is the case, firearms are seen as tools that can be used by their possessors to accomplish the very practical task of defending themselves, others, or their property from those bent on doing harm. Whether many firearms owners are ever actually called upon to defend themselves with their weapons, whether it is probable that they could or could not defend themselves if called upon to do so, and whether they should or should not be encouraged to attempt to defend themselves, are questions of no concern to this study. What is important is that many people acquire and possess firearms because others have helped them to feel that they need firearms to cope with the world as others have helped them to see it.

When firearms function practically in people's lives, they function as tools, and tools are created or selected by their users according to the tasks the users feel they must accomplish with them. And given the perspective upon which this study is based, prospective tool users consider conditions "out there" in the "real world," as these conditions have been socially defined and subjectively experienced, in order to determine what their tasks will be. It follows, then, that in different parts of what is now considered to be the modern world, different sorts of people have used different sorts of firearms to cope with different sorts of objective conditions as these conditions have been filtered through different socially constructed frames of reference. For instance, in areas where large wild animals were present and seen by men as primary sources of food, where hunting rather than trapping or some other method was seen as an acceptable means of acquiring food, and where a technology capable of producing firearms was present or accessible, it would not be surprising if the guns developed for the hunters eventually took the shape of rifles. Substitute "wild-fowl" for "large wild animals" in the preceding sentence, and it would not be surprising if the hunter's gun eventually took the shape of a shotgun. In times and places where men made their livings in ways not requiring the use of weapons, but where street offenses such as robbery were common and self-defense was seen as being largely the responsibility of the individual, the demand for small guns easily carried on one's person would obviously be great. In the pasts of some parts of the modern world, therefore, shotguns, for instance, might be expected to have functioned practically in the lives of many people, while rifles and handguns functioned practically in the lives of few if any people. In some areas firearms of various kinds might be expected to have functioned practically in the lives of only a relatively small number of individuals --say an aristocracy--while in other parts of the world each of the three basic types of civilian firearms-- rifles, shotguns, and handguns--might be expected to have functioned practically in the lives of many ordinary citizens. Once firearms are fitted into sociohistorical perspective, in other words, one would expect to find that the practical functioning of firearms and the popular attachment to firearms are related. If firearms are examined within a phenomenologically-informed perspective, the means through which past practical endeavors have helped shape present practical and

27

non-practical endeavors are hardly mysterious, as will be seen in the following discussions of the derivative recreational and symbolic functions of firearms.

Before shifting the discussion to the derivative functions, however, another point must be made concerning the practical use of firearms. So far it would seem that firearms function practically in the lives of those who possess them because they enable such persons to acquire food or to cope offensively or defensively with their enemies--human or otherwise. But since the ability to use tools of any kind with skill is not inborn and can only be acquired through practice, a third practical function derives from those functions likely to be considered more basic. Through their use, firearms enable their possessors to acquire the skills needed by those engaged in the more serious business of hunting for food and coping with enemies. Therefore, target shooting, in its more basic forms at least, can be a practical pastime for some persons. Target shooting also may be one of the main links between the practical function and its recreational derivative, as shall be seen shortly.

RECREATIONAL FUNCTION

In the preceding pages the ability of men to create and use tools has been mentioned often; however, as some social scientists would be quick to point out, men are not only creators and users of tools. Possibly more significantly, men are symbol creators and users. Through their ability to interact symbolically with others, all persons concerned come by an ongoing picture of reality (and of themselves and others as they relate to reality) that they more or less share with those with whom they generally interact. This point was made earlier as it was stressed that men do not respond directly to objective reality. It was noted that sociologists of knowledge, phenomenologists, and symbolic interactionists share an awareness of this human predicament. While sociologists of knowledge and phenomenologists have been primarily interested in understanding how men come to see the world as they do, symbolic interactionists have been more interested in understanding how their ability to use symbols enables men to act and interact with each other.[25] Symbolic interactionists, therefore, have been particularly cognizant of certain needs peculiar to humans—needs having to do with

28

man's ability to create and use symbols.

From Charles Horton Cooley and George Herbert Mead
to modern scholars, symbolic interactionists have
argued that a person's image of himself is arrived at
and maintained or transformed through the person's interaction with others. It follows from the symbolic
interactionist argument that the maintenance or enhancement of socially acquired self-images quite often takes
precedence over the satisfaction of needs that insure
physical survival.[26] If their argument is accepted, all
sorts of human activities, utilitarian and otherwise,
take on added significance as men strive to meet what
they believe to be the expectations of their significant
others. Men acquire desired self-images to the extent
that they see indications that they have met these expectations.[27] This point cannot be emphasized too
strongly, because it seems generally to be taken for
granted that men are motivated to accomplish certain
tasks simply because the tasks themselves cry out to be
accomplished. It is further assumed that once aware of
the task at hand, men will address it directly. Given
this commonly accepted view, the hunter, for instance,
hunts to provide food for himself and those dependent
upon him in order that he and they might survive physically. It is assumed that the techniques the hunter
uses are those he has reason to believe will enable him
to accomplish his task. But when viewed in this fashion, the web of expectations that allow the hunter to
orient himself to the point where the desirability of
physical survival can be taken for granted is obscured
along with the logic of his assignment to do the hunting.

The symbolic interactionist might well argue that
the hunter hunts primarily because through his interaction with others he has come to see himself as a
hunter and provider. He has, therefore, come to see
himself as a person of whom others have certain expectations. Consequently, the hunter has acquired certain
expectations of himself. The techniques he utilizes
are likely to be those he feels others, particularly
other hunters, expect competent hunters to utilize. If
he innovates, it is likely to be as much due to the fact
that he feels others expect hunters to be innovative,
or that he sees himself as a maverick who is expected
by others to violate their expectations, as it is due to
the fact that the previously accepted hunting techniques
no longer seem to work.

The preceding discussion of various sociopsychological phenomena that have been conceptualized in terms
of looking-glass self, generalized other, significant
others, reference groups, etc., has been tremendously
over-simplified. But it is hoped that the discussion
will suffice to demonstrate the relevance of these concepts to the questions under consideration: How did the
recreational function derive from the practical, and why
do firearms function recreationally? It would seem to
follow from the sociopsychological considerations mentioned above that since skill in the use of firearms is
likely to be honored in a society in which the members
find themselves dependent upon the use of firearms, the
practical sessions that enable men to acquire such
skills are likely to become competitive. Being known
as the best shot in the community would be quite reward-
ing. And given these considerations, target shooting
could become a worthwhile activity in and of itself
apart from its practical justification. An interest in
target shooting could thereby survive after the skills
of the hunt are no longer required to provide men with
sustenance, and after men are no longer called upon to
protect themselves with firearms. Individuals who have
never been called upon to hunt their own food or to
confront their enemies with firearms, therefore, may
acquire great pride in their ability to shoot through
their association with others who seem to appreciate
shooting skills. And some minimal familiarity with
firearms could easily become widely associated with
manliness--but for reasons better understood in interactional rather than Freudian terms. Such would not
likely be the case, however, in societies where firearms
have never functioned practically in the lives of many
persons.

Now and again writers of various sorts have commented on the relationship between various forms of
recreation and various practical endeavors. In discussing the transformation of wrestling from work--possibly
the most "primitive" form of combat--to play, sociologist Gregory P. Stone, for example, has pointed out that
"an important function of play is the recreation and
maintenance of obsolete work forms, making history a
viable reality for mankind. Thus, canoeing, archery,
and horseback riding persist in society today as play.
Wrestling is no exception."[28] One would certainly have
no difficulty thinking of other obsolete or obsolescent
work forms still with us in the form of games and sports
--fencing, "bronco busting" and other rodeo events,

30

logrolling and other lumberjack sports and games, and dogsled racing, to list a few obvious activities apart from those being discussed involving firearms. Social commentator and pop sociologist Tom Wolfe has even suggested that modern stock-car racing has evolved from the business activities of the "whiskey runners" of Appalachia.[29] However, little attention has been given to the sociopsychological and sociological processes that make the transformation from work forms to recreational forms possible. John S. Oelker, a track coach, has touched on these processes but he did not carry his investigation very far. After briefly discussing the survival value that the ability to run, jump, and throw must have had for "primitive" man, Oelker writes that

> some naturally became more skillful than others and liked to demonstrate this superiority not only in cases of necessity but also in practice before the group or tribe. They soon noticed that their superior strength, speed, agility or skill impressed everyone, particularly the desirable females, and so the faint stirrings of many motives behind man's actions, as we know them today, began to play a part in how well the primitive creatures performed these physical acts.[30]

Though all too brief, this explanation of the evolution of track and field from primitive work forms is in line with the explanation offered above for the derivation of the recreational function of firearms from their practical function.

If the recreational function derives from the practical through man's ability to use symbols and through the concerns with self-images and the expectations of others that come with his symbol-using ability, several things might be expected to accompany such a derivation. First, the popular recreational uses to which firearms are put should reflect the practical uses from which they have evolved. For instance, where formal pistol duels between gentlemen were once common, it would not be surprising to find that target shooting with pistols had survived as a gentlemanly pastime, and that something of the duel had been carried over in different types of shooting matches and in the design of target pistols. If practice sessions held when duels were

31

still common were to be useful to those likely to be called upon to defend their honor, the rules of the target session and the weapons used would have to be similar to the rules and weapons used in the duel. Duel rules and weapons, therefore, would serve as a base from which less practical matches and weapons would evolve. But while gentlemen might be expected to have retained an appreciation for pistol marksmanship, for reasons of the sort outlined previously, where would a common citizen of the same society have acquired an appreciation for the formalities of a pistol match, or the time and money to pursue such an appreciation in the unlikely event that he had acquired it?

In areas where it was once considered a burgher's duty to defend his city as a member of a city militia, when the need arose, and where the right to keep and bear arms for such purposes was considered to be a hard-won privilege, community rifle shoots capable of outlasting the conditions that helped foster such competitions could be expected to be popular. The common man's familiarity with weapons suitable for military use, and matches designed to test his marksmanship with such weapons, could be expected to have the support and encouragement of the whole community. Also, where many people once acquired much or most of their food through hunting, and where game is still available, sports hunting barely distinguishable from practical hunting could be expected to be popular. In fact, to the extent that the game taken is eaten by the hunter and his family and friends, sports and practical hunting overlap. The image of the hunter as provider and an appreciation for practical marksmanship and for general hunting skills, including game calling and stalking, can thereby continue to exist long after other food sources have become available to those who once were dependent upon hunting.

If the recreational derives from the practical in the aforementioned manner, one would also expect to find that those deeply committed to a particular recreational form involving firearms might at the same time consider other recreational forms involving firearms popular in other areas or among different social classes or ethnic groups to be uninteresting, meaningless, frivolous, unsporting, crude, irresponsible, or dangerous. An example of a gun sport considered by many gun enthusiasts to be irresponsible and dangerous is provided by the "fast draw" craze that some Americans were caught up

32

with after television and "adult westerns" introduced
them to a highly romanticized and artificial version of
the western gun fight. A number of rather highly publicized accidents occurred as individuals practiced
this art, and even though fast draw enthusiasts have
formed clubs, held competitions, and worked to make
their sport safe, the "responsible" members of the firearms fraternity still tend to view the Hollywood
western version of "fast draw" as the roller derby of
the gun sports. Even articles concerning practical fast
draw techniques for policemen and military personnel
seldom, if ever, appear in the official journal of the
National Rifle Association, the American Rifleman, and
nothing concerning the activities of the Hollywood
western fast draw clubs, or of the techniques and equipment used in their sport, is ever mentioned in the pages
of this magazine.

And finally, if the recreational derives from the
practical as claimed above, one would expect recreational forms involving firearms, but not necessarily their
use, to develop. Firearms are durable, and where their
possession has been widespread, their possession is
likely to continue to be widespread even after the
practical uses to which firearms have been put have
faded away. In such areas many people become firearms
collectors of a sort through inheritance, while others
put a great deal of effort into collecting firearms.
As some people collect antique furniture, coins, stamps,
bottles, or tools, others collect firearms. The same
sorts of socio-psychological factors cited earlier in
connection with shooting can make collecting worthwhile
--though other factors may also be involved, as shall
be pointed out later. Within the "status community" of
collectors of any variety, a person can acquire prestige
because he owns a particularly sought after piece or
because he has a complete or nearly complete collection
of a certain sort.[31] Collectors of firearms may not
even be interested in firearms in the way that hunters
or target shooters are interested in them. Some collectors do not even fire the guns they own; they simply
collect artifacts that others have helped them to feel
are worth collecting.

And while firearms are durable, they are also in
need of repair or modification from time to time. Professional gunsmiths and engravers are available, of
course, but some individuals work on firearms as a
hobby. As some "do-it-yourself" hobbyists make, repair,

or refinish furniture, others convert obsolescent military rifles to sporting rifles, accurize guns designed for other purposes in order that they might be used for target shooting, make or refinish stocks, carve or engrave wooden or metal parts, or experiment with cartridge loadings. A person whose hobby is refinishing rifle stocks, for example, may well acquire as much prestige and prestige-related self-satisfaction through this sort of activity as he acquires through hunting, target shooting or collecting firearms.

In the preceding discussion it has been pointed out that, given a symbolic interactionist frame of reference, it appears that men do not act in terms of what "objective conditions" demand of them. Rather, men act in terms of their self-images and the expectations of others, their awareness of self as well as their awareness of the expectations of others being made possible through the human ability to use symbols and through the symbolic interaction with others that this ability makes possible. If men act in these terms, not only those human activities that seem to be calculated to insure physical survival but those that seem to threaten survival--such as war--and those that might seem to have little to do with such "serious" matters-- such as art, games, sports, and hobbies--can be rather easily understood. Interaction in any of these contexts makes it possible for individuals to orient themselves with respect to others as well as to the physical world around them. Where individuals cannot so orient themselves, anomie exists and physical survival is not likely to be taken for granted as desirable. But there are other ramifications connected with man's symbol-using abilities that can help us to understand other ways in which firearms function in people's lives and how these other functions have derived from the practical.

SYMBOLIC FUNCTION

After having stated that receiving their first real rifle seemed to serve as "veritable rites of passage that certified their arrival at manhood" for many American boys, Hofstadter noted that

> it is still argued by some defenders of our
> gun culture, and indeed conceded by some
> of its critics, that the gun cannot and
> will not be given up because it is a basic

symbol of masculinity. But the trouble
with such glib Freudian generalities is
that they do not explain cultural variations: they do not tell us why men elsewhere have not found the gun essential to
their masculinity.[32]

A symbolic link of the Freudian variety between firearms
and masculinity would certainly be called into question
by the existence of cultural variations. But a Freudian
interpretation of a possible linkage of this sort is not
necessary, as Hofstadter inadvertently acknowledges
later on in his essay. "The gun," he wrote, "though it
had a natural place in the South's outdoor culture, as
well as a necessary place in the work of slave patrols,
was also an important symbol of white male status."[33]
But rather than attempt to explain how firearms or any
other artifact can come to be symbolic of anything,
Hofstadter simply dismisses possible symbolism of this
sort as irrational and anachronistic. Given the assumptions upon which this study is based, however, the
symbolic function of firearms in some socio-cultural
settings is not difficult to explain, and little about
the popular attachment to firearms wherever such an
attachment can be found can be understood unless such
symbolism is considered.

Man the symbol-user emerges from the discussion in
the previous section as a creature who situationally
responds to objective conditions as they are filtered
through a socially acquired subjective frame of reference in terms of the image he has, or would like to
have, of himself, and in terms of the expectations he
feels that others, particularly significant others,
have of a person of his kind. It was even suggested
that the maintenance or enhancement of socially acquired
self-images quite often takes precedence over the satisfaction of needs that insure physical survival when
there is a choice to be made between them. Within this
context, it was then shown how various sorts of activities generally assumed to have little if any utilitarian
function or survival value--activities commonly referred
to as recreational and more specifically labeled sports
or hobbies--could evolve from more "practical" activities, take a particular form, and come to be considered
meaningful and worthwhile, even all-important, to those
who engage in them. Target shooting can become a desirable pastime even for those who worry little about
having to defend themselves or to hunt their own food.

35

And similarly, collecting firearms can become a desirable pastime for those who may have little desire to fire the weapons they collect. Such activities simply become meaningful through symbolic interaction with others, and having become meaningful, enable individuals engaged in the activities to orient themselves toward others and the world around them. However, not only activities but artifacts can be expected to acquire meaning for man the symbol-user, if the assumptions upon which this study is based are accepted.

Various practical as well as recreational activities center around automobiles, boats, cameras, parachutes, skis, postage stamps, old furniture, etc., all of which have, or have had, their practical uses. But to men as symbol users, these artifacts can become other than means to practical and social self-realizational recreational ends. Since they have been used in certain ways by certain people to accomplish certain tasks that various others have viewed with favor, disfavor, or indifference, these objects are not simply objects; they are objects invested with meaning. As objects invested with meaning, they may be used as badges that enable those individuals displaying them to mark themselves off from those who do not display them. The badge-bearer can lay claim to a certain status or to certain privileges both objectively, in that the badge shows those who recognize it that the bearer is so entitled, and subjectively, in that the badge enables the bearer to feel that he is so entitled.[34] Those displaying such objects, may also lay claim to certain "character traits" and other qualities supposedly possessed by others of "their kind," and others may accept their claim. An automobile, for example, provides us with a means of transporting ourselves from one place to another, but it also provides us with a means of showing off. Before the "energy crisis" and the related trend toward more economical small cars, new Cadillacs or Lincolns were the cars of the "successful" man, the man who obviously had what it took to get to the top. These were the cars of the doctor or lawyer in the "respectable" middle class world, and they are still the cars of the pimp in the ghetto. They were also the cars of the man who desired to look successful. The "sports car" was the car of the happy-go-lucky, carefree young modern and those not so young or modern who wished to look so. Before the advent of the pocket calculator, the slide rule encased in a leather holster dangling from the belt of a student marked him off as someone

majoring in engineering, "science," mathematics or some
such "difficult" subject, and, therefore, it marked him
off as someone with "intelligence" and "ambition" enough
to put that intelligence to "good use." With respect to
weapons, the sword, for instance, has symbolized warrior
or noble status and has thereby been linked with such
traits as "courage" and "honor."[35]

Given the preceding, it is not surprising that
firearms also can become "status symbols," not only for
the soldiers and hunters for whom they are tools of the
trade, but also for those who through their interaction
with others have come to identify with firearms users
of one variety or another. For some boys, therefore,
receiving their first real gun may well serve as something of a rite of passage. However, other people in
one way or another, if only inadvertently, will have had
to encourage him to define his acquisition in this way
before he can so define it. In areas where firearms
have functioned practically or recreationally in the
lives of many people, such assistance may often be
forthcoming, but due to "differential association," such
assistance may not always be forthcoming.[36] Hence, in
the United States not all young men are interested in
acquiring a real gun while some young women _are_ interested in acquiring one. Therefore, where the acquisition of a firearm helps mark its new owner off as a
"responsible" person or something of the sort, the
reasons for this state of affairs are no more mysterious
and difficult to understand than are those which allow
an automobile, for example, to function in the same
fashion.

But artifacts of various sorts, including firearms,
can function symbolically in people's lives in a more
subtle fashion. As badges or status symbols, artifacts
enable people to mark themselves off from one another or
to link themselves to others with whom they identify.
Symbolic interactionists are particularly interested in
this sort of symbolic function, the sort that enables
people to _interact_ with one another, to know what to
expect of others and to know what others expect of them.
Phenomenologists, however, are more likely to be interested in the everchanging, ongoing, pictures of reality
that men acquire through their symbolic interaction with
others. These pictures enable men to _make sense_ of the
objective world with which they must cope.

From the phenomenological point of view, therefore,

37

artifacts of various sorts can serve as symbolic links
to the past, the future, cherished associations, far-
away places, a way of life, heroic individuals, great
events, or anything else that can be subjectively experienced within the context of the socially-constructed
world views subscribed to by interacting individuals at
any given time. Artifacts of various sorts, then, can
be vital to the preservation of these world views.[37]
Firearms, for instance, can become more than weapons,
pieces of sporting equipment, or badges signifying
membership in a certain group, newly come-by responsibility, masculinity, or other such qualities or traits.
Firearms can become artifacts positively or negatively
associated with Daniel Boone, the Civil War, the
elemental lifestyles of the frontier, war in general,
crime, masculinity in the abstract, adventure, civic
responsibility or irresponsibility, slavery or freedom.
Negative symbolism, in fact, has probably hampered
efforts to understand the phenomenon with which this
study deals. Note, for instance, that when television
news commentators report increases in the crime rate, a
drawing of a pistol often accompanies the statistics as
they are flashed on the screen even though firearms have
not been involved in many of the categories of crime
being discussed. In the eyes of the media and political
"liberals," firearms, particularly handguns, and crime
are symbolically linked.

Positive gun symbolism, of course, is hardly rare.
The Kentucky, or, more properly, Pennsylvania rifle, for
instance, is more than just an old gun to many Americans. It is the gun of the legendary pioneers who
pushed through the Cumberland Gap to clear the wilderness and begin "building a nation"--the gun of Daniel
Boone, Davy Crockett and other "heroes" of days gone
by. Similarly, the Colt Single Action Army revolver,
thanks to Hollywood and to writers of pulp westerns,
has become symbolically linked with the "Old West" even
though many other makes and models of handguns were
carried by the cowboys, soldiers, and gunfighters on the
frontier. It would be surprising if these kinds of
associations did not overlap status community motives
for collecting firearms, since possession of such artifacts can provide symbolic links in the present to an
otherwise hazy past reality upon which the present is
assumed to be based. Symbolic associations of the sort
being discussed, however, are not likely to be widespread in societies where the possession and use of
firearms has never been widespread. On the other hand,

where firearms ownership and use for practical purposes has been widespread, one might expect to find that antique firearms of the types most associated with past "glories," modern replicas of such weapons, and modern arms bearing some of their features are popular.

SUMMARY AND THESIS STATEMENT

The following thesis statement summarizes the phenomenologically-informed perspective on the popular attachment to firearms that has been presented in this chapter:

1. Firearms are basically tools developed by men to enable them to cope with objective conditions as these conditions are socially defined and subjectively experienced.

2. Due to the ramifications of man's social shaping through symbolic interaction, recreational and symbolic functions tend to derive almost automatically from the practical uses to which firearms have been put, the derivative functions beginning to develop almost simultaneously with the practical.

3. Where objective environmental and sociocultural conditions, as they have been socially defined and subjectively experienced, foster widespread practical use of them, firearms will thereby tend to acquire widespread recreational and symbolic significance which, in terms of the type of firearms involved, their design, and the form which the sports and hobbies involving them take, bear the stamp of the practical.

4. This tendency will insure that the widespread interest in and attachment to firearms will survive the fading of their practical function, or, if certain objective conditions continue to exist and be defined as threatening, support the continuation of the practical function.

Relating these four propositions to Chapter I's discussion of firearms possession in the United States and other parts of the modern world, adds two more propositions to this thesis statement:

5. Objective environmental and sociocultural condi-

tions in the United States, as they have been
socially defined and subjectively experienced, have
fostered the widespread practical use of shotguns,
rifles, and handguns, while conditions, as they
have been socially defined and subjectively experienced, that have prevailed in other parts of the
urban industrial world have fostered the use of none
or only one or two of these types of firearms.

6. Differences in, and for that matter, similarities
between the United States and other urban industrial
nations with respect to the civilian possession of
firearms and related phenomena, can thereby be adequately accounted for in terms of the preceding.

FOOTNOTES

1. Richard Hofstadter, "America as a Gun Culture," _American Heritage_, October, 1970, pp. 7 & 10.

2. Ibid., 6.

3. Ibid., 82.

4. Ibid., 7 & 84. See pictorial treatment of the recreational uses of firearms.

5. See the firearms regulations section of the _Reader's Guide to Periodical Literature_, 1959 to date. While there are a few exceptions, the overwhelming majority of the gun control articles listed in _Reader's Guide_, other than those appearing in outdoor magazines, accept the cultural lag-vested interest explanation for the American attachment to firearms. Also see Carl Bakal, _The Right to Bear Arms_ (New York: McGraw Hill Book Company, 1966), and George D. Newton, Jr. and Franklin E. Zimring, _Firearms and Violence in American Life_ (Washington, D.C.: U.S. Government Printing Office, 1969).

6. Hofstadter; and Newton and Zimring.

7. Bakal, 68-92.

8. See practically any editorial in the _American Rifleman_, _Guns_, or _Guns and Ammo_. See the firearms regulations section of the _Reader's Guide to Periodical Literature_, 1959 to date. The gun control articles listed in _Reader's Guide_ appearing in the outdoor magazines accept the utilitarian explanation for the American attachment to firearms. Also see F.S. Meyers, "Right of the People to Bear Arms," _National Review_, July 5, 1968, p. 657; and Don B. Kates, Jr., "Handgun Control: Prohibition Revisited," _Inquiry_, December 5, 1977, pp. 20-21. Books based on the utilitarian explanation include James E. Serven, editor, James B. Trefethen, compilor, _Americans and Their Guns: The National Rifle Association Story Through Nearly a Century of Service to the Nation_ (Harrisburg, Pennsylvania: Stackpole Company, 1967); Bill R. Davidson, _To Keep and Bear Arms_ (New York: Arlington House, 1969); James B.Whisker, _Our Vanishing Freedom_

(McLean, Virginia: Heritage House Publishers, 1972); Robert J. Kukla, Gun Control (Harrisburg, Pennsylvania: Stackpole Books, 1973).

9. Liberal civil liberties lawyer Don B. Kates, Jr. has managed to penetrate this barrier to bring several articles and a book sympathetic to the utilitarian explanation to these audiences. See his Restricting Handguns: The Liberal Skeptics Speak Out (North River Press, Inc., 1979); "Against Civil Disarmament," Harper's, September, 1978, pp. 28-33; and "Why Gun Control Won't Work," Commonweal, March 13, 1981, pp. 136-138.

10. Karl Mannheim, Ideology and Utopia: An Introduction to the Sociology of Knowledge, trans. Louis Wirth & Edward Shils, A Harvest Book (New York: Harcourt, Brace & World, Inc., 1955), pp. 55-108.

11. Konrad Lorenz, On Aggression, trans. Marjorie Kerr Wilson (New York: Harcourt, Brace and World, 1966), Motivation of Human and Animal Behavior (Van Nostrand Reinhold, 1973), and King Solomon's Ring, trans. Margorie Kerr Wilson (New York: Crowell Publishers, 1952); Robert Ardery, African Genesis (London: Gollins, 1961), The Social Contract (New York: Atheneum, 1970), and The Territorial Imperative (New York: Atheneum, 1966); and Desmond Morris, The Naked Ape (New York: McGraw Hill, 1967).

12. The ethological perspective has been given much exposure through the works of Ardrey and Morris cited above. An example of the way Freudian views have been worked into modern fiction is provided by Ian Fleming's James Bond spy thriller, The Man With The Golden Gun (New York: Signet Books).

13. Bakal, 68-92.

14. See Mark Kram, "Of Arms and Men They Sing," Sports Illustrated, May 7, 1973, p. 62. Kram notes that handgun shootings most sophisticated ideologist, Jeff Cooper, is well grounded in the writings of anthropologist Raymond Dart and ethologist Lorenz. Cooper indicates that this is the case in the introduction to Fighting Handguns (Los Angeles: Trend Books, 1958), p. 4.

15. See Ashley Montagu, ed., Man and Aggression (London, Oxford, New York: Oxford University Press, 1973).

16. A standard dictionary definition of intelligence is the "capacity for reasoning, understanding, and for similar forms of mental activity; aptitude in grasping truths, facts, meanings, etc." Rational is defined as "having or exercising reason, sound judgment, or good sense," and reason as "the mental powers concerned with forming judgements or inferences" and "sound judgement, good sense."

17. Kenneth Page Oakley, Man the Tool-Maker, Phoenix Books (Chicago: The University of Chicago Press, 1958), p. 1.

18. Hofstadter, 82.

19. Newton and Zimring, 61.

20. Ibid., 68.

21. Ibid.

22. See the Armed Citizen in any issue of The American Rifleman.

23. Newton and Zimring.

24. See Peter L. Berger and Thomas Luckmann, The Social Construction of Reality: A Treatise in the Sociology of Knowledge (Garden City, New York: Anchor Books, Doubleday & Company, Inc., 1966).

25. Hugh Dalziel Duncan, Symbols in Society, (New York: Oxford University Press, 1968), p. 13. Duncan makes the point as follows:

> In the American sociological tradition of James, Mead, Dewey, Park, Cooley, and Burke, the tradition of the 'act' is very different from the European tradition of 'culture' analysis. . . . Action theory is very different from culture theory. Art, science, religion, and philosophy in the European tradition are systems of knowledge (how we 'apprehend' the

world), in the American they are
systems of action (how we 'act' in
the world).

26. Jack D. Douglas, American Social Order (New York:
The Free Press, London: Collier-MacMillan Limited,
1971), p. 144. Douglas claims that "the central
idea of the symbolic interactionist perspective . . . is that social definitions of one's
self and of actions are the major reasons why individuals perform actions." See Glenn M. Vernon,
Human Interaction: An Intro to Sociology, (New
York: The Ronald Press Co., 1972) for a consistent application of the interactionist perspective
to various social and socio-psychological phenomena
including motivation. pp. 445-462.

27. This argument has been criticized by Dennis H.
Wrong in "The Oversocialized Conception of Man in
Modern Sociology," American Sociological Review,
26 (April, 1961), 183-193. More precisely, Wrong
criticizes those who argue that "people are so
profoundly sensitive to the expectations of others
that all action is inevitably guided by these expectations." But while his criticism might cause
some discomfort to those who see man as an acceptance seeker or a status seeker, it does not undermine those who see man as an identity seeker
who must know who he is before he can orient himself to the world around him. Man the identity
seeker must concern himself with the expectations
of others in order to orient himself, but he will
not necessarily feel obliged to meet these expectations as he interprets them. In fact, to the
extent that he has, through interaction with
others, come to think of himself as a non-conformist, he may feel obliged to violate the expectations he thinks others have of him in order to
meet those of some non-conformist ideal.

28. Gregory P. Stone, "Wrestling--The Great American
Passion Play," in Sport: Readings from a Sociological Perspective, edited by Eric Dunning
(Toronto: University of Toronto Press, 1972), p.
302.

29. Tom Wolfe, The Kandy-Kolored Tangerine-Flake
Streamline Baby, (New York: Farrar, Straus &
Girous, 1965), p. 139.

44

30. John S. Oelkers, "Track and Field," in Motivation in Play, Games and Sports, ed. Ralph Slovenko and James A. Knight, (Springfield, Illinois: Charles C. Thomas Publishers, 1967), p. 472.

31. See Joseph Bensman, "Classical Music and the Status Game," in Games, Sport and Power, ed. Gregory P. Stone (New Brunswick, New Jersey: Transaction Books, 1972), pp. 163-177. Bensman applies Max Weber's concept of "stand" or "status community" to those whose lifestyles center around classical music. Also see Max Weber, The Theory of Social and Economic Organization, trans. A.M. Henderson and Talcott Parsons (New York: The Free Press and London: Collier Macmillan Limited, 1964), p. 347n.

32. Hofstadter, 82.

33. Ibid., 84.

34. See Duncan, 213; Orrin E. Klapp, Collective Search for Identiy (New York: Holt Rinehart and Winston, Inc., 1969), pp. 73-115; Kurt Lang and Gladys Engel Lang, Collective Dynamics (New York: Thomas Y. Crowell Company, 1961), pp. 480-481; and Gideon Sjoberg, The Preindustrial City; Past and Present (New York: The Free Press and London: Collier-Macmillan Limited, 1960), pp. 126-133. These are only a few of the works that point out how dress, speech, and mannerisms are used by people to mark themselves off from some and identify themselves with others.

35. Lee Kennett and James LaVerne Anderson, The Gun in America: The Origins of a National Dilemma (Westport, Connecticut & London, England: Greenwood Press, 1975), p. 6, and Noel Perrin, Giving Up the Gun: Japan's Reversion to the Sword, 1543-1879 (Boston: David R. Godine, Publisher, 1979) p. 36.

36. The concept "differential association," though applied to a different phenomenon here, is used in essentially the same sense as its creators intended it to be used. See Edwin H. Sutherland and Donald R. Cressey, "Learning to be Deviant," in The Study of Social Problems: 5 Perspectives, ed. Earl Rubington and Martin S. Weinberg (New York, London and Toronto: Oxford University Press, 1971), pp. 143-144.

37. See Alfred Schutz, <u>Alfred Schutz: On Phenomenology
    and Social Relations</u>, ed. Helmut R. Wagner (Chicago
    and London: The University of Chicago Press,
    1970), p. 296

CHAPTER III

METHODOLOGICAL CONSIDERATIONS

Having discussed the works of several prominent sociologists who have been classified by themselves or by others as phenomenologists, sociologists of knowledge, symbolic interactionists, ethnomethodologists, and so forth, Irwin Deutscher wrote:

> The unifying element, the core which permits all of these diverse sociologists to be called "phenomenological," is that they share a perspective on human behavior and social processes. What they have in common is that each of them insists that the proper study of man must attempt to understand the world as its actors do—to view it from their perspective. The phenomenological orientation always sees reality as constructed by men in the process of thinking about it.[1]

This study, which draws on various "subjectivist" sociological perspectives, is phenomenological in the preceding sense. In the previous chapter it was argued that if we are to understand the popular attachment to firearms wherever that attachment exists, we must consider the ways in which man's tool-creating and -using abilities are affected by his symbol-creating and -using abilities. And we must also consider the socially constructed realities that man's symbolic abilities make possible. The six propositions listed at the end of Chapter II amount to a phenomenologically-informed attempt to spell out the ways in which man's symbol-creating and -using abilities might be expected to have affected his firearms-creating and -using efforts, and to show how these social and existential considerations might help us to understand the popular attachment to firearms as that attachment exists in the United States and elsewhere.

In order to support the preceding propositions, the development and use of the basic types and modifications of firearms likely to be found in civilian hands must be linked to the people who developed and used these guns, and to the efforts of these people to cope with the world of their time and place as they, but not

47

necessarily all others of their time and place, perceived that world. To accomplish this linkage, it is
necessary to penetrate the worlds of the gun creators
and users of various times and places, and in this chapter the means of accomplishing this penetration will be
discussed as each proposition is examined separately or
paired with another.

PROPOSITION I Firearms are basically tools developed
by men to enable them to cope with objective conditions
as these conditions are socially defined and subjectively experienced.

    Symbolic interactionist Glenn M. Vernon has written
concerning objects: "They proclaim the intentions of
those who use them."[2] Taken out of context, this statement is simplistic and somewhat misleading. As most
symbolic interactionists would probably be quick to
point out, nothing in the "world out there" tells us
about itself. Everything must be interpreted or read;
therefore, everything--the words on this page, the objects that "proclaim the intentions of those who use
them"--can be misinterpreted or misread. Yet whether
read as intended or not, the words on this page were
selected to convey a certain meaning, and whether interpreted accurately or not it is assumed that the user of
a tool had something in mind when he selected or created
that tool to accomplish a certain task. It is assumed,
therefore, that meanings are "out there" to be read,
and it is the phenomenologist's task to get at those
meanings created and held by others.[3] In this qualified
sense, therefore, objects "proclaim the intentions of
those who use them." And if this is the case, a reading
of the design characteristics of various types of firearms can help us to determine whether they were intended
to serve as tools (practical function), as pieces of
sporting equipment (recreational function), as badges
or as symbolic links to something or other (symbolic
function), as the following examples illustrate.

    Modern rifles differ in many ways from those that
were produced in the 16th century, and yet rifles of all
periods have something in common that sets them apart
from other types of firearms likely to be found in
civilian hands. Rifles all have rather long barrels--
measuring from about 16 inches or so for carbines to
four feet or more. Rifles also have shoulder stocks.
But while these features generally mark them off from
pistols, they do not mark rifles off from shotguns or

smoothbore muskets. What rifles have in common that sets them off from these other firearms is that their relatively long barrels are spiral grooved on the inside. Their barrels are, in other words, rifled. This rifling causes bullets fired through such barrels to spin, giving the bullets stability after they have left the barrel, thereby making accurate and consistent shot placement possible at some distance. With the rifle held in both hands and the stock held to his shoulder, the shooter achieves steadiness and can align his sights with his target to take advantage of the accuracy built into his weapon. Given these central characteristics of the rifle, therefore, it seems obvious that a great deal of thought has gone into producing a weapon that can hit targets at some distance if the shooter has the skill to use it properly.

Interpretation has certainly been involved in this analysis of rifles; this interpretation would have been difficult for those who have not acquired some firsthand familiarity with such weapons. But for those familiar with them, the very design features of the rifle seem in a certain sense to "speak for themselves." Yet these design features do not tell us everything. They do not tell us, for example, why anyone should be interested in developing such a weapon, or why certain "kinds of people" but not others would be interested in acquiring rifles. To answer these questions, the development and use of rifles must be put into social-historical context.

When we discover, with the help of firearms historians, that rifles were developed in central Europe where they became popular with those who hunted for food, the intentions of their creators and users begin to come into focus. When we take into consideration that these hunters had access to large animals, but that the mountainous terrain of the area often made it difficult to get within effective smoothbore or crossbow range of these creatures, the "world out there" with which these ancient riflemen were trying to cope is brought into sharper focus. The rifle was originally a tool quite rationally developed to enable those who used it to cope with that which they had good reason to be concerned about in the "world out there" as they saw it. And the very specific link between this tool and the tasks to be accomplished with it in the "world out there," as its users saw that world, is emphasized by the fact that the vast majority of the soldiers in

European and American armies continued to use the far less accurate smoothbore musket for 300 years or so after the principle of rifling was known. If we consider the design characteristics of the musket and place them in context, the existence of such a state of affairs is quite understandable, as shall be seen later. But for now, suffice it to say that until certain changes were made in the rifle and in infantry tactics, the features that made the rifle suitable for hunting also made it less than suitable for ordinary military purposes.

The purpose of the preceding discussion has been to demonstrate that firearms in a sense "proclaim the intentions" of those who created their various types, as well as the intentions of those among whom the various types of firearms became popular. In proclaiming these intentions, firearms allow us a glimpse of the worlds with which others far off in time and space were trying to cope. But the purpose of the preceding was also to demonstrate that the subjective intentions, the meanings associated with firearms use, can be brought into sharper focus only if such as the following are considered: When and where were certain basic types of firearms--shotguns, rifles, and handguns--and basic modifications thereof--repeating shotguns, rifles, and pocket pistols, for example--developed? When and where did they become popular? Among what "kinds of people" were they popular? With what kinds of activity was their use associated? What were the conditions in the "world out there" with which these people had to cope at these times and places?

To expand a bit on the last three questions, it would seem safe to assume that wars during feudal periods were experienced differently by the aristocracy than they were experienced by the peasantry. Also, though roads in 18th century England were infested by highwaymen, there is reason to believe that the wealthier classes who had occasion to travel were more concerned about this state of affairs than were the poorer classes who seldom traveled and possessed little that was worth stealing. And the presence of bears in the forest is likely to present human forest dwellers with problems that persons who share their home areas with animals no larger than rabbits never have to face. In other words, if firearms are to be fitted into meaningful frames of reference, questions such as the following must also be considered for their periods of development and use:

How was society stratified? How did people support themselves? How did lifestyles differ from one major group to another? Were people geographically mobile or bound to the land? Was game present? What kind? Was it hunted? By whom? How? Was human conflict common? Between individuals or collectivities or both? What classes of people were directly involved? How did firearms fit into the picture? Were firearms easily obtainable? What types were used? For what? By whom? Were attempts made to regulate the use of firearms? To whom did the regulations apply? By whom were the regulations advocated? Were certain classes of people encouraged to use firearms? How? By whom?

This means of reading firearms to determine whether various basic types and modifications thereof are essentially tools, pieces of sporting equipment, badges, or symbolic links, is similar to the "verstehen" approach to the study of the actions of men advocated by Max Weber and Wilhelm Dilthey.[4] It will be expanded upon in the discussion of PROPOSITION II.

PROPOSITION II Due to the ramifications of man's social shaping through symbolic interaction, recreational and symbolic functions tend to derive almost automatically from the practical uses to which firearms have been put, the derivative functions beginning to develop almost simultaneously with the practical.

As mentioned above, all rifles, ancient as well as modern, are precision instruments in that they are designed to enable their users to place single projectiles accurately at some distance. But as anyone familiar with such weapons is well aware, some types of rifles have much more accuracy built into them than have other types, though both types are products of the same time and place. An expert marksman armed with the best modern hunting or military rifle available, could hardly be expected to hold his own in formal target competition with a marksman of equal skill armed with the best target rifle available for that specific type of match. Yet a price is paid for this extreme accuracy, and those rifles designed especially for formal target shooting are too cumbersome, too fragile, or both, for long term hunting or military service. Ever more sophisticated target refinements that make weapons less than satisfactory for hunting in the wilderness or coping with enemies on the battlefield, therefore, would seem to provide us with something of an indicator concerning the

51

importance those who use such rifles attach to doing
well in shooting matches. When we find that at various
times and places the winners of formal shooting matches
have been richly rewarded at impressive community ceremonies, much can be inferred concerning the maintenance
and enhancement of the self-images of the competitors.

Those who are familiar with firearms are likely to
be aware that modern military, hunting, and target rifles differ significantly from each other. Such individuals are also likely to be aware that these modern
firearms differ significantly from their predecessors
of the muzzleloading era. The most obvious difference
between muzzleloaders and modern guns, is that the latter can be loaded by simply placing a cartridge containing both powder and bullet into its chamber or magazine,
while the former must be loaded by pouring just the
right abount of loose powder down the barrel and ramming
a lead ball in on top of it, a rather tedious and time
consuming process. But there are other differences.
The smokeless powder used in modern guns produces flat-
ter bullet trajectories and greater accuracy than does
the old black powder used in muzzleloaders,and it also
makes it much easier to keep guns clean. Black powder
is quite corrosive, and unless guns using it are washed
carefully after having been fired, they can be ruined
rather quickly. Add to all this the fact that the latest military rifles and most of the latest hunting rifles are repeaters that can be fired a number of times
and quite rapidly before reloading, while the great
majority of muzzleloaders were single-shots, and the
relative convenience and efficiency of the modern firearms is difficult to overlook. Therefore, rifles produced in recent years possessing the features of these
ancient arms--single-shot, muzzleloading, etc.--and in
some cases resembling the old guns so much that only
experts can tell them apart, seem to tell us something.
And when we find moderns paying as much for these non-
antiques as they would have to pay for a rifle of modern
design, and wearing frontier buckskins while hunting or
target shooting with these replicas of old guns, it is
difficult to think of such guns as being merely tools
or pieces of sporting equipment. Though interpretation
is obviously still involved here, when placed in context
these guns seem almost to tell us that those with whom
they are popular are attempting to link themselves symbolically to the heroic lifestyles associated with our
nation's past.

No claim is made above that all target shooting is done with firearms especially designed for the sport, or that all target matches are formal and have lavish award ceremonies, or that symbolic linkages with this or that are always accomplished with firearms as obviously designed for the purpose as those described. These extreme, yet quite common examples have been chosen in order to demonstrate that when firearms are put into social-historical context they can "tell us" whether their designers and those with whom they became popular saw them as tools, pieces of sporting equipment or symbols. They were also chosen to demonstrate that various designs in context make the links between the practical functions on the one hand and the recreational and symbolic functions on the other seem rather obvious. But, as noted earlier, while the design features "tell us" a great deal, they do not "tell us" all. If the meanings associated with the recreational and symbolic uses of firearms and the ties between these and the meanings associated with their practical use are to be gotten at and brought into sharper focus, questions such as the following must be considered: What kinds of recreational activities involving firearms have people participated in at various times and places? What classes of people have participated in them? What sorts of social recognition have they received? From whom have they received it? How have firearms been displayed on the person in various societies at various times? How have they been ornamented? On what sorts of occasions, other than those associated with their practical or recreational use, have firearms been carried? What types have been carried on these occasions? By whom? What eras, events, lifestyles, etc., other than the contemporary, have been reflected in the interest in firearms in any given period? What sorts of community or overall sociocultural support have these various manifestations of interests in the past received? What classes of people were involved with them?

PROPOSITION III Where objective environmental and sociocultural conditions, as they have been socially defined and subjectively experienced, foster widespread practical use of them, firearms will thereby tend to acquire widespread recreational and symbolic significance which, in terms of the types of firearms involved, their design and the form which sports and hobbies involving them take, bear the stamp of the practical.

PROPOSITION IV This tendency will insure that the wide-

spread interest in and attachment to firearms will survive the fading of their practical function, or, if
certain objective conditions continue to exist and be
defined as threatening, support the continuance of the
practical function.

To the extent that PROPOSITIONS I and II can be
supported in the manner set forth above, PROPOSITIONS
III and IV should also be supported. But to restate
III and IV at this point serves to remind us why I and
II are important to this study and to link these four
propositions to the central thrust of the studies
thesis, as made explicit in PROPOSITIONS V and VI.

PROPOSITION V Objective environmental and sociocultural conditions in the United States, as they have been
socially defined and subjectively experienced, have
fostered the widespread practical use of shotguns, rifles and handguns, while conditions, as they have been
socially defined and subjectively experienced, that
have prevailed in other parts of the urban industrial
world have fostered the use of none or only one or two
of these types of firearms.

PROPOSITION VI Differences in, and for that matter,
similarities between the United States and other urban
industrial nations with respect to the civilian possession of firearms and related phenomena, can thereby be
adequately accounted for in terms of the preceding.

If PROPOSITIONS V and VI are to be supported, differences between the United States and the rest of the
modern, urban, industrial world should emerge as firearms designs are analyzed and placed in social-historical context by way of attempting to support PROPOSITIONS
I through IV. But with what other parts of the world
should the United States be compared?

When subscribers to the cultural lag-vested interest
explanation for the widespread popular attachment to
firearms in the United States compare the firearms situation here to that in other nations, those other nations are generally the "free nations" of Europe--Great
Britain, France, Belgium, the Netherlands, West Germany,
Austria, Italy, Switzerland and the Scandanavian coun-
tries--plus Japan, Australia and Canada. These nations
seem to be considered more urban, industrial, and modern than, for example, Mexico, Brazil, or Egypt. And
these nations are viewed as being more democratic than

the countries behind the Iron Curtain and other nations such as South Africa. It is assumed that unlike citizens of the "underdeveloped nations," the citizens of modern nations no longer need firearms. And it is also assumed that the citizens of modern "free world" countries have rid themselves of "gun cultures" because as free and enlightened persons they chose to do so through their duly-elected representatives, not because they were forced to do so through the application of the police state methods of the totalitarian states.

Canada and Australia are specifically cited as proof that even those nations barely removed from the frontier have, in Hofstadter's words, "succeeded in modifying their old gun habits." Only vested interests combined with the inherent weaknesses of the federal system of government, therefore, could have kept the United States from ridding itself of its "gun culture." Since all of these assumptions are being called into question in this study, the nations with which the United States will be compared in the following pages will be those of "free" Europe listed above, plus Japan, Canada, and Australia. For reasons that will become apparent, the European nations and Japan will be grouped together and classified as "Old World" societies for purposes of analysis, and Australia and Canada will be treated together with the United States as "New World" societies.

If the basis of the practical function of firearms and the relationship between it and the other functions as stated in PROPOSITIONS I through IV can be shown to hold for (1) the now modern formerly Old World societies, (2) the now modern formerly frontier societies apart from the United States, and (3) the United States, these propositions are supported at the same time that the basis for comparison necessary for the support of PROPOSITION V and VI is provided. This is the method employed in this study; however, for reasons having to do primarily with the availability and accessibility of sources, the testing of PROPOSITIONS I through IV can be expected to be more thorough for the United States than for the other societies. Nevertheless, treatment of the other societies, particularly with respect to PROPOSITION I, should still be more than adequate for the accomplishment of the task at hand.

While this book is informed by the author's own first-hand experience and familiarity with guns and with people who collect guns or keep them for protection or recreation, it relies heavily on sources such as the following: social, military, sports, costume, and arms histories; memoirs and travelers' accounts; the works of students of ethnic relations, social stratification and deviance; gun catalogs and advertisements; and the literature of the firearms fraternity--hunters, collectors, target shooters, and others.

FOOTNOTES

1. Irwin Deutscher, *What We Say/What We Do* (Glenview, Illinois and Brighton, England: Scott, Foresman and Company, 1973), p. 328.

2. Glenn M. Vernon, *Human Interaction: An Introduction to Sociology* (2nd ed., New York: The Ronald Press Co., 1972), p. 192.

3. This is not meant to imply that this phenomenological task can ever be fully accomplished.

4. Max Weber, *The Theory of Social and Economic Organization*, trans. A.M. Henderson & Talcott Parsons (New York: Free Press and London: Collier Macmillan Ltd., 1964), pp. 94-96.

CHAPTER IV

THE EVOLUTION OF THE GUN

POWDER AND BALL AND ONE SHOT: ? TO 1850

Credit for the invention of both gunpowder and the gun has often been given to the Chinese, who, according to some of the early translators of ancient manuscripts, were using gun powder and guns hundreds of years before they came to be known in Europe.[1] A number of firearms historians, however, are now suggesting that there are several good reasons for questioning these claims.[2] But the question hardly needs to be resolved here, for wherever gunpowder and the gun were invented, the technological developments that have made firearms what they are today have, for the most part, occurred in Europe and its North American extension, the United States.

There is evidence to the effect that firearms existed in Europe at least as early as 1326, and while these early guns were cannons, arms small enough to be held and fired by one man may have been known in Italy and southern Germany as early as 1340 and in Britain by 1371.[3] These "hand cannons," as their name implies, were simply miniature versions of the standard sized cannons of the time, and they consisted of shaft- or pole-mounted iron tubes with one end welded shut and provided with a touchhole.[4]

In order to load a primitive portable firearm of this sort, the desired amount of powder was first poured down its barrel from its upturned muzzle, and then a wooden disc was tamped down over the powder with the aid of a ramrod. The disc separated the powder from the lead, brass, iron, or bronze ball that was rammed down the barrel next, and its primary function was to increase compression. Then a little powder was poured into a small hole at the breech end of the barrel to make contact with the charge inside the gun and the weapon was ready to be fired.[5] Firing was then accomplished by setting off the powder in the touchhole with the aid of a glowing wire or fuse. When the charge inside the gun went off, a back-flash erupted from the touchhole.

When a "hand cannon" was fired, the pole upon which the gun was mounted was planted on or in the ground, or it was passed under the arm pit. Such weapons were merely pointed rather than aimed, therefore, and much luck was involved if the shooter hit his mark at more than a few yards distance. However, there is some reason to believe that these primitive guns could do considerable damage when fired point-blank into . masses of unarmored men at ranges of sixty yards or less, and under twenty yards they could pierce armor.[6]

Though formidable in some ways, the hand cannon was still incredibly cumbersome. The tedious loading process described above had to be repeated after every shot to prepare the weapon for the next shot--if the gun was still in one piece. A fire source had to be readily accessible if the touchfuse used to fire the gun was to be kept lit. And since the gun could only be pointed rather than aimed, nowhere near the accuracy attainable with such contemporary weapons as the longbow or the crossbow could be achieved with the hand cannon.

Between 1440 and 1470 the ignition and aiming deficiencies of the hand cannon seem to have been overcome to a certain extent as gunstocks essentially the same as those used today gradually replaced the poles upon which the hand cannons had been mounted and as the matchlock was developed.[7] With respect to loading, however, the tedious and time-consuming loading process associated with the hand cannons of the 14th century remained basically the same for all firearms developed before the middle of the 19th century. This means that until 130 or so years ago, the great majority of firearms users in even the most industrially "advanced" parts of the world had at their disposal one shot per gun. Before a second shot could be fired from the same gun, it had to be loaded with powder and ball and primed more or less as described above.

Of course, guns with two barrels, though not the norm, were known during the muzzle-loading era, and these made two reasonably quick shots available to their users. Guns with more than two barrels were also made occasionally, and single-barreled repeaters utilizing revolving cylinders or magazines were made as far back as the 15th and 17th centuries respectively.[8] But the guns with three or more barrels were too cumbersome to become popular, and the repeaters, though ingenious, were fragile, intricate, expensive, unreliable, or dangerous to their users until revolvers were perfected and mass produced toward the middle of the 19th century.[9]

And prior to the invention and perfection of metallic cartridges around the middle of the 19th century, each chamber of these various types of multibarreled guns and repeaters had to be loaded with powder and ball. Before the invention of the percussion cap earlier in the 19th century, each chamber also had to be primed as has been described. Until approximately 130 years ago, there-fore, the great majority of firearms produced since their first recorded appearance in Europe of the 14th century, were single-shots that had to be loaded with loose powder and ball. Once firearms are placed in social-historical context in later chapters, the implications of the limitations of these muzzle-loading single-shots should become apparent.

The transformation of the hand cannon into something approaching a functional firearm along modern lines was made possible by the development of the matchlock. The matchlock, which consisted of a Z- or S-shaped "serpentine" pivoted in the middle, one end of which held the lit match while the other end served as a trigger, made it possible for the shooter to aim and light the gun while holding it with two hands.[10] Once this device allowed the gun to be aimed and fired while being held with two hands, the way was opened to the development of the shoulder stock that would facilitate aiming.[11]

While the matchlock may have been invented independently in various parts of Europe by men trying to produce less cumbersome guns, Robert Held is inclined to believe that it originated in Genoa around 1440.[12] Regardless of when or where it first appeared, however, the matchlock and the guns to which it was fitted improved a great deal before the end of the 15th century.

Yet though the matchlock made possible a portable firearm that could be aimed and fired by one man, it had not liberated firearms from a fire source. In order to be able to bring such a weapon into action quickly, its match had to be kept lit, and the glowing match could give away either the hunter's or the soldier's position.[13] The lit match also could prove something of a hazard to a shooter trying to keep it from coming into contact with the powder he had to pour down the barrel and into the flash pan of his weapon in order to reload it.[14] And, of course, as long as a lighted match cord had to be relied upon to set off a firearm, the pistol was not a practical weapon, since "one essential quality of an effective pistol, apart from being light and handy, is that it shall be capable of being carried for immediate action."[15] Weapons of this sort apparently did not seem impractical to the Japanese, however, since they made matchlock pistols from the 16th century until Japan renewed contact with the west after Perry's arrival in 1853.[16]

With the invention of the wheellock, possibly as early as 1480 in northern Italy or as late as the early 1500's in southern Germany, portable firearms that once loaded with powder and ball could be carried ready for firing at a moment's notice were finally made possible.[17] Fire was still needed to set off the priming powder, of course, but the wheellock mechanically produced the ignition fire in much the same way that a modern cigarette lighter produces the spark that lights its fluid. Through a spring and chain arrangement, a wheel with a serrated edge could be brought into contact with a piece of pyrites and sparks were thereby produced that would ignite the priming powder.[18] To prepare the lock for firing, it had to be wound up with a key three-quarters of a turn or so until it locked into place.[19] Once wound, the weapon could be carried ready for firing, though 16th century springs might be expected to weaken if left wound for months at a time. To fire the weapon, the shooter merely lowered the "dog-head" holding the pyrite so that the latter made contact with the serrated wheel, and when ready activated the wheel by pulling the trigger.

While the wheellock made the one-hand gun practical and came to be used on the better quality longarms of the 16th and early 17th centuries, the longarms of the ordinary European infantryman and of the poorer classes of hunters were still equipped with matchlocks until near the end of the 17th century or later.[20] This is not surprising, since the wheellock was obviously a complicated, fragile, and expensive device. With the perfection of a less complicated and cheaper spark-producing lock, the flintlock, the matchlock finally faded from the scene in the technologically more advanced parts of Europe. In Japan, however, the great majority of firearms produced before Perry's arrival in 1853 were matchlocks little different from those the Portuguese had taken to the islands in 1543.[21]

The flintlock is also a spark-producing device, but its spark is produced by a flint striking a flat piece of steel situated over the priming powder. The flint is held in the jaws of a spring-activated cock that is released by the pull of the trigger. The flat steel piece that the flint strikes is pushed out of the way as it is struck so that the sparks can ignite the priming powder.[22] The loading process for guns equipped with this lock, it should be remembered, was still essentially the same as that for the ancient hand cannons, though powder flasks and other devices had existed since early matchlock days to facilitate loading and priming.

Howard L. Blackmore feels that there is reason to believe that Germans, possibly Germans working in a Swedish armory, invented the flintlock toward the middle of the 16th century, though he acknowledges that it may have been known in Italy as early as 1522.[23] Held, however, seems to believe that the flintlock originated in the Netherlands toward the middle of the 16th century.[24] Whichever the case may be, the popularity of the flintlock spread during the 17th century until it became the most common lock to be found on European guns from the latter part of that century until the advent of the percussion cap in the early 19th century.

The percussion lock developed in England, France, and America during the first quarter of the 19th century, was the last major firearms ignition system developed during the powder-and-ball era. With the almost simultaneous invention of the percussion cap in England and America between 1814 and 1820, the percussion system was perfected.[25] This cap, containing a small amount of fulminate of mercury, was placed over a drilled-out nipple. When detonated by a spring-driven cock released by a pull of the trigger, the cap sent a jet of flame through the hollow nipple to set off the propellant charge in the gun's chamber.[26] It should be noted that while guns equipped with such locks still had to be loaded with powder and ball, the percussion lock, unlike its various predecessors, did not require priming. After loading, the shooter needed only to place a new cap on the nipple of his gun. Not only was this procedure more convenient, but it made shooting in damp weather somewhat more easily accomplished.

In the following chapters, the guns equipped with these early ignition systems will be placed in sociohistorical context, but the purpose of this discussion has been to familiarize the reader with the cumbersome (by modern standards) characteristics of these weapons.

Now attention will be shifted to the special features of the basic types of small arms to be touched upon during the course of this book, since all of these features originated early in the powder-and-ball era.

The inside of the barrels, the bores, of the ancient hand cannons and the early matchlock guns were smooth, or as nearly so as the technology of the time would permit them to be. For reasons that will become clear shortly, even the best marksmen needed much luck to hit a target the size of a man or deer at 100 yards with a ball fired from such a barrel. And it was no sure thing for marksmen so equipped to hit duck- or rabbit sized targets at 30 yards or more. Chances of hitting small targets at close range could be improved considerably, however, if such guns were loaded with a handful of pellets rather than with a single ball. The pellets would tend to spread once they had left the barrel, and the probability was great that at least some of them would hit the target. The first shotguns came into being, therefore, when the first portable firearms were loaded with pellets. Yet air resistance against the lighter pellets insured that the effective range of a gun loaded with them would be much less than the range of a gun loaded with a single heavier ball; therefore, the problem of accurate bullet placement at a distance still remained.

The technical explanation for the inaccuracy of balls fired from smoothbores is that such balls turn in flight as their heaviest or densest side shifts forward, and this turning combined with air friction causes the ball to wobble and curve unpredictably.[27] If the ball can be made to spin about its central axis, however, the gyroscopic effect eliminates the wobble and curve, reduces air turbulence, and thereby increases both the range and the accuracy of bullet placement. Rifling, or parallel spiral grooves cut into barrel bores, spins a ball in such a fashion, and once this principle was discovered, much more accurate shooting became possible. While this explanation of the effects of rifling would likely satisfy a product of the 20th century who filters the world through a "scientific" frame of reference in order to make sense of it, it would hardly have satisfied a product of the 15th or 16th centuries, as will be seen later.

Spinning arrows may have provided men with insight into the principles of rifling, according to Held, but however acquired these principles were applied to guns between 1450 and 1480.[28] Evidence exists to the effect that firearms with rifled barrels were known in Italy and Germany prior to 1477, and by 1525 fine rifles were made in various parts of Europe, with Germany leading the field.[29] The accuracy of these rifles, compared to that of their smoothbore contemporaries, is attested to by the fact that target matches at ranges of more than 200 yards were apparently arranged for rifles as early as 1477.[30] Yet all through the powder-and-ball era the great majority of firearms produced in Europe were smoothbores. The reasons for the less accurate smoothbore's popularity are not difficult to understand, however. The smoothbore could be used with either bird shot or a single ball, even though a ball fired from a smoothbore was far less accurate and far reaching than was a ball fired from a rifle.[31] The rifle, on the other hand, could be used only with ball, since the spiral grooves of its barrel tended to swirl pellets ineffectively. And the spiral grooves of the rifle also made it more difficult to load than a smoothbore, since the raised portion of the grooves had to cut into the ball to make it spin, and the ball had to fill the hollows of the bore to prevent gas seepage and loss of compression. The rifle ball had to be hammered down the barrel with ramrod and wooden mallet, therefore, "a laborious and lengthy procedure wholly unsuited for the heat of battle and slow to find acceptance among hunters."[32]

Of course, if the rifle could have been loaded at the breech rather than the muzzle, all of this effort would not have been necessary. But while attempts to produce breechloaders were made as far back as the 14th century, and 17th and 18th century efforts were reasonably successful, powder-and-ball breechloaders also had their shortcomings and the really successful guns of this type came after the development of the metallic cartridge.[33] Eventually, however, a means was discovered through which the muzzleloading rifle could be loaded with somewhat less effort. This procedure involved using a ball small enough to fit the bore without being cut by the raised portion of the rifling grooves, but wrapping that ball with a greased patch of thin material that increased its diameter enough to take the grooves and maintain compression.[34] While this method reduced the exertion required to load a rifle, however, wrapping the ball added something more to the operation.

While the earliest smoothbore longarms were capable
of firing "hail shot," they were not specifically designed to do so and could not be considered true shotguns. However, by the early 17th century smoothbores
measuring five and a half or six feet or more in length
were being used by fowlers, and it is assumed that they
were loaded primarily with shot.[35] And as ignition
systems improved enough to make shooting at airborne targets practical, fowling pieces specifically designed for
shot--but capable of firing a ball--were developed.
Well before the end of the powder-and-ball era, therefore, two basic types of longarms were in use, those
with rifled barrels and those with smoothbore barrels.
And of the smoothbores, some--muskets--were used primarily with ball, and others--fowling pieces or shot-
guns--were used primarily with shot. The blunderbuss,
a third variety of smoothbore shoulder-stocked firearm
which was loaded with several musket or pistols balls or
with shot of various sizes, seems to have originated
with the Dutch in the early 17th century.[36] With its
short barrel and its muzzle flared to as much as two or
more inches in diameter, the blunderbuss was a short
range weapon, the predecessor of the modern sawed-off
shotgun or riot gun.

The firearms discussed to this point have all been
equipped with shoulder stocks, and to take advantage of
such accuracy as was built into them, they had to be
fired from the shoulder using two hands or a rest.
Though the blunderbuss and the cavalry carbine (originating in the 16th century), were short weapons measuring only two feet or so in length, the muskets, rifles,
and fowling pieces carried by foot soldiers or hunters
ranged from four to almost six feet in length and from
9 to 20 or more pounds in weight. Such guns were obviously too cumbersome for the horseman, or for regular
carrying by a person whose everyday activities did not
ordinarily involve the use of firearms. The one-hand
gun, or pistol, just as obviously had no such shortcomings. Where or when such weapons had their origin no
one knows, but Claude Blair reasons that they must have
been invented at about the same time in Germany and
Italy shortly after the invention of the wheellock made
the one-hand gun practical.[37]

The earliest pistols carried by horsemen were often
huge weapons with barrels 12 to 16 or more inches in
length that fired balls well over one-half inch in diameter (.50 caliber), but tiny pocket pistols measuring

less than 5 inches overall were available to be carried
on the person by the 18th century or earlier.[38] But as
should be clear by now, firearms features that could be
viewed as desirable for some purposes might be considered less than desirable for other purposes. The pistol
could be fired from one hand, but not with the steadiness fostered by two-hand shooting with the aid of a
shoulder stock. Consequently, pistols have generally
been regarded as short-range weapons though some accurate long-barreled pistols have been provided with de-
tachable shoulder stocks with which they could be con-
verted to carbines and made more effective at longer
ranges. Of course, the pistol cannot "shoot as hard" as
a longer-barreled gun loaded with the same amount of
powder and a ball of the same size and weight, "all
other things being equal," for the longer barrel acts as
a more efficient combustion chamber.[39] And a powder
charge in the smaller and lighter pistol produces more
recoil than an equal charge produces in a heavier musket
or rifle; therefore, pistols are likely to use reduced
loads, further reducing their "power." These are hardly
serious shortcomings, however, since pistols were not
developed to compete against the longer arms.

THE CARTRIDGE AND THE REPEATER: 1850 TO DATE

The earliest forms of the three basic types of
small arms to be found in civilian hands in the modern
parts of the world today--shotguns, rifles and pistols--
all date back to the beginning of the 16th century or
earlier, as the preceding discussion makes clear. But
at the beginning of the 19th century, though firearms
had changed in a number of significant ways in the
course of 400 years or more of trial and error modification and experimentation, they were still almost as
tempermental and as tedious to load as their ancient
predecessors. Between 1830 and the turn of the century,
however, this state of affairs was changed by the introduction of smokeless powder, the "Minie" ball, metallic
cartridges, and repeating mechanisms.[40]

The advantages of smokeless powder over black powder have already been discussed in Chapter II, and the
"Minie" ball, which made ramless muzzleloading possible, needs no elaboration because it was quickly made
obsolete by the perfection of metallic cartridges.
Cartridges tremendously simplified the loading of firearms, since they brought ball, powder, and percussion

cap together in one container that could easily be slipped into the firing chamber at the breech end of a gun.

While single-shot and double-barreled breechloading cartridge-firing firearms of each of the basic types are still produced, the majority of firearms made since the perfection of cartridges have been repeaters of some kind or other. Handguns are either revolvers or semiautomatics. Revolvers have a rotating cylinder containing several chambers (often six) within which cartridges are loaded. In the so-called "single-action" revolver, the cylinder rotates and is locked into place for firing as the hammer which detonates the cartridge is pulled back and locks into place. When the trigger is pulled, the hammer falls, strikes the rear of the cartridge containing the equivalent of the percussion cap and the gun fires. With a "double-action" revolver the cylinder is cranked around and the hammer is pulled back automatically as the trigger is pulled, a task that requires more effort than is necessary to pull the trigger of a single-action. Most modern revolvers can be fired either way. With semi-automatic pistols, cartridges are loaded into a clip which, as the weapon is fired, slips them into the firing chamber as an action operated by recoil or gases generated by the previous firing recocks the gun and ejects the spent cartridge. The trigger must be pulled to fire each shot. Such actions are also used on rifles and shotguns. A similar action, the full automatic, operates in like fashion but continues to fire as long as the trigger is held back and ammunition lasts. Such actions are found on submachine guns and many modern military rifles and carbines. Other rifles and shotguns have repeating actions manually operated by bolts, levers, or slides. Except for the revolver, which dates back to the 15th century and was perfected during the first half of the 19th century, all of the preceding repeating mechanisms were invented and perfected during the last half of the 19th century.[41] And all of these mechanisms, including the revolver, were invented and perfected in Europe and the United States.

From the middle to the end of the last century, therefore, firearms were transformed greatly, a fact with many interesting ramifications which will be explored later as firearms are fitted into social-historical context. By way of placing firearms into such a context, attention will now be shifted from their mechanical features to the Old World "world out there" into which firearms were introduced. The mechanical

characteristics of firearms, however, will be expanded
upon in social-historical context in the following chapters.

FOOTNOTES

1. Noel Boston, <u>Old Guns and Pistols</u> (London: Ernest
    Limited, 1958), p. 20.

2. Robert Held, <u>The Age of Firearms: A Pictorial
    History</u> (Northfield, Illinois: Gun Digest Company,
    1970), p. 15; and Howard L. Blackmore, <u>Guns and
    Rifles of the World</u> (New York: The Viking Press,
    1965), pp. 1-2.

3. Held, 23.

4. Ibid.

5. Ibid., 24.

6. Ibid.

7. Ibid., 26-27

8. Held, 43 and Claude Blair, <u>Pistols of the World</u>
    (New York: The Viking Press, A Studio Book, 1968),
    p. 54.

9. Held, 177.

10. Blackmore, 9.

11. Woodcuts of early firearmed hunters using match-
    locks, show them with the butt of the stock held
    against the right hand at shoulder level. It is
    difficult to understand how they could have fired
    their weapons in this fashion. Charles Chenevix
    Trench, <u>A History of Marksmanship</u> (Norwich, Great
    Britain: Harrold & Sons Ltd., 1972), p. 106. Some
    early stocks were designed to be held against the
    chest, rather than against the shoulder. See Held,
    29.

12. Held, 26.

13. Ibid., 45.

14. Ibid., 39.

15. Blair, 2.

16. Held, 43.

17. Blair, 3 & Held 47.

18. Blackmore, 19.

19. Held, 48.

20. Ibid., 57, 73, 105.

21. Blackmore, 41. Also see Noel Perrin, Giving Up the Gun: Japan's Reversion to the Sword, 1543-1879 (Boston: David R. Godine, Publisher, 1979), pp. 67-70.

22. Blackmore, 28.

23. Ibid.

24. Held, 70.

25. Ibid., 174.

26. Ibid.

27. Ibid., 138.

28. Ibid.

29. Ibid., 36.

30. Ibid.

31. Ibid.

32. Ibid., 36-37.

33. Blackmore, 58 & Held, 140, 150-151.

34. Held, 139.

35. Ibid., 80 & 81; and Gunnar Brusewitz, Hunting (New York: Stein and Day Publishers, 1969), pp. 88-89.

36. Held, 102-104.

37. Blair, 5.

38. See Blair, plates 11, 15, 24, 25 for examples of the large pistol and 310 and 311 for examples of the small ones.

39. Michel H. Josserand and Jan Stevenson, *Pistols, Revolvers, and Ammunition* (New York: Crown Publishers, Inc., 1972), p. 10.

40. Held, 183.

41. Ibid., 185.

CHAPTER V

THE SOCIAL-HISTORICAL CONTEXT: THE OLD WORLD

THE EUROPEAN SOCIAL CONTEXT

At the time that firearms arrived on the scene in the Old World and for some time thereafter, the economic basis of society was agricultural, the great majority of people lived in rural areas, and few people experienced either social or geographic mobility or were encouraged to do so. Now the economic basis of Old World society is largely industrial, the majority of people live in urban areas, and social and geographic mobility is far from uncommon. As Old World society was transformed, landscapes and the physical environment in general were altered. Also altered were the symbolic frames of reference that had allowed people to make sense of and relate to the physical world as well as to other human beings. And over the centuries much human conflict--conflict between individuals and conflict between groups--has been associated with these various transformations. This is the context into which firearms must be fitted if we are to understand the ways in which they have functioned in the lives of those who have possessed them in the Old World.

But changes of the sort touched on above notwithstanding, perhaps the most important point to take into consideration when attempting to place firearms in context in the Old World is that whether invented there (as may have been the case in Europe) or introduced from the outside (as was the case with Japan and may have been the case with Europe) firearms were inserted into ongoing systems. That is, firearms were inserted into worlds that people had already "mapped out" and made sense of through their interaction with others and with the physical environment. While the lines marking off the different strata of society from each other, for example, may not have been as clear-cut as they have sometimes been depicted, there is reason to believe that the great majority of those considered by others to be peasants thought of themselves as peasants and that the great majority of those considered by others to be aristocrats accepted the label themselves. For the most part peasants and aristocrats knew, or thought they knew, what others of their own rank as well as other social levels expected of them and what they could ex-

73

pect of others. And while the gradual transformation of
these normative expectations over the years indicates
that they were not always reinforced through social
interaction, their overall continuity indicates that for
the most part they were so reinforced. Those at various
social levels not only generally knew how they related
to others; they knew how they related to the land, other
creatures (wild as well as domestic), and to the tools
associated with various tasks assigned those at various
levels of society. Most probably they also knew <u>why</u>
everything was related to everything else as it was.

     To be sure, if the assumptions upon which this
study is based are accepted, socially constructed realities are quite tenuous, and the mere insertion of firearms into the picture could be expected to cause that
picture to be altered somewhat.[1] Yet, while the introduction of firearms into feudal Europe and Japan could
be expected to have forced some modification of the
various frames of reference existing at the time, firearms could hardly completely change these frames. And
firearms could not be developed and made sense of themselves except in terms of these frames of reference,
modified though they might be.

     The Europe into which firearms were introduced in
the 14th century or earlier was an overwhelmingly agricultural world of rural-based and tradition-bound peasants and aristocratic feudal lords. The peasants, who
constituted the majority, farmed the land and depended
on the aristocrats for protection, or at least that was
the case at one time. The aristocrats, a warrior elite,
were in turn supported by the peasants in exchange for
protection. The origin of the distinction between warrior and peasant in some parts of Europe dates back to
ancient times, but in the Middle Ages the distinction
spread in large part due to the expense of the military
equipment that was used at that time. As Stanislaw
Andrzejewski has explained,

> We cannot be sure in the case of western
> European lands that the military service
> has been restricted because the armament
> became costlier, as this restriction was
> a legacy of the Roman past, and moreover
> the Germanic invasions would tend, as
> usually /sic7 in such cases, to narrow or
> at least maintain this restriction.

74

Nevertheless, it can be said with certainty that the medieval military technique would prevent the extension of military service even after the ethnic fusion took place. It has been calculated that several years' income of the whole village was necessary to cover the cost of equipping one knight. And nothing could oppose a warrior clad in protective armour on an armoured charger. So, ineluctably, the peasant masses were militarily useless and helpless.[2]

Not all peasants were helpless before the armored knight, as Andrzejewski acknowledges elsewhere and as will be seen shortly, but, for the most part, it seems that the above can be accepted.[3] Yet the feudal lord operating out of his castle was not just a parasite to the peasants working his fields--or at least he had not always been a parasite. "The feudal lord lived by the prosperity of his lands, but his prosperity was due in large measure to himself," writes Frantz Funck-Brentano. "He made his domain safe; his sword enabled the merchants to traffic on it, and his labourers to work; he added useful improvements."[4] But the time came--Funck-Brentano implies that it came as early as the end of the 13th century in France--when, partly due to the efforts of the feudal lords themselves, the protection their swords and castles afforded their peasants was no longer needed. The feudal lords, however, continued to levy numerous and varied tolls and dues in the towns as well as in the country districts.[5]

The feudal aristocracy had become established. Aristocratic lifestyles and related world views which had evolved over the centuries as aristocratic warriors had fought or acquired the skills necessary to do so could not be expected to disappear. According to the medieval societal division of labor, knights existed to fight, just as peasants existed to work and the clergy existed to pray. And since knights existed to fight, they felt that it was only fitting that they be allowed "to monopolize the arms-bearing privilege, both for fighting and hunting."[6] There were certain honorable ways to fight and certain honorable weapons to be used-- those that the nobility could afford and with which they were familiar, the sword among them--and attempts were made to ban other weapons such as the crossbow and the gun, which gave the lowborn the advantage, from the field of battle.[7] The days of the armored knight and heroic combat in the style of the Middle Ages were numbered in the 14th century, however, and not simply because of the invention of the gun. The feudal order, in the words of V. G. Kiernan, "was meeting with growing resistance from below, and its military resources for coping with both internal and external challenges were obsolescent."[8]

The feudal order was also undermined by the revival of international trade, which by the middle of the 13th century had generated a noticeable increase in wealth.[9] International commerce had not come to a complete halt during the Middle Ages, of course, but the new trade involved manufactured goods and luxury items rather than the simple cross-regional exchange of raw products. Cities such as Florence, Milan, Nurnberg, Marseilles, and Venice, became famous for the things they produced-- fine weaving and dyeing, metal work, glass wares, and so forth--and those who produced and sold these items in the cities prospered. Historians Richard A. Preston and Sydney F. Wise have written the following concerning the impact these prospering "middle-class" businessmen and artisans and their cities had on the feudal scene:

> The appearance of a wealthy, numerous middle class had important consequences. The old simplicity of peasant, lord, clergy, and king was gone, disrupted by the addition of a dynamic class which was profoundly anti-feudal in character. In countries like Italy and Germany, where the central government was weak, growing towns shook off the hold of adjacent lords and became in effect independent city states. In England, however, and to a lesser degree in France, where the feudal duchies were strong, the towns became allies of the crown against the feudal aristocracy. Moreover, the growth of urban population and the spread of a money economy associated with trade had a strong impact upon the life of the countryside. Urban demands for food and raw materials made farming for profit possible; rising prices and a more plentiful money supply gave the peasant the means to purchase his freedom or commute his labor services for a money rent. In England, for example, enfran-

chisement and agricultural prosperity
created a rural class of small farmers,
the yeomen, who filled the ranks of English armies in the late Middle Ages.[10]

Towns and cities had existed in Europe all through
the Middle Ages, but they and their inhabitants had always been somewhat marginal to the feudal system. Being
neither aristocrats nor peasants, the townsmen--burghers,
bourgeoisie--were a class in between, a middle class as
they, or at least the merchants and the artisans among
them, eventually came to be known.[11] Given the effect
their commerical activities had on those around them, it
is not surprising that this middle class and the feudal
aristocracy whose lifestyles and world views they
threatened came to antagonize one another. Attention
will be centered here on the ways in which the middle
class undermined the aristocracy's monopoly of fighting
skills--the basis of the aristocracy's very existence.
The burghers themselves were not fighters, though some
had fought, using feudal methods, to free their cities
from feudal obligations, and cities had fought each
other for the protection and development of their trading spheres.[12] Being business-oriented, however, the
burghers were not interested in fighting their own battles. Consequently, the burghers eventually came to
hire footloose men to do the fighting for their cities
or for the absolute monarchs whom the burghers supported.

Mercenaries, or soldiers--those who fought for pay--
though not part of the feudal system "had constituted
a major export trade of the Middle Ages."[13] Often they
had been "pauperized or bastard gentlemen, offscourings
of feudality," but increasingly during the late Middle
Ages they were peasants from outside the more heavily
settled areas of feudal Europe.[14] Archers from the
south of Wales proved to be particularly effective fighters, and it was from their wars with the Welsh that the
English acquired the longbow that enabled English yeomen
in conjunction with feudal cavalry to humble French armored knights time after time during the Hundred Years
War.[15] And then there were the Swiss, the peasants who
had never been ruled by an aristocracy, who with their
pole arms, the halberd and the pike, and their disciplined and mobile formations took to the offensive
against the armored cavalry and defeated them regularly
without the assistance of cavalry of their own.[16] There
were others such as the Genoese crossbowman who provided
the infantry for many medieval armies, and who were prob-

ably recruited from the Ligurian hills, Corsica, and
Sardinia.[17] As Kiernan has noted concerning the re-
cruiting grounds for such mercenaries, they

> lay in mountainous regions on the fringes
> of Europe, inhabited by alien peoples
> such as Celts or Basques. In an age when
> the cultivators of the settled plains had
> been disarmed by their noble "protectors,"
> and ravaged by famine and pestilence,
> these sturdy, needy hillman were still
> ready for war.[18]

Due to the dislocations brought on by changes in
the economic sphere mentioned earlier, town populations
had grown, and peasants separated from the soil and not
belonging to the guilds provided the burghers with a
local source for the recruitment of soldiers.[19] Though
this source was taken advantage of by cities in search
of fighting men, for some time the national armies recruited by the absolute monarchs and financed by the
bourgeoisie were composed of outlanders. The reason for
foreign recruitment will become clear later.

Even before firearms came into general use, therefore, the feudal warrior aristocracy had been dealt
several setbacks. The kings who had once depended on
them for military support could now, with the help of
the wealthy middle classes, buy fighting men capable of
defeating the feudal lords on the field of battle. But
the townsmen not only undermined feudal military techniques and those who practiced them with money; they
eventually undermined them further with new weapons.
The cannons that could pound down castle walls and the
muskets that could penetrate armor were, after all,
manufactured by the artisans of the cities.[20] While
the feudal lords themselves sometimes employed firearmed
mercenaries, they seldom used them effectively, for the
lords were generally contemptuous of all missle weapons--
the longbow, crossbow, and the gun, portable and otherwise.[21] This point is made clear by Kiernan who writes:

> More than once on the battlefield the
> haughty /French/ knights had ridden down
> their own Genoese crossbowmen, as contemp-
> tible plebeians. The Swiss were ostenta-
> tiously plebeian, but the bluest-blooded
> gendarme could not fail to respect their
> prowess, all the more perhaps because they

78

fought hand to hand, not with long-range
missiles like the Genoese.[22]

The burghers, on the other hand, had no such pre-
judices against missile weapons and guns in particular,
as indicated not only by the fact that they produced
guns but that they were also among the first to use
guns. "The first undoubted reference to guns," according to historians A. V. B. Norman and Don Pottinger,
"is an order by the Council of Florence in 1326, to prepare iron bullets and cannon of metal for the defense
of the Republic."[23] And though some mercenaries were
slow to accept firearms, others were not.[24] Professional fighting men competing for employment were more likely than others to keep up with technical progress. Experts from the industrially advanced regions played a
leading part in spreading the use of firearms. In
England, the first hand-gun soldiers were Flemings and
Germans hired for the War of the Roses.[25] Thus the
weapons as well as the money of the urban middle classes
contributed greatly to the downfall of feudalism.

Yet, as Kiernan has put it,

> under the auspices of absolute monarchy,
> by what might be described as a sort of
> "managerial revolution," the aristocratic
> order achieved a remarkable recovery,
> though it had of course to undergo im-
> portant changes.[26]

And this managerial revolution seems to have come about
in large part due to the reluctance on the part of the
middle class to take a hand in directing the new standing armies that their economically motivated efforts
and alliances with kings had inadvertently helped to
bring into existence. Hiring men to do their fighting
for them appealed to the business-oriented middle
classes, since once the fighting was finished the soldiers could simply be paid off and sent away to be paid
again only if and when they were needed again. Mercenaries often did not simply go away after their jobs were
finished, however, and they possessed the means of making rather serious nuisances of themselves.

In 1445 France took several mercenary companies
into permanent royal service, in part in order to cope
with other mercenaries who were no longer needed and had
become troublesome, and in doing so France established

the first European standing army since Roman times.[27]
Permanent armies thereby resulted from efforts to avoid
permanent armies.[28] Other national armies followed, but
the bourgeois was not interested in leading the armies
for which he paid, and the princes thereby found themselves in a position to start and end wars.[29] The
princes then turned the direction of the standing armies
over to the aristocrats whose order, paradoxically, was
thereby saved by the default of the middle class and by
the very establishment of the standing armies--financed
by the middle class and equipped with weapons developed
by urban artisans--that had made feudal military techniques and the aristocratic warriors who practiced them
obsolete. The following statement by Alfred Vagts, who
has traced linkages between the old and the new warrior
aristocracies in some detail, neatly summarizes this
transformation.

> Although the bourgeois left the direction
> of war to the princes, the princes did
> not themselves control their armies en-
> tirely in the beginning: rather they con-
> tracted with private entrepreneurs for
> the collection, organization, disciplin-
> ing, and feeding of forces. Thus the
> bourgeois financed wars they did not start--
> **kings** started wars they did not fully
> manage. These war entrepreneurs, who
> continued their activities under new names,
> had already been noblemen in the majority
> of cases, usually of the lesser and impe-
> cunious brackets. The higher aristocracy
> did not bestir itself so energetically as
> a Monluc, a Wallerstein, a Marlborough.
> These men indicated what forces were still
> left in a class that had, for a time,
> seemed likely to go down helplessly be-
> fore the rising, money-making bourgeoisie.
> They became the true beneficiaries of
> the standing army, whereas the bourgeois
> profit through armies were largely re-
> stricted to the purveyor's business.
> The nobility even officered the standing
> army more than the old impermanent forces
> of the condottieri. It was essentially
> created in their favor, for the employ-
> ment and sustenance of a feudal class
> which could not make a living otherwise,
> after the feudal system broke down.[30]

In England the middle classes were able to keep some control over the army through Parliament, because the insular situation of the country kept almost everyone concerned from feeling caught up in a power struggle. But on the Continent the middle classes were not so successful. Where the power of the middle classes matched that of the aristocracy, the monarchs and their bureaucracies benefited from the power struggle. Gaining the upper hand, the monarchs, who had managed to bring the aristocrats under control with the money, mercenaries, and weapons provided by the middle classes, tended to favor the aristocrats with whom the monarchs felt they had more in common, giving them "preference and honors, while granting the bourgeois, instead of honor, a chance to build up manufactures and commerce. Thus a silent deal was consummated at the expense of the peasantry and the common laborer, the beasts of burden of Absolutism, as a military and industrial system."[31]

When force was needed to keep the peasants in their place, or to make them serfs where they had not been before as was the case in Brandenburg-Prussia, the foreign mercenaries of the standing armies could supply that force. Ironically, the Swiss, who had no aristocratic overlords and were so envied by their German neighbors, "became the chief watch-dogs of tyranny."[32] This is not to imply, however, that the Swiss were the only mercenaries employed.

The transformation of the aristocracy enabled patterns of social stratification that had originated in feudal times to survive in Europe until the industrial and political revolutions of the late 18th and early 19th centuries and beyond. Though much more industrial at the end of the 18th century than it had been during the 14th century, when firearms had appeared on the scene, and though the middle classes had become much more prominent and were about to become dominant, Europe of the late 18th century was still overwhelmingly rural and agricultural, most of its people were still peasants, and its aristocracy was still dominant. Since this was the case for approximately the first 500 years of the 650 years or so after firearms became available, a brief look at the lifestyles and concerns of European aristocrats and peasants seems called for since they constituted the majority of Europeans among whom guns produced by the urban classes were introduced.

European aristocrats have never been a homogeneous
lot clearly marked off from the members of other classes
by their warrior origins and skills. "There was enor-
mous difference . . . between a great duke with lands
and power a king might envy, and an impoverished baron
caught in the squeeze between rising prices and a small
fixed income," writes E. Harris Harbison of the early
16th century European nobility.[33] The situation was
more of less the same at the end of the 18th century
when poverty-stricken aristocrats were hardly a rarity,
and when there were only a few magnates of great
wealth.[34] The poverty-stricken aristocrat was still an
aristocrat, however, or at least he was in those countries where a rather clear-cut distinction was made between the highborn and commoners. In some places, however, this distinction was blurred. Still dealing with
16th century Europe, Harbison notes that

> in some countries, as in England and
> Castile, the nobility shaded off at its
> base into a rural middle class of gentry,
> whose titles were not hereditary but who
> were definitely something more than yeo-
> men or free farmers.[35]

The distinction was blurred even at the "higher" social
levels in England where noble origins, though important,
were "endowed with fewer privileges than on the Continent," and where one could come to be recognized as a
gentleman through his acquisition of a fortune or in
some other way.[36] In Sweden where, according to
Andrzejewski, feudalism had never existed, "the main
difference between the nobles and the peasants was that
the former possessed more land. No judicial or admini-
strative powers over the peasants were vested in the
nobles, except in those who were at the same time royal
officials."[37]

Though the nobility generally felt themselves to be
separated from commoners by blood or birth, for centuries wealthy merchants had purchased land and titles to
go with it, and the absolute monarchs came to make it a
practice to elevate their bureaucrats to the nobility,
a nobility of the robe thereby taking its place alongside the nobility of the sword.[38] And in the days before the standing armies were established, those colonels
who founded mercenary companies were commonly knighted
if, as was not often the case, they were not already of
noble origin.[39]

In spite of the rather nebulous picture cf the aristocracy painted above, however, it would seem safe to state that its members generally shared an "intense sense of status."[40] Just how intense this sense of status could be can be seen from the story Funck-Brentano relates of a poor cousin of Chateaubriand who had been offered the post of tutor in the house of the Duc de Bourbon. The poverty-stricken aristocrat, an Abbe, replied: "Those belonging to my House may engage tutors, they are themselves never tutors to anyone."[41]

Typically aristocrats also possessed

> a particular sense of honor. In Prussia
> aristocratic honor was given legal recog-
> nition, and an aristocrat's word was ac-
> cepted in court without affidavit. In
> most places sense of honor was expressed
> in dueling. Aristocratic honor abhorred
> commercialism and usually commerce itself.
> Slavery to the earning of money and the
> petty, dishonorable haggling that this
> entailed were to be shunned.[42]

Other characteristics of the aristocracy particularly significant for the purposes of this study were its cultivation of physical bravery and its concern with manners and lifestyle. With respect to bravery, as might be expected from the preceding discussion, the aristocratic code typically expressed itself through military service and leadership and it continued to do so through the revolutionary period in Europe.[43] Even the nobility of the robe saw the military as a desirable profession for their sons.[44] With respect to manners, Stearns writes of the European nobility of 1800:

> The aristocracy felt itself to be the
> bearer of a distinct and superior code
> of manners and culture. It was a leisure
> class, devoted to activities inaccessible
> to the crowd. It strove to maintain a
> peculiar style of life. This effort took
> the form of dandyism for the British court
> aristocracy, of widespread gambling, which
> provided excitement and showed scorn for
> money, of adoption of French language and
> culture by many Russian nobles, of distinc-
> tive homes and clothing in many areas,
> and of the perpetuation of exclusive hunt-

83

ing rights almost everywhere. In the
concepts of distinctive honor, manners,
bravery, and public service the aristocracy saw the fulfillment of its superior
status.[45]

The European peasants, about whom little has thus
far been said, have been no more homogeneous than the
aristocrats. One would expect the world views and
lifestyles of a 14th-century French peasant to differ
somewhat from those of his 19th-century counterpart, but
differences also have existed between contemporaries.
Some peasants, such as the Swiss--who were never ruled
by an aristocracy--and the English yeomen--who did have
to contend with an aristocracy--were "free," while
others, such as the serfs of Brandenburg-Prussia, were
bound to the land by their noble overlords. And differences existed between the wealthier peasants of any time
and place and their poorer cousins of the same time and
place. Yet European peasants of all times and places
have had much in common with each other, as have peasants
everywhere, or at least scholars have felt that this has
been the case.

The Old World peasants were farmers in that they
raised crops and made their livings primarily from the
land; yet for the most part, they differed considerably
from the farmer that Americans know. To begin with, in
most regions peasants lived not on isolated farms but in
villages which were surrounded by their fields. Peasant
society in Europe at the beginning of the 19th century
was built around and had long been permeated by the village and the family, and to a great extent peasants lived
to perpetuate their families through marriage and children.[46] The village, though "an economic unit producing
most of the goods the peasant required," generally
amounted to "a collection of several extended families
who were themselves often closely related" and few
peasants had much experience beyond the village.[47] The
towns that they visited to attend fairs, the traders that
brought them goods plus entertainment and news, the tax
collectors, recruiters, and rural police who brought the
central government into their lives, provided peasants
with only occasional and intimidating contacts with the
world outside their villages, and the village priest was
generally one of their own with little more formal education than the peasants themselves possessed.[48]

The preceding comments probably describe the ex-

periences, for the most part, of common rural folk of
all parts of the Old World prior to their having been
fully exposed to the disruptive forces of modernism in
the 19th and 20th centuries. Interacting almost exclusively with other members of their own village, peasant horizons were limited by the standards of the "educated" modern, their world views were clearcut, they
were collectivity-oriented and tradition-bound, and
their informal social controls were formidable. Just
how formidable these controls could be will be seen
later when the Japanese peasantry is discussed.

For reasons of the sort mentioned above, peasants,
whenever and wherever they existed, were bound into
their communities and into frames of reference constructed within these communities until these frames of
reference have been disrupted. Until these disruptions
occurred, peasants thereby possessed some measure of
psychological and economic security. Economic security,
however, was typically minimal and the peasants' lot was
generally trying. Even as late as 1800 in the rich agricultural areas of Europe they often shared their small
rude, dirt-floored, clay and log, poorly ventilated and
lighted huts with their farm animals; wore crude wool or
linen clothing; went barefoot; subsisted on potatoes or
course black bread; suffered from such diseases as tu-
berculosis; did hard farm labor for three seasons of the
year; and either practically hibernated to conserve energy or engaged in weaving or some other arduous domestic manufacturing during the winter.[49] Even the wealth-
iest peasants suffered greatly when the harvest was bad,
but though the wealthy still worked hard they normally
lived reasonably comfortably in solid houses, possessed
elaborate celebration costumes, and had more food including meat and milk once or more a week, and wine and
beer.[50]

The reference to celebrations above implies that
peasants did take some time off from their labors, and
in fact religious and other holidays were fairly fre-
quent in some areas.[51] Yet peasants have seldom had an
easy time of it, and their problems were brought on
largely by certain features of pre-industrial agriculture which it will not be necessary to elaborate upon
here.[52] It should be mentioned, however, that wherever
aristocrats existed in Europe they helped keep peasants
near the subsistence level. Prior to the French Revolution, French aristocrats still lived largely off of
what they could collect from their peasants.[53] And an

effort was made during the 18th century to restore
"feudal rights and dues where they had been allowed to
fall into neglect."[54]

From the late 18th century through the middle of
the 19th century, Europe, or at least those parts of the
Continent that are being considered here, was greatly
transformed by political and industrial revolution and
was well on its way to becoming more urban than rural
and more industrial than agricultural. The aristocracy
survived the political revolutions and was able to hold
on to some special privileges for some time afterwards,
though their feudal rights over the peasantry were taken
from them in western Europe by 1800 and in central Europe by 1850.[55] The aristocracy still had disproportion-
ate voting power in France until 1848 and in Prussia as
late as 1918, but it continued to decline until it
merged to a great extent, if not completely, with the
upper-middle class to form a new European upper class.[56]

The peasantry also survived the revolutionary period, but many peasants were forced off the land and into
the cities as the population of Europe increased tremendously after the middle of the 18th century and land
grabs such as the enclosure movement in England changed
patterns of land use in the countryside.[57] Those peasants who remained on the land had to make some adjust-
ments to market agriculture, and as years passed they
came to benefit materially from these changes. As they
came to have more contacts with the outside world
through education and military service, peasant horizons
broadened somewhat. Yet those peasants who remained on
the land remained traditional, and family, village,
land, and religion were still important to them.[58]
Those who left the land to find work in the cities
caused city populations to zoom upward and swelled the
ranks of a social class that, while hardly new, did not
become significant until the industrial revolution: the
working class. According to Harbison, only a half-dozen
or so European cities had populations exceeding 100,000
at the beginning of the 16th century.[59] By 1800, according to Stearns, there were still only 22 European
cities of this size or larger.[60] By 1895, however, 10
per cent of Europe's total population lived in 120
cities of 100,000 or more.[61] Britain was more than half
urban by 1850 and 80 per cent urban by 1900.[62] France,
which had been 80 per cent rural in 1800 and 75 per cent
rural as late as 1850, was 50 per cent urban by 1930,
and Germany, 65 per cent rural in 1850, was 50 per cent

urban by 1900.[63] Between 1870 and 1900, German cities
with populations of 100,000 or more increased in number
from eight to forty-one, and by the latter date five of
these cities had populations of 500,000 or more.[64]

In discussing the composition of the 16th century
European bourgeoisie, Harbison notes that "at the bottom
journeymen and apprentices constituted a small but growing industrial proletariat in some towns."[65] For some
time this proletariat's numbers remained small, but due
to the dislocations mentioned earlier, the modern European working class was taking shape during the early
part of the 19th century. As peasants forced off the
land came to the cities to find work, even though they
seldom brought skills with them, slums populated by ir-
regularly employed transients--the dangerous class--
expanded.[66] As industrialization increased this class
did not disappear; "they were the people who lived in
the most crowded and filthy slums, whose food and clothing was still barely sufficient for survival."[67] But as
the number of factories and their sizes increased, many
of these people and others fresh from the rural areas
or recruited from the artisan ranks, became more regularly employed, and they formed a new social class of
factory workers by the middle of the 19th century. By
the last decade of the century, a large part of the
lower classes and a third of the populations of such advanced industrial nations as England and Germany were
composed of factory workers.[68] Though the working conditions, pay, and job security of the early factory
worker left much to be desired, they may have been better off materially than those who had stayed on the
land. Yet factory and city existence did not provide
the psychological security of the peasant's village, and
the workers were cut off from the out-of-doors. But by
the time that the majority of factory workers were the
sons and grandsons of factory workers, they had developed traditions of their own and ties with the country and
peasant life had faded. By then factory workers were
becoming increasingly materialistic, and though their
material conditions were steadily improving, rising expectations also increased their level of discontent.[69]

These, then, were the potential firearms owners and
users of Europe--the aristocrats with their traditional
ties to weapons and war; the peasants, free and otherwise, of limited horizons and traditional ties to the
family, village, and land; the city-based artisans, some
of whom developed and fabricated firearms, and their

fellow town-dwellers, the businessmen and professionals
of the dynamic middle class; and the uprooted who were
transformed in the cities from the dangerous class to
the modern working class. While European society was
being transformed, however, in that the aristocracy was
blending with its middle class rival at the upper level
to form a new European upper class and at least part of
the rural peasantry was becoming an urban working class,
the European landscape was also being changed apprecia-
bly. Cities of 100,000 cover much more ground than do
those of 10,000, and, as has been seen, there were many
more of the former after the middle of the 19th century
than there had been at the beginning of the century.
Networks of roads--surfaced roads--came with urbanism
and industrialism, and new parts of Europe were thereby
opened up to trade and agriculture and put in closer
touch with each other.[70] Between 1800 and 1900, the
population of the whole of Europe, not only its cities,
increased from 188,000,000 to 401,000,000.[71] Even the
countryside, therefore, became more crowded. What does
all of this have to do with firearms? As shall be seen,
as the European landscape was transformed the natural
habitat of certain types of large wild animals was destroyed, and these animals thereby disappeared from much
of the Continent and consequently could no longer be
hunted there.

                 THE JAPANESE SOCIAL CONTEXT

        The Japan into which firearms were introduced by
the Portuguese toward the middle of the 16th century,
resembled in several respects the Europe into which
firearms had been introduced two centuries or so earlier. As still was the case in Europe, the two most prominent social rankings in the overwhelmingly rural Japan
of that time were the rural-based and tradition-bound
peasantry and the warrior aristocracy--the samurai. Of
course the samurai were the dominant class, but by the
16th century footsoldiers recruited from the peasantry
were quite common.[72] Since the Provincial Wars that had
begun during the previous century were still in progress, both the samurai and the common soldiers that
they commanded were kept quite busy. But by the end of
the 16th century these wars were over, and Japan was
unified under the rule of the usurping Tokugawa Sho-
guns--the commanders of the Emperor's armies who became
military dictators.[73] Before the Tokugawas came into
power, however, attempts had already been made to disarm

the sometimes rebellious peasants and to establish or
re-establish the distinction between farmers and soldiers.[74] Hideyoshi, a pre-Tokugawa shogun, tried to
disarm the peasantry through the "sword hunt" of 1588,
and he also issued decrees establishing peasants as
residents of the countryside and samuari as residents
of castle towns controlled by feudal lords—daimyos.[75]
In this way Hideyoshi hoped not only to separate peasant
and samurai, but to keep both peasant and samurai from
associating with artisans and merchants.

Once in power, the Tokugawas retained and attempted
to enforce Hideyoshi's policies, and their efforts
helped to shape, though they did not of themselves produce, patterns of social stratification and other social
arrangements that remained more or less intact from
around the beginning of the 17th century until past the
middle of the 19th century. In 1639 Japan's rulers cut
off practically all contacts with the outside world, and
kept Japan virtually isolated until Commodore Perry's
arrival in 1853. Through this isolation, strict sumptu-
ary laws, and other means, the Tokugawas tried to maintain the prevailing social order, and despite some even-
tual problems with merchants of the towns, the order did
prevail.[76] In Japan merchants could not cope with their
powerful military dictators as easily as European merchants could cope with their fading feudal aristocracy
through foreign trade and alliances with kings. Consequently well into the Tokugawa period merchants ranked
behind soldiers, farmers, and artisans in the social
hierarchy, though, as George Sansom has noted, merchants
eventually made their presence known.

> Tradesmen--merchants and shopkeepers--
> came lowest in the social scale /except
> for outcasts7, but as the economy of
> Japan developed and expanded in times of
> peace, merchants in particular were to
> gain increasing power, until by the eigh-
> teenth century they were able, by their
> financial strength, to break down barriers
> in the social structure which the Tokugawa
> Shoguns had erected. By then the rich
> merchants were employed regularly as govern-
> ment contractors, and their services were
> indispensable to the members of the mil-
> itary class. Even trade guilds, to which
> the government was in principle opposed,
> were used to collect certain taxes.[77]

Nevertheless, Japan remained rural and the samurai and the peasantry remained prominent until well into the 19th century, with the samurai acting as retainers to their overlords--daimyo--in the castle towns to which they had been assigned at the end of the 16th century. Practically all peasant villages were within twenty miles of a castle town, and this proximity enabled the samurai to collect taxes from the peasants in order to support the town.[78]

According to Barrington Moore, there were 194 daimyo who ranked directly below the Shogun in 1614, and the number had increased to only 266 shortly before the Restoration of the Emperor in 1868.[79] Beneath these great lords was the main body of samurai. And as H. Paul Varley has written:

> The samurai occupied an anomalous position in isolated Japan of Tokugawa times. These warriors, who along with their families constituted between seven and ten percent of the national population, were guaranteed superior social prerogatives and hereditary stipends by the statutes of both Hideyoshi and the Tokugawa. They alone, moreover, enjoyed the privilege of wearing swords, the visible symbols of their ascendant rank, and had the theoretical (although presumably seldom exercised) right to cut down any member of another class who chanced to offend or displease them. Yet, whatever their special rights and privileges, the samurai of this age were in fact warriors who had no wars to fight. Unable to pursue the profession that supposedly justified their existence, they were obliged to seek employment in other fields--such as government or teaching--or simply to remain idle and attempt to get by on their stipends, which in nearly all cases were either held constant or were reduced while prices rose steadily.
> Nevertheless it appears to have been precisely because they were unable to engage in warfare that the samurai of this era became particularly self-conscious of themselves as a class and of their unique role in Japanese history. They came, for

example, to romanticize the deeds and
behavior of their ancestors, to find all
glory and manliness in the conduct of
earlier samurai even when that conduct
had obviously sprung from the most savage
emotions.[80]

From this romanticizing of the samurai past, evolved an
ultimate moral standard--bushido--by which the samurai
was to conduct his life, and which called for his absolute loyalty to his daimyo.[81]

All samurai, however, did not fit neatly into the
system. Those who could not subsist on their stipends
cut their ties with their lords and became wondering,
masterless ronin; troublesome men whose eagerness for
action helped make the late Tokugawa period turbulent.[82]
Ronin may have numbered as many as 500,000 at one
time.[83] While in Europe aristocratic warriors who for
one reason or other did not fit into the system could
offer their services as mercenaries or leaders of mercenaries and find a war in which to fight, the samurai
of isolated warless Japan of the Tokugawa period could
not cope with their lack of employment in this fashion.
Some ronin in one way or other worked their way back to
farming, while others became merchants even though they
were forbidden to do so.[84] Some impoverished samurai
sold their status, though such sales were prohibited,
while others adopted the sons of wealthy merchants to be
their heirs.[85] In this way warriors became merchants
and merchants became warriors, and as had been the case
in Europe, supposedly clearcut class distinctions based
on blood became blurred. Yet the samurai remained formidable past the middle of the 19th century. After the
Restoration in 1868, however, the samurai lost their
social, economic and political privileges.[86]

Until modern times the peasantry seems to have constituted as much as eight-tenths of Japan's population.[87] As was the case over much of those areas of
Europe being considered in this study, the Japanese
peasant lived in villages rather than on isolated farms.
However, as suggested earlier, the Japanese village may
well have been even more tightly knit than its typical
European counterpart. The following, by Barrington
Moore, implies as much:

> The Japanese village displayed a
> fierce demand for unanimity that recalls

the Russian sbomost'. Personal affairs
were given a public character lest they
lead to deviant opinion or behavior. Since
anything secret was automatically sus-
picious, a man with private business to
conduct with someone in another village
might be obliged to conduct it through
his headman. Gossip, ostracism, and more
serious sanctions, such as assembling at
a man's gate and beating pots and pans in
unison, or even banishment (which meant
cutting a peasant off from human society
so that he must soon starve or run afoul
of the law), all helped to create a con-
formity that was probably far more severe
than any lamented by modern Western intellectuals. Only after he had learned the
sense of the community by careful consul-
tation with other leading figures, did the
headman express his own opinion on any important issue. Villagers would go to great
lengths to avoid any open conflict of opinion. Smith mentions one village where, as
recently as the period after World War II,
the village assembly met privately on the
day before its public meeting in order
that decisions might be unanimous. Similarly a headman in Tokugawa times would
bring together the parties to a boundary
dispute to reach a compromise. Only after
the compromise had been reached and the
matter settled, would he issue an "order."[88]

While Japanese peasants occasionally were rebellious, they were generally kept in line by the informal
social controls described above, combined with the more
formal controls encouraged by the Tokugawa rulers, systems of land use and taxation, and other features of
Japanese society. One of the more formal methods of
social control was the five-man group. The land-holding
heads of these groups were held responsible for the behavior of the members of each group, and every inhabi-
tant of a village had to belong to such a group.
Through five-man groups and other means, marriage, adop-
tion, succession, inheritance, individual conduct, dispute settlements, and religious practices were strictly
controlled, and prohibitions against peasant firearms
possession and sword-carrying were strictly enforced.[89]

92

Though, as has been indicated above, the Japanese peasant's ties to his village and its consequent control over him still existed at least as late as the period following World War II, the Restoration and the Meigi regime that came with it affected the peasant in at least one way significant for the concerns of this study. With the Meigi came a conscript army, and through that army the peasant was reintroduced to the military affairs and weaponry that the ruling classes had tried to keep from him for almost 300 years. For the most part, the Japanese peasants seem to have opposed conscription.

> Conscription with its three years of mili-
> tary service deprived the peasantry for an
> appreciable period of the strongest hands
> on the farms, and with no mechanization
> of agriculture such an absence would be
> acutely felt. Further, it prognosticated
> fresh tax burdens, and finally . . . it
> strengthened the repressive powers of the
> state.[90]

During the tumultuous times that resulted in the Restoration, anti-feudal agrarian revolts had cropped up again and the conscript army composed mostly of peasants was used against the peasantry.

The conscript army established in 1872-73 was also used against the disgruntled samurai whose feudal privileges, including the right to wear the sword, had been stripped away after the fall of the Tokugawas. Conscripted peasants first met the samurai in battle at Satsuma in 1877 and defeated them. While it might seem surprising that an army recruited from a peasantry kept from military service for almost 300 years could defeat one composed of professional warriors, even though the former outnumbered the latter 65,000 to 40,000, the reasons for such an outcome are not hard to find.[91] The samurai of warless, isolated Japan had not altered their weapons and tactics for 300 years or so, and when they met the conscripts the samurai insisted on using their traditional weapons, the bow and arrow and the sword, as they had done when they had been called upon to fight on one side or the other in other battles leading to the Restoration.[92] Many samurai who were offered the new muzzle-loading, percussion rifle muskets--firing the Minie ball--that were being acquired from the West refused to use them, but the conscripts did not hesitate to do so, and they had become reasonably proficient in the use of these weapons.93 With the samurai relying primarily on their swords and the conscripts using their rifles, it is not surprising that the latter won.

The state of affairs described above tells us much about the place of firearms in Japanese history. For 300 years as firearms were becoming ever more sophisticated in Europe and North America, Japan's tradition-bound professional warriors with no wars to fight and isolated from the rest of the world would have little if anything to do with guns, though they had been used in the Provincial Wars of the 16th century. Over this same period the peasantry that constituted the great majority of the population was stricly forbidden to possess weapons of any sort, and Japan's isolation plus the collectivist features of Japanese peasant society seems to have insured that firearms would be both difficult for peasants to acquire and if acquired, difficult to keep secretly. When the peasant was reintroduced to firearms in the third quarter of the 19th century, this reintroduction was accomplished within a military rather than a civilian context, and the gun still had no place in village life. While formal regulations against firearms ownership by ordinary citizens still existed, they do not seem to have been needed.

SUMMARY

The preceding description of Old World stratification patterns and their evolution over the past 600 or so years has admittedly been brief and oversimplified, but since its purpose is to set the social stage for that which is to follow it is hoped that it will be adequate. It will be noted that little has been mentioned concerning the modern social scene in Europe and Japan. This did not seem to be called for, however, since the Old World into which firearms were introduced and in which related traditions took shape over a period of hundreds of years was largely a world of peasants and aristocrats on the way to becoming a world of the middle class and the working class. The social scene past and present will be filled out further as the firearms described in chapter IV are, in the next chapter, fitted into the social setting described in this chapter.

FOOTNOTES

1. For an example of how the insertion of a new tool
into an ongoing system, though admittedly a "primitive" one by western standards, can affect that
system, see Michael Banton's description of the
effect the introduction of the steel axe had on a
tribe of Australian aborigines. Michael Banton,
"The Fragility of Simple Role Systems," The Sociological Perspective, ed. Scott G. McNall (Boston:
Little, Brown and Company, 1971), pp. 180-181.

2. Stanislaw Andrzejewski, Military Organization and
Society (London: Routledge & Kegan Paul Ltd.,
1954), pp. 38-59.

3. Ibid., 65.

4. Frantz Funck-Brentano, The Old Regime in France
(New York: Longman's, Green & Co.; London: Edward Arnold & Co., 1929), p. 74.

5. Ibid., 76-77.

6. Alfred Vagts, A History of Militarism: Romance and
Realities of a Profession (New York: W.W. Norton
& Company, Inc., 1937), p. 39.

7. Ibid., 42-43; and Richard A. Preston and Sydney F.
Wise, Men in Arms: A History of Warfare and Its
Interrelationships with Western Society (New York
& Washington: Praeger Publishers, 1970), p. 75.

8. V. G. Kiernan, "Foreign Mercenaries and Absolute
Monarchy," in Crisis in Europe 1560-1660, ed. by
Trevor Aston (New York: Basic Books, Inc., 1965),
p. 117.

9. Preston and Wise, 82.

10. Ibid., 82-83.

11. E. Harris Harbison, The Age of Reformation (Ithaca,
New York: Cornell University Press, 1955), pp. 8-
11.

12. Vagts, 41 and Preston and Wise, 95.

13. Kiernan, 121.

14. Ibid., 122.

15. Ibid., and Preston and Wise 87-88.

16. Ibid., 92-94.

17. Kiernan, 122.

18. Ibid.

19. Vagts, 41.

20. Ibid., 43.

21. Ibid.

22. Kiernan, 125.

23. A. V. B. Norman and Don Pottinger, Warrior to Soldier 449 to 1660: A Brief Introduction to the History of English Warfare (London: Weidenfeld & Nicolson, Limited, 1964), p. 98.

24. Kiernan implies that the Swiss were slow to use firearms, but Charles Oman indicates that they used them by the middle of the 15th century. See Kiernan, 124 and Charles Oman, A History of the Art of War in the Middle Ages, Vol. II, 1278-1485 (New York: Burt Franklin, 1924), pp. 257-258.

25. Kiernan, 121.

26. Ibid., 117.

27. Ibid., 119, Preston and Wise, 91, and Vagts, 44.

28. Vagts, 45.

29. Ibid., 46.

30. Ibid.

31. Ibid., 47.

32. Kiernan, 130.

33. Harbison, 9.

34. Peter N. Stearns, European Society in Upheaval:

Social History Since 1800 (New York: The Macmillan Company; London: Collier-Macmillan Limited, 1967), p. 15; and Funck-Brentano, 99-105.

35. Harbison, 9.

36. Vagts, 72.

37. Andrzejewski, 60-61.

38. Stearns, 13, Vagts, 69, and Barrington Moore, Jr., Social Origins of Dictatorship and Democracy: Lord and Peasant in the Making of the Modern World (Boston: Beacon Press, 1966), p. 48.

39. Vagts, 42.

40. Stearns, 12.

41. Funck-Brentano, 139-140.

42. Stearns, 13-14. Emphasis mine.

43. Ibid., 14.

44. Vagts, 69.

45. Stearns, 14. Emphasis mine.

46. Ibid., 22.

47. Ibid., 23-24

48. Ibid., 24.

49. Ibid., 28.

50. Ibid., 29.

51. Ibid.

52. Ibid., 4-6.

53. Moore, 41.

54. Ibid., 63 and Stearns, 19.

55. Stearns, 89.

56. Ibid., 91 & 290.

57. Ibid., 58-66.

58. Ibid., 95 & 386.

59. Harbison, 8.

60. Stearns, 113.

61. Ibid.

62. Ibid.

63. Ibid., 3 & 113.

64. Ibid., 112.

65. Harbison, 10.

66. Stearns, 36-37.

67. Ibid., 119.

68. Ibid., 249.

69. Ibid., 253.

70. See Paul Mantoux, The Industrial Revolution in the Eighteenth Century: An Outline of the Beginnings of the Modern Factory System in England (Harper Torchbooks, The Academy Library, New York & Evanston: Harper & Row Publishers, 1961), pp. 112-120.

71. Stearns, 58. Europe's population had increased by only 3% between 1650 and 1750.

72. H. Paul Varley with Ivan and Nobuko Morris, Samurai (New York: Dell Publishing Co., Inc., 1970), p. 93.

73. E. Herbert Norman, Soldier and Peasant in Japan: The Origins of Conscription (New York: International Secretariat Institute of Pacific Relations, 1943), pp. 10-11.

74. The distinction between warrior and farmer can be traced back to the 8th century according to George Sansom, A History of Japan 1615-1867, v. 3 (Stanford, California: Stanford University Press, 1963),

p. 29.

75. Varley et al, 114-115.

76. Moore, 230-231.

77. Sansom, 31.

78. Moore, 232-233.

79. Ibid., 231.

80. Varley et al, 121-122.

81. Ibid., 122-123.

82. Moore, 236.

83. Sansom, 32.

84. Ibid., 34 and Moore, 237.

85. Moore, 237.

86. Ibid., 276-277.

87. Sansom, 29.

88. Moore, 262-263.

89. Ibid., 261-262.

90. Norman, 49.

91. Ibid., 45.

92. Ibid., 44-45.

93. Ibid., 34 & 45.

CHAPTER VI

THE GUN IN THE OLD WORLD

THE GUN IN EUROPE

Since no one is certain when or where the first
hand-portable firearms were produced, it is obvious that
no one can be sure of either the purposes for which they
were first produced or for what they were first used.
The earliest known written references to such guns, however, link them to city armories, and the earliest
known paintings and woodcuts depicting their use show
them in the hands of soldiers.[1] These clues, plus the
design characteristics of these primitive guns as they
have been described earlier, would seem to indicate that
the hand cannons were developed as tools of war, as were
the cannons from which it is believed they derived.[2]
Given the shooter's dependence on a separate fire
source, the time-consuming and touchy procedure involved
in setting these guns off, the good possibility that
they would not fire properly coupled with the equally
good possibility that even if they fired the target
would be missed, it is difficult to imagine anyone carrying such a weapon for personal protection. Considering the difficulty involved with these primitive firearms in hitting the object being fired upon, it is also
difficult to imagine that those who hunted to put food
on their tables would enthusiastically take to such
weapons. However, some attempts to hunt with hand cannons might well have been made at an early date.

While it might seem that these shortcomings would
also disqualify the hand cannon as a military weapon,
especially since such relatively far more accurate and
far reaching missile weapons as the crossbow and the
English longbow had long been available, this is not the
case. As noted previously, these early guns were ar-
mor-piercing at close range. Accuracy was scarcely important if they were fired point-blank into an advancing
column, since under these conditions something would
most probably be hit. Even their temperamental nature
could be compensated for, to a certain extent, on the
battlefield if they were fired in numbers large enough
to insure that enough of them would work properly and
do damage to the enemy. And such numbers could be quite
easily achieved since these weapons, relative to other
missile weapons, were easy to make and easy to learn to

101

use.

It took a bowyer about two weeks to make a crossbow, two more weeks to make the windlass used to pull
the bow into cocked position, and over an hour to make
each quarrel, while hand cannons could be made in half
a day and a dozen balls could be cast in a minute.[3]
And while five hundred longbowmen were as effective as
two thousand gunners against infantry, it took a lifetime of daily practice to make a good archer, but only
a few weeks to make an acceptable shooter out of a peasant.[4] Peasants thereby became potential soldiers to
their feudal lords, rather than expendable draft animals.

Considering what was said earlier concerning the
relationship of the feudal lords and their peasants toward the end of the Middle Ages, however, the former
may well have been reluctant to put such weapons into
the hands of the latter, unless the peasants were being
shipped off to serve as mercenaries for someone else and
therefore be no threat to the lord himself. City
militias might have been the first fighting units to
take firearms seriously, as the order for 500 hand cannons in 1364 by the burghers of the town of Perugia,
Italy would seem to indicate.[5] Modena had four in its
armory in 1365 and Augsburg had thirty in 1381.[6] Hand
cannons did get into the hands of peasants, but it would
seem more likely that they were put there by burghers
or by noble founders of mercenary companies than by
those feudal lords who had a vested interest in the
feudal system and its traditional military weapons and
tactics. According to Charles Oman, the Hussite rebels
of Bohemia, for the most part burghers and peasants,
were the first to use hand cannons in battle on a large
scale.[7] They did so in their rebellion against the Holy
Roman Empire (1420-1454). Once their army was disbanded, Bohemian soldiers armed with hand cannons became
mercenaries.[8] The Swiss free peasant mercenaries, who
relied primarily on their pole arms, often used crossbowmen and handcannonmen as skirmishers. By the middle
of the 15th century, the latter weapon--most likely
having acquired a stock of some sort by that time and on
the verge of becoming a matchlock--began to prevail for
such purposes.[9] And, as mentioned earlier, the first
gun-equipped soldiers on English soil were Flemish and
German mercenaries.

While it seems that some city militias were familiar with hand portable firearms as early as the 14th century, and mercenary companies equipped with such weapons were not uncommon by the middle of the 15th century, it was not until well into the 16th century that firearms came into their own as military weapons with the standing armies of the absolute monarchs. By the late 15th century the matchlock had made its appearance; consequently, firearms had become more effective. As they became more sophisticated, firearms also became more expensive, and only rich nations such as Spain, with its abundance of American gold, could readily afford to equip large numbers of troops with them.[10] France began to increase systematically the number of firearms in its infantry only after having been exposed to their effectiveness in the hands of her enemies at Pavia in 1525.[11] And in England, where the national weapon for several centuries had been the longbow, the gun did not win out over that still formidable weapon until 1595.[12] By that time, of course, the wheellock and the flintlock were both known, but the latter was still too expensive and the former too expensive and fragile to put into the hands of large numbers of troops.

It would seem likely that the hand cannons of the 14th and 15th centuries were fired at animals on occasion, though for reasons mentioned previously, it seems doubtful that they were very effective hunting tools. There appears to be no evidence to the effect that they were used in this manner, however. In fact, firearms historians and those who have chronicled the history of hunting cite no evidence to the effect that guns were used for hunting prior to the very late 15th or early 16th centuries. The presence of the matchlock and, in some parts of Europe, the rifled barrel, however, makes it difficult to believe that guns were not so used much earlier. The shooting match at 200 yards held in 1477 indicates that guns which could have been utilized for hunting were available by that time.

By the 16th century, however, there is an abundance of evidence that firearms were used for hunting by all classes, but especially by peasants. The Emperor Maximilian I (1459-1519) complained bitterly about the peasants' use of firearms for hunting and attempted to bring this usage to a halt by passing harsh regulations.[13] And the Emperor himself, on the one hand an enthusiastic advocate of the military use of firearms, but on the other hand an outspoken critic of their use for hunting

by members of any class, is nevertheless shown firing
one at a chamois in a painting done for him in 1504.[14]
In England, Acts of Parliament as early as 1508 seem to
have been aimed at curbing the use of crossbows and guns
by the poorer classes who used them for hunting. In
1542 a "statute established the world's first officially
issued hunting licenses."[15] In Italy, the author of a
book on field sports, writing of the area around Rome
in 1548, claimed that deer had been alarmed and dis-
persed as the result of the use of firearms.[16] "In 1517
the Duke of Wurtenburg decreed that any peasant found
off the main paths in the woods and fields of the game
preserves, carrying a gun, crossbow or any other firearm
shall lose both his eyes."[17] And woodcuts depicting
firearmed hunters, often peasants, in the Netherlands
and other parts of Europe during the second half of the
16th century are apparently quite common.[18]

     While the gun seems to have originated as a tool
of war, therefore, by the beginning of the 16th century,
if not several decades earlier, it was becoming a tool
of the hunt and it was well established as such, especially with the peasantry, by the second half of that
century. A civil use for the gun thereby took its place
alongside of its military use, and a second line of development, on occasion related to but in many ways independent of the original, came into being. It is this
civil use of firearms with which this study is primarily
concerned. But before the three main types of firearms
to be found in civilian hands--shotguns, rifles and
handguns--are placed in social-historical context, one
type at a time, a discussion of the spreading use of
firearms and of the effects of early attempts to regulate their possession and use seems called for.

     Given the earlier observations concerning the aris-
tocracy and its attempts to monopolize the arms-bearing
privilege for both fighting and hunting and concerning
the peasants' limited horizons and feudal obligations,
it might seem surprising to find that peasants, in any
significant number, were using firearms for hunting by
the beginning of the 16th century. Some loss of control
over the peasantry may have occurred as the aristocracy
was being undermined by the aforementioned middle-class
alliance with the absolute monarchs. However, not only
the nobility of Europe but its royalty generally attempted to discourage their subjects from keeping and
using firearms, as some of the earliest references to
firearmed hunting cited above indicate. There seem to

have been several reasons for this stand being taken by various ruling groups. The most obvious concern might have been that firearms in the hands of commoners could prove troublesome to other commoners as well as to the ruling elites themselves. One reason that mercenary soldiers were so popular with the absolute monarchs seems to have been that the latter did not trust their own subjects enough to arm them.[19] This seems to have been particularly true on the Continent, although even in England, which had long encouraged every able-bodied man to keep arms and be prepared for militia service, there were many misgivings when it came to putting firearms into the hands of the people at large.[20]

While these misgivings were quite similar to those held by the ruling classes of England's continental neighbors, the English rulers were also afraid that the use of guns by their subjects would cause those subjects to neglect their longbows and thereby be unprepared in the event of war.[21] The longbow still had many supporters in Tudor England, and they believed, with some justification, that it was a better military weapon than the guns then available.[22] Be that as it may, the gun, especially if "hail shot" was used (the shotgun, in effect) could more easily put food on the table. And if hail shot was used, gun marksmanship of the sort that might be of use on the battlefield was not even fostered.[23] This reference to hunting with firearms brings to the fore still another reason for the ruling classes' efforts to discourage possession of firearms by peasants and other commoners. Hunting was for the upper classes, as C. G. Cruickshank writing of the late Tudor era in England makes clear. "A royal proclamation referred to the widespread illegal use of fowling and birding pieces which was despoiling all parts of the country of pheasant, partridge and all sorts of game which should serve for the delight of her majesty, the nobility, and other men of quality."[24]

It is difficult to determine what effect attempts to regulate the use of firearms by the peasantry and others of the poorer classes actually had, but the wording of various regulations down through the centuries and other bits of evidence suggest that in England, France, and at least parts of Germany and Austria, the poorer classes continued to possess and use firearms legally or otherwise.[25] This state of affairs should hardly be surprising, since formal social controls that do not have the support of those to whom they apply seem at best to be only superficially effective. The Swiss free peasants, of course, seem to have encouraged those in good standing in the community to possess and familiarize themselves with weapons of various sorts, including firearms. The fact that peasants evidently acquired and used firearms in spite of attempts to discourage them from doing so is less surprising than the fact that such typically tradition-bound people of limited experience in the world apart from their village wanted to acquire and use guns.

While it is difficult to reconcile his writings with numerous other accounts of English peasants using firearms during the period of which he writes, Lindsay Boynton claims that rustic militiamen would have nothing to do with the smoking, fire-flashing, noisy guns of late Tudor England.[26] From what others have written, it would seem that many rustics overcame any fear of firearms they may have had upon first being exposed to them. However, such original fear as they may have experienced is surely understandable if we take into consideration what moderns would feel to be the superstitious world view of people in general and peasants in particular of those days gone by. In his _A History of Shooting_, Jaroslav Lugs devotes twenty-five pages to a discussion of "shooting magic and superstitions."[27]

Taking into consideration the rootedness, the limited horizons, the "superstition," etc., of the peasants, one might wonder how they ever came to accept firearms at all. But from the previous discussion it can be seen that while the typical European peasants of the 19th century and earlier seldom left their villages, over the years significant numbers of peasants were uprooted. Furthermore, the discussion of mercenaries points out that over a period of several hundred years significant numbers of these peasants from certain parts of Europe became soldiers. When these men returned to their homes, particularly if they did so in large numbers as must have been the case occasionally in such countries as Switzerland, the weapons with which they had become familiar on far-off battlefields certainly came with them and were thereby introduced into otherwise conservative, tradition-bound settings. And while many mercenaries came from outlying areas where no aristocracy existed, some did not. According to Kiernan, "in the insurgent areas of Austria and south-west Germany during the Peasants' War many peasants had seen military service, and were thus much better armed and organized than in Thuringia, where there were few ex-soldiers."[28] He goes on to quote Engels to the effect that the peasants of Allgaeu not only had soldiers and experienced commanders in their ranks but possessed "numerous well-manned cannon" as well.[29] And in commenting on the introduction of gunpowder into the field of sport, Michael Brander writes:

> One may be sure that the soldier, or more often the sailor, returned from adventure overseas, having seen the deadly effects of a "handgonne" on the enemy, was not slow to try it out on the rafts of wild-fowl on the marches, or on the king's deer in the forests, even though a slow fuse or matchlock and a stand for the gun was required. Such a man, who had possibly travelled halfway round the known world, was not likely to submit tamely to having his liberty curbed at home. If he did not own land or have a grant of warren, he was likely to poach or take game as and when he felt like it. The sturdy independence of the average Tudor Englishman was such that any law to the contrary would have been considered a challenge.[30]

It would seem reasonable, therefore, to assume that rustics in various parts of Europe were introduced to firearms by those of their number who brought them back from far-away wars. In England--and probably else-where--it seems that returning soldiers who did not wish to put their weapons to further use themselves were only too ready to sell them in spite of the fact that the guns were the property of various counties and therefore not theirs to sell.[31] English soldiers in Ireland even sold their weapons to the rebels.[32] On the Continent, in some areas, the peasants' first exposure to firearms may have been brought about through their contacts with roving bands of mercenaries from areas other than their own. If this were the case, there is a good chance that the contact was less than pleasant since mercenaries could scarcely be characterized as a gentle lot. More-over, outside of their home areas the mercenaries tended to treat all civilians in the same manner whether those civilians were the subjects of their employer, or of his enemies, or whether they had an employer or not.[33]

107

While the first firearms used for hunting may well
have been military weapons, and while military weapons
are still used by some for hunting, as noted earlier,
once firearms were put to civilian use a separate line
of development, to which attention will now be shifted,
gradually began to evolve. Attention will be given
first to the shotgun, since it could be argued that it
has the fewest links with the military of the three
types of firearms to be discussed here; furthermore, it
seems to be the firearm most likely to be found in
civilian hands in the parts of Europe being considered
in this study.

SHOTGUNS

Originally, shotguns--or, more properly, smoothbore
longarms loaded with hail shot--seem to have been the
hunting weapons of peasants and other poor commoners,
and, for the most part, the game at which these guns
were fired was commoners' game. At first, however,
firearms merely augmented ancient methods of trapping
game: nets, snares, lime rods, intoxicating baits, etc.
Even after the use of firearms became more common, these
other means of putting food on the table were still
utilized.[34] Given what has been said earlier about
European peasant life prior to 1800 and even later, one
might safely assume that these hunting and trapping activities were serious business to people who were essentially farmers rather than hunters and trappers.

Woodcuts from the 16th century show peasant hunters
crouched just a few yards from the sitting birds at
which they have just fired their cumbersome matchlocks,
a technique which some of their ancestors may have used
with hand cannons a century earlier and which their descendants might still be using a century later. For
these poor people, a gun, at least after matchlocks came
into use, must have been quite an investment, unless it
was carried home from militia or other military duty.
Also, powder and lead must have been expensive enough
that an effort had to be made to make every shot
count.[35] After all, people back there in the village
were depending on the hunter to augment their generally
meager food supply, and he was utilizing some of their
precious resources in the effort. Given the limitations
of his weapon, if an attempt was to be made to make
every shot count, the hunter had to get as close as possible to his quarry and, if small game was being hunted,

use hail shot. The stalking skills that enabled the peasant hunter to get close to his quarry, the shooting skills, modest though they might have been by modern standards, that enabled him to hit his target more often than his friends hit theirs, and the warm reception the successful hunter must have received from his family and friends--all surely added a satisfying, recreational aspect to the serious business of hunting. The possession of a gun may also have symbolically marked off its owner from fellow villagers who did not possess one. The symbolic interactionist would certainly expect all this to be the case, but historians, it seems, have yet to provide him with supporting evidence. That the long gun capable of firing hail shot functioned practically in the lives of those peasants who hunted with them, however, seems certain.[36]

The European peasant down to modern times hunted and trapped primarily to eat, whatever else these activities might have afforded him. The aristocrat hunted for other reasons, however; consequently, unless he was poverty-stricken, he was likely to consider trapping and stalking to be beneath him.[37] Though he might have occasionally used gun and hail shot for amusement when they were first introduced, he hardly considered using them for serious hunting.[38] Throughout the Middle Ages and into the age of firearms, hunting had enabled the noble to develop and display the riding skills and the skills with such traditional weapons as the spear and sword that would prepare him and keep him prepared for fighting. Of the wild creatures available to him, therefore, he was primarily interested in those that would give him a good chase on horseback or those that could give him a stiff fight. Consequently, such large wild creatures as were available in various parts of Europe were generally reserved for the royalty and aristocracy. The animals available in those parts of Europe being considered here, at the time that firearms were introduced, included such swift creatures as the stag, or red deer, and the fallow deer, and such formidable ones as the wildboar. The roe deer was classified as noble game in Sweden, and the wolf and bear were also considered to be worthy of the attention of the nobility. However, both of the latter were considered to be outlaw animals, and all able-bodied men, including commoners, were obliged to aid in the elimination of wolves and bears whenever possible.[39] To hunt the fierce wild boar, which was considered to be the very personifica-: tion of evil, with boar sword or spear was seen as particularly heroic.[40]

During the time that firearms were working their way into the sporting scene, with certain exceptions, small game and birds could be legally hunted and trapped by peasants, while large game was reserved for the nobility.[41] However, as Gunnar Brusewitz has noted, "a striking reversal of the social position of game belonging to the lowest group was . . . to take place when fire-arms had developed so much that rapid wing shots were possible."[42] Strictly speaking, there was no reversal, since the nobility retained their rights to large game and took over much of the commoner's claim to small game. The development of the wheellock, which only the wealthy aristocrat, or burgher, could afford, seems to have helped the aristocrat acquire an increased interest in firearms for hunting as well as fighting. As his appreciation for marksmanship increased, he turned his attention to creatures that peasants had previously netted or shot sitting from a few yards distance. The matchlock, with its lit fuse and slow ignition, made hitting moving targets a matter of luck. The relatively quick ignition of the wheellock and the later flintlock made shooting flying possible, though difficult; therefore, such shooting could be considered a test of marksmanship.[43]

But in some parts of Europe there were also other reasons for the development of the aristocrat's interest in bird shooting: he had little else to hunt. As Trench has written:

> Several factors combined to produce, particularly in Britain, a craze for birdshooting which, beginning in the seventeenth century, lasted some 200 years. Foremost among these was the disappearance of the forests of medieval England. The demands of iron-smelting, house- and church-building, and above all of shipbuilding almost destroyed the forests, and no one did any systematic re-planting. With the forests went the wild deer, red and fallow, the hunting of which had been the great sport first of the Court and the nobility, then of the richer squirearchy until about the end of the sixteenth century. By the Restoration wild deer had disappeared from most of

the country and sportsmen had to look
elsewhere. At the same time improvements
in arable farming, more acreage under
corn and root-crops, created conditions
in which pheasants and partridges flourished; the Game Laws forbade the killing
of game for all, broadly speaking, but
owners of land worth Ł100 a year; and
increasing prosperity encouraged these
fortunate "qualified persons" to regard
shooting more as a sport or perhaps a
status-symbol than as a means of food
procurement. Shooting, not hunting with
hounds, became the characteristic upper-
class sport.[44]

Urbanization, industrialization, and new agricultural patterns transformed most of Britain into shotgun
country at a rather early date, as large game was driven
out and small game thrived. France and Italy were similarly transformed to a great extent at a later date.[45]
And as bird and small game hunting became ever more popular with the aristocracy, and later with the wealthier
members of the middle class who acquired aristocratic
tastes, several things occurred. For one, the shotgun,
which had originated as a smoothbore hand cannon or
matchlock capable of firing either ball or shot, was refined and refined again until by 1800 or so its expensive versions had become quick-pointing sporting guns
fit for the most demanding of the wealthy sportsmen of
the period and capable of hitting birds on the wing.
But long before that time, finely finished fowling
pieces, often elaborately decorated, were made for those
who could afford them and, as Held writing of Henry
VIII's time has noted, for some who could not.

Even a nearly bankrupt young baronet or a
lawyer with a modest income (Ł100-a-year-
plus) went shooting (if he ever did so at
all) with the finest German, French, Italian or Spanish gun he could buy, beg or
borrow, not because one shot better than
the other but because it was almost ex-
actly like the one which the Duke of
Gloucester had been seen at Windsor on
Wednesday last.[46]

And, according to Held, as shooting became ever more
popular with high society, some gentlemen appear to have

111

acquired fowling pieces without entertaining "the faintest intention of putting them to more strenous use than as insignia of rank."[47]

With the aristocratic and upper class interest in hunting birds and small animals came efforts to preserve such creatures, preservation efforts having previously been reserved for large game. In France the following decree reserving hunting privileges exclusively for the nobility was passed in 1669:

> We forbid merchants, artisans, bourgeois and inhabitants of towns, boroughs, parishes, villages and hamlets, peasants and all persons of humble birth of whatever condition and quality, not being in possession of fiefs, seigneuries and high magisterial functions, in any place, form or manner, to hunt any fur or feathered game whatsoever.[48]

By law, violation of the above could result in condemnation to the galleys, confiscation of goods or even execution.[49]

According to Funck-Brentano,

> throughout the extent of a capitainerie /areas of special hunting right jurisdiction and restriction/ it was forbidden to enclose a property with walls, hedges or ditches, which would have interfered with hunting; a man was forbidden to keep arms in his house and to walk abroad with a dog; unless it had a billet of wood hanging from its neck; he was forbidden to reap before the end of June, and to enter his own fields between the 1st of May and the Feast of St. John--by the Feast of St. John the partridges are fledged, and néither my lady partridge, nor setting pheasant must be disturbed.[50]

While the English upper classes were far less autocratic and less sharply defined than were the French, they nevertheless guarded their shooting privileges, restricting them to men of "worth," as noted previously. But where game was as jealously protected as it was in France, even small creatures through sheer numbers came to constitute a hazard to the peasants' crops. When this occurred, the peasants occasionally rose against these creatures as they did in France in 1754.[51] Even where and when peasant crops were not ruined by game, however, the poor country folk were deprived of a food source when they were not allowed to hunt. Therefore, as small game hunting became the sport of the aristocrat and the wealthy, poaching, which had existed since hunting restrictions of any sort had been imposed, became a sport as well as a practical activity to the simple country folk.[52] In fact, all sorts of people poached or were in some way involved with poaching, including otherwise respectable clergymen, magistrates, and even the gamekeepers whose job it was to ward off poachers.[53] In some English villages everyone old enough to poach did so, and eventually gangs formed and poaching became a commercial endeavor.[54] According to Richard Heath, who wrote in the 1890's of the earlier part of the 19th century,

> these gangs were co-operative societies, for they not only provided guns and other instruments, but hired men at wages little above that given to the gamekeepers to do the actual poaching while they took the booty, or at least the lion's share of it, and if these servants of the gang were arrested, money was forthcoming to pay the penalties.[55]

Pitched battles between poachers and gamekeepers were not rare, and all sorts of traps, including guns that would fire down the line that triggered them when the line was tripped over, were used to guard the game parks of various estates.[56] Poachers, however, have continued their activities with net as well as gun into the 20th century.[57]

Still another phenomenon that evolved along with the increasing interest in shotguns and bird shooting on the part of the aristocracy, and eventually on the part of the wealthy in general, was competition shooting with the shotgun. While it seems quite likely that peasant hunters compared bags after a day of hunting, they have left little evidence to this effect. Not so the aristocracy and gentry. As shall be seen later, the nobility and royalty often kept meticulous records of the various kinds of animals they had taken in one way or another during their lives, and this record-keeping carried over

113

to bird shooting. Brander cites an entry in the shooting chronicle of Peter Hawker to the effect that he had beaten all of his neighbors in partridge shooting for a particular month in 1852.[58] He also cites the recorded accomplishments of another early 19th century sportsman--"100 pheasants with 100 shots, 97 grouse with 97 shots, and 20 brace of partridge with 40 shots."[59] And according to A. E. Richardson

> betting . . . often accompanied partridge and game shooting, wagers being laid on the number of winged game which could be killed between sunrise and sunset . . . It is on record that Coke of Holkham, in 1801, killed as many as 726 partridges in five days.[60]

Coke may well have achieved this record by having the birds blocked by nets, causing them to fly back toward the shooter. This utilization of nets was a common practice with society shooters of his day, particularly when large numbers of shooters were involved as in a well-organized and socially fashionable "grand battue." According to F. M. L. Thompson,

> game books in which were entered each day's shooting party and each day's bag, seem to have made their appearance /in England7 towards the end of the eighteenth century, a sign of growing organization of the sport. . . . The height of organization in execution, the grand battue in which carefully nurtured birds slothful from too good living were methodically slaughtered in droves, was reached in the decade after 1815; the remaining excitement in this branch of the sport seemed to lie in the establishment of national records for the largest single day's bag which was put at 525 pheasants in 1823, shot at Ashridge by twelve guns.[61]

From about 1870 to 1914, beaters were used to drive birds back over the shooter for these large shoots.[62]

Around 1856 or so, fashionable competition shooting with the shotgun became even more formalized as pigeon shoots on ranges especially designed for the purpose were introduced in England and quickly spread to the

Continent.[63] International matches were arranged, the more famous of these being held in France at Monaco, Cannes, Paris, Dieppe, Bordeaux, Reims, Boulogne and Pau; in Belgium at Brussels and Spa; in Germany at Baden-Baden and Enns a. Donau; in Italy at Milan, Florence, Rimini, Venice, and Lido Island; in Spain at San Sebastian and Seville; and in Bohemia at Prague.[64] For these matches pigeons were released from traps to be shot by individual shooters competing against others in accordance with elaborate rules. The champions of these matches became quite well known in higher circles, although some were already well known, such as the Spanish King Alfonso, who won the Silver Cup at Seville in 1910.[65] But at the major ranges such as Monte Carlo, gambling was more important than sport and bets were placed on each pigeon.[66] Since the sport was opposed by many as being cruel, it was finally prohibited, with England holding out until 1921.[67] By that time, however, "clay pigeons" and traps to hurl them had been perfected and competition shooting with the shotgun continued at local, national, and international levels.[68]

Needless to say, the grand battue, pigeon shooting in competition, or even clay pigeon shooting were not for the peasant or others of the poorer classes.[69] These pastimes were for the aristocrats and the wealthy who could not only shoot legally, but who could also afford fine and sometimes quite specialized guns as well as the other trappings of high society. Commenting on those who created the hunting attire for the 19th century socialite hunters, Brusewitz writes:

> They created elegant and tastefully patterned costumes which were often not even suitable for walking along a well-trodden footpath. There almost seems to have been a conscious effort to stress the social status of the hunting gentleman by making his attire as "distinguished" as possible. The idea was to be able to spot from afar that it was a gentleman who was approaching in the woods and not just some shabby stalker.[70]

In England, shooting (that is, small game and especially bird shooting with the shotgun) seems to have remained an upper class sport to this day. T. H. Pear, in his 1955 study of English social differences, found that the ruling group shared the following attributes much more often than did the members of the social levels below it:

> Family--Titled and Professional.
> Education--Public and Grammar School,
>   University education.
> Occupation--None or Professional.
> Clubs--Carlton and Brooks.
> Recreation--Shooting and Golf.[71]

And he goes on to say that

> it is hardly necessary to say that the
> American, wider use of the word "hunt-
> ing" is not acceptable to the English.
> Shooting retains much of its social ex-
> clusiveness, since in order to shoot, it
> is necessary to own or hire the shooting
> rights of a preserve. Most of the best
> shooting is in Scotland, and to a lesser
> degree on the Yorkshire moors. Because
> of its exclusiveness, it is regarded as
> socially very desirable, and the dream of
> many "climbers" is to be invited to some-
> one's shoot. This is often a mark of great
> favour from a host, who naturally wishes
> to restrict his house-party to people of
> his own sort, who, he feels, will under-
> stand, appreciate and enjoy the sport and
> with whom he can relax. To be well equip-
> ped is a necessity for any guest: it
> would be a serious error to use the host's
> cartridges, though they are always pro-
> vided.[72]

On the Continent, however, the hunting privileges of the aristocracy faded away after the political revolutions, and hunting in France became particularly democratized, as many visitors have noted. An Englishman visiting that country in the 1930's wrote:

> In France shooting may be said to be one
> form of out-door exercise which is prac-
> ticed by everyone. Nearly every profes-
> sional man living in a town goes out to
> the country to shoot on Sundays and takes
> his dogs with him. Indeed, there are, dur-
> ing the season, special trains back to
> Paris on Sundays at the hours when chasseurs

will be likely to be returning home, and
special carriages on those trains reserved
for them and their dogs, and so marked.
As for the peasant farmers who live
in the villages, everyone of them will go
out shooting on Sundays, and everyone of
them will have his dogs.
If shooting is socially so widely-
spread a pastime, it is because preserving
on a large scale is far rarer than in
England. Of course, there are rich men who
have big shoots, as there are men who breed
pheasants and organize drives; but they are
the exception rather than the rule.[73]

A German visitor of the late 1930's described
French outdoor life in an almost identical fashion, and
referred to France during hunting season as "a nation in
arms--shotguns to be exact."[74] Both authors cite hares,
rabbits, and partridges as the quarry almost always
sought by French hunters, although boar, deer, chamois,
and ibex exist in some parts of France, with the latter
two animals to be found in the Alps and Pyrenees respectively.[75] According to the English author, however,
"for most Frenchmen . . . la chasse does not extend to
such fancy game."[76] The hunting of small game has survived World War II in France, as noted in Chapter I,
with game having to be imported to meet the demand.
Game was already so scarce before the war, however, that
it was the practice of French hunters, who generally
seem to have hunted in groups, to gather around and con-
gratulate any of their number who bagged anything.[77]
The social-psychological implications of these prac-
tices--hunting in groups and celebrating the success of
a companion--would be obvious to the symbolic interactionist.

Before leaving this discussion of the shotgun, it
should be pointed out that considering the game to which
most Englishmen and Frenchmen have access--small animals
and birds--the shotgun is their most practical hunting
or sporting tool. It should also be pointed out that
until recently little effort has been made in either
country to regulate the possession of such weapons.
Long guns, most probably smoothbores capable of firing
hail shot, were evidently possessed by French peasants
even before the Revolution.[78] And Josserand writes of
the post-World War II period

117

that although the authorities seem horri-
fied at the thought of a pre-World War I
military rifle in private hands, no one
gets excited about the two and a half million or more shotguns in France. Loaded
with buckshot or slug, the shotgun is a
formidable combat weapon, as the Germans
must have been well aware, since they
made great haste to confiscate all they
could locate when they occupied France in
1940.[79]

In Great Britain, according to Colin Greenwood, Chief
Inspector West Yorkshire Constabulary, stricter regulation of shotguns is being urged by some, and shotgun
possession has already become subject to more regulation
than existed prior to 1968. Yet a different sort of
certificate is needed to possess shotguns legally than
one needs to possess other firearms legally.[80] To obtain a shotgun certificate a person need not show "good
reason" for acquiring such a weapon; he is entitled to
the certificate if he is "of good character."

A further contrast with the firearms certificate is that a shotgun certificate refers only to a person and permits him to
hold any number of weapons without further
formalities, whereas the firearms certificate refers both to the person and to specific weapons, authorizing the possession
only of those weapons detailed in the certificate.[81]

Similar distinctions between shotguns and other types of
firearms are made in the Scandinavian countries and in
other parts of Europe.[82] Over most of Europe, however,
regulation attempts have generally centered on hunting
privileges rather than on shotgun ownership. And hunting restrictions, in conjunction with industrial revolution in England and political as well as industrial
revolution in France, have succeeded in making hunting
of a type for which shotguns are best suited the sport
of the higher classes in the former nation and of all
classes in the latter. For similar reasons, shotguns
are the most common hunting and sporting guns in Italy
and much of the rest of Europe, though, as shall be seen,
the rifle is also popular in some countries.

RIFLES

The following statements by Blackmore and Held, respectively, help to explain in part why rifles have been much more popular in some parts of Europe than they have been in other parts of the Continent.

> In eighteenth-century Britain, with
> the destruction of forests and the enclo-
> sure of waste lands, the herds of wild deer
> were banished to the barren moors of Devon
> and Scotland, and the opportunities for
> using a rifle began to dwindle rapidly.
> When a demand for rifles arose during the
> American Wars, the British Board of Ordance
> was hard put to find gunmakers in England
> capable of producing rifled barrels in any
> quantity.[83]

> The rifle was naturally the gun of
> Germany and Switzerland, where big game
> abounded in the lush forests and stark
> mountains. By 1700 the gunmakers of Bavaria
> had developed short, massive, heavy wheel-
> lock and flintlock rifles which could kill
> bears and deer at two hundred yards with
> ease, while shots beyond four hundred were
> not unknown.[84]

But while central European terrain and the animals to be found there certainly must have accounted for the rifle's popularity as a hunting tool in these areas, other factors added to the weapon's overall popularity. Central Europe of the 15th and 16th centuries and later was the home of the Swiss free peasants who supplied mercenaries for all of Europe. In Germany and Bohemia there were many free cities, and to the east of Bohemia --whose people had first used large numbers of firearms in battle--was the military frontier with the Turks, who were using firearms themselves by the middle of the 15th century.[85] In other words, central Europe of that time was a place where firearms were military tools as well as hunting tools to burghers and many peasants. Conse-quently, whether or not the principle of rifling was first discovered there, it was in central Europe that rifled long arms first came into general use. And there is an abundance of historical evidence to the effect that rifles came to function recreationally and symboli-cally as well as practically in the lives of those cen-

119

tral Europeans who possessed them.

Shooting guilds came into existence in Switzerland, and as a reaction to the Turkish threat, in the Holy Roman Empire during the 15th and 16th centuries. The first such guilds used crossbows in their matches, with targets set at 130 meters, but by 1466 Lucerne had a gun guild and before rifling became common such guilds shot over the shorter range of 100 meters. According to Trench, competitors used their own weapons, but the authorities provided the ammunition for Sunday target competitions.[86] Trench goes on to claim that the prizes for these matches were breeches, hose, and other such utilitarian items. But according to Lugs, who treats such matches in great detail, the prizes were more varied and became less utilitarian as the years passed. Ready-made clothes and material for clothes were awarded, but so were richly ornamented domestic animals--ranging from geese to horses, with a pig for the worst shot-- and rifles, powder flasks, swords, spears, and various pewter utensils were particularly popular prizes. Tumblers, dishes, bowls, rings, hat buckles, and neck chains made of gold or silver also came to serve as prizes, and strictly ornamental gold trophy cups for display in the winner's home or shooting club became popular in the 15th century.[87] Medals and plaques, similar to those still awarded at shooting matches, made their appearance in the 17th century.

These shooting competitions were colorful and extravagant affairs, and over much of central Europe they became extremely popular with spectators as well as with the participants. The Zurich matches of 1504 had something for everyone--dancing, feasting, displays of swordsmanship, jousting, horse racing, games, strolling players, Gypsies, and prostitutes, etc. Participants in these matches numbered 460 crossbowmen and 236 arquebusiers, and they came from as far away as Innsbruck and Frankfurt-am-Main.[88] The festivities generally started at an inn from which the marksmen, after much drinking and socializing, would march to the shooting range behind the target keeper, who was colorfully attired as a medieval jester, and a band, and ahead of the spectators.[89]

These festivals were community affairs "par excellence," and the communities that sponsored them paid for them, often using lotteries to do so.[90] According to Lugs, who describes these events in marvelous detail, songs and poems similar to those used to commemorate medi-

eval tournaments were written in honor of shooting festivals, their contestants, and the richness of the towns
that had sponsored them.91 The social and communal aspects of these events is further attested to by Lugs'
comments concerning the shooting brotherhoods.

As public corporations, these shooting
associations played a considerable role
in social life. At that time townspeople
were united in corporations only according
to their crafts--into separate guilds.
These were, moreover, considerably restricted by their regulations and ancient,
outmoded ceremonials, and also by their
restricted spheres of activity, and they
offered no opportunity for developing a
more integrated social life. Shooting
brotherhoods kept to old traditions, but
could easily adapt their more elastic
regulations to different times and conditions. How much they were changed can
be seen from the articles of these associations. Whereas the articles of the
first shooting brotherhoods contain religious commands, shooting articles of
more recent times state the aim of the
association to be general entertainment
and recreation besides perfection in
handling arms.92

While guns gradually came to outnumber crossbows
at shooting festivals, the guns used did not always have
rifled barrels. In fact, rifled barrels were at times
expressly prohibited for match use.93 While the reasons
for such prohibitions may well have differed in each
case, they may have been prompted occasionally by the
belief that the spinning rifle bullets were guided by
demons. Demon guidance was proven to the satisfaction
of those concerned in Mainz in 1547 when two marksmen,
one using ordinary lead bullets, the other using demon-
proof silver bullets engraved with a crucifix, fired
twenty shots each at a target 219 yards away. Nineteen
of the twenty regular bullets hit the target while none
of the silver did. Rifles were then seized and destroyed, and anyone who continued to produce them risked
being burned at the stake.94 The decree was soon forgotten, however. No one suspected at the time that the
silver balls were less accurate than lead balls because
the rifling stripped silver instead of biting into it,

121

thereby reducing compression, and that the engraved crucifixes compounded the problem by throwing the ball out of balance and creating air turbulence.[95] At least this is a modern explanation for the inaccuracy of such projectiles, but it should be noted that exorcism of rifle bullets is still known in South Germany.

As central European rifle makers and the hunters and target shooters who used their products tried to build more accuracy into these long range precision instruments, trigger mechanisms and sights became more sophisticated. Set triggers, the second of which required only a very light pull after the first had been pulled, became standard on the more expensive rifles during the 17th century.[96] Sights that could be adjusted were in use by the 17th century, and optical sights had also made their appearance by that time.[97] But such refinements seem to have been applied to rifles in general with specialized rifles for target shooting taking some time to develop. By the early 19th century, however, target rifle barrels had become heavier, stocks, butt plates, and palm rests to facilitate off-hand shooting (the standing position) had been developed, and more sophisticated sights were available.[98] The target rifle had come into its own.

Many town shooting associations perished during the Thirty Years' War, and though they were revived after that war, they never again matched the military importance that they had achieved during the 16th century and retained until the 17th century.

> In the 17th and 18th centuries, governments no longer favoured shooting associations as they were superfluous to the needs of the regular armies which had been introduced by them. Thus, shooting became a symbol of the jealously-protected privilege of townsmen to use weapons. The greatest adversaries of town shooting associations were two typical absolute sovereigns, the Prussian Kings Friedrich Wilhelm I, and his successor Friedrich II. In Austria Emperor Joseph II tried to cancel shooting association and bird shooting in the year 1785.[99]

Interest in rifle marksmanship never disappeared completely from the central European scene, however, and the revolutionary period of the early 19th century prompted many middle-class members of town and national guard units to form new rifle associations.100 The popularity of target shooting reached its peak at that time, and many men let the sport rule their lives. Those men, consumed by their desire to be shooting champions, ignored family and work responsibilities to concentrate on their sport, which often required travel, and shooting matches often encouraged gambling and the losses that could result from such activities.101

As noted earlier, specialized target rifles had made their appearance by the early 19th century, and these rifles must have been expensive. With the advent of the breechloader and metallic cartridges in the second half of the 19th century, the expense of these special rifles increased to the point that the ordinary citizen could not afford them.102 The shooting associations began to fail, and their ranges, which could not accommodate the powerful new rifles, fell into disuse. While some shooting festivals continued well into the 20th century, central European target matches had lost much of their folk character. For those who can afford it, however, target shooting has remained a popular sport there. With the perfection of metal cartridges, smallbore rifles--.22 caliber and 4 millimeter--became practical, and rifles patterned after the high-powered match rifles, but chambered for the smaller cartridges, came to be used on small indoor as well as outdoor ranges. These smallbore target rifles were approximately the same size and weight as the larger-caliber match rifles, and they also possessed the target refinements of the latter--set triggers, adjustable sights, hooked butt plates, etc. Fine air rifles with these special features have also been produced for match shooting.103

With the possible exception of the Scandinavian Peninsula and the mountainous parts of France and northern Italy, the kind of grass-roots support for rifle marksmanship that was rather widespread in central Europe seems never to have existed in the other parts of Europe being considered here. The terrain and game of central Europe in a sense demanded the rifle's long-range accuracy and power, while the shooting associations, which at first encouraged military preparedness with the crossbow and smoothbore guns, came to prefer the rifle as they became more interested in precision shooting. At the time, the rifle was of limited military usefulness because it took so long to load. Until

the early 19th century, the smoothbore musket, though
not nearly as accurate as contemporary rifles, was the
better military weapon, given the infantry tactics in
use. The loose-fitting musket balls allowed a musketeer
to fire five shots in the two minutes that a rifleman
required to reload his weapon to get off a second
shot.[104]

Where the rifle was not used for hunting, therefore, military factors alone were hardly sufficient to
foster grass-roots interest in precision shooting of the
sort that rifles could provide. This state of affairs
changed somewhat, however, as such developments as the
"Minie ball," and later the cartridge-firing breechloaders, made rifled longarms effective military weapons
toward the middle of the 19th century. In 1937 L. H.
Weir wrote that

> much attention is given to training young
> boys how to shoot in most of the European
> countries. In Sweden instruction in shoot-
> ing in the boys' schools is obligatory.
> The cost is borne by the state. In London
> there is an organization of school boys
> under the name of "Lord Roberts Boys" that
> has for its object training in shooting.
> They spend several weeks of each year on
> the military shooting ranges. They are
> uniformed and camp in tents during the
> shooting period. Shooting instruction is
> given in the schools of France, Italy,
> Roumania, etc. In the latter country in-
> struction in all the schools has been ob-
> ligatory since 1906. In Austria-Hungary
> before the World War shooting instruction
> using the army weapon was carried on in
> the four upper classes of the gymnasia.[105]

Yet while various national governments encouraged
their citizens to become proficient with the rifle as
they set about building armies, conscript and otherwise, with which they could acquire empires and defend
themselves against their neighbors, a grass-roots interest in rifle shooting does not seem to have developed
in areas where the rifle was not a practical hunting
weapon. And it should be noted that governmental support of rifle shooting in Europe has generally been
qualified. Organized training sessions in a controlled
setting were encouraged in some countries, but civilian

possession of rifles, particularly those of a caliber sufficient for military use, has been discouraged in many of the same countries--a notable exception being Switzerland. In England an applicant for a firearms certificate must convince the certifying agency that he has "good reason" to own such a weapon before he can legally acquire even a .22 caliber rifle. However, "active membership of an approved rifle club is normally considered to be good reason. . . ." if the applicant's rifle is suitable for target work.[106] In France, attempts have been made to control the possession of military long arms, rifled or otherwise, since such weapons came into use. During the Franco-Prussian War, however, as Josserand puts it, "French citizens were vigorously encouraged to do what the year before they had been proscribed from doing: to arm themselves."[107]

As noted in Chapter I, World Wars I and II have undermined efforts to enforce European firearms regulations, and there is reason to believe that many rifles are in private hands in such places as France and Norway and possibly even England.[108] Of the last nation, Greenwood writes that during World War II "millions of men of many nationalities were under arms in this country and, in addition to the regular soldiers, such reserve units as the Home Guard were fully equipped with rifles, sub-machine guns and other small arms, many of which were kept in men's homes."[109] And in Germany approximately two million army rifles were left unaccounted for after the end of World War I.[110] The illegal possession of military rifles in parts of Europe, where no previous grass-roots attachment to such weapons existed, does not seem to have fostered an interest in rifle shooting, however. Private citizens who possess such weapons seem to hold on to them just in case another emergency comes along. The British citizenry apparently was so short of militarily effective small arms, shotguns as well as rifles, at the beginning of World War II that American private citizens were requested to donate personal weapons to equip the British Home Guard.[111]

Since the possession of rifles in England was not regulated until 1920, the apparently small numbers of these weapons in civilian hands there prior to World War II cannot be credited to firearms regulations.[112] As noted several times previously, the Industrial Revolution and the circumstances leading up to it had made England shotgun country by the 17th century as far as hunting was concerned. Those Englishmen wealthy enough to go after big game on the Continent, or in Africa or Asia, used rifles; consequently, the English have produced some very fine custom-built rifles for use on elephants and other large game. But such hunting obviously has not been for the common man. Aside from the silencer-equipped .22 rifle sometimes used on small game by English poachers, therefore, ordinary Englishmen have evidently had little civilian contact with rifles. They have apparently felt no need for rifles, considering the type of game available in England, and due to the fact that legal shooting is the sport of the wealthy in their country.

It has been mentioned several times that the rifle has been a popular hunting weapon in the more rugged areas of Europe, but such hunting has yet to be discussed to any great extent. As noted in the course of the preceding discussion of the shotgun, from the Middle Ages through the political revolutions of the late 18th and 19th centuries, the European aristocracy had attempted to reserve the privilege of hunting the larger more formidable game animals for itself. Though it was every man's duty to eliminate wolves and bears, the aristocracy and royalty reserved for themselves the stag or red deer (similar to the North American elk), the fallow deer, the wild boar, the chamois of the Alps (after the Emperor Maximillian took an interest in hunting them), and sometimes the roe deer and the European elk (similar to the North American moose).113 In outlying areas where there was no aristocracy, as was the case in Switzerland, and in areas where it was difficult for the aristocracy to enforce hunting regulations, commoners hunted such animals if they were available. In areas where hunting could be regulated more stringently, the aristocracy went to great lengths to protect its game animals. According to Brusewitz:

> The lengths to which the European princes were prepared to go to satisfy their craving for hunting wild boar may well be called one of the darkest chapters in the history of hunting. In many areas the peasants were forbidden to fence their fields and, if they were allowed to do so in some generous cases, it was on the explicit condition that the poles were not made so high or pointed that the animals might injure themselves when they jumped

126

over. With the increase in population
and cultivated land, the damage done by
game finally became almost disastrous for
the farming community: this once caused
Martin Luther to preach a fiery sermon
about the hunting-mad princes who forbade
the peasants to protect their property
against destructive animals, without a
thought of providing compensation for the
losses.[114]

Not only wild boar but other game, small as well as
large, was so guarded once small creatures came to be
regarded as worthy of the aristocracy. However, when
elaborate hunts were conducted, the goal was to shoot
as many creatures as possible. Whereas hunting had once—
ideally at least—served as a test of the warrior aristocrat's horsemanship and courage as he pursued a stag
on horseback or faced a wild boar with a hunting spear,
it came to pass that deer and other creatures were shot
down literally by the thousands as they were, with the
aid of screens and nets, driven past shooting stands
full of aristocratic "hunters."[115] Sometimes hurdles
were set up to slow the animals as they passed the
shooters. The carcasses were often buried in hugh lime
pits.[116] Such "hunts" were quite popular with the
French and German aristocrats of the late 17th and 18th
centuries.[117] As was the case with bird shooting, once
it became fashionable with the aristocracy and upper
classes, records were meticulously kept and these helped
noble "hunters" build their reputations. Electors of
Saxony, Johann Georg I (1611-1656) and Johann Georg II
(1656-1680) lifetime records were as follows:

	I	II
Red deer	35,421	43,649
Fallow deer	1,045	2,062
Roe deer	11,045	16,864
Wild boar	31,902	22,298
Bear	238	239
Wolves	3,872	2,195
Lynx	217	191
Hares	12,047	16,966
Foxes	19,015	2,740
Beavers	37	597
Badgers	930	1,045
Otters	81	180
Wildcat	149	292[118]

With the waning of the aristocracy's privileges, commoners acquired the right to hunt legally in some parts of Europe where they had not previously been able to do so. But both holdovers from the past and urbanization and industrialization have transformed big game hunting in Europe. This transformation might be discerned from the following comments made at different periods by three observers of the European scene. In 1903 an English-speaking visitor in a Germany where status and class difference were still very pronounced wrote:

> While the masses have their special outdoor pastimes, the classes have theirs. Germany is still a country of great hunters, and large game flourishes and offers much sport as well as profit to those who are fortunate enough to possess hunting rights. This is due not more to the abundance of forest and other preserves than to the great interest in the preservation of game and the regulation of its destruction and sale, in the day of forest laws. Red deer, roe, elk, fallow deer, wild boar, and moor and field game are amongst the sportsman's possible quarry. A curious arrangement has been legalized in some parts of Germany,--Prussia is an example. The owners or tenants of large estates--that is, estates of about four hundred acres--may exercise the right of shooting game subject to the ordinary legal restrictions: but smaller estates or holdings are combined, and the shooting rights are sold or leased by the local authority, which divides the proceeds amongst those entitled to them in proportion to the extent of their land, due compensation being given to the owners or holders in the event of damage being done to land or crops by either sportsmen or game. . . . Poaching is not so common as might be supposed from the abundance of game. The reasons are the severity of the law, the careful watch that is kept by fiscal and private foresters, and the restrictions which apply to the sale and transmission of "Wild" of all kinds, for these alone make the risk of detection so

great that the modern would-be poacher has
found them not to be worth the candle.[119]

In the 1930's another observer, apparently a German, wrote:

> France and Italy know only the shotgun.
> In England hunting is a sport. The art
> of venery is dead; there is no word for
> it in modern English. It has only the
> terms "hunt" and "chase." Nowhere but in
> Germany will you find so many antlers and
> boars' heads decorating the walls, and
> every third room seems to be hung with a
> picture of a stag breathing clouds of
> steam into the autumn air. The most pop-
> ular regiment in the army has always been
> the "Jager" (hunters). . . .
> For many people Germany is one huge
> intricate hunting map. . . . Sport is
> subject to much restriction and limita-
> tion, and much annoyance from neighbours,
> stray dogs, poachers, and so on. It leads
> its devotees down every sort of path and
> track, for there is not an acre of German
> ground without its paths or glades. The
> paths are often bespattered with game
> droppings, and tracks of bird and beast
> can often be seen in the mud and leaf
> mould by the side of the road. As one
> walks through the fields, flocks of crows
> circle above one's head and frightened
> hares dart away over the stubble. The dog
> barking from the neighbouring village and
> the church tower in the distance only
> serve to increase the sense of loneliness
> which the landscape for all its crowded
> population manages to convey. In this
> sportsman's landscape many a German ex-
> periences the greatest moments of his
> life.[120]

And in the early 1970's an American outdoorsman
wrote of Europe in general:

> The status of Europe's big game animals
> is exactly what might be expected in a
> part of the world so densely populated and
> so intensively developed for industry and

agriculture. Some animals have long been extinct or are nearly so now. Nowhere, with the possible exception of the Soviet Union, is there an abundance of big game. . . .[121]
　　Summed up, the best place to see European big-game animals is in zoos.[122]

From the above it would appear that ancient shooting privileges still existed in some form, however modified, in the Germany of 1903 and that the effects of urbanization and industrialization were not yet worthy of comment, at least to a visitor. The second observer, a German, writes of traditions, but not of privileges, and of good hunting in a crowded countryside. (That there was still much game to be hunted in the Germany of the 1930's is to a certain extent supported by Weir, who reports that the annual bag there during that period was 20,000 tons.[123] How much of this was big game--rifle game--is not reported, however.) The third observer, an American writing in the 1970's, is impressed by the scarcity of big game in Europe, including Germany, and by the crowded conditions there. Of course, game may well have been considered scarce and conditions crowded in the Germany of 1903 as judged by the standards of the American. Since no numbers are provided for comparison, it is impossible to determine from the above to what extent, or even whether, big game populations have decreased in Europe during this century. Yet it would seem safe to assume that there is less game in Europe calling for the use of rifles now than in the past, and certainly that there is less game there than is to be found in land areas of comparable size in North America.

Before leaving this discussion of the rifle in Europe, it should be mentioned that long guns equipped with both rifle and shotgun barrels are popular on the Continent. With such a gun the hunter is equipped to take either large or small game. The latter can still be found all over Europe, but not the former. In areas where hunters have been likely to find either type of game in the same vicinity, the combination rifle-shotgun has apparently been reasonably common.

HANDGUNS

While it took several centuries for the rifle to evolve to the point that it was accepted as the sol-

130

dier's basic weapon, and while the shotgun and other
smoothbore multi-projectile firearms such as the blunderbuss have seen only occasional action with the military over the centuries, the military accepted the one-
hand gun almost as soon as it became available. Cavalrymen quickly accepted the pistol, and by the middle of
the 16th century they had devised a new tactic based
upon its use. The caracole brought line after line of
cavalry up to fire point-blank at masses of enemy pikemen, and then the cavalry would retreat.[124] But while
pistols were being used on the battlefield at a time
when shotguns and rifles were primarily tools of the
hunt or pieces of sporting equipment, civilians also
found use for them.

Anyone familiar with European history is likely to
be aware of the fact that that part of the world has
often been less than peaceful, and the references to the
various wars fought during the period covered by this
study serve as reminders to that effect. During these
wars, down through the 17th century at least, non-com-
batants often had cruelties visited upon them by roving
mercenary bands, even those employed by their own
rulers.[125] On occasion, then, even civilians--peasants,
burghers, or aristocrats--found it necessary to take up
arms against other men if they were to avoid, or attempt
to avoid, such mistreatment. Continental travelers of
the 17th century reported that peasants at various times
and places carried arms as they worked in their
fields.[126] Disbanded soldiers often became robbers, and
in fact, according to E. S. Bates, "between soldier and
robber . . . the difference was merely that of official,
and unofficial, employment."[127] During the 18th century, wars, though numerous, became more limited in
scope and civilians were less directly caught up in
them. This did not mean, however, that civilians no
longer felt the need to keep arms.[128] While the mercenary bands were no longer a problem, robbers remained
troublesome to those who possessed anything likely to be
considered valuable. Even in England, which had generally been spared the problems the mercenaries had posed
on the Continent, highwaymen and footpads were common.

Christina Hole, writing of England from 1500 to
1800, states that

> discharged soldiers, vagrants, profession-
> al thieves, and men dispossessed and ruined
> by the upheavals of two troubled centuries

all helped to swell the number of those
who made a living by highway robbery.
Young gentlemen sometimes took to the road
for the sake of adventure, or to ease a
temporary financial difficulty, and afterwards returned to normal life without necessarily forfeiting the regard of their
friends. Travellers were forced to go
heavily armed and whenever possible in
companies, but they were usually a poor
match for the organized bands that infested open heaths and moorlands, or the
solitary, well-armed and well-mounted
highwaymen who knew every yard of his
chosen territory.[129]

And the streets of the growing cities of the 16th
through the early 19th centuries were equally fraught
with peril for those who possessed anything likely to be
defined as worth stealing, or for that matter, for anyone else. Cecile Hugon writes that serious crimes were
committed in broad daylight in 17th-century Paris, and
that "it was believed that from eight to ten thousand
ruffians haunted the streets."[130] Writing of 18th century England, J. H. Whiteley states that

> newspapers of the first half of the cen-
> tury contain countless chronicles of acts
> of robbery with violence, in broad day-
> light. Riots broke out on the slightest
> provocation. Lecky's pages abound in al-
> most incredible stories of vice and crime,
> open and rampant in the streets of the big-
> gest towns. Ladies attending Court func-
> tions had to be guarded by servants armed
> with blunderbusses "to shoot at the
> rougues". . . . In 1782 Horace Walpole
> writes: "Owing to the profusion of house-
> breakers, highwaymen and footpads-- and
> expecially because of the savage barbar-
> ities of the two latter who commit the
> most wanton cruelties--if one goes abroad
> to dinner, you would think one was going
> to the relief of Gibraltar.[131]

Small wonder, therefore, that civilians found use
for pistols as soon as these small firearms were made
practical by the development of the wheellock. For
several reasons, however, the pistol was not for every-

one. To begin with, in its wheellock form it was fragile and too expensive for any but the wealthy to afford. And though some gentlemen evidently hunted from horseback with the pistol as early as the latter part of the 16th century, such hunting was not likely to be seen as practical by the poorer classes who could not afford either the pistol or the horse, and who were primarily interested in supplementing their food supply through hunting.[132] For these poorer people, if they could afford to buy or otherwise obtain a gun at all, a smoothbore long arm that could fire either ball or shot was by far the most practical hunting weapon. And such a weapon, though cumbersome, could also be kept within easy reach in house or field and used for defensive purposes, since compactness was of little importance to peasants who seldom traveled more than a few miles from their villages and fields. Within the peasant villages residents were not likely to feel the need for personal weapons any more sophisticated than knives, since, though peasant life could be rough and tumble, informal social controls seem to have provided more security on village streets than was likely to exist in the larger towns.[133]

Though the poorer classes of city dwellers may well have possessed little worth stealing, they lived in a violent world and could easily be caught up in situations that endangered their lives. Yet knives, clubs, and other weapons were less expensive than pistols and were more easily acquired. Such weapons were also adequate for defensive purposes, since the poorer city folk seldom had to face others armed with firearms. The reasonably wealthy, however, could afford pistols and they were likely to feel a need for them since they were more likely to be the target of robbers, many of whom were firearmed themselves. The wealthy were also more likely to travel in cities and cross country, making themselves more vulnerable to robbers.[134] For several centuries, therefore, the pistol in Europe as it was used by civilians was the relatively compact defensive weapon of those whose everyday affairs normally did not involve the use of weapons. And of course, the pistol's compactness and concealability also made it a favorite weapon of those who operated outside the law.

From the time that pistols started to come into general use, various ruling classes seem to have been uneasy about such easily concealed guns. According to Blackmore, the Emperor Maximilian I banned wheellocks from Lower Austria in 1517 primarily due to the fact

133

that such locks made it possible to construct guns that could be carried loaded and concealed.[135] This ban was extended to all the territories of Maximilian's empire in 1518, and in 1532 a ducal edict imposed a similar ban on concealable guns in Brescia, Italy.[136] Similar restrictions were attempted in England and Scotland through the 16th and 17th centuries, though it should be noted that individuals with incomes above certain levels were not affected by the law and that official attempts to completely control the possession of pistols in England did not come about until the early 20th century.[137] In France, attempts were made to prohibit the manufacture of all firearms at the beginning of the 16th century (before even the French military accepted guns), and an edict of 1666 prohibited the manufacture of pistols, daggers, epees and other "secret weapons."[138] Such prohibitions had little effect, and pistols were sold in broad daylight and their prices appeared in the tax books in 1697.[139] A later edict of 1728 seems to have been no more effective.[140]

In spite of such early attempts to regulate the manufacture and possession of pistols, they eventually took their place alongside the sword as gentlemen's weapons. And although pistols were used by those on the other side of the law, major design features and variations evolved as the "respectable" attempted to defend themselves. If the pistol, the most conveniently portable of the portable firearms, was to serve as a defensive weapon for the traveler, it had to be readily available to him at all times. Therefore, it had to be carried on his person or within easy reach on his horse or in his carriage. Changes in the design features of pistols carried by civilians for defensive purposes, therefore, in many ways not only reflected technological developments related directly to firearms, but changes in modes of transportation as well. As travel by coach and private carriages became more common and travel by horseback less common during the 18th century, civilians relied less on heavy horse pistols and more on middle-sized belt or carriage pistols.[141]

The horse pistol was a hugh weapon often having a barrel a foot or more in length; therefore, it was more likely to be carried in a holster attached to the horse's saddle than on one's person. Since most horse pistols were single-shot, at least two were generally carried on the horse in this fashion. The smaller carriage or belt pistols, on the other hand, could readily be carried in pairs inside traveling cases in the carriage or on one's person in or out of the carriage.[142] Carriage pistols, however, though smaller in overall size than the horse pistols, were still formidable weapons.

Once highway robbery had been stamped out in England, due at least in part to the establishment of an effective police force during the second quarter of the 19th century, the interest in traveling pistols faded, and defensive pistols of all sorts became less formidable in power as well as size.[143] Tiny "muff-pistols," many less than 5 inches in overall length, were not uncommon at this time.

Travel by carriage, rather than by horse, also may have helped to convince gentlemen that the pistol was a more practical weapon than the sword. Even in its single-shot muzzle-loading form, the pistol had an advantage over the sword because women and older men could conceivably use the pistol to defend themselves. Yet the sword remained an effective weapon--it did not have to be reloaded--for those, whether afoot or on horseback, who were skilled in its use. Inside a stage coach, however, the sword was almost useless.[144] By the last quarter of the 18th century as stage travel became common, even the small sword, which had been not only fashionable with the English gentry, but which had served as a symbol of their very status, faded from use.[145]

As the pistol took its place alongside, and later supplanted, the sword as the personal defensive weapon of aristocrats and other gentlemen, it also took its place alongside the sword as a dueling weapon for those--aristocrats, military officers and other gentlemen--likely to be concerned with defending their honor. According to A. V. B. Norman and Don Pottinger, "after 1530 the wearing of the sword with civilian dress became much more common, and instead of quarrels being settled in the lists in full armor dueling with swords came into fashion. Since the opponents were unarmoured, a lighter blade could be used than on the military weapon."[146] Dueling with swords seems to have originated in Italy. Italian fencing masters, and later the Spanish, not only taught their art to the rest of Europe, but helped develop the civilian thrusting sword--the rapier, direct ancestor of the small sword--in the process.[147] At this time, richly decorated swords and daggers "began to be part of fashionable dress, used rather to display the taste and wealth of the owner than for offence."[148] Yet as long as swords were carried, they were commonly used for dueling by those prone to involvement in such "affairs of honor." However, since the pistol had been accepted as a cavalry weapon quite soon after its invention, and since military officers were often of the honor-obsessed aristocracy, it is not surprising to find that these weapons were used in duels as early as the second half of the 16th century and that these early duels were based on the cavalry tactics of the time.[149] The duelists typically rode at each other on horseback, fired their pistols at each other, and then, if necessary, continued the duel with their swords. It seems, however, that duels were seldom fought with pistols alone until the end of the 18th century, when sword wearing was no longer fashionable.[150]

The first pistols used in duels were ordinary military or civilian types. As pistol duels became more common, however, pistols especially designed for that purpose were made. Though the dueling "ritual was not as rigid or elaborate as is generally supposed," certain rules came to be generally followed and pistols were designed with these rules in mind.[151] Held states that

the final test of a dueling pistol was the elusive quality of "coming up." While most were fitted with carefully centered front and rear sights, the rules prohibited pausing for as much as an infinitesimal instant to take any deliberate aim. Combatants faced each other with pistols ready cocked at arm's length at their sides, and upon signal raised and fired instantly. It was a matter of life and death that the pistol be perfectly balanced--too light in front presented the danger of shooting too high, too heavy of shooting too low. The angle of butt and barrel had to be such that when the pistol was held in a natural, uncramped position with an extended arm, it would throw its ball precisely in the line from shoulder to index finger. A skilled marksman did not aim but "feel" his pistol dead on target merely by extending his arm toward his opponent.[152]

Considering the care that was taken to produce pistols with the qualities Held describes, some might be surprised to find that British and American dueling pistols were generally not allowed to be rifled because the accuracy of such weapons was considered to be too great at the traditional dueling distance of twenty yards.[153] In France rifled dueling pistols were the rule, but in England and America such weapons were intended to be used on targets rather than in duels.[154] It might also be pointed out that while dueling pistols were superbly crafted they were not ornate since gold or silver inlays or other shiny ornaments might reflect the sun and the glare could momentarily blind the duelist. Ornate "dueling" pistols were made for presentation to important personages and were not intended to be used on the "field of honor."[155] On the one hand, then, much was done to make the dueling pistol a very effective weapon, but, on the other, in England and America at least, the traditional opposition to rifled duelers increased the element of chance involved in such affairs.

Well into the 19th century dueling seems to have been generally accepted by aristocratic gentlemen in most parts of Europe as an honorable means of settling personal disputes and affronts. Yet, the practice was illegal almost everywhere and it was often punishable by death.[156] When there was a choice to be made between defending one's honor and protecting one's career or even one's life, however, the gentleman often chose to protect his honor and dueling flourished. Dueling even became an obsession to some aristocratic adventurers in 18th century France, and they looked for any excuse to fight.[157] For the most part, however, duels were more or less confined to the dueling set. While duels were an everyday occurrence for those attempting to build their reputations within these circles, outside of them duels were rather rare.[158] Nevertheless, once pistols came to be used in duels,

the mere fact that it /dueling/ existed as an established, if not legalized, institution was enough to make careful training in the art of pistol shooting as necessary a part of the education of an Englishman of this period as a knowledge of fencing had been in earlier generations, and to cause the English gunsmiths to devote their utmost skill to the perfection

137

of the pistol as a weapon for target and dueling use.

It was therefore in the dueling period, at the close of the eighteenth and during the first quarter of the 19th century, when pistol shooting was receiving greater attention in England than at any period either before or since, that the English flintlock pistol attained its greatest perfection, and that the English enjoyed the reputation both of being the best gunsmiths and the most formidable pistol-shots in Europe.[159]

It has been suggested that dueling with pistols rather than swords became more generally accepted in England, Ireland, and America than in other places because the standard of swordsmanship was generally lower in these parts of the world.[160] In any case, the sword was used to some extent in France after it had been almost completely discarded for dueling purposes in England and America.[161]

There seems to be little doubt that target shooting with pistols came into existence as gentlemen attempted to acquire the skills that would serve them well in a pistol duel, and that target pistols evolved from dueling pistols. The connection between dueling and target shooting has been made by George and also by Dixon, who states that as the sword faded from the scene as a defensive and dueling weapon "the aristocrat was not to be deprived of the opportunity to excel with his prowess at arms and it was soon the rage to spend as much time in the gunsmith's shooting galleries at target practice as it was previously in the fencing academy."[162] And Lugs has noted that the shape, size, sights, hair-trigger, and finish of the single-shot target pistol are those of the dueling pistol, and that ballistic information acquired with dueling pistols was eventually used to improve target pistols.[163]

Long after metallic ammunition and repeating mechanisms had been perfected, pistols designed for target shooting remained single shots and retained something of the classic lines of the dueling pistol.[164] In fact, the modern "free pistol" used in Olympic and other international competition is single shot, and much of the old dueler's design is retained under assorted improvements in sights and grips.[165] Toward the latter part

of the 19th century, however, revolvers with target refinements were produced, and semi-automatic pistols so
refined were available by the early part of the 20th
century.

While pistols especially designed for target shooting were produced as far back as the late 18th century,
formal target matches for the pistol are not nearly as
old in Europe as are matches for the rifle or even the
shotgun. According to Lugs, pistol shooting in Germany
did not become popular until 1890.[166] At about the same
time, pistol-shooting clubs were being established in
Austro-Hungary, England, and France, and international
competitions were under way by the turn of the century.[167] But in Europe, pistol shooting never became
as popular as rifle shooting.[168] Pistol matches in
Europe never acquired the folkish quality of the ancient
rifle matches, nor did they seem to capture the attention of the community as rifle matches had done. This
should not be considered surprising, since from the
previous discussion it would seem obvious that the pistol had been a gentleman's weapon in Europe and the common man had had relatively little experience with it.
And though the pistol had been used by the military
prior to the middle of the 16th century, the military
had been little concerned with fostering pistol marksmanship.[169] George notes that

> this low opinion of the pistol was not,
> however, founded so much upon its actual
> powers as upon a species of military pre-
> judice, originating in a reaction against
> the seventeenth century practice of per-
> mitting cavalry to halt and to fire with
> the pistol at excessively long ranges, in-
> stead of charging home with the sword,
> and culminating in a deliberate neglect of
> pistol shooting, which endured almost to
> the end of the eighteenth century, and
> only ceased when, as has already been re-
> counted, the decline of the civilian fash-
> ion of wearing swords brought the pistol
> into prominence as a dueling arm.[170]

Formal pistol matches had, and still have, traces
of dueling practice left in them. In shotgun competition, the shooter stands waiting for the bird or clay
pigeon to be released, and he fires at the moving target from a standing position much as he would fire at a

139

bird in the field. In rifle competition, there are
matches that require the shooter to fire from a standing
position (offhand), while other matches require the
prone position. Either position might be used by the
hunter or the soldier in the field. In Scandinavian
countries, rifle shooting and skiing are combined in a
competition of obvious military value in that part of
the world--a competition which has in recent years been
incorporated into the Olympics.[171] Some international
competitions even include moving target matches. In
other words, all of these types of matches involving
rifles and shotguns are directly related to practical
forms of marksmanship of use to the soldier or hunter,
though regulations and the very specialized equipment
that have come to be used in such matches detract somewhat from their practicality. When it comes to pistol
shooting, however, the practical connections are less
obvious unless it is a duel for which one is practicing.

The pistol shooter in the standard European pistol
match, or in the standard American match for that matter, stands erect facing his target with his pistol held
at arm's length. In some matches he cannot raise his
pistol, which is held angled downward, before the target
rotates into view. Such competition certainly does not
test one's ability to get a pistol into action quickly,
nor does it test one's ability to hit a moving target as
might be necessary if the pistol were being used as a
defensive weapon. Neither does such competition take
advantage of the accuracy built into a good pistol. To
benefit from this accuracy, a two-handed grip, a rest,
or something other then the standing position would be
called for. Matches designed to foster combat or long-
range two-hand shooting with the pistol are becoming
very popular in the United States and will be examined
later, but the standard pistol match here and in Europe
is still built around the old duelist's stance. The
targets used in some European matches are man-sized silhouettes, and shooting at them was originally referred
to as "duel-shooting."[172]

From the preceding discussion two points, one of
which has been made several times previously, should be
clear. The first point is that although the pistol once
figured rather prominently in European civil life both
as a defensive and as a dueling weapon, only a relatively few Europeans, and these of the upper and aristocratic classes, seem to have been very familiar with these
weapons. The second point is that aristocratic interest

in pistol shooting peaked before modern cartridge-firing repeating pistols became available toward the middle of the 19th century.

In England, dueling came to be considered disreputable shortly after the end of the Napoleonic Wars when many ex-officers and others who claimed to have been officers eked out a living by cheating at gambling and challenging those who accused them of cheating to duels.[173] And as the highways became safer and railroads were built, the practice of traveling "armed to the teeth" faded by the middle of the 19th century. This is not to say that Englishmen and other Europeans stopped acquiring pistols, however. In fact, though little seems to have been written on the subject, pistol ownership may have become more widespread in Europe after modern means of mass production made it possible to produce cheap versions of the new cartridge-firing revolvers. Large numbers of these cheap revolvers were manufactured in England, Belgium, Germany, and other parts of Europe, and though many of these weapons were exported to other parts of the world, many of them evidently stayed in the countries which produced them.[174] And after the semi-automatic pistol had been perfected, toward the beginning of the 20th century, tiny pocket pistols of this sort seem to have become quite popular on the Continent. But these small pocket revolvers and semi-automatics were guns kept for emergencies rather than guns whose use would foster a widespread interest in pistol shooting. Such weapons were not accurate at any great distance, and if the American experience with such pistols is typical, those who acquired them seldom fired them.

As noted earlier, attempts have been made to control pistol ownership in many modern parts of Europe since these weapons were invented. As also noted, however, all-inclusive restrictions on their possession in Britain came into being after the turn of the century.[175] Given what has been said above, it would seem that early attempts to control pistols had little, if any, effect at all, but many American advocates of strict pistol controls claim that modern European controls are quite effective. English Chief Inspector of Police Greenwood does not think that they are. In Britain a person must convince the authorities that he needs a pistol before he can obtain a firearms certificate and legally acquire one. But Greenwood claims that there is good reason to believe that there are more illegal pistols in England and Wales than there are legal ones.[176] France has attempted to regulate pistol possession since the 16th century, and in 1939, in reaction to the Cagoule Plot, a very strict law aimed at regulating pistols and weapons of all sorts--except shotguns-- was enacted.[177] But as noted in Chapter I, Paris police estimate that only approximately 10 per cent of the pistols in that city are registered. While the world wars have made it next to impossible to enforce such regulations in most European countries, such efforts are undermined further by smugglers. Frenchman Josserand writes that

> a reworked smuggler's car will carry at
> the least three hundred automatic pistols
> under the false floorboards; we know this
> from experience. And maritime contraband,
> though it requires better organization,
> also yields a lot more freight. During
> the late 1950's and early 1960's entire
> arsenals entered France illegally through
> the Mediterranean ports.[178]

The wave of bank robberies in France during the 1970's tends to support Josserand's claim, since the robbers were well armed with pistols as well as with submachine guns.[179]

Before leaving this discussion of the pistol, it should be mentioned that even during the time that gentlemen commonly carried pistols for personal defense and at times used them for dueling, such weapons were not commonly displayed on the person as was the sword. In fact, dueling pistols were not carried on one's person at all. An attempt was generally made to provide the duelists with pistols from a matched set with which neither was familiar.[180] Even defensive weapons were not commonly worn openly, however. For the most part, defensive pistols were carried out of sight in greatcoat pockets, etc.; and consequently, they were not a distinguishing feature of the gentleman's costume as the sword had once been.

Only in some areas peripheral to those being considered here was the pistol carried openly. In Scotland the distinctive all-metal flintlocks of that nation were prominently displayed clipped to the waists of lords, as evidenced by numerous portraits of these gentlemen that have come down to us from the 18th century and earli-.

er.[181] And in Montenegro, in Europe but not in the area covered by this study, it might nevertheless be worthy of note that through the 1920's a revolver was a prominent part of the national dress of all males who could afford one.[182] In these outlying areas the pistol seems to have functioned as a status symbol of the badge variety; however, this was not the case throughout Europe proper. This is not to say, of course, that in Europe proper handguns had not functioned symbolically in the lives of those who possessed them. It is rather to say that the practice of carrying pistols concealed has kept them from readily being used as badges of manhood and nobility. And perhaps this tradition of keeping handguns out of sight is at least partially responsible for the impression that Europeans do not have easy access to pistols, while, if we can believe Greenwood, Josserand, and others, there are actually many pistols in civilian hands in Europe. Little attention is paid to the pistol: it may seldom be shot and never paraded, but it is there in the dresser drawer, half-forgotten, to be available if needed for protection or for guerilla activity during any future occupation.

THE GUN IN JAPAN

As mentioned several times previously, the Portuguese took matchlock muskets to Japan in 1542. The Japanese were quite impressed by these weapons, and they soon started producing guns of their own in such numbers that, according to Noel Perrin, "they had fought battles in the late sixteenth century using more guns than any European country possessed."[183] In one battle fought in 1575, 10,000 of the 38,000 men of one of the opposing armies were equipped with matchlock muskets.[184] But while matchlocks made the peasant foot-soldiers equipped with them so effective against mounted swordsmen that use of the latter was soon abandoned, and while cannons encouraged castle builders to make their structures more massive and to protect castle doors, bridges, and casements with metal, the gun's long-term impact on Japan was not great. As Sansom has noted, in Japan muskets and cannons

> did not have the same effect as in the West upon the structure of society, for they did not accelerate the breakup of feudalism. The professional fighting man, the samurai whose weapon was the sword,

143

retained his high position and was not
displaced, as had already been the mounted
knight in Europe, by infantry armed first
with the long bow and later with the gun.
The dominating idea of the rulers of Japan
from the 16th century was having achieved
stable institutions, to see that they were
not changed. They therefore resisted,
consciously or unconsciously, any innova-
tion which tended to alter their existing
arrangements, finally taking the extreme
step of closing the country completely so
as to exclude all alien influences.[185]

Japanese armies of the latter 16th and early 17th
centuries were equipped in much the same way as were
their European counterparts. The matchlock musket was
used in Europe as well as in Japan, and in both areas it
seems that these muskets were the weapons of the common
soldier. Pikes were used in Japan as they were in European countries until the European invention of the bayonet in the latter part of the 17th century.[186] While
the bow was still an important Japanese weapon, the
English also used the bow until the late 16th century.
Horsemen carried swords at that time in both Europe and
Japan, though the pistol, made possible by the wheellock
and flintlock, was well on its way to becoming a formidable cavalry weapon in Europe. Since muskets were single shot and took a considerable length of time to reload, swords were carried as backup weapons by both
European and Japanese musketeers. Pikemen or spearmen
also carried swords as secondary weapons. And of course,
in both Europe and Japan, the sword remained the gentleman's weapon, the very badge of his status in times of
peace as well as war, for centuries after firearms became available.[187] In 1853 the Japanese were still using
swords, bows, spears, and matchlock muskets, however,
while Europeans and Americans had long abandoned these
arms, with the exception of the sword which was still
used by cavalry.

While Europeans and their North American descendants were developing ever more sophisticated and specialized firearms for civilian as well as military use as
they fought each other or moved out to conquer the
wilderness, the isolated, consciously conservative Japanese made no attempt to go beyond their matchlock technology. In fact, the Japanese continued to use the
matchlock more than two hundred years after the flint-

lock was known to them. A Dutch trading expedition presented a dozen flintlock pistols to the Shogun in 1636,
and in 1643 another Dutch ship brought flintlocks to the
attention of a group of provincial samurai, but the Japanese did not adopt the flintlock.[188] When they
were introduced to the matchlock in the middle of the
16th century, the Japanese had been involved in a civil
war, and they quickly recognized the military effectiveness of guns. But they were also quick to recognize,
as Europeans had discovered a century or more earlier,
that guns enabled common soldiers recruited from the
peasantry to shoot down aristocratic horsemen and
swordsmen. This recognition that guns could constitute
a threat to the established social order led the Tokugawas to de-emphasize firearms and their development once
the shoguns established their strong centralized government. And of course, the shoguns had the support of the
samurai in their efforts to de-emphasize guns, because
the samurai had a vested interest in preserving the
traditional fighting techniques for which they had been
trained, thereby preserving the social distinction between themselves and the peasantry. Since the shoguns
were in power by the time that the flintlock was introduced in Japan, it is no wonder that this new firearms
ignition system was ignored.

As noted several times previously, the Tokugawas
attempted to regulate the possession of all weapons and
to control the manufacture and sale of firearms. While
Japan's isolation and other features of Japanese society
mentioned earlier seem to have aided the shoguns in
their efforts to control the possession of weapons,
these efforts still were not completely successful. Yet
with weapons possession being a privilege of the samurai
aristocracy and firearms being scarce, it is hardly surprising that, as Blackmore has written,

> the possession of such arms became a mark
> of distinction among noblemen, and the gun-
> makers were encouraged to fashion highly-
> decorated pieces. The traditional skills
> of the swordsmakers were easily turned to
> this task. The laborious technique de-
> voted to the forging of a sword blade were
> applied to the making of a barrel, the
> iron being folded and welded many times
> to temper it. . . .
>   The decoration applied to the barrel
> is usually a rich nunome (overlay) of gold

and silver in appropriate dragon, wave or scroll motifs. The owner's family badge or Mon is given a prominent place near the breech. This badge was sometimes repeated in gilt on the stock.[189]

As best as can be determined from the sources available to the author, all pre-Perry Japanese firearms were smoothbores. If this actually was the case it would not be surprising, since though the rifling principle may have been known over much of Europe by the early 17th century, the rifle was not the weapon of the Portuguese or of the other seafaring Europeans who visited Japan in those days. And though information on the subject appears to be quite rare in the West, Japan seems never to have been "big game country." The incentive to produce accurate long-range weapons for hunting purposes, therefore, seems not to have existed there. Samurai who preferred swords and bows for war did hunt birds and other small game with their matchlock long arms, but it is not clear whether they used ball or shot or both.[190] According to sketches in a book on firearms written in Japan in 1612, "young Japanese bloods shot flying birds from horseback while at a gallop."[191] Perhaps "shot at" would describe their activities more accurately than "shot," however, because to hit one's target under such conditions with any kind of gun, much less with the matchlock long arms depicted, would require much more luck than skill, even if shot were used. Whether those privileged few who possessed firearms regularly and seriously engaged in shooting of this sort, however, is not known.

It has been mentioned previously that the Japanese seemed to be the only people to produce any significant numbers of matchlock pistols. The larger of these pistols, according to Perrin, "were designed for use on horseback--and hence were to be fired only by members of upper samurai families," since the lower samurai were not permitted to ride horses.[192] The necessity of keeping a fuse lit in order to have the gun ready for action, and the difficulty of accomplishing this when the pistol is being carried on one's person undoubtedly limited the usefulness of these weapons, however.

After Perry's arrival, the Japanese were quick to abandon their matchlocks for modern firearms--first percussion muzzle-loaders, then metallic-cartridge repeaters.[193] As noted in the previous chapter, the soldiers

146

of Japan's new conscript army accepted these weapons, but the traditional samurai, the warrior elite whose privileges were being stripped from them after the Restoration, generally would not use modern rifles. But while the Japanese soon caught up with the rest of the industrial world with respect to military small arms and weaponry in general, civilian versions of these modern small arms apparently were never produced--at least not in great numbers.[194] Nor, in a tradition-bound peasant society in which firearms had long been the playthings and status symbols of a warrior aristocracy rather than practical everyday aids to survival, does there seem to have been any great civilian demand for the new firearms once they were introduced in Japan. Even if various socio-cultural factors working against a widespread popular interest in firearms had not existed, the game available in Japan would hardly have fostered interest in the rifle. The traditional ways of trapping birds and other small game were still practical to a people who had not been exposed to the modern shotgun. In addition, informal social controls of the villages seem to have worked well enough that the personal protection afforded an individual by the handgun was not likely to have been seen as necessary, particularly since the great majority of civilians had probably never seen a modern handgun.

It would appear, therefore, that the great majority of Japanese have had little to do with firearms down through the centuries, even though their nation's 20th century military ventures and the samurai in their past have caused Westerners to view them as a warlike people. It might be significant to note in this regard that although the Japanese soldiers of World War II were considered fanatically brave and physically fit, those who fought against them were far from impressed by their rifle shooting skills.[195]

SUMMARY

Later it will be necessary to review in some detail what has been said above in terms of the various propositions of the thesis statement presented earlier, but at this time a brief summary of the major points made during the course of this chapter seems called for. These are as follows:

1. Portable firearms seem first to have been used

in Europe by city militiamen and mercenaries during the 14th and 15th centuries. The warrior aristocracy, for the most part, appears not to have been interested in guns as serious tools of war until well into the 16th century.

2. Peasants may have used firearms to supplement their food supplies as early as the 15th century, but guns were seldom used in the recreation hunts of the aristocracy until the late 16th or early 17th centuries.

3. The smoothbore long gun loaded with hail shot was used by common hunters of the early 16th century to take small animals and birds considered by the aristocracy of the time to be unworthy of their attention. Once improvements in firearms had made them efficient tools of war and marksmanship thereby came to be considered a respectable martial skill, shooting, even shooting at small game, came to be of interest to the aristocracy and aristocrats generally attempted to reserve the game-shooting privilege for themselves. Nevertheless, the shotgun remains the common man's weapon in those parts of Europe where the common man hunts.

4. The rifle seems to have been used as early as the late 15th or early 16th centuries by hunters and target shooters of those parts of Europe that were mountainous, forested, and possessed large wild animals, but a grass-roots interest in long-range marksmanship of the sort of which rifles are capable seems never to have been very widespread in other parts of Europe. The rifle was not accepted as a primary military weapon in Europe until the early part of the 19th century.

5. The pistol, made possible by the invention of the wheellock, was accepted as a military weapon in the first half of the 16th century. Civilians also accepted it as a defensive weapon--and highwaymen as an offensive weapon--at about the same time, but the pistol seems from the very beginning to have been a much more popular weapon at the upper levels of European society than elsewhere. By the late 18th century it had become-- alongwith the sword--a dueling weapon, and by the early 19th century it was the dueling weapon.

6. Formal shooting competitions with ball-loaded smoothbores were held as early as the second half of the 15th century. Rifle matches are almost as old,

while shotgun matches date from the middle of the 19th century, and pistol matches from the second half of the same century.

7. Some evidence to the effect that guns have served as status symbols in Europe has been presented, but the pistol seems seldom to have been worn openly by civilians and consequently does not seem to have acquired the badge qualities of the sword.

8. Portable firearms development in Japan from the time guns were introduced there by the Portuguese toward the middle of the 16th century to the time of Perry's arrival in the middle of the 19th century was practically nil. And though the Japanese used firearms as tools of war and of the hunt and as status symbols during this period, the Japanese civilian's exposure to firearms over the centuries has been nowhere near that of the Europeans.

FOOTNOTES

1. Charles Oman, A History of the Art of War in the Middle Ages, Vol. II, 1278-1485 (New York: Burt Franklin, 1924), p. 228; Robert Held, The Age of Firearms: A Pictorial History (Northfield, Illinois: Gun Digest Company, 1970), p. 23; Howard L. Blackmore, Guns and Rifles of the World (New York: The Viking Press, 1965), pp. 5-7.

2. Oman, 228.

3. Held, 25.

4. Ibid.

5. Oman, 228.

6. Ibid.

7. Ibid., 229.

8. Ibid., 366.

9. Ibid., 257-258; Richard A. Preston and Sydney F. Wise, Men in Arms (New York & Washington: Praeger Publishers, 1970), p. 105.

10. Preston and Wise.

11. Ibid., 103.

12. Ibid., and C. G. Cruickshank, Elizabeth's Army (At the Clarendon Press, Oxford, 2nd ed., 1966), p. 102-129.

13. Howard L. Blackmore, Hunting Weapons, (London: Barrie & Jenkins, 1971), p. 216.

14. Ibid., 216-217.

15. Held, 63-65.

16. Blackmore, 220.

17. Jacob Salwyn Schapiro, "Social Reform and the Reformation," Studies in History, Economics and Public Law, ed. by the faculty of Political Science of Columbia University, Vol. XXXIV, No. 2. (New York:

Columbia University Press, 1909), p. 336.

18. See Plates in Held, 38 & 65; Charles Chenevix Trench, A History of Marksmanship (Norwich, Great Britain: Harrold & Sons Ltd., 1972), p. 106, 110, 111, 114, 127, & 131; Blackmore, 221, 223, & 224.

19. V. G. Kiernan, "Foreign Mercenaries and Absolute Monarchy," Crisis in Europe 1560-1660, ed. Trevor Aston (New York: Basic Books, Inc., 1965), pp. 118 & 128.

20. Cruikshank, 110-111; and Lindsay Boynton, The Elizabethan Militia 1558-1638 (London: Routledge & Kegan Paul; Toronto: University of Toronto Press, 1967), pp. 57 & 119.

21. Cruikshank, 102ff; and Held, 62-63.

22. Ibid., 102-129 & 282.

23. Trench, 117.

24. Cruikshank, 102-103.

25. Held, 63. Funck-Brentano, in his history of the old regime in France, refers several times to the peasant's possession of firearms and seems to indicate that such possession was reasonably widespread. Frantz Funck-Brentano, The Old Regime in France (New York: Longman's, Green & Co.; London: Edward Arnold & Co., 1929), pp. 104, 128, 272.

26. Boynton, 57. Writing of the army rather than the militia of the same period in England, Cruikshank states "though musketeers had to pay for their powder out of their own pockets there was no difficulty in finding men to carry firearms. Why? Partly because the musket had a prestige value, and partly because it could earn its keep in non-military activities--poaching, or worse." p.116 C. H. Firth, however, writing of Cromwell's Army states that

> the pike was held more honourable because it was the more ancient weapon. It was also held more honourable because all adventurous gentlemen who enlisted to see the wars preferred,

as the phrase was, "to trail a pike."
Therefore the pikeman was regarded
as a gentleman compared to the musketeer. . . .
    A third reason was that pikemen
were usually finer men physically than
the musketeers. Physical strength
was not so necessary for shooting as
for managing the pike.

C. H. Firth, Cromwell's Army: A History of the
English Soldier during the Civil Wars, the Commonwealth and the Protectorate (London: Meuthuen &
Co., Ltd., New York: Barnes & Noble Inc., 1962),
pp. 70-71.

27. Jaroslav Lugs, A History of Shooting: Marksmanship, Dueling and Exhibition Shooting (The Centre,
Feltham, Middlesex: Spring Books, 1968), pp. 189-
214.

28. Kiernan, 129.

29. Ibid.

30. Michael Brander, The Hunting Instinct: The Development of Field Sports Over the Ages (Edinburgh &
London: Oliver & Bond, 1964), pp. 71-72.

31. Cruickshank, 113, 116, 126.

32. Ibid., 126.

33. E. S. Bates, Touring in 1600: A Study in the Development of Travel as a Means of Education (Boston
and New York: Houghton Mifflin Company, 1911), p.
351.

34. Held, 80.

35. Ibid., 57.

36. Ibid., 80.

37. Gunnar Brusewitz, Hunting: Hunters, Game, Weapons
and Hunting Methods from the Remote Past to the
Present Day (New York: Stein and Day, Publishers,
1969), p. 111.

38. Held, 80.

39. Brusewitz, 110-111. In France a wolf hunting unit
    with officers recruited from the regular army was
    created and flourished particularly during the 17th
    and 18th centuries. In Sweden and elsewhere wolf
    hunting was a community affair. pp. 182-188.

40. Ibid., 138.

41. Ibid., 110.

42. Ibid., 111.

43. Trench, 126.

44. Ibid., 128.

45. Eugen Diesel, Germany and the Germans (New York:
    The MacMillan Company, 1931), p. 42.

46. Held, 78.

47. Ibid., 92.

48. Funck-Brentano, 128.

49. Ibid., 127.

50. Ibid., 128.

51. Ibid., 129.

52. Christina Hole, English Home-Life 1500-1800 (Lon-
    don, New York, Toronto, Sidney: B. T. Batsford
    Ltd., 2nd ed. 1949), p. 133; and Stella Margetson,
    Leisure and Pleasure in the Eighteenth Century
    (London: Casswell & Company, Ltd., 1970), p. 124.

53. Margetson, 125.

54. Richard Heath, The English Peasant; Studies: His-
    torical, Local, and Biographic (London: T. Fisher
    Unwin, Paternoster Square, 1893), p. 34.

55. Ibid.

56. Brander, 119; Heath, 33-35; Hole, 133; Clifton
    Johnson, Among English Hedgerows (New York: The

MacMillan Company, 1899), pp. 192-193; and F. M. L. Thompson, English Landed Society in the Nineteenth Century (London: Routledge & Kegan Paul; Toronto: University of Toronto Press, 1963), p. 142.

57. Brander notes that the silencer equipped .22 rifle; is often used by modern English poachers, p. 62. Also see Greenwood, 149; Johnson, 191; Clifton Johnson, Along French Byways (New York: The Mac-Millan Company, 1900), pp. 76-77; and Philip Carr, The French at Home: In the Country and in Town (New York: The Dual Press, 1930's?), p. 149.

58. Brander, 143.

59. Ibid., 138.

60. A. E. Richardson, Georgian England: A Survey of Social Life, Trades, Industries & Arts from 1700 to 1820 (Freeport, New York: Books for Libraries Press, Inc., 1931), p. 79.

61. Trench, 137.

62. Ibid., 155.

63. Lugs, 115.

64. Ibid., 117.

65. Ibid., 119.

66. Ibid.

67. Ibid.

68. Ibid., 120-125.

69. Clay pigeon shooting required elaborate ranges as well as expensive equipment. See Lugs, 120-125.

70. Brusewitz, 101.

71. T. H. Pear, English Social Differences (London: George Allen & Unwin Ltd., 1955), p. 78.

72. Ibid., 255.

73. Carr, 149.

74. Friedrich Sieburg, Who Are These French (New York: The MacMillan Company, 1938), p. 182.

75. Carr, 147-149; Sieburg, 184.

76. Carr, 150; and Johnson, Along French Byways, p. 77.

77. Sieburg, 182-184.

78. Funck-Brentano, 104, 128, 272.

79. Michel H. Josserand and Jan Stevenson, Pistols, Revolvers and Ammunition (New York: Crown Publishers, Inc., 1972), p. 288.

80. Colin Greenwood, "British Gun Controls Don't Work!" Guns & Ammo (December, 1972), 102.

81. Colin Greenwood, Firearms Control, (London: Routledge & Kegan Paul, 1972), p. 190.

82. Nils Kvale, "Gun Laws in Scandinavia, The American Rifleman, Vol. 114 (July, 1966), 19-21.

83. Blackmore, Hunting Weapons, p. 276.

84. Held, 140.

85. Oman, 357.

86. Trench, 105-107.

87. Lugs, 50-51.

88. Trench, 107.

89. Lugs, 54.

90. Trench, 107.

91. Lugs, 56.

92. Ibid., 47.

93. Ibid., 21.

94. Held, 138.

95. Ibid.

96. Blackmore, <u>Hunting Weapons</u>, 269. Such triggers were also used on crossbows in the 16th century.

97. Ibid.

98. Lugs, 24.

. 99. Ibid., 47. Emphasis mine.

100. Ibid., 49.

101. Ibid.

102. Ibid.

103. Bill R. Davidson notes that "air rifle and air pistol shooting are very advanced in Europe. But they tend to predominate in sections of Europe with long, dreary winters." Bill R. Davidson, <u>To Keep and Bear Arms</u> (New York: Arlington House, 1969), p. 174.

104. Held, 105.

105. L. H. Weir, <u>Europe at Play</u> (New York: A. S. Barnes & Company, 1937), pp. 222-223.

106. Greenwood, <u>Firearms Control</u>, p. 208.

107. Josserand and Stevenson, 274 & 271, 279-280.

108. Page 8.

109. Greenwood, <u>Firearms Control</u>, p. 71.

110. Richard Watt, <u>Kings Depart: The Tragedy of Germany: Versailles and the German Revolution</u> (New York: Simon and Schuster, 1968), p. 509.

111. Greenwood, <u>Firearms Control</u>, p. 71.

112. Greenwood, <u>Guns and Ammo</u>, 33.

113. Brusewitz, 110-111, 128-129.

114. Ibid., 140-141.

115. Held, 122.

116. Ibid.

117. Ibid., and Blackmore, Hunting Weapons, p. 272-273.

118. Blackmore, 270.

119. William Harbutt Dawson, German Life in Town and Country (New York & London: G. P. Putnam's Sons, The Knickerbocker Press, 1903), p. 222-223. Emphasis mine.

120. Diesel, 41-42. Emphasis mine.

121. Erwin A. Bauer, Big Game Animals (New York, Evanston, San Francisco, London: Harper & Row/Outdoor Life, 1972), p. 359.

122. Ibid., 366.

123. Weir, 224.

124. Blackmore, Hunting Weapons, 308.

125. Bates, 352.

126. Ibid., 350.

127. Ibid., 353.

128. Preston and Wise, 133-134.

129. Hole, 34-35.

130. Cecile Hugon, Social France in the XVII Century (London: Methuen & Co. Ltd., 1911), p. 158.

131. J. H. Whiteley, Wesley's England: A Survey of XVIIIth Century Social and Cultural Conditions (London: The Epworth Press, 1938), p. 199.

132. Blackmore, Hunting Weapons, 309.

133. See Mildred Campbell, The English Yeoman: Under Elizabeth and the Early Stuarts (New York: Augustus M. Kelley Publishers, 1968), pp. 364-365; John Finnemore, Social Life in England: From the Nineteenth Century to the Present Day (London: A & C Black Ltd., 1956), p. 21.

134. See John Nigel George, English Pistols and Re-
     volvers (London: The Holland Press, 1938), p.
     46; Rosamond Bayne-Powell, Travellers in Eighteen-
     th-Century England (London: John Murray, Albe-
     marle Street W., 1951), pp. 34-39; G. D. H. Cole
     and Raymond Postgate, The British People, 1746-
     1946 (New York: Alfred A. Knopf, 1947), p. 17;
     Richardson, 33-34, 94; and Joan Park's, Travel in
     England: In the Seventeenth Century (London:
     Humphrey Milford: Oxford University Press, 1925),
     pp. 166, 169-170. Park: writes that "to travel
     well-armed was an ordinary precaution. Weapons
     gave the traveller heart to set out on his jour-
     ney, though when the test came the sword might
     never be unsheathed and the pistol never cocked."
     p. 166. She also notes that the country folk on
     occasion rose against the highwaymen. pp. 182-
     184. While all of the above deal with highwaymen
     as hazards of travel in England, Funck-Brentano
     mentions French brigands several times. pp. 80,
     85-86.

135. Blackmore, Hunting Weapons, 307.

136. Ibid., 308.

137. Ibid., 309; and Greenwood, Firearms Control, 7-44.

138. Josserand and Stevenson, 271-272.

139. Ibid., 272.

140. Ibid.

141. George, 46.

142. Norman Dixon, Georgian Pistols (York, Pennsylvan-
     ia: George Shumway, Publishers, 1971), p. 22.

143. George, 129-130.

144. Dixon, 22.

145. Ibid., 22. Dixon also notes that another reason
     for the small swords going out of fashion may have
     been that the sword carrying privilege of the gen-
     try became an embarrassment as the Age of Revolu-
     tion got underway.

146. A. V. B. Norman and Don Pottinger, Warrior to Soldier 449 to 1660: A Brief Introduction to the History of English Warfare (London: Weidenfeld & Nicolson, Ltd., 1964), p. 169.

147. Ibid., 170. "The name 'rapier' was at first given to any civilian sword and only later came to mean a thrusting weapon when these became almost universal."

148. Ibid., 171.

149. Lugs, 135-138.

150. George, 69. Lugs notes that in some areas "pistol duels were preferred because they gave an equal chance to older combatants, whereas in small sword duels younger and taller opponents had the advantage." p. 140.

151. Held, 165.

152. Ibid.

153. Ibid., 166.

154. Ibid., and George, 85.

155. Held, 166.

156. Lugs, 139-140; George, 73.

157. Lugs, 140.

158. George, 75-76.

159. Ibid., 76.

160. Trench, 226.

161. Held, 165.

162. Dixon, 22-23.

163. Lugs, 72.

164. See Lugs, 70, 74-75.

165. See Lugs, 74.

166. Lugs, 126.

167. Ibid., 127-128.

168. Ibid., 128.

169. George, 88.

170. Ibid., 89.

171. Davidson

172. Lugs, 128.

173. George, 128.

174. George, 227; and A. W. F. Taylorson, The Revolver
     1889-1914 (New York: Crown Publishers, Inc.,
     1971), p. 19.

175. Greenwood, Firearms Control, 20. According to
     Greenwood, Montenegro, Norway, Sweden, Denmark,
     Serbia and Switzerland had no restrictions at all
     on the carrying of arms by civilians as late as
     1889. Concealed firearms were prohibited at that
     time in the Duchy of Coburg, Hesse, Saxony, Wert-
     emberg and France. "In the Duchy of Baden and in
     Germany the carrying of firearms at public meet-
     ings was prohibited and in the Netherlands the
     carrying of firearms on roads or in public places
     was forbidden with some exceptions." In Bulgaria,
     Belgium, Greece, Italy, Portugal, Spain and with
     some exceptions Austria, Romania, Russia and Tur-
     key a permit was required to carry any type of
     firearm. But it seems that such laws as existed
     were not always well enforced. "The Ambassador
     of Belgium reported, 'I am informed that the
     existing regulations, even about the carrying of
     pocket pistols, are rarely, if ever, enforced; and
     no serious effort has yet been made to check the
     growing use of cheap pocket pistols.'"

176. Ibid., 239. Judging by the thousands of illegally
     possessed pistols that are surrendered each year,
     Greenwood feels that the sources are not drying
     up and that there could well be more than 63,000
     illegal pistols in England and Wales.

177. Josserand and Stevenson, 278-281.

178. Ibid., 282-283.

179. "Hands Up!" Newsweek, (February 18, 1974), 57.

180. Lugs, 151.

181. John Telfur Dunbar, History of Highland Dress (Edinburgh & London: Oliver & Boyd, 1962), plates 9, 12, 16, 18, 19, 29, 33, 44.

182. Greenwood, Firearms Control, 20-21; Melville Chater, "Dalmatian Days: Coasting Along Debatable Shores Where Latin and Slav Meet," The National Geographic Magazine, Llll (January, 1928), photograph, Plate X; and George Higgins Moses, "Greece and Montenegro," The National Geographic Magazine, XXIV (March, 1913), photographs pp. 283, 284, 286, 289, 290.

183. Noel Perrin, Giving Up the Gun: Japan's Reversion to the Sword, 1543-1879 (Boston: David R. Godine, Publisher 1979), p. 4.

184. Ibid., 19.

185. George Sansom, Japan: A Short Cultural History (New York: D. Appleton-Century Company, Incorporated, 1936), p. 412.

186. Norman and Pottinger, 200.

187. Perrin, 36. According to Perrin, the sword was even more important as a symbol of nobel status in Japan than it was in Europe, since the sword was the only badge of rank that a samurai wore. The beautifully made sword "was the visible form of one's honor--'the soul of the samurai,' in the Japanese phrase."

188. Ibid., 68.

189. Blackmore, Guns and Rifles of the World, 17.

190. Perrin, 31.

191. Trench, 128.

192. Perrin, 33-34.

193. Held, 43.

194. It is interesting to note that while Japan has
      never been known for its sporting guns, the Jap-
      anese are now making long guns for such prominent
      western arms makers as Browning, Smith & Wesson,
      and Winchester.

195. Davidson, 120.

CHAPTER VII

THE SOCIAL-HISTORICAL CONTEXT: THE NEW WORLD

NEW WORLD vs. OLD

Approximately 150 years after the first recorded
appearance of hand-portable firearms in Europe, the age
of European exploration and colonization began with
Columbus' "discovery" of the New World. As European
explorers and settlers journeyed both to remote parts of
the world previously known to them and to the newly discovered lands--first the Americas and much later, in the
17th century, Australia--they carried with them hand-
portable firearms in their various early forms. Consequently, firearms have been part of the New World scene
from the very beginning of large-scale European exploration and settlement in these areas; guns were not inserted into ongoing systems as they had been in the Old
World. To be sure, the American and Australian aboriginals were introduced to firearms by outsiders, but the
descendants of these outsiders rather than those of the
aboriginals are the typical Americans, Canadians, and
Australians of today.

Though the modern New World is, for the most part,
the work of transplanted Europeans and their descendants, it has never been simply Europe transplanted. As
might be expected, the uprooted Europeans who settled
the New World were not typical of those more thoroughly
bound to the social systems that the uprooted had left
behind. Therefore, the uprooted could scarcely be expected to attempt to duplicate the old system. Exploration and colonization of the New World was in many ways
a commercial venture from the very start (consider Columbus' search for a shortcut trade route to the far
east) and therefore the dynamic business-oriented European middle class had much more reason to take part personally in the adventure than did the tradition-bound
aristocracy. To be sure, aristocrats came to the New
World; some as governors and administrators, and
others, the poorer ones, in search of fortune. But the
poor aristocrats had little vested interest in the old
system, and the governing aristocrats were seldom in a
position to introduce into the commercially-oriented New
World a relatively static system already increasingly
being undermined by commercial activity in the Old
World.

Even when and where an attempt was made to transplant something European, atypical though it might be, to the New World, that something was soon transformed almost beyond recognition, for conditions in "the world out there," the objective world as Europeans experienced it, were far different from the conditions experienced by them in the Old World. As noted earlier, the great majority of Europeans from the Middle Ages down through the 19th century, and in some areas into the 20th century, were peasants bound legally, traditionally, or by practical necessity to the land and agriculture. As populations increased, the countryside as well as the cities became ever more crowded and arable land became increasingly scarce, a condition compounded by changing patterns of land use. In the New World, vast continents were sparsely settled by "savages" who, in the eyes of the Europeans, were not putting the land and natural resources available to them to good use.[1] Operating at the "frontiers" of civilization as they saw it, some Europeans saw the New World as a "wilderness" to be "tamed"--transformed into farm lands and town sites-- while others were less interested in changing this "wilderness" than they were in exploiting it for its precious metals and furs.[2] To do either--and both were done--was to foster geographic mobility, beginning with the trip to the New World, and to encourage much more social mobility than had existed in the Old World. Old World lifestyles and world views and the stratification patterns and ties to the land that these lifestyles and world views encouraged, therefore, were even less appropriate to the New World setting than they were becoming in the Old World.

The New World differed significantly from the Old in terms of the physical environment, and it also differed in terms of the social arrangements that the transplanted started to fashion upon their arrival. On the one hand, land and other resources valued in Europe were in abundance and apparently for the taking in the New World. On the other hand, Old World ways of allocating and otherwise relating to these valuables hardly seemed to apply in the new setting and might well be called into question if an attempt was made to apply them. The traditional ways utilized in the Old World of defining one's place and keeping one in his place were, for the most part, even less effective in the New World than they eventually became in the Old. New ways of defining place and keeping people in their place, of course, took shape in the New World, and they were more often based on fluctuating economic factors than on lineage. But as people differing from one another in physical appearance, or culture, or both, came into contact with each other as they roamed about the New World, definition of place in terms of "race" and ethnicity also occurred. Of course, contact between culturally different peoples had also taken place in Europe, but ethnic groups there tended to be more segregated. Consequently, contact with others, for the most part, was made at the periphery of the group on the frontier between its holdings and those of its neighbors.[3] As shall be seen, ethnic interaction in the New World has been quite different. Before moving on, however, it should also be noted that the distinction between fighter--or warrior--and non-fighter--or civilian--that the peoples of much of Europe had taken for granted for ages were undermined by conditions in parts of the New World almost from the very beginning of settlement.

The New World differed from the Old, therefore, in such ways as have been briefly described above, but as differences had existed from one part of the Old World to another so did they exist from one part of the New to another. In other words, all frontiers were not alike. The remainder of this chapter will be devoted to a consideration of some of the major ways in which the New World frontiers differed, and to the ways in which the nations that developed behind these frontiers still differ.

FRONTIER DIFFERENCES--GEOGRAPHIC AND SOCIAL

The term frontier means different things to different peoples. In other parts of the world, frontiers--the boundary lines between nations--are likely to be associated with restrictions, but in the United States frontier is more likely to be associated with openness and opportunity.[4] Of course, other modern nations--Canada and Australia among those covered by this study, various Latin American countries and Siberia among those not covered--have had, and in some cases still have, frontiers that some scholars have taken to be similar to the American frontier. But these other frontiers differed from the American variety in terms of the exploitability of their physical environments, in terms of the traditions of their settlers, or in terms of both of the preceding.[5]

Latin America was settled by the Spanish and the Portuguese, who brought much more of feudal Europe with them than did the English-speaking peoples who gradually moved across North America from east to west. And only on the pampas of southern Argentina and the plains of Brazil did the Spanish and Portuguese find anything other than jungles, semiarid plateaus, and mountains.[6] Therefore, where Latin-American pioneers were not kept by both the suitability of the physical environment and the remnants of feudal world views and related life-styles from moving out on their own to conquer the wilderness, the remnants of feudalism were generally enough to keep them from doing so.

In Canada and Australia, by contrast, the first settlers came from nations well advanced in modern concepts of capitalism and middle class values, but physical conditions precluded the emergence of a frontier spirit identical with that of the United States. In Australia frontiersmen during the 1850's and 1860's pushed through gaps in the coastal mountains as had American pioneers through the Appalachians nearly a century before; but instead of finding the rich plains of a Mississippi Valley, they encountered semiarid lands and uninhabitable deserts. With the pioneer pastoralist driven back by lack of water for farming, the continent's interior remained either unsettled or the province of wealthy capitalists whose resources could support the large-scale sheepherding operations that alone were profitable there. In Canada frontier expansion was blocked by the Laurentian Shield, a tangled mass of brush-covered hills and sterile soils that deflected migrants southward into the United States. Not until railroads penetrated this barrier in the later nineteenth century could settlers reach the lush lands of the prairie provinces; those who did so came directly from the East and brought with them established practices that had not been loosened by a recurring pioneering experience.

Only in eastern Canada during the seventeenth century and in Russian Siberia

during the nineteenth did pioneers find
a physical environment comparable to that
of the United States.[7]

But, according to Ray Allen Billington, absolute rulers
and tyrannical traditions kept pioneers in these areas
from developing the "go ahead" spirit associated with
the American frontier, though the hold of both the rulers and the traditions were weakened on these other
frontiers.

Through the preceding comparisons of various frontiers, Billington attempted to pinpoint the source of
the "go-ahead" spirit that, while not a uniquely American trait, was to him particularly pronounced in the
United States. For the purposes of this study, however,
what he has written may give us reason to believe that
the frontier experienced by Americans was significantly
different from those frontiers experienced by Canadians
and Australians. The English pioneers in what is now
the United States went off into the wilderness for the
most part to acquire land and to settle on it, and the
land they found was capable of supporting them. The
lifestyles and world views fostered by collective attempts to cope with a raw, unforgiving new environment
have, therefore, been those of a significant number of
those Americans at any given time during the first 300
years or so of American history. There was a wilderness
to move off into and tame for nearly that length of
time. A frontier experience of a particular kind,
therefore, has been a significant part of the American
scene from the beginning of large-scale European settlement of what is now the United States until the recent
past. It is within this context that the American attachment to firearms, or at least part of it, must be
understood. Further exploration of the differences between frontiers should make this point clear.

As Europeans and their descendants moved off to
settle unclaimed New World lands, they often found it
necessary to hunt for their food. Since large as well
as small game of many varieties was abundant in most
areas, hunting guns—ball- or shot-firing longarms—obviously functioned practically in the lives of pioneers
in North America, Australia, and elsewhere. Since some
of the animals that these pioneers came into contact
with—bears, wolves, mountain lions, etc.—were quite
formidable and could be dangerous to men, firearms were
often used defensively against them. For the time

being, however, attention will be focused on the pioneers' attempts to cope with other human beings rather
than on their attempts to cope with other creatures.

THE ABORIGINAL, THE PIONEER, AND AMATEUR SOLDIERING

In all parts of the New World, Europeans and their
descendants eventually came into contact with aborig-
ines--people who had occupied these areas for some time
before the Europeans arrived in numbers. Though the
aboriginals in any given area are often thought of as a
single group of people--for example, all American Indians are thought to be the same--there were as many
ethnic groupings among these earlier occupants of the
New World as there were among the various newcomers--
Spanish, Portuguese, English, French, Dutch.[8] Though
conflict, in some form or other, was usually generated
sooner or later as new came into contact with old, where
the lifestyles and world views of the peoples concerned
did not cause them to threaten each other--as was the
case with the French and at least some Indian tribes in
Canada--relations could be relatively peaceful for long
periods of time. In many areas, however, relations between old and new were, more often than not, anything
but peaceful. When aborigines and the newcomers faced
each other in battle, the former, due to their relatively unsophisticated weaponry, tactics, and organization,
were often at a distinct disadvantage--as was the case
with the Australian Aborigines. In some areas, however,
aboriginal military techniques were more effective and,
with European weaponry supplementing their own, the aborigines could face the invaders in battle on more or
less equal terms--at least in the short run. This was
the case with many Indian tribes throughout what is now
the United States.

Of the three frontiers to be considered in this
study, the aboriginal resistance to the expansion of
Europe was the most fierce on the American frontier, and
armed conflict between red man and white was an almost
continuous part of the American scene for nearly 300
years. Often this conflict was widespread enough that
it was referred to as war, and while the war-oriented
lifestyles and world views of some Indian tribes could
in part account for the conflict that occurred, the
English settlers and their descendants also did much to
bring it on. As the number of English settlers increased and what the colonists viewed as wilderness was

transformed into farm land, Indians were driven off or exterminated. In New England especially, land hunger combined with Protestant zeal as settlers cleared the North Atlantic seaboard of Indians by 1740. "America was the New Canaan, a promised land set apart by God for his elect. The Indians who encumbered it were pagans 'of the cursed race of Ham'; the Reverend Richard Mather, on hearing of the Pequot Massacre, rejoiced that 'on this day we have sent six hundred heathen souls to hell.'"[9]

The French colonies in Canada were based on fur trade rather than agriculture, and since the former required Indian assistance and cooperation, the French did not pose as much of a threat to the Indians as did the English further south. Consequently, with the exception of the strong Iroquois Confederacy who found it to their advantage to compete with the French and cooperate with English fur traders, the French got along quite well with their Indian neighbors.[10] And once the Iroquois exhausted themselves through continuous warfare, the French could afford to be less vigilant and live in relative peace with the red men.[11]

In Australia, the English considered the Aborigines to be something less than human, and treated them accordingly. In Tasmania the colonists went so far as to hunt the natives for sport.[12] Though the Aborigines on occasion retaliated using sheer numbers--bands of one hundred or more--to overcome small numbers of firearmed settlers, they were generally unwarlike and militarily ineffectual against the whites.[13] When compared to the warfare between red and white on the American frontier, the armed conflict between black and white in Australia seems a mere parody of war.[14]

In Canada, therefore, the Europeans and their descendants did little to provoke conflict between red and white, and relations between aboriginal and settler were generally peaceful even on the plains frontier of the late 19th century. In Australia, the natives were certainly provoked, but they did not possess the means to do much about it. On the American frontier, however, not only were the Indians provoked by the settlers, but some tribes were only too willing and able to give as much as they received--at least in the short run. And ironically, the competition between the various colonizing powers and their commercialism helped to make the more warlike tribes even more formidable by putting firearms into their hands.

The North American Indians had not shown much interest in obtaining matchlock muskets of the sort used by the early European explorers and settlers, but by 1650 all New World Europeans except the Spanish were illegally trading guns to the Indians.[15] Europeans found it quite profitable to trade firearms for furs, and the Dutch even seemed unconcerned that the Indians might use these guns against Dutch settlements elsewhere.[16] It was the Dutch, according to historian Carl P. Russell, who helped make the Iroquois so formidable by supplying them with guns.[17] With these guns the Iroquois rampaged not only against the Hurons, their traditional foes who had benefited greatly by their trade relations with the French, but also against the French themselves.[18] And the Iroquois harassment of the French served to benefit the English, with whom the Iroquois became allied. The gun trade with the Indians can thereby be seen to have served yet another purpose for the various colonizing powers--it enabled them to obtain effective Indian allies for their campaign against European rivals in the New World. During the American Revolution the British made certain that their Iroquois allies "were fully equipped with the best armament that England could supply."[19] Even after the New World rivalries between the English, French, Dutch and Spanish had faded away, however, the firearms trade with the Indians continued. By the early years of the 19th century, cheap but effective muskets and rifles were being designed especially for the Indian trade.[20] By the latter part of the 19th century, Indians on the plains, including those who were often at war with settlers as well as neighboring tribes, were receiving rifles of the latest design. Some students of the West claim that in some cases the Indians were better equipped than the soldiers sent to chastise them.[21] In many cases, therefore, the red men that the American frontiersmen encountered as they gradually pushed westward were willing to fight and had access to firearms almost as good as, and in some cases better than, their white opponents.

Historian Daniel Boorstin has written that to the American frontiersman

> the Indian was omnipresent; he struck without warning and was a nightly terror in the remote silence of backwoods cabins. The New England settlers, Cotton Mather

recalled, felt themselves "assaulted by unknown numbers of devils in flesh on every side"; to them Indians were "so many 'unkennel'd wolves.'" Every section of the seacoast colonies suffered massacres. The bloody toll of the Virginia settlements in 1622, and again in 1644, was never forgotten in the colony. In Virginia in 1676, Nathaniel Bacon's Rebellion expressed the demand of western settlers for more aid against the Indians. We have already seen how the Indian massacres of the mid-18th century sharpened the crisis of the Quaker government of Pennsylvania. Such nightmares shaped the military policy of settlers until nearly the end of the 18th century. The Indian menace, which haunted the fringes of settlement through the whole colonial era, remained a terror to the receding West well into the 19th century. Not until ten years after the massacre of Custer's troops in 1876, when the few remaining Indians had been removed to Indian Territory or to reservations, did the Indian threat disappear.[22]

The Indian, therefore, was far from helpless, though he would eventually be overwhelmed by the descendants of the Europeans. He could give as much as he received and more, since as a rule those who fell captive to him were tortured.[23] To the whites, he was a terrible foe, and one that could not be dealt with in the standard European manner. The Indian's omnipresence and hit-and-run tactics made traditional European armies and tactics useless. He struck civilians where no army was present and was gone before troops arrived on the scene. If civilians were to be defended, therefore, they had to be prepared to defend themselves as they cultivated the land and provided themselves with food and shelter.[24] Thus the armed citizenry as the basis of the American version of the militia came into existence at a very early date.

Militias had existed in Europe for centuries, but the American version differed from them in a number of significant ways. On the American frontier the militia was very loosely organized. It fought as a unit when there was time to call it out and when the numbers of

the enemy made it necessary. Otherwise, individuals and
family units had to take care of themselves. In America, therefore, the armed individual, or at least those on
the frontiers of settlement, provided the basis for the
militia.[25] In Europe it tended to be the other way
around; the individual was armed through the militia.
In Europe, where militias existed, individuals often had
to be pressured into equipping themselves or their local
units with acceptable military weapons and gear. To a
great extent, this was also the case in those parts of
what is now the United States that were far enough from
the frontier for the populace not to be worried about
attacks by the Indians or the French.[26] On the frontier, individuals tended to arm themselves for their
own defense--and to provide themselves with food--apart
from any formal requirement that they do so. The threat
to their very existence was obvious and continuous; they
needed no prodding. And in European militias, Switzerland being a notable exception, firearms were kept in
community armories and issued when the militia was
called out. This procedure would hardly have been
practical on the frontier.

Frontier militia men, having had to rely so much
on their individual weapons and having learned Indian
tactics, were formidable fighters when called upon to
protect their own communities from attacks by Indians
or by the equally formidable militia fielded by the fur-
trading French. But the frontier militiamen were not
disciplined soldiers, nor were they generally interested
in engaging in long-term large-scale military opera--
tions.[27] Apart from Virginia and Kentucky frontiersmen
and such units as Roger's New England Rangers, however,
the colonial English and later American militia were
composed mostly of ill-trained peaceful farmers from
long-settled areas and they were not very effective
fighting units.[28]

When and where settlers had to be on guard continually, their defensive efforts, sometimes based on a
more or less formal militia organization, could be formidable. But from early times, efforts to maintain a
ready reserve of effective citizen soldiers across the
country have met with mixed success in the United States.
By 1850 most Americans considered the one or two muster
days a year required by the traditional standing militia
to be a nuisance, and though militiamen were supposed to
arm themselves, they often appeared with rusty weapons,
or--in some western states--"cornstalks, sticks, umbrel-

las, ramrods," and "other make-believe weapons."[29]

The well-to-do and those with connections could in any number of ways evade their militia obligations, while those who were compelled to serve were generally not the most enthusiastic part-time soldiers.[30] Consequently, militia musters often appeared comical, even ludicrous, to those who observed them or took part in them.[31] While the militia may seldom have had much popular support when and where danger from human enemies has not been imminent, however, amateur soldiering has at times been quite popular in the United States, as indicated by the volunteer movement of the 19th century and earlier. The volunteer companies—some of which were organized in the late 18th century in response to crisis—were not part of the state militias, though most had militia designations.[32] The early volunteer companies amounted to exclusive social clubs, and they carefully screened prospective members.[33] By the 1820's and 30's, however, volunteer companies composed of clerks, artisans, and even hoodlums, were organized, and immigrant companies became numerous. Such companies were very popular with the Irish and German immigrants, and though target shoots were popular with all the volunteer groups, such organizations allowed the Germans to transplant their old country rifle clubs in the United States.[34]

The volunteer companies supplied their own uniforms, which were patterned after those of such colorful foreign regiments as the French Zouaves and the Scottish Highlanders, but they often rode hired or borrowed horses and carried muskets borrowed from state arsenals.[35] These units often took part in annual encampments where they paraded, shot at targets, and otherwise played soldier. However, their social functions seem to have gone far beyond their military functions.[36] The encampments were the sites of barbecues as well as of target shoots and drills.[37] And during the year, companies entertained other companies from their own or other cities with military balls or dazzled parade onlookers with intricate marching maneuvers. There was much of the latter-day college fraternity and the lodge, of the Shriners, cheerleaders, and marching bands about the volunteer companies.[38]

Whether the volunteer companies were effective military units or not has been the subject of much debate, but they seem to have functioned quite effectively

173

as police in some areas.[39] "Slave-patrolling in some parts of the South and action against city mobs in the North gave them a quasi-military raison d'etre."[40] But regardless of their effectiveness as either soldiers or policemen, the volunteer companies, the militia, and the National Guard that evolved from them have done much to blur the distinction between soldier and civilian in the United States. And though evolving democratic traditions and distrust of standing armies lent ideological support to amateur soldiering as did social conditions behind the frontier, attempts by settlers on the frontier to cope with hostile Indians first put arms into the hands of numbers of ordinary civilians and made serious part-time soldiers out of them.[41] Such a stimulus to part-time soldiering seems generally to have been lacking in Canada after the Iroquois threat to the French had faded in the 18th century. In Australia, such a stimulus to part-time soldiering as may have existed seems not to have been long lived or widespread.[42]

LAW AND ORDER AND AMATEUR POLICING

While the aboriginal often posed a formidable threat to those who lived along the frontier of settlement in what is now the United States, anyone familiar with "western movies" is probably aware of the fact that the invading whites often and in various ways threatened each other. Of course, the movies may have depicted the frontier as being much wilder than was actually the case, but there is certainly reason to believe that, by modern middle-class standards at least, the frontier was in actuality a very rough-and-ready place. In the early days of settlement, people who shared a more or less common world view and a consciousness of kind--such as the Puritans--often built a community around a collective way of life to which they were all quite dedicated. As a result, social control in such communities did not pose much of a problem.[43] Social control could generally be accomplished through ostracism, ridicule, and other informal or semi-formal means of the same sort that were used in the older and well-established peasant villages and small towns of Europe. The more individualistically oriented, however, set out by themselves or with their families to make their own way in the wilderness, and the isolated lands they cleared and farmed were, more often than not, too far from the nearest settlements to fall within the effective range of control of these

174

settlements. Settlers, therefore, often had to look out
for themselves and to protect themselves not only from
Indians but from opportunistic renegade whites who would
take advantage of the settlers' isolation. While there
may not have been as many renegades as legend and the
movies would have us believe, the opportunism that
brought many individuals to the frontier coupled with
the lack of effective law enforcement in some areas undoubtedly produced enough renegades to keep the isolated settler on guard.

But human threat to life, limb, and property on the
frontier did not always reside beyond the city limits.
While some relatively peaceful communities, inwardly at
least, were established along or just behind the west-
ward-moving frontier of settlement by religious groups
or new immigrants attempting to develop or preserve
their unique ways of life, many, if not most, frontier
communities did not originate in such an organized manner.[44] Some communities grew up around the trading
posts where trappers rendezvoused to sell their furs,
buy supplies, and socialize. Others materialized practically overnight in areas where gold, silver, oil, or
other valuable minerals had been discovered. Still
others grew up around military forts or at railheads.
Order did not come naturally to such communities, since
they tended, as did the frontier as a whole, to attract
men "on the make."[45]

On the American frontier in town as well as country, in other words, there were many--business entre-
preneurs, gamblers, bandits; one could not always be
distinguished from the other --who were more than willing to take advantage of the fact that settlement there
often preceded the establishment of law and order.[46]
In fact, it might well be argued that in a very real
sense the business entrepreneur in many cases differed
from the bandit only in that the former used different
methods and ended up on the right side of the law that
he helped to make and enforce.

Even after it had been established, law and order
on the frontier left much to be desired. And the tenuous nature of law and order on the frontier drew outlaws and outlaw gangs bent on taking advantage of the
unsettled state of frontier society. As Richard Maxwell
Brown has noted:

Law enforcement was frequently inad-

175

equate. Throughout most of the 19th century (and not just on the frontier) it was pinned down to the immediate vicinity of county seat, town, or township. Localities lacked the economic resources to support constables, policemen, and sheriffs in long journeys of pursuit after lawbreakers. A really large expenditure of funds for the pursuit, capture, jailing, trial and conviction of culprits could easily bankrupt the typical frontier county or town.[47]

The very emptiness of the frontier, its rugged vastness, combined with the limitations of available transportation, further hindered law enforcement. There were many places that a fugitive could hide, therefore, and if he had much of a lead he might very easily evade his pursuers.[48]

Brown also points out that

linked with inadequate law enforcement was an uneven judicial system. Through fear, friendliness, or corruption, juries often failed to convict the criminal. Lack of jails (in the early days) or their flimsy condition made it nearly impossible to prevent those in custody from escaping. The system presented numerous opportunities for manipulation by outlaws who could often command some measure of local support. Whenever possible outlaws would obtain false witnesses in their behalf, pack juries, bribe officials, and, in extreme cases, intimidate the entire system: judges, juries, and law enforcement officials. Such deficiencies in the judicial system were the source of repeated complaints by frontiersmen. They made the familiar point that the American system of administering justice favored the accused rather than society. The guilty, then /sic/ charged, utilized every loophole for the evasion of punishment. Compounding the problem was the genuinely heavy financial burden involved in maintaining an adequate "police establishment" and judicial system in a sparsely

176

settled and economically underdeveloped
frontier area.[49]

Considering the lack of law and order at some times
and places on the American frontier, and its tenuous
nature at other times and places, it should not be surprising that ordinary citizens occasionally took the law
into their own hands. Those who did so have commonly
been referred to as vigilantes, though they sometimes
took other names--such as regulators--for themselves.
The first recorded vigilante movement took place from
1767 to 1769 in Piedmont, South Carolina. From then
until around 1900 such movements were common across the
United States, particularly in those states west of the
Appalachians.[50] Some 500 or so vigilante movements may
have occurred in the United States during that period,
but only 326 are currently known.[51] It is interesting
to note that vigilante movements did not make their appearance in what is now the United States until frontier expansion speeded up to the point where adequate
law enforcement efforts could not keep pace with it.[52]

While vigilantism tended to appear where the law
left something to be desired, it could also appear where
the law was functioning adequately.[53] The latter variety came about (1) through efforts to promote local political and fiscal reform, as seems to have been the
case in San Francisco in 1856; (2) through efforts by
the upper levels of a community to get newcomers with
strange and offending lifestyles in line; or (3) through
efforts to reduce the cost of local government.[54]

Some vigilante committees were quite small, numbering only a dozen or so members, while others had thousands of members--the San Francisco committee of 1856,
for example, had from 6,000 to 8,000 members.[55] Where
community consensus tended to support the vigilantes,
they usually disbanded once order had been established
or reestablished to almost everyone's satisfaction.[56]
This was generally the situation when the vigilantes had
been organized by the "respectable" people of the community to cope with those they considered to be lower-
class troublemakers or outlaws. Where community consensus did not exist, antivigilante coalitions tended
to develop and wars between the two factions continued
for some time, as exemplified by the war between the
Regulators and the Moderators in east Texas from 1840
to 1844.[57]

Private citizens have taken the law into their own hands through the various vigilante movements and related movements such as the Ku Klux Klans. But on occasion citizens have become their own policemen and at the same time remained within the law, as was the case with the anti-horsethief movement that came into existence just after the Revolutionary War and spread all across the United States.[58] Members of the various anti-horsethief societies turned the culprits that they captured over to the law, and eventually constabulary power was given to such societies by some states.[59]

As can be seen from the above, the American on the frontier, whether he lived in town or off by himself, was occasionally called upon to do his own policing, legally or otherwise, as well as his own soldiering. On the American frontier, therefore, not only was the distinction between civilian and soldier blurred, but that between citizen and policeman as well. These distinctions do not seem to have been blurred on either the Canadian or the Australian frontiers, as shall be seen.

As law and order does not seem to have posed much of a problem to the English settlements of the slowly advancing frontier east of the Appalachians, neither does it seem to have posed much of a problem to the early French settlements of eastern Canada. In fact, social control in the French-Canadian communities may have been further fostered by the feudal world views and lifestyles that the French brought with them, though the frontier tended to undermine these world views and lifestyles to a certain extent. By the time the Canadian frontier had moved to the western plains, the English controlled Canada. Taking advantage of their experience with constabulary forces in Ireland and India, the British established such a force in Canada.[60] That force, the centrally-controlled Northwest Mounted Police, preceded the settlers to the Canadian west and had established itself and a respect for law and order before large-scale settlement got under way.[61]

The differences between the American and Canadian methods of law enforcement in their respective wests is dealt with at length by Paul F. Sharp in his history of the northern plains.[62] Citing some of the limitations of the American system--a system that had survived almost intact over some two hundred years of frontier experience before it moved out on to the plains--Sharp goes on to claim that

many thoughtful Americans urged a similar
system /to the Canadian7 in their West as
they learned of the success of the Northwest Mounted Police. But western communities, intensely jealous of their traditional powers in the administration of justice,
refused to accept such a system. It appeared to be synonymous with a military
rule that undermined local government and
abandoned traditional guarantees of personal freedom.63

While the centrally-controlled Northwest Mounted
Police may well have had much to do with making the
Canadian West a much less threatening place than that
found south of the border, if we accept what Billington
has argued earlier in the chapter, their job may not
have been nearly as difficult as it would have been for
a similar organization south of the border. According
to Billington, large-scale settlement of the Canadian
West was postponed until the railroads had penetrated
the Laurentian Shield in the late 19th century. The
settlers of the Canadian prairies, therefore, as has
already been noted, "came directly from the East and
brought with them established practices that had not
been loosened by a recurring pioneering experience." If
this were the case, the lack of a recurring pioneering
experience, as much if not more than the presence of
the Mounties, may have accounted for the "stronger
tradition of respect for the institutions of law and
order" that supposedly existed on the Canadian fron-
tier.64 Be that as it may, law and order on the Canadian frontier does not seem to have been as difficult
to achieve as it was on the American frontier. And
Canadian frontiersmen, unlike their American neighbors,
seldom seem to have felt called upon to take the law in
their own hands.

With respect to law enforcement, the Australian
frontier resembles, superficially at least, the Canadian
frontier more than it does the American frontier. This
might be expected, given the close official relationship both Australia and Canada have had with Great Britain. And some Australian observers have credited the
British system of justice with keeping "gun-slingers"
and "bounty-hunters" from becoming a part of the Australian frontier.

In North America, they generally elected

their sheriffs, marshals and judges, and grew tolerant of the incompetence and corruption inevitable in functionaries who depend on the popular vote for their livelihood. In Australia the British system of government appointments prevailed and, whenever a new settlement began, there moved in a unit of the official police force. Lawless men there were in plenty in the Australian colonial days, but these were never allowed to stalk through towns with guns in their belts. If they persisted in their malefactions they had to hide in the hills. They became bush-rangers who, when in need of funds or horses, stuck-up or bailed-up, stage-coaches, sheep stations and, occasionally, banks. If one of these men singly showed his face in a township he would be promptly put in gaol by the local police. Billy the Kid could never have arisen in Australia. At the outset of his career he would have had his bottom kicked, and his little pistol taken away from him. Likewise, that loathsome phenomenon, the bounty-hunter, was never spawned in Australia where it was held, that given the establishment of a proper police force, it was their job, except in very unusual circumstances, to bring bad men to justice. The acceptance of blood-money was held to be an outrage to bush morality. In Australia a bounty-hunter would have found nobody to drink with.[65]

If we take the above at face value, we are led to believe that a centrally-controlled police force on the order of the Canadian Northwest Mounted Police, a police force supported and respected by the populace at large, brought law and order to the Australian frontier. But considering what many others have written about Australia, this does not seem to have been the case. The Australian frontier communities themselves may well have had less gunplay than their American counterparts due in part to the existence of a centrally-controlled police force. Australian police, however, seem never to have had a great deal of public support. To a certain extent, this lack of support for the police may be accounted for by the fact that white Australia origi-

180

nated as an English penal colony. As late as 1851, 59 percent of the 187,243 white inhabitants of New South Wales, Australia's oldest colony, were convicts, emancipated convicts, or native-born lower class who had little in common with the free immigrant and official classes and much in common with the convicts and emancipists.[66] While one could hardly expect convicts, emancipated convicts, and those who more or less shared their views to have much regard for the police, the relations between the police and a good part of the Australian population were further strained because the first Australian policemen were themselves convicts and the police were largely recruited from convicts and emancipated convicts until the second half of the 19th century.[67] This police recruitment pattern was necessary in part because the "Currency Lads," or native-born, were so negative toward police service that only convicts or emancipated convicts were available for such work.[68] But

> from the point of view of the convicts, and of a great many other Australians who were strongly influenced by their outlook, those who became policemen and overseers were not the best prisoners but the worst. By consenting to act as constables they broke, in the most flagrant possible way, the first principle of "government men" and bushworkers; that of loyalty to one's mates. Whatever else might be added to them of spiritual grace or worldly perquisites, they forfeited utterly the respect of their fellows.[69]

In other words, the police themselves were regarded as bounty hunters.

Ward states that it is doubtful

> whether the police force of any English-speaking country, except Ireland, has ever been more thoroughly unpopular than were those of most Australian colonies of the last century. Even special corps like the Queensland Native Mounted Police, in sorry contrast with such bodies as the Royal Canadian Mounted, established a reputation for ferocity rather than gallantry.[70]

181

Another Australian observer has pointed out that Australians are still largely anti-police.[71]

In spite of lack of popular support, however, the Australian police, past as well as present, have evidently been a power to be reckoned with. They have not hesitated to use "strong-arm" methods. As H. C. Allen has observed, "in a one-time penal settlement one would not expect universal support for the agencies of law and order."[72] This state of affairs may account for the lack of "large-scale lawlessness of the American frontier type" even during the Australian Gold Rush of the mid-19th century, on the one hand, and the existence of bushrangers--Australian outlaws--who were worshipped as folk-heroes, on the other hand.[73]

The early bushrangers were generally convict "bolters," or escapees, but later the native-born took to the road on occasion.[74] Taken together, the social origins of the bushrangers, the fact that they constituted professional opponents of the unpopular police, and the apparent limitations of the Australian environment "which allows economic success only to the few," may help account for the bushranger's widespread support among those Australians at the lower socio-economic levels.[75] While the respectable urban middle classes (whose numbers and influence increased after the gold discoveries) and the propertied and official in general tended to see things differently, to the country folk and the working classes the bushrangers were Robin Hoods.[76] While they may not have always given to the poor that which they took from the rich, bushrangers often "singled out for special attention those squatters /pastoral employers7 who had the reputation of being hard or unjust taskmasters," and thus came to be considered protectors of the working class whom they seldom bothered.[77] Of course, the latter possessed little worth stealing. But even when the bushrangers robbed the rich, they seem generally to have taken "pains to avoid 'unnecessary' violence."[78] According to Ward

> it paid bushrangers to avoid bloodshed because such a policy greatly increased the esteem in which they were held by wide sections of the community. It is clear that, both before and after the Gold Rush decade, the desperadoes could not have existed for long if it had not been for the almost universal sympathy

and support of the bush proletariat.[79]

The bushrangers' avoidance of bloodshed seems to
have been made possible largely due to the fact that
they seldom encountered much resistance from those whom
they robbed. One 19th-century writer, who had talked
with twenty or so persons who had been robbed by bushrangers, comments on the lack of resistance on the part
of these victims: "Indeed, I was sometimes surprised
how they /the bushrangers/ were allowed to walk the
course, even under circumstances where defence would almost, to a certainty, have been attended with success."[80]

From what has been covered in this section, it
would seem reasonably safe to conclude that, with respect to the issue of law and order, the Canadian and
Australian frontiers were far less threatening places in
the eyes of those who experienced them than was the
American frontier to those who experienced it. On the
plains of British Canada of the late 19th century,
transplanted easterners did not present much of a law
enforcement problem to each other, and the crime that
existed could be handled by a respected, efficient, centrally-controlled constabulary. In Australia, an unpopular, but apparently reasonably effective, centrally-
controlled constabulary had enough crime to deal with,
but most of the populace seemed not to have felt threatened by the outlaws. Australians, therefore, did not
attempt to take the law into their own hands. In the
United States, over a period of some three hundred years
of frontier history, no centralized police force existed
and those on opposite sides of the law, such as it was
defined at any given time, were seldom gentle with each
other. On the American frontier, private citizens did
take the law into their own hands, but they did not do
so, on a large scale at least, on the Canadian and
Australian frontiers.[81]

BEHIND THE FRONTIER--INDUSTRIALIZATION,
URBANIZATION, IMMIGRATION AND WAR

It cannot be known what percentage of those Americans who lived on or near the frontier at one time or
another during its approximately three hundred years of
existence ever took up arms to do their own soldiering
against the Indians or some other enemy, or to bring law
and order to their community. But from the accounts of

183

the Indian-settler battles and vigilante movements that
have come down to us, we have good reason to believe
that hundreds or even thousands of Americans were occasionally involved in such activities at the same time
and place. And we have reason to suspect that many more
Americans were aware of the involvement of their fellow
citizens in these policing and soldiering activities,
and of the conditions that brought on their involvement.
Whether or not they were ever called upon to fight,
therefore, it would seem safe to assume that many, if
not the majority, of those who lived on the American
frontier had to live with the awareness that hostile
Indians or whites or both might be in the neighborhood;
that the army or the local law enforcement agencies, for
one reason or other, might not be able to protect them
from these hostiles; and consequently, that they might
be called upon to defend themselves. From what has
been said in the previous section, it would seem that
though human threats to life and limb certainly existed
on their frontiers, Canadians and Australians had less
cause to be preoccupied with them. Therefore, if one
is trying to understand the part the frontier has played
in helping to bring about the American attachment to
firearms, he can hardly afford to treat the American
frontier as if it were the same as the other two. The
similarities are at best superficial.

But by focusing our attention on their frontiers,
other differences between these three nations that can
shed light on the different ways firearms have fitted
into their respective histories are left unexamined.
The United States, Canada, and Australia have all had
frontiers, as different as these frontiers may have been
from one another, but they are now all "modern" nations
by western standards. While all three nations still
have large tracts of unsettled "wilderness," practically
all of the land that a use has been found for has been
put to that use--settlement, agriculture, etc.--and all
three nations have become industrialized and urbanized.
In each, 70 percent or more of the population lives in
urban areas. But here the resemblance ends. Australia
is 2,967,909 square miles in area, but has a population
of only about 14,250,000--a population density of 4.5
persons per square mile--86.6 percent of whom live in
cities scattered around the coastal fringes of the island continent. Canada is 3,851,809 square miles in
area, but has a population of only about 23,700,000--a
population density of 6.1 persons per square mile--76.1
percent of whom live in cities most of which are situ-

ated in the southern part of the country near the United States border. The United States, between Australia and Canada in area at 3,615,122 square miles, has a population of over 218,000,000, more than six times larger than that of Australia and Canada combined--a population density of 59 persons per square mile--73.5 percent of whom live in cities situated in the eastern half of the nation and along the west coast, but to a certain extent scattered all across the country. And in the sphere of economics, the Gross National Product of the United States is over $975,240,000,000 compared to Canada's approximately $79,130,000,000 and Australia's $38,660,000,000.[82] It would seem therefore, that while the United States, Canada, and Australia are all "modern" nations that have been carved out of the "wilderness" during the past three hundred years or less, the transformations that have occurred in the United States have been far more extensive than the transformations have been in the other two countries. And these extensive American transformations, which have often been thought of in terms of progress, have not come about smoothly or without cost to those who made them possible.

As Americans developed a largely rural-agricultural society behind the frontier and then transformed it into a largely urban-industrial society, human threats to individual and group security did not automatically fade away. Several wars have been fought on American soil since the United States has existed, and these wars have to a great extent taken place behind the frontier. The Revolutionary War, which brought the United States into existence, set not only American against British, but, where some Americans did not desire independence, neighbor against neighbor.[83] And the Civil War, which pitted the urban-industrial North against the rural-agricultural South, also often set neighbor against neighbor, at least in the border states. The issue of slavery had helped to generate warring factions in some areas such as Missouri and Kansas even before the Civil War began. And after the war, the Reconstruction period bred more civil strife. Before the Civil War, white southerners who lived in areas where there were many slaves often worried about slave insurrections, and these insurrections occasionally occurred. After the war, white southerners had to cope with the Yankee occupation and with freed slaves, and the freed slaves had to contend with the first Ku Klux Klan. Canada has been spared such full scale wars between white powers and their repercussions since the British overcame the French toward the middle of the 18th century, and Australia has been spared such conflict altogether.

Banditry also continued to exist after the frontier had moved on or faded away. Such famous "western" outlaws as the James brothers operated in what would now be considered the Midwest—Missouri and its adjacent states—after the Civil War when the wilderness, or Indian frontier, had been pushed back to the Great Plains and to the mountains further west. The first great train robbers—the Reno brothers—took up their trade in the 1860's even further back east in Indiana. And gangs of bank robbers operated across the Midwest as late as the Depression and the 1930's. To many subsistence-level farmers and other rural and small-town folk at the lower socio-economic levels, such outlaws, many of whom themselves came from such backgrounds, became folk heroes; but these outlaws constituted a menace to the moneyed.[84]

While family feuds occurred in the ranching West and Southwest, which in many ways could still be thought of as frontier, such feuds also occurred in rural areas far removed from the late 19th century frontier in or across the state lines of states such as Kentucky and West Virginia. In the southeastern United States, such feuds as occurred in the late 19th and early 20th centuries often seem to have amounted to continuations of the Civil War—the involved families having fought on opposing sides.[85]

From the above, it can be seen that the American countryside well behind the frontier still posed security problems to those who inhabited it. But so did—and do— the larger towns and cities pose security problems for those who inhabit them. Considering the spectacular way in which many American cities mushroomed into existence, one could hardly expect to find them orderly places in the early days. According to urban historian Blake McKelvey, the first nine American cities to reach a population of one hundred thousand all exceeded the growth rates of the fastest growing English industrial cities, "and several doubled or tripled the growth rates of their closest British counterparts."[86] Chicago grew "from zero to 109,000 between 1830 and 1860."[87] With people streaming into the new American cities at such an incredible rate, it might well be expected that those people jostled and in many ways threatened each other as individuals or groups attempted to establish themselves and an order beneficial to themselves and to the groups to which they belonged. And when the diverse lifestyles and world views of those who crowded into the American cities are taken into consideration, the magnitude of the threats these people posed to one another can be appreciated.

The United States has been considered to be part of the English-speaking world since it came into existence, but from its beginning, the ethnic origins of large numbers of those who have lived within its boundaries have been other than English. Before the Europeans came, many different Indian ethnic groups lived in what is now the United States. French, Dutch, Germans, Scotch-Irish and Africans of varied ethnicity, the last having been brought over against their will to be slaves, also were here in large numbers before the American Revolution, and as the United States expanded to the Pacific Coast, areas long settled by Spanish speaking peoples were annexed. By way of contrast, the "original mix" in Canada, apart from the varied aboriginals, was French and English, and all of Australia's original European inhabitants were from the British Isles. And immigration over the past two hundred years has increased the ethnic diversity of the United States, while Canada, which may have had a proportionately larger number of immigrants during this period, and Australia have not been so affected.[88]

From 1851 to 1950, over half of Canada's immigrants came from the British Isles or the United States, and as late as 1947, 89 percent of Australia's white population originated in the British Isles.[89] By way of contrast, only a third of those immigrants who came to the United States between 1820 and 1945 came from the British Isles, while 57 percent came from Italy, what was once Austria-Hungary, Germany, Russia, Poland, and Scandinavia, and many of the rest came from such places as French Canada, Mexico, Greece, Japan, Finland, Armenia, the Netherlands, Portugal, and the Arab countries.[90] And though in some parts of the United States some of these ethnic groups were able to establish their own towns or neighborhoods, in other parts of the country they have lived in close proximity to each other. The ethnic origins of the populace of the United States are more diverse than those of any other nation. And the diversity, overlooked when the United States is classified simply as an English speaking nation, becomes even

187

more remarkable when we consider that of those immigrants who have come here from Germany, for instance, some were Protestant, some Catholic, and some Jewish. Also many Americans are distinguished from others by skin color and other physical features commonly thought to be classifiable in terms of "race."91

All immigrants did not settle in the city, but many did.92 Over half of those persons living in Chicago, Milwaukee, and St. Louis during the Civil War period were foreign-born.93 In 1890, 25 percent or less of the populations of Milwaukee, New York, Chicago, Detroit, San Francisco, Buffalo, St. Paul, and Cleveland were **white** native of native parents, and Jersey City, St. Louis, Cincinnati, Brooklyn, Pittsburgh, Boston, Rochester, New Orleans, Newark, Minneapolis, Allegheny, Providence, Louisville, Philadelphia, Baltimore, Washington, and Omaha all had 50 percent or less of their populations falling in this category.94 San Francisco, New Orleans, Louisville, Baltimore, Washington, and Kansas City each had 10 percent or more of their populations categorized as non-white by 1890, with Washington's non-white population exceeding 30 percent of the whole.95

Sociologist Robert K. Yin has written the following concerning American cities and ethnic and race relations:

> The city has been the focus of race and ethnicity for two reasons. First, most racial and ethnic groups migrated into the city in large waves, either related to migration from foreign countries, or in the case of the black people, to migration from another region of the United States. Second, the groups created segregated settlements or neighborhoods within the city. The attraction of the city for these groups was predominantly an economic one: the city offered both easy entry jobs and cheap housing located relatively near to the jobs. The attraction was also a cultural one, as the new migrant was more likely to find others of his own language and national background in the city, which meant being able to live with people having similar values and customs.
> It also meant the development of var-

188

ious urban neighborhoods, most having
some sense of turf or territoriality. . . .
The sense is perhaps most strongly evi-
densed by the desire to remain in one's
neighborhood and to prevent attempts by
outsiders (usually government) to change
the neighborhood, whether by urban renewal,
scatter-site housing, block-busting, or
school busing. Territoriality was also
maintained in those neighborhoods where
several different ethnic groups lived in
the same small area with each group re-
taining its own identity.[96]

As industrialization progressed in Europe, uprooted
peasants crossed national boundaries--sometimes only
newly established--to find employment in industrial
cities of other nations--Irish to England, Italians to
France and Germany, etc.--but these migrations have not
been as varied or of the same magnitude as those experienced by the United States.[97] In American cities
"white native American" Protestants, white Irish Catholics, swarthy south Italian Catholics, Jews from Germany, Poland, Russia and elsewhere, "black native American" Protestants from the rural South, Spanish-speaking
Catholics--some "white," some "black,"--from Puerto Rico
or elsewhere, and, in some areas, "yellow" Chinese or
Japanese--some Christian, some not--constitute only some
of the major ethnic, religious, and racial groups that
have, in some combination, had to cope with each other.
The lifestyles and world views of the members of any one
of these groups were often in themselves enough to make
them appear to be subhuman to the members of other
groups with which they came into contact. But such differences were brought into even sharper focus when, as
was--and still is--often the case, those subscribing to
one lifestyle - world view set were forced to compete
with those who subscribed to another set.[98] The segregated communities each group attempted to carve out for
itself were often created at the expense of another
group. The early Irish eventually infringed upon "native American" turf. The later Italians infringed upon
Irish turf. Now blacks are infringing upon Italian,
Slavic, etc., turf. And members of various ethnic
groups have often found it necessary to compete with
those defined as outsiders for jobs. As American cities
were mushrooming in the 19th century, so was American
industry, and industrialists were not averse to using
immigrant labor to keep wages low or to break strikes.

189

Strike breaking, of course, could hardly be expected to endear immigrants to the native workers or to the workers of the other immigrant groups affected.[99]

Cultural differences and ethnic vested interests have thus fostered much urban unrest in the United States, past and present. Perhaps riots with racial or ethnic overtones have been the most obvious manifestations of this sort of unrest, but there have been others. Just as in the past an Italian, for example, may have had good reason to fear for his safety if he happened to wander into an Irish section of town, and vice versa, now a white of practically any ethnic background often has good reason to fear for his safety in a black section of town, and vice versa.[100] And streets in those parts of a city where turf is being contested can be quite threatening to all who have occasion to walk them.[101]

In the early American cities these various peoples had to look out for themselves, since the cities were no better off than the frontier with respect to law enforcement. Before 1844 no urban police systems existed in the United States, and when police forces finally were established they seem to have been primarily concerned with coping with urban rioting.[102] Urban rioting was part of the American scene long before large scale immigration began. But toward the middle of the 19th century, immigration combined with urban and industrial expansion created sprawling slums, and political and economic conditions fostered even more urban turmoil.[103] Cunliffe claims that much of the rioting of this period was "paramilitary in flavor," and he goes on to make some interesting connections between the volunteer fire companies that were often involved in these riots and the volunteer companies that were discussed earlier in connection with the militia.

> Nativism, minority sentiment and political
> faction formed a curious amalgam. The
> fire companies were a perfect epitome of
> this. Their members, whether in Boston,
> New York, Philadelphia or New Orleans,
> were volunteers. They wore uniforms.
> They were competitive, high-spirited and
> reckless. Some were hostile to immigrants
> others were made up of Irishmen. They
> were closely involved in ward politics and
> were linked with military companies (so

190

> that they were ready-made recruits for
> the Zouave companies of 1860-1861). A
> short-lived periodical, the New York Pio-
> neer, began publication in 1840 with the
> announcement that it was "devoted to the
> Military and Fire Department." A similar
> claim was made by the E'clairlur, another
> New York militia periodical which ran in
> the 1850's. . . .
>   It was not always easy to tell wheth-
> er the New York fire companies were for
> or against the law. More precisely, they
> were their own law--their own standing
> army. Street gangs of obviously criminal
> propensity also uniformed themselves
> like private armies.[104]

Cunliffe goes on to note that these uniformed gangs
freely used clubs, stones, and pistols on bystanders as
well as rival gangs when they clashed, and the militia
sometimes had to be used to put down their uprisings.

    Fire in the cities of the mid-19th century and
earlier could be disastrous--consider Chicago--so the
fire companies were quite necessary. But these companies were not always concerned with putting out fires.
Occasionally as they were on their way to a fire, or
once they had got there and were attempting to extin-
guish it, they were set upon by rowdies hired by an opposing faction.[105] If the fire was in the enemy's territory, they were inclined to let it burn.[106] And fire-
men occasionally acted as "expert arsonists" during
riots.[107]

    The police forces that were established to bring
order to the cities were also linked to various factions, and the police sometimes took a major part in the
rioting. Occasionally police forces even fought each
other, as the Municipal Police and the Metropolitan
Police did in New York in 1857 when the latter force was
established to replace the former.[108] Neither side
could smash the other and the city suffered as the police gangs continued to clash. There is reason to believe that in 1858 the senior members of the police
force and fire service led the assault on the Quarantine
Station on Staten Island and its wards of yellow fever
victims.[109] That assault eventually resulted in the
hospital's being burned down, and fire company arsonists assisted in the operation.

As the urban police became more firmly established, they refrained from such behavior and set about attempting to enforce the law, but this does not mean that they became apolitical and attempted to provide members of all groups with the kind of protection the various groups desired. Given the ethnic and economic diversity of the populations of American cities, even-handed law enforcement would have been--and still is--difficult, if not impossible, to accomplish, even if the police had dedicated themselves to the task. Peter K. Manning's discussion of the "social function" of criminal law points out the difficulties involved.

> A society's laws, it is often said, reflect its customs; it can also be said that the growth of the criminal law is proportionate to the decline in the consistency and binding nature of these mores. In simpler societies, where the codes and rules of behavior were well known and homogeneous, sanctions were enforced with much greater uniformity and predictability. Social control was isomorphic with one's obligations to family, clan, and age group, and the policital system of the tribe. In a modern, differentiated society, a minimal number of values and norms are shared. And because the fundamental, taken-for-granted consensus on what is proper and respectable has been blurred or shattered, or, indeed, never existed, criminal law becomes a basis of social control. As Quinney writes, "Where correct conduct cannot be agreed upon, the criminal law serves to control the behavior of all persons within a political jurisdiction."
> Social control through the criminal law predominates in a society only when other means of control have failed. When it does predominate, it no longer reflects the mores of the society. It more accurately reflects the interests of shifting power groups within the society. As a result the police, as the designated enforcers of a system of criminal laws, are undercut by circumstances that accentuate the growing differences between the moral code and the legal order.[110]

Manning's claim that the criminal law "reflects the interests of shifting power groups," is, as shall be seen later, important to this study; consequently, his claim calls for some elaboration by way of support. Some scholars have argued that the law, here as well as elsewhere, tends to function as the handmaiden of the propertied, and members of the working classes in the industrialized world have often had reason to agree. In the United States, the development of the National Guard as a replacement for the obsolete State militia would seem to provide support for this argument. After all, the National Guard developed rapidly in the northern industrial states after the labor riots of 1877; prior to World War II the Guard was often called out during periods of labor violence; wealthy industrialists have sometimes helped to subsidize the Guard; and Guard officers have generally been businessmen or professionals.[111]

Time after time, once the labor movement got underway in the 19th century and even before, miners and other laborers--often but not always immigrants--with what they considered to be legitimate grievances, came up against the militia or National Guard. Sometimes the workers were rioting or engaged in vandalism, but at other times they were apparently simply on strike. John Higham relates the story of a strike that took place in Pennsylvania in 1891, in which strikers, commonly thought to be Hungarians but actually led by British and Americans, rioted and vandalized after the company brought in non-union workers.

> In this tense situation, a crowd of "Huns," returning from a mass meeting, passed a frightened detachment of state militia guarding a company store. Someone fired a shot, the strikers fled, and the militia fired two volleys after them. Ten dead and fifty wounded immigrants littered the road. According to the /New York/ Tribune, the militia's action was "upheld by businessmen and all law-abiding people in the entire region."[112]

Higham tells of another Pennsylvania strike during which 150 unarmed Polish and Hungarian strikers on their way to urge miners in a nearby town to join them were intercepted by a sheriff's posse numbering 102 deputies.

> As the strikers came in sight, the sheriff
> ordered them to return. Someone struck
> him, frightening him into commanding the
> deputies to fire. They poured volley af-
> ter volley into the surprised and ter-
> rorized crowd as it stampeded in flight.
> They killed twenty-one immigrants and
> wounded forty more. The sheriff, a form-
> er mine foreman, explained that the crowd
> consisted of "infuriated foreigners . . .
> like wild beasts." Other mine foremen
> agreed that if the strikers had been
> American-born no blood would have flowed.[113]

Occurrences of the sort described above have not
been rare in American history, and the Kent State University incident of 1971, when demonstrating college
students were fired upon by National Guardsmen, is
enough to remind us that such occurrences have not always been related to labor-management conflict. But to
conclude that those who have come up against the forces
of the law in such circumstances have been unfairly vic-
timized by those forces is to overlook the two-sidedness
of any conflict. Continuing with the example of labor,
miners and other laborers have not always hesitated to
shed blood in an effort to achieve their goals. During
the decade following the Civil War, Pennsylvania mine
owners and managers were terrorized by Irish miners belonging to the secret Molly Maguires.[114] In 1922 striking coal miners near Herrin, Illinois laid siege to a
mine occupied by strikebreakers and guarded by armed
company guards, and after the latter had surrendered
following a battle, at least 19 strikebreakers and
guards were massacred by the enraged miners, who had
promised them safe conduct out of the area.[115] And
Colorado experienced thirty years of strikes and vio-
lence--1884 to 1914-- generated by "economic, class,
and ethnic tensions."[116] In 1914 a battle between strikers and the militia resulted in the burning of the strik-
er's tent city and the deaths of women and children.
The striking miners responded to this event with a rebellion that lasted for ten days, covered 250 miles of
southern Colorado, and had to be put down by federal
soldiers.[117] In other words, as was the case with the
American Indian, those on the "other side" of labor and
other conflicts in the United States have, occasionally
at least, been able to give as much as they received,
and in doing so they have threatened the status quo.

However, those who have acquired power after once having been on the wrong side of the law have found that they have moved to the right side of the law. Once this shift had occurred, the law could be used to the advantage of those who had previously been powerless. Richard E. Rubenstein has observed that

> debtor-farmer uprisings are part of our national heritage; as late as the 1930's, debt-ridden farmers were obstructing mortgage foreclosures, burning crops, and buying foreclosed properties for pennies at "shotgun sales." Working men struggling to unionize were even more accustomed to using violence to gain their objectives; as a recent report states: "The United States has had the bloodiest and most violent labor history of any industrial nation in the world." Businessmen hired their own private armies or allied themselves with gangsters in order to defeat the union movement. The immigrants in urban areas fought each other and the police for control of the streets, participated in race riots, and engaged in a style of politics not meant for those with weak fists. They created organized crime in the United States and (as Daniel Bell has suggested) used criminal activity both as a way of exercising community control and as a road to economic advancement when other routes were closed. The same groups which began their rise to surburban respectability and middle-of-the-road politics in the 1930's and 1940's were the Molly Maguires, Wobblies, gangsters, and anarchists of an earlier age. But they did not hesitate, once power had been obtained, to employ official violence through control of local government and the police against emerging groups as violence-prone as they once had been.[118]

The last sentence of the preceding quotation serves to high-light another aspect of Manning's point concerning criminal law and its enforcement. If law "reflects the interest of shifting power groups," power shifts can result in groups finding themselves on the wrong side as well as the right side of the law. From the earliest

times in the United States, many "ordinary Americans"--
working men, farmers, immigrants, blacks, students,
etc.--have on occasion had good reason to view the law,
and its enforcers, as something from which they needed
to be protected rather than as something that provided
them with protection. All sides involved in labor,
ethnic, and other conflicts have attempted to use the
law to their own advantage, and to the extent that any
one side has succeeded, their opponents have viewed the
police and the National Guard as "oppressors" rather
than as "protectors." Some American private citizens,
behind the frontier as well as on it, became, on occasion, their own policemen. Other Americans, by virtue
of the fact that the law at the time was being made,
interpreted, and enforced by their opponents, became,
to the extent that they challenged the law, criminals.[119]
And the organizations that the latter have formed by way
of offering resistance--unions, the first and third if
not the second Ku Klux Klan, the Black Panthers, the Students for a Democratic Society, for example--have been
viewed with considerable suspicion by "law-abiding" citizens as well as by the enforcers of the law.

As can be seen from the above, threats to life,
limb, and property did not disappear from the American
scene with the passing of the frontier. The large cities,
the smaller industry-spawned mining and mill towns, and
the territories surrounding cities and towns have produced their share of threats to life, limb, and property.
Given the multiplicity of lifestyles and world views of
the various peoples who comprise the population of the
United States and the economic and political conditions
that these people have created and modified as they have
interacted, it is no small wonder that Americans have so
threatened each other. Much of that referred to as
"crime in the streets" can be tied directly into the
broader ethnic, racial, and class conflicts discussed
above, since those on the other side of these ethnic,
racial, and class boundaries are often defined as acceptable targets for aggression by members of any given
group. Street crime that cannot be so accounted for,
can to a great extent be tied directly into the lifestyles and world views subscribed to by the members of
various groups. Willingness to use one's fists or a weapon, for instance, may be linked to masculinity at the
lower socio-economic levels across a number of ethnic or
racial boundaries, but such willingness is likely to be
defined as troublesome by those higher up the socio-economic ladder.[120] Since the police who attempt to enforce

the law--and who in doing so create the crime statistics--are the agents of those at the higher social levels, those at the lower social levels by just "doing their own thing" are responsible for much of the crime on the streets.

Be that as it may, however, it is not surprising that many American city or town dwellers, present and past, have considered their streets to be unsafe. And given what has been said above, it is no wonder that many Americans have not been willing to trust the police to protect them. The police might be in the "enemy camp," and at best be unwilling to do much protecting. Blacks, since they have become more vociferous, have often complained that little law enforcement effort has been expended in their part of town unless a white person has been accosted. But even where the police have been efficient and have wanted to provide protection for everyone, or at least for members of a favored group, they have not been able to be present everywhere at once. And in communities where racial tension, for example, is building up, threats to life and limb may be, or at least appear to be, omnipresent. The black family that has dared to move into a white neighborhood where it is unwelcome and the white storekeeper in a section of town that has become predominantly lower-socio-economic-level black may both have good reason to fear for their safety. With respect to personal security, therefore, conditions in American cities, as experienced by many of their past or present inhabitants, have been little different from conditions on the frontier where people felt called upon to protect themselves and possessed the means of doing so.

Cities in other parts of the modern world have not been completely free of the conditions that have caused many American city dwellers to fear for their safety. As Europe modernized, social control through the criminal law increased, and the propertied used the police and militia units to cope with the "criminal behavior" and the rioting of the disgruntled "dangerous classes."[121] And it is interesting to note that while European demonstrators have often done much property damage, the troops and police trying to control demonstrators have done most of the blood letting.[122] Many Europeans at the lower socio-economic levels, therefore, have also had reason to believe that the law and its enforcers were more threatening than protecting. As might be expected from the previous discussion of law and order on the

frontier, the same has been true of Australia, and not
surprisingly, since attempts to maintain law and order
in industrializing England brought Australia into
existence as a penal colony. According to McGregor,

> the police force demonstrates the hostility
> which marks the relations between the or-
> dinary people and those in power over them.
> Relations between the police and the pub-
> lic are probably worse in Australia than
> anywhere else in the world. Some commen-
> tators have traced this back to convict
> days and the conflict between the author-
> ities and the people which has character-
> ized the Australian scene from the early
> days of the penal colonies--a conflict
> which broke out again in the abortive
> and bloody rebellion of miners at Eureka
> Stockade, the great maritime strikes at
> the end of the nineteenth century and la-
> ter the bitter clashes and hunger marches
> of the Depression. Today most sections
> of Australian society still regard the po-
> lice with suspicion and antagonism even
> if they do not regard them as enemies;
> among working people this attitude is par-
> ticularly strong, but it extends through
> quite unexpected social levels.[123]

In Europe, however, civil turmoil during the urban
industrial era has centered around clear-cut class conflict. This conflict was, for the most part, uncompli-
cated by ethnic factors which tended to pit those of the
same socio-economic level against one another on a daily
basis. Consider the revolutionary period from 1789 to
1848. Northern Ireland is an exception to the rule, but
there, as has been the case in parts of the United States,
the common man, whether Catholic or Protestant, has also
had reason to consider the streets unsafe.[124] The Flems
and Walloons of Belgium have no great liking for each
other, but aside from the capital city of Brussels, they
tend to live apart from one another in different sections
of the country.[125] In ethnically diverse Switzerland,
the major political units--cantons--tend to be ethnically
homogeneous, but, to the extent that they are not homogeneous, the communities within them are.[126] The same
holds true for Yugoslavia, which, for reasons cited in
Chapter III, is peripheral to the Old World areas being
considered in this study.[127] England proper has been

quite homogeneous until recently, though over the years it has absorbed Irish immigrants.[128] Since World War II, however, England has acquired a "colored" population of about 1 million, or 2 percent of the population, from the West Indies, India, and Pakistan.[129] Along with the infusion of the "colored" population, England has acquired some of the ethnic tensions that the United States has experienced.[130] The same has been true of France, which since World War II has acquired several hundred thousand Algerians from its ex-colony, a few hundred thousand "blacks" from other colonies, large numbers of Italians, and in addition smaller numbers of Spaniards, Belgians, Poles, Germans, and Swiss.[131] The ethnic diversity and immigration experienced by these two countries during the past thirty years, however, can hardly be compared to that which the United States has experienced since it came into existence. All of the European countries considered here have had Jewish minorities, but they have been small. Though discriminated against, since the Revolutionary period Jews had tended to blend in with their fellow countrymen well enough that the Nazis had to make them wear arm bands to make them recognizable. In Canada and Australia, as noted earlier, the ethnic mix has not been great, though again things have changed somewhat since World War II.

It should also be pointed out that the diverse peoples that immigrated to the United States came at a time when urbanization and industrialization were occurring, even in areas not far removed in time or space from the rawness of the frontier. In Europe, urbanization was well underway before industrialization began and the disruption of the established order associated with either, as great as it was, was not unduly complicated by ethnic diversity or immigration. In Canada and Australia, industrialization never reached the magnitude that it reached in the United States. And the industrialization that did occur in Canada and Australia, being controlled to a great extent from England, was not of the helter-skelter, get-rich-quick, every-man-for-himself type experienced in the United States. It was, therefore, less disruptive of the social order still taking shape in these areas.

SUMMARY

Though the New World might well be considered an extension of Europe, it is not simply Europe transplanted. And while all parts of the Americas and Australia that have been settled were at one time or another frontiers of the New World variety, we have seen that there has been a great deal of variation from one frontier to another. Even in those areas where the "wilderness" was "conquered" primarily by English speaking peoples, the frontier experience was different from place to place. For the most part, the land itself presented challenges to the Canadian and Australian frontiersmen that it did not present to Americans. The aborigines on the American frontier put up much stiffer resistance to the invasion of the whites than did those of Canada and Australia. And "law and order" on the American frontier was much more tenuous than was the case on the other two frontiers. Even between English-speaking nations, however, New World differences have not all been related to frontiers and the frontier experience. A glance at population figures and the gross national products for these three nations is enough to show that while all three have been transformed from "wilderness" to "modern" nations since their settlement by Europeans, much more transformation has occurred in the United States than has occurred in Canada and Australia. Therefore, it is hardly surprising, especially when the ethnic, "racial," and economic diversity of its population is considered, that "law and order" behind the frontier in the United States has been much more tenuous than it has been in Canada and Australia. The importance of the differences and similarities between these three nations will be seen in the next chapter, as firearms are placed into the New World social-historical context.

FOOTNOTES

1. Murray L. Wax, Indian Americans: Unity and Diversity (Englewood Cliffs, New Jersey: Prentice-Hall, Inc., 1971), p. 16.

2. See David D. Anderson, ed., Sunshine and Smoke: American Writers and the American Environment (Philadelphia, New York, Toronto: J.B. Lippincott Company, 1971), pp. 7-86.

3. See Chester L. Hunt and Lewis Walker, Ethnic Dynamics: Patterns of Intergroup Relations in Various Societies (Homewood, Illinois: The Dorsey Press, 1974), pp. 24-93, 298-327, 363-398.

4. Ray Allen Billington, "Frontiers" in The Comparative Approach to American History, ed. by C. Vann Woodward (New York and London: Basic Books, Inc., Publishers, 1968), p. 76.

5. Ibid., 77.

6. Ibid., 77-78.

7. Ibid., 79.

8. See Wax, 3-25 concerning ethnicity among the American Indians.

9. Richard A. Preston and Sydney F. Wise, Men in Arms (New York & Washington: Praeger Publishers, 1970), p. 165.

10. Ibid., 165-166; and Carl P. Russell, Guns on the Early Frontier: A History of Firearms from Colonial Times Through the Years of the Western Fur Trade (Berkeley and Los Angeles: University of California Press, 1962), p. 17.

11. Preston and Wise, 166.

12. Tamotsu Shibutani and Kian M. Kwan, Ethnic Stratification: A Comparative Approach (New York: The Macmillan Company and London: Collier-Macmillan Ltd., 1965), pp. 123-124.

13. Manning Clark, A Short History of Australia (New York and Scarborough, Ontario: A Mentor Book, New

American Library 1963), p. 73.

14. Russel Ward and John Robertson, ed., Such Was Life: Selected Documents in Australian Social History 1788-1850 (Sidney and London: Ure Smith, 1969), pp. 46-53.

15. Russell, 11-12.

16. Ibid., 12.

17. Ibid., 24.

18. Ibid., 17.

19. Ibid., 51. It is hardly surprising that the Iroquois sided with the British, since unlike the American colonist they were not altering the landscape and pushing the Indians off of their land. See Preston and Wise, 166.

20. Russell, 103-141.

21. Such claims are probably exaggerated, however. See John E. Parsons and John S. du Mont, Firearms in the Custer Battle (Harrisburg, Pennsylvania: The Stackpole Company, 1953), pp. 25-32.

22. Daniel J. Boorstin, The Americans: The Colonial Experience (Vintage Books New York: Random House, 1958), p. 348.

23. Ibid., 347.

24. Ibid., 354.

25. Joe B. Frantz, "The Frontier Tradition: An Invitation to Violence," in The History of Violence in America: A Report to the National Commission on the Causes and Prevention of Violence, ed. by Hugh David Graham and Ted Robert Gurr (New York, Toronto, London: Bantam Books, 1969), p. 151.

26. Boorstin, 355.

27. Ibid., 357-372.

28. Preston and Wise, 169. It might be noted that in Canada the French provided militiamen with muskets

and allowed them to keep their weapons in their own home. Preston and Wise, 168.

29. Marcus Cunliffe, Soldiers & Civilians: The Martial Spirit in America 1775-1865 (Boston and Toronto: Little, Brown and Company, 1968), p. 205.

30. Ibid., 205-208.

31. Ibid., 186-192.

32. Ibid., 217-218.

33. Ibid., 219-220.

34. Ibid., 223.

35. Ibid., 236.

36. Ibid., 230-235.

37. Ibid., 250.

38. Ibid., 131 & 134-135.

39. Ibid., 235-254.

40. Ibid., 236.

41. Boorstin, 347-350.

42. The militias of British Canada and Australia were more on the order of the European militias, or of the American militia behind the frontier. See Leslie E. Hannon, Canada at War (Toronto: McClelland and Stewart, 1968), pp. 14-15; and Robert Nelson, Frank Morgon, Peter Breen, Stuart Reid, and David Evans, A Pictorial History of Australians at War (London, Sydney, New York, Toronto: H. G. Paul Hamlin, 1970), pp. 29-31.

43. Richard Maxwell Brown, "The American Vigilante Tradition," in The History of Violence in America ed. by Graham and Gurr, 167.

44. Ibid.

45. Frantz, 128-129.

46. Sharp, 109.

47. Brown, 178. Also see Sharp, 109.

48. Ibid.

49. Ibid., 178-179.

50. Brown, 154. He also notes, pp. 204-208, that vigilantism cropped up again in the 1960's.

51. Ibid., 154, 218-226.

52. Ibid., 158.

53. Ibid., 188.

54. Ibid., 189 & 167-171.

55. Ibid., 171.

56. Ibid., 184-190.

57. Ibid., 185-190.

58. Ibid., 191.

59. Ibid., 190-191.

60. Sharp, 110.

61. Seymour Martin Lipset, "The 'Newness' of the New Nations," The Comparative Approach to American History, ed. Woodward, p. 70.

62. Sharp, 78-132.

63. Ibid., 110.

64. Lipset, 70.

65. Jock Marshall and Russell Drysdale, Journey Among Men (Hodder & Stoughton, 1962), p. 99.

66. Russel Ward, The Australian Legend (Melbourne, London, Wellington, New York: Oxford University Press, 1958), p. 15.

67. Ibid., 144-145; and H. C. Allen, Bush and Back-

woods: A Comparison of the Frontier in Australia and the United States (Sydney, London, Wellington, Melbourne: Angus & Robertson and Michigan State University Press, 1959), p. 104.

68. Ward, 144-145.

69. Ward, 145; and Allen, 104.

70. Ward, 144.

71. Craig McGregor, Profile of Australia (London: Hodder and Stoughton, 1966), pp. 81-85.

72. Allen, 103. Also see 104-105.

73. Ibid., 103-104.

74. Ward, 141.

75. Ibid., 136, 144; and Allen, 105.

76. Ward, 142-163.

77. Ibid., 142.

78. Ibid., 140.

79. Ibid. Also, for a discussion of the phenomenon of social banditry, see Eric Hobsbawm, Bandits (New York: Dell Publishing Co., Inc., 1969).

80. Ward, 140.

81. Brown, 154, 156, claims that vigilantism is a uniquely American phenomenon.

82. Population densitys, urban residence percentages, areas, and GNPs were taken from "Australia," "Canada," and "The United States," The New Encyclopaedia Britannica, Micropaedia, 15th ed., Vol I, p. 662; II, p. 496; X, 272, and hold for the early 1970's. Population sizes were taken from John Paxton, ed., The Statesman's Year Book 1980-1981 (New York: St. Martin's Press, 1980), pp. 96, 260, and 1367, and hold for 1978.

83. John Adams, according to Alistair Cooke, said "the colonial population divided up into one third that

took arms, one third that was either openly or
secretly loyal to the British, and one third that
didn't give a damn . . ." Alistair Cooke's America
(New York: Alfred A. Knoph, 1973), p. 109. The
Loyalist third did not have it easy after the war.
pp. 126-127.

84. See Hobsbaum on social banditry and Richard Maxwell
Brown, "Historical Patterns of Violence in America," The History of Violence in America, ed. Graham and Gurr, pp. 46-47.

85. Brown, 48-49.

86. Blake McKelvey, American Urbanization: A Comparative History, (Glenview, Illinois and Brighton,
England: Scott, Foresman and Company, 1973), p.
27.

87. Ibid., 33.

88. John Higham, "Immigration," in The Comparative Approach to American History, ed. by Woodward, p. 96.

89. Ibid., 97.

90. Ibid.

91. The very usefulness of the whole idea of race has
been questioned by many scientists, social and
otherwise, but other scientists and the man-on-the-
street take it for granted that rather clear-cut
races exist in some objective sense. For a short
but neat critique of the concept of race, see Ina
Corinne Brown, Understanding Race Relations (Englewood Cliffs, New Jersey: Prentice-Hall, Inc.,
1973), pp. 27-32.

92. Many Germans headed for the farming areas that had
been opened up behind the frontier with the express
purpose of establishing a new German nation in
North America, according to Nathan Glazer, "Ethnic
Groups in America: From National Culture to Ideology," in Minority Responses, ed. by Minako Kurokawa (New York: Random House, 1970), p. 76. Many
of these Germans settled in Texas, and during the
Civil War they supported the Union. Some of

the Texas feuds that occurred after the war seem
to have come about due to the conflicting loyalties
of the pro-Union German settlers and native Southerners. Brown, "Historical Patterns of Violence
in America," 49.

93. Higham, 96.

94. McKelvey, 72.

95. Ibid.

96. Robert K. Yin, ed., Race, Creed, Color, or National
Origin: A Reader on Racial and Ethnic Identities
in American Society (Itasca, Illinois: F. E. Peacock Publishers, Inc., 1973), pp. 126-127.

97. See Stearn, 114.

98. See Herman R. Lantz with the assistance of J. S.
McCrary, People of Coal Town (Carbondale, Illinois:
Southern Illinois University Press & London and
Amsterdam: Feffer & Simons, Inc., 1971), pp. 37-
87; John Higham, Strangers in the Land: Patterns
of American Nativism (New York: Atheneum, 1970),
pp. 26, 65-67; and Joseph Lopreato, Italian Americans (New York: Random House, Inc., 1970), pp.
110-113.

99. Lantz, 49-54; Higham, Strangers in the Land, 45-52;
and Roger Daniels and Harry H. L. Kitano, American
Racism: Explorations of the Nature of Prejudice
(Englewood Cliffs, New Jersey: Prentice-Hall, Inc.,
1970), pp. 35-45.

100. See Lopreato on Italian-Irish conflict, p. 111.

101. Paul Wilke, "As the Blacks Move In, The Ethnics
Move Out: Its not much fun to go home again," New
York Times Magazine, (January 24, 1971).

102. Brown, "Historical Patterns of Violence in America," 60.

103. Ibid., 53.

104. Cunliffe, 89-90. Emphasis mine.

105. Ibid., 89.

106. Ibid., 90.

107. Ibid., 93.

108. Ibid.

109. Ibid.

110. Peter K. Manning, "The Police: Mandate, Strategies, and Appearances," in Criminal Justice in America: A Critical Understanding, ed. by Richard Quinney (Boston: Little, Brown and Company, 1974), pp. 177-178. Emphasis mine. Also see Stuart L. Hills, Crime, Power and Morality: The Criminal Law Process in the United States (Scranton, London, Toronto: Chandler Publishing Company, 1971).

111. Brown, "Historical Patterns of Violence in America," 61.

112. Higham, Strangers in the Land, 89.

113. Ibid., 90.

114. Brown, "Historical Patterns of Violence in America," 74.

115. Paul Angle, Bloody Williamson: A Chapter in American Lawlessness (New York: Alfred A. Knopf, 1962), pp. 3-71.

116. Brown, "Historical Patterns of Violence in America," 74.

117. Ibid., 75.

118. Richard E. Rubenstein, "Rebels in Eden: The Structure of Mass Political Violence in America," in The New American Revolution, ed. by Roderick Aya and Norman Miller (New York: The Free Press and London: Collier-Macmillan Limited, 1971), p. 107. Emphasis mine.

119. See H. L. Nieburg, "Uses of Violence," in Civil Strife in America: A Historical Approach to the Study of Riots in America, ed. by Norman S. Cohen (Hinsdale, Illinois: The Dryden Press Inc., 1972), pp. 229-230.

120. For insight into the differences in world views that are likely to get those at the lower socio-economic levels into trouble with the law enforcement agencies supported by those at the higher levels, see Edward C. Banfield's controversial The Unheavenly City: The Nature and the Future of Our Urban Crisis (Boston & Toronto: Little, Brown and Company, 1968), pp. 159-184; and R. Lincoln Keiser, The Vice Lords: Warriors of the Streets (New York, Chicago, San Francisco, Atlanta, Dallas, Montreal, Toronto, London, Sydney: Holt, Rinehart and Winston, 1969), pp. 29-30, 49-52, 56-80. For insight into the uneven treatment of class, ethnic and racial "outsiders" by the legal system, see Charles E. Reasons and Jack L. Kaykendall, ed., Race, Crime and Justice (Pacific Palisades, California: Goodyear Publishing Company, Inc., 1972).

121. Charles Tilly, "Collective Violence in European Perspective," in The History of Violence in America, ed. by Graham and Gurr, pp. 4-45; and Allan Silver, "The Demand for Order in Civil Society: A Review of Some Themes in the History or Urban Crime, Police, and Riot," in Criminal Justice in America, ed. by Quinney, pp. 152-169.

122. Tilly, 42.

123. McGregor, 81-82.

124. Hunt and Walker, 31-41.

125. Ibid., 29-30.

126. Ibid., 42.

127. Ibid., 363-397.

128. Ibid., 301-302.

129. Ibid., 303.

130. Ibid., 314-317.

131. Ibid., 317-321.

CHAPTER VIII

THE GUN IN THE NEW WORLD

THE INTRODUCTION OF FIREARMS INTO THE NEW WORLD

By the time that Columbus "discovered" the Americas in 1492, hand-portable firearms had been known and used in Europe for some 150 years. Consequently, guns were included in the armament carried to the New World by European explorers from the very beginning of full-scale exploration. Firearms, however, were not the chief personal missile weapons of the early explorers and the soldiers who accompanied them. While the few hand-portable guns they carried, and their cannons, seem to have frightened the aboriginals, the most dependable portable missile weapons of the Europeans were the crossbow and the less common longbow.[1] Since the matchlock and even the wheellock and rifling all seem to have been invented and put to use by 1500, some rather sophisticated firearms had been developed in Europe by the time New World exploration got underway. However, though these guns existed at the time, it is not likely that they came to the Americas with the very first explorers, since the Spanish and Portuguese were not among the early leaders in firearms technology. The first portable firearms to reach the New World, therefore, may well have been "little advanced beyond the ancient hand-cannon stage," and these guns were less effective than the crossbow under New World conditions.[2]

By the early 16th century, however, Spain had used its New World gold to equip its army with matchlock muskets, and these muskets soon reached the Americas. Matchlocks were carried on expeditions into Mexico as early as 1519, and even the wheellock seems to have gotten there with Coronado as early as 1540.[3] France, having only begun to equip its army with firearms after Pavia in 1525, introduced the matchlock to the St. Lawrence region in the 1530's.[4] The first portable firearms that reached the Americas in numbers, therefore, came in the hands of the explorers and soldiers of the expeditions that the explorers headed. These guns were of the same type, smoothbore matchlock muskets, with which European armies were beginning to be equipped at the time. In other words, these guns were tools of war and they remained so for some time, though the Spanish, Portuguese, and French soldiers who carried them certainly must have occasionally used them as hunting tools.

Once colonization got underway in North America, however, civilians as well as soldiers came to the Americas in numbers, and the former as well as the latter found use for firearms. In fact, in the New World the very distinction between civilian and soldier became blurred almost beyond recognition for reasons discussed at length in the preceding chapter. If the various colonies were to be defended from attacks by Indians or rival Europeans, the colonists themselves, civilian or otherwise, had to do the defending. Even in the hands of civilians, therefore, firearms served as weapons of war. But if the colonists--English, French, or Dutch-- were to survive, they also had to provide themselves with food. It is not surprising, therefore, that hunting became a common means of supplementing diets in a land where wildlife, large as well as small, was plentiful and restrictions on hunting were impossible to enforce. In North America, therefore, civil and military uses of firearms dovetailed as they had not generally done in Europe.

The firearms that the early 17th century colonists brought with them from Europe were generally quite similar, if not identical to, those used by their national armies. The matchlocks the Dutch brought to their Hudson settlements in 1613 were legally established military standard.5 And the matchlock musket was carried by most of the English who established colonies at Jamestown (1607), Plymouth (1620), and Boston (1630).6 The English, however, also brought a few wheellocks and flintlocks and even crossbows and longbows to these colonies with them.7 The civilian use of firearms in the North American New World, therefore, goes back at least as far as the very early 17th century, but in terms of the weapons used and the context within which they were used, civil and military overlap considerably. Before elaborating on this point, however, a difference between firearms usages in North America and Australia should be noted.

Australia was discovered by Europeans during the early 17th century, but it was not colonized until 1788.8 By the time that Europeans settled in Australia, therefore, the flintlock was the most common ignition system used on firearms in the western world, and very reliable smoothbored or rifled long guns and pistols were being fabricated in various parts of Europe and European-in-

212

fluenced North America. The first Australian "colonists" did not have ready access to the firearms at the time, however, since they were convicts. Of course, the marines and the military and civil officers who accompanied the convicts had guns, but only the free civilians, whose numbers were relatively small well into the 19th century, could be allowed to possess weapons. When Irish convicts rebelled in 1804 and set out to conquer Sydney, they were armed primarily with sticks, staves, and hoes, though they did manage to acquire a few guns.[9] The widespread civilian use of firearms in the Australian New World, therefore, goes back only as far as the early 19th century, and given what has been said in the previous chapter with respect to the differences between frontiers, one would not expect civil and military gun usages to have overlapped much in Australia. This point will be elaborated upon further in the following sections.

SHOTGUNS

The buckskin-clad frontiersman and the "cowboy" mounted on his horse and wearing a broad-brimmed hat and a bandana tied around his neck are central figures of America's frontier heritage, and the weapons they carried, the longrifle of the frontiersman and the "six-shooter" of the cowboy, are symbolic of that heritage. But on the early frontiers, North American as well as Australian, the smoothbore longarm, rather than the rifle or handgun, was the primary military, defensive, and hunting tool. As noted several times previously, the rifle did not become an effective military weapon until the early 19th century. With the exception of a few special units, therefore, European armies in the New World as well as the Old World carried smoothbore muskets into the 19th century. But civilians also had reason to prefer the smoothbore over the rifled long gun, for the smoothbore could be used with shot as well as ball and to hunt small game as well as large. And particularly important in the New World, the smoothbore could be used as a tool of the hunt and as a tool of war. When used as a tool of war, the quick loading of the smoothbore was as important to the civilian part-time soldier as it was to the professional soldier. But while these practical reasons for the civilian preference for smoothbores existed, it is doubtful that many English, French, or Dutch colonists down to the early 18th century had ever seen a rifle. The rifle, after all, as noted in

213

Chapter VI, was developed in Central Europe and little attention was paid to it elsewhere. Thus, the Minutemen of 1775 as well as the Pilgrims of 1620 were armed with smoothbore muskets--the latter matchlock, the former flintlock.

As noted earlier, the smoothbores used by the early English, French, and Dutch colonists in North America were like those used by the military. But as civilian fowling pieces evolved from muskets in Europe, immigrants began to bring fowling pieces to the New World. The fowling piece, of course, was the forerunner of the modern shotgun, but it would be some time before most North Americans would be concerned with acquiring guns intended to be used almost exclusively with shot. In North America, the wealthy acquired these sporting weapons from Europe as they became available. Ordinary people, however, had even less use for specialized guns than did the poorer people of the Old World, since, as arms historian Warren Moore has noted, "the colonist usually had only one gun which he used for hunting, protection, and militia duty."[10] Since even the poorer colonists had access to large as well as small game, and since Indians and rival Europeans had access to the colonists, the colonists needed reliable all purpose guns capable of firing ball as well as shot.

And long after rifles became available, the shot-or ball-firing capability of the smoothbore musket was still appreciated by the Indians and many white hunters of French Canadian and Creole descent on the western frontier. As Russell has noted:

> The inaccuracy of the musket at long range was not a disadvantage to this /Indian/ buffalo hunter, for he commonly rode alongside his lumbering quarry and discharged his gun point-blank into the vitals of the beast. This practice, together with the prevailing mode of hand-to-hand combat in intertribal war tended to perpetuate the big bore and the heavy ball of the musket.[11]

From the beginnings of colonization well into the 19th century, therefore, musket and fowling piece were, for all practical purposes, one and the same to the ordinary North Americans, red as well as white, who had occasion to fight each other or to hunt for their food.

Even when guns designed primarily to fire shot wound up
on the frontier, they were often used to fire ball.
Some traders of the first half of the 19th century, according to Russell, "preferred sporting shotguns . . .
to the standard light trade musket or the heavier military musket."[12] And Russell quotes one Captain Levinge,
a sports hunter of the 1840's, as follows:

> One word as to the best sort of gun for
> Upper Canada. There is not the facility
> of carrying about several kinds of guns,
> and a smooth-bore "double gun" which will
> throw ball true at 60 yards,--and most
> guns will--is the best weapon for deer
> shooting, as most of the shots got in the
> woods are within that distance. It is,
> therefore, available for small game.[13]

Once the North American frontier had moved on and
the land behind it became ever more transformed, first
by agriculture and later by urbanization and industrialization, the shotgun in its purer form came into its
own in much the same way as it had in Europe. At first
the shotgun was the sporting gun of the wealthy who
mimicked the lifestyles of the European aristocracy and
upper class, and who could afford to own specialized
weapons the finer examples of which had to be obtained
from Europe until well into the 19th century.[14] By the
late 18th century, the fowling pieces produced in Europe
no longer had barrels six feet or more in length, and
the thickness of the barrel walls had been reduced to
the point where the related reduction in weight made
double-barreled guns practical. Of course, these thin-
walled barrels could be damaged if fired with ball, but,
on the one hand, such damage could be avoided if the
precautions recommended by Levinge were followed, and,
on the other hand, the sportsmen who acquired these guns
to use on wild fowl and other small game had no reason
to fire ball through them. Behind the frontier, hunting
became, from the middle socio-economic levels on up at
least, ever more a recreational rather than a practical
activity, and by the early 19th century shooting flying
finally began to catch on in North America.[15]

As was the case in Europe, competition shooting
with shot-firing weapons in North America seems to have
begun when hunters compared their bags after a day's
hunt, but by the early 19th century, formal competition
was beginning to evolve. In 1832 the Cincinnati Inde-

pendent Shooting Club was formed, and its members accumulated a certain number of points for each type of animal they took during a specified period. Each deer, bear, or swan was worth 50 points, each goose 25, pheasant 10, rabbit 2, quail 1, etc.[16] The person who accumulated the most points for the season was the champion hunter. Since ball was probably used on the deer and bear, such competition was obviously not restricted to shotguns. But by 1842 the club was trying trap shooting using live pigeons, and formal shotgun competition in North America was underway.[17]

As had been the case in Europe, live pigeons were eventually replaced by clay pigeons and the modern sports of trap and skeet shooting began to take shape in the New World. In fact, Americans seem to have played a leading role in developing clay pigeons and other inanimate aerial targets as well as the apparatuses that threw them.[18] While Europeans tended to use inanimate aerial targets for bird hunting practice, inanimate aerial target shooting became a sport unto itself in the United States.[19] Some 3400 clay bird shooting clubs with a combined total of 111,000 members were active by 1915 in the United States, and there were approximately 150,000 additional unregistered shooters.[20] Competitive shotgunners claim that the Grand American Trapshooting Tournament, held annually since 1900, is "America's oldest national sports championship."[21]

In order to avoid giving certain shooters an advantage in these early clay bird competitions, it became necessary to make a distinction between the professionals and the amateurs. Some of the best shooters were being supplied with guns and ammunition by various manufacturers of such products, and eventually some shooters were even hired to shoot for these companies all by way of promoting sales. In the 19th century, firearms in the Old World as well as the New World came to be mass produced in factories rather than hand-fabricated by gunsmiths in their small shops.[22] The arms industry in the United States had benefited tremendously from conditions on and behind the frontier, and even before the Civil War, various arms companies competed vigorously with each other for government contracts and the business of the frontiersman and the sportsman.[23] It should be noted that ties to England and conditions on their respective frontiers did not encourage either Canada or Australia to develop their own small arms industries. As recreational shooting became ever more popular in the United

216

States, arms manufacturers developed specialized sporting guns and ammunition and competed with each other in drawing attention to their respective products. One way of accomplishing this objective, was to get one's products into the hands of those shooters likely to win major shooting matches. Another marketing ploy was to hire expert shooters to travel around the country giving shooting exhibitions or competing in tournaments using the guns or ammunition produced by their sponsors.[24] Since these men and women who made their living shooting at targets, or at least had their hobby partly subsidized by an arms producer, had much more practice and experience than the other shooters, the amateurs could seldom compete on equal terms with the professionals.

Of all the competition shooters, clay-bird shooters seem to have been most affected by this head-on competition between the professionals and the amateurs. Eventually those clay-bird shooters who were subsidized to any extent came to be officially classified as professionals, and though they were still allowed to compete against the amateurs, the professionals were not eligible to win prizes.[25] Paradoxically, the amateurs shot for cash prizes. Professionals, however, could arrange matches for themselves where all contestants could win cash, and amateurs could compete in such matches against the professionals without endangering their amateur standing. Those amateurs who shot well enough might desire to become professional, since their shooting expenses would then be paid by their sponsors. However, as shall be seen, fewer amateurs than expected may have been interested in becoming professionals.

The expense associated with clay-bird competition was, and probably still is, of little concern to the majority of those interested in the sport. For social as well as economic reasons, competition shooting with the shotgun has not been for everybody in North America or Europe, if we are to believe shooting enthusiast and authority Bill R. Davidson. He has observed that "trap and skeet have evolved differently in the United States" from those competitive shooting sports involving arms other than the shotgun. Trap and skeet "are 'country-club' sports that draw more affluent people--economically in the same brackets as those who join the country clubs to play golf. Trap and skeet cost more to shoot, round for round, in most instances. There is more socializing attendant to trap and skeet."[26]

His reference to country clubs would seem to indicate that by "socializing" Davidson was referring to the type of activities that would be of interest to a society editor. Of course, this linkage between skeet and trap and the more socially prominent is consistent with the linkages that have been made several times previously between the socially prominent of Europe, as well as North America, shooting flying, and the evolution of the shotgun as a sporting weapon. When social class is considered, the distinction made between amateur and professional clay-bird shooters takes on added significance. After all, the western upper classes have traditionally been staunch supporters of amateurism, as Ned Polsky has pointed out in his sociological study of the game of pool:

> The point of the remark falsely attributed to Herbert Spencer, "To play a good game of billiards is the sign of a well-rounded education, but to play too good a game of billiards is the sign of a misspent youth," is precisely the point made in that locus classicus for the ideology of the "gentleman," Lord Chesterfield's letters to his son, when Chesterfield : warns his son against becoming too good a flute player: the upper class must uphold the distinction between the amateur and the professional, and the true gentleman takes care that he cannot possibly be mistaken for a professional or vice versa.27

This upper class support of amateurism in sports and games might well reflect survivals in a capitalistic socio-economic system of the traditional aristocratic disdain for money earning; to shoot for a living is hardly the same as to shoot for cash prizes. To shoot for a living is to become a hired performer whose skills can be appreciated, but who must be kept in place with respect to those in a position to do the hiring. To shoot for cash prizes is to engage in the sporting life appropriate for those at society's upper levels who are called upon to consume conspicuously.

From what has been said above, it can be seen that in North America as in Europe the unspecialized smoothbore that could fire ball as well as shot was used by ordinary men to put food on the table and, especially in

North America, to protect themselves, while the special-ized shot firing weapons that evolved from these smoothbores were originally used by those at the upper levels of society for recreational purposes. In North America as well as in Europe, however, the shotgun in its pure form eventually became the arm of the "common man," also. Though, according to Newton and Zimring, there were some four million more rifles than shotguns in civilian hands in the United States in the late 1960's, of those households who possessed any firearm at all, 33 percent possessed shotguns while only 29 percent possessed rifles and 20 percent possessed hand-guns.[28]

    In North America, at the same time that mass pro-duction techniques resulted in the production of large numbers of cheap firearms of all types, industrializa-tion--of which mass production was a component part--and the urbanization that accompanied industrialization were transforming rather large sections of the United States into shotgun country as far as hunting was concerned. In some areas of the East and Midwest where deer, bear, wolves, and even bison had once been common, only small animals such as rabbits, squirrels, foxes, and various land and water birds such as quail, ducks, and geese remained by the end of the 19th century. Not only the destruction of habitat, but market hunting had helped to wipe out certain species such as the bison of the prairies and western plains and the passenger pigeons of the East.[29] By the time that serious attempts were made to regulate the taking of game and the destruction of habitat, the deer populations of such midwestern states as Illinois had been reduced to nearly zero. In these areas where only small game remained, the shotgun became a principal weapon of hunters who were becoming ever less dependent on hunting as a primary source of food, though as shall be seen in the next section, small-caliber rifles also came to be used for squirrel and rabbit hunting. And even in densely settled areas where they have been reintroduced by conservationists, these animals often cannot be legally hunted with the high-powered rifles designed for such hunting. In Illinois, where conservation efforts have increased white-tail deer populations to the point where after 1957 they could be legally hunted again, and several other states, hunting deer with modern firearms is legally restricted to the shotgun whose range when firing single slugs or large buckshot is considerably less than that of a mod-ern deer rifle. As Davidson has explained it:

The maximum lethal range of the more
modern high-powered rifle calibers can
be 2.75 miles or even more than that in
a few instances. The maximum lethal
reach of the rifled slug fired from a
shotgun is under a mile--usually well under it. The maximum lethal reach of buckshot is less than 600 yards. The problem
is, the accurate range of the rifled slug
on big game is usually under 100 yards,
and for buckshot the accurate coverage
is about half that. Hunting with shotguns in built-up areas is thus an attempt
to compromise between efficiency and safety.[30]

Davidson goes on to say that the accurate range of the
high-powered rifle for hunting purposes is 400 to 500
yards.[31]

Since the perfection of cartridges and the breechloader, the smoothbore in Europe as well as in North
America has become increasingly specialized as a shot-
firing weapon, though cartridges loaded with a single
ball or slug have long been available for use with such
guns. But with shotguns being used for deer hunting in
some parts of the United States, smoothbores designed
primarily to fire single slugs, the modern equivalent of
the old smoothbore muskets, are now being produced.
Remington Arms, for example, produces a "shotgun" with
rifle type front and rear sights and a barrel "choked
for use with rifled slugs and buckshot." This "shotgun"
is called the "Deer Gun."[32] Such weapons as these would
not be adequate for bird or small game shooting, or for
trap or skeet.

Given what has been written above, therefore, the
findings of a 1968 Harris poll cited in Newton and Zimring and already referred to in part earlier in this
section, should not be surprising, though they should be
taken with a grain of salt.[33] Of those rural, town, sub-
urban, and large city households that possessed any
firearms at all, the type possessed expressed in percentages of households possessing them were:

	Rural	Town	Suburbs	Large Cities
Handguns	19	22	16	21
Rifles	42	29	25	21
Shotguns	53	36	26	18^{34}

Of those eastern, midwestern, southern, and western
households possessing any firearms at all, the types
possessed expressed in percentages of households possessing them were:

	East	Midwest	South	West
Handguns	15	20	18	29
Rifles	22	26	35	36
Shotguns	18	40	42	29
Percent of Households possessing any gun	33	51	59	49^{35}

To the extent that this poll reflects firearms possession in the United States reasonably well, therefore, the
shotgun is the most popular firearm of those who dwell
in rural areas--it has long been associated with the
farmer in the popular imagination--and it is by far the
most popular firearm in the Midwest and South.

It has been stated several times previously that
the unspecialized smoothbores of the 19th century and
earlier were used primarily by common folk to procure
food and, in North America, to protect themselves, while
the specialized smoothbores were used at the upper levels of society for recreational purposes. But even the
practical hunting activities of common folks had their
recreational aspects. As will be seen in the next section dealing with the rifle, it was once a common practice to compare bags after a day's hunt, and this practice has survived to this day as a part of the somewhat
practical hunts of even those individuals at the lower
socio-economic levels. Formal competitive shooting with
the shotgun in the United States, however, has not generally been the sport of the common man.

One form of shotgun competition that seems to be
reasonably popular with middle income folk in parts of
the country where the shotgun is particularly popular,
involves much less shooting skill than luck. In the

221

modern version of the turkey shoot, no turkey is actually shot at all. Shooters take their turns firing their shotguns at a stationary piece of cardboard with a spot marked on it that has been set up at a specified distance, a fresh target being provided each shooter for each shot. The shooter who places a BB nearest the spot with a single shot wins the match and takes home the turkey. Second place may win a ham, and so forth. Since shotguns spray BBs from their barrels, individual BBs cannot be placed accurately.. Therefore, the BB ending up nearest the spot is determined less by the shooter's marksmanship than by the choke of the gun, which determines the spread of the shot, and luck. Such shoots are generally sponsored by various organizations, such as the Junior Chamber of Commerce, to raise funds. The shooters are charged so much for each shot they fire in the competition.

Much of what has been said so far in this section concerning smoothbore and shotgun usage in the United States applies to Canada as well. But while large sections of the United States have been transformed by industrialization and urbanization into shotgun country where hunting is concerned, this has not been the case in Canada. Though two survey based estimates of Canadian gun ownership, one conducted in 1974 and the other in 1976, disagree considerably concerning the number of guns in civilian hands in that country, they agree that approximately 59 percent of those civilian guns are rifles while only about 34 percent are shotguns.[36]

Information concerning the types of firearms carried by the early European inhabitants of Australia is difficult to come by, in the United States at least, but even though the island continent was settled almost two hundred years after North America, it would seem safe to assume that smoothbore longarms predominated. The British military of the late 18th and early 19th centuries was still equipped with the smoothbore musket, though a special unit commanded by Major Patrick Ferguson had been at least partially equipped with a unique breechloading rifle of that officer's own invention during the American Revolution.[37] Since the free civilians who began to settle Australia in the early 19th century came from the British Isles, as did the convicts who preceded them, it is likely that they brought smoothbore muskets, fowling pieces, and specialized shotguns with them, for, as noted several times previously, the rifle was not a common weapon where they came from. Some evidence to this effect is provided by Russel Ward and John Robertson in their documented social history of Australia from 1788 to 1850. The writers of the period whom they cite make reference to immigrants coming out armed with muskets and pistols for protection against bushrangers, to bushrangers armed with double-barrelled guns (shotguns) and pistols, and to the shooting of pigeons, parrots, and other shotgun game near Sydney.[38]

The smoothbore longarm, musket or shotgun, therefore, served the Australian's purposes during the muzzleloading era as it served those of the Canadians and Americans who used it. Such guns were used against the Aboriginals who, unlike their North American counterparts, seldom used either gun or horse. Smoothbores were used to cope with bushrangers, and they were used by bushrangers. And smoothbores were certainly adequate for hunting purposes, given the wild life the early settlers found in Australia. Unlike North America, Australia at the beginning of European settlement had no "large game"--moose, elk, deer, bear, wolves, etc.--with the possible exception of the wild buffalo of the remote Northern Territory. The smoothbore firing shot was needed for hunting native birds, therefore, and with ball it could be used to hunt kangaroo. After settlement began, many animals including deer and wild boar were introduced into Australia, and with the advent of the repeating rifle this weapon was used to hunt these larger animals.[39]

As in North America, hunting in Australia has been free of the class restrictions common to the Old World; consequently it has been engaged in by people at all social levels. However, the picture that Edgar Waters paints of hunting in Australia leads one to suspect that it differs somewhat from the Canadian and American varieties.

> Hunting is much less important than fishing as a sport for a number of reasons: the relative lack of interesting game, the lack of hunting grounds near the main centers of population, and the stringent laws governing licenses for the possession of firearms. There is a good deal of rather casual shooting of small game by country dwellers /a very small percentage of the population as noted in the previous chapter7; duck shooting is undertaken in a

223

more planned and definitely organized fashion. A few, sufficiently wealthy and sufficiently adventurous in temperment, shoot buffalo or crocodiles in the Northern Territory. In many pastoral districts big Kangaroo shoots are sometimes organized, as much for utilitarian reasons--keeping down the number of animals which compete with sheep and cattle for grass--as for sport.[40]

If hunting is primarily engaged in by countryfolk in an Australia that is 85.5 percent urban, not many Australians could be expected to hunt if game is difficult to get to.

If we accept what Newton and Zimring have to say, Australian firearms regulations should have little effect on shotgun hunting since these regulations impose no restrictions on the ownership of shotguns.[41] As far as competition shooting with the shotgun is concerned, in Australia as elsewhere, cost alone would tend to limit such activity to the wealthy.

As can be seen from the preceding discussion, in "modern" parts of the New World as well as the Old World, where there is game to be hunted the shotgun is ubiquitous. And in the New World as well as the Old, few, if any, restrictions have been placed on shotgun ownership. But in the New World as opposed to the Old, the rifle is more numerous than the shotgun. Even in Australia, recent estimates claim that 64 percent of the guns in civilian hands there are rifles while only 32 percent are shotguns.[42]

RIFLES

Smoothbores came to North and South America and Australia in the hands of those Europeans currently credited with discovering these New Worlds and starting the great age of exploration and colonization, and in the hands of the civilian settlers who filled out these New World colonies. Where there were Europeans in the New World, there were smoothbored muskets and later the fowling pieces and shotguns that evolved from these muskets. This was not the case with the rifle, which evidently was not introduced into the New World until the early 18th century, and which took some time to be-

come popular in areas outside of those into which it had
been introduced. The rifle, as has been mentioned several times previously, was not an important weapon to
the English, French, Dutch, Spanish, and Portuguese who
had done the early exploring and colonizing; indeed, it
may hardly have been known to some of these peoples.
It was an important weapon to the Germans and Swiss;
however, these peoples were relatively late arrivals in
the New World. When the Germans and Swiss did arrive
in numbers at the beginning of the 18th century, most of
them settled in what is now Pennsylvania where they came
to be known as Pennsylvania Dutch. They brought with
them not only the rifles that they had used in Europe,
but also gunsmiths who knew how to make these rifles.
Most of these gunsmiths set up shop in what came to be
called, after 1729, Lancaster County.[43]

According to historian Roger Burlingame:

> The rifle moved out of Pennsylvania to
> the frontiers of New York and Virginia.
> By the time of the Revolution, it had got
> occasionally into the hands of the "Green
> Mountain Boys" of Vermont. It could be
> found almost anywhere in the Allegheny
> foothills. It was used in warfare against
> Louisburg. The English could have seen
> it there and experimented with it but the
> English were conservative.
> Yet all this time, it seems not to
> have reached the coast of the colonies.
> In any case, it was unknown in Massachu-
> setts where the war began.[44]

The rifle came from Europe first to what is now
the United States, therefore, not to Canada or Australia, and it became the preferred weapon of those who
were continually pushing off into the wilderness to
clear new land, not of the settled colonial farmer or
even, for the most part, of the fur traders. The rifle
that the American frontiersman eventually adopted, however, was considerably different from the European variety that the Germans and Swiss had brought with them.
The central European rifle, though much more accurate
than the smoothbore musket, was too cumbersome for frontier use and it had to be modified considerably before
it came to be popular with the American frontiersman.
To describe the shortcomings of the European rifle and
the modifications that transformed it into the legendary

Kentucky, or, more properly, Pennsylvania rifle, enables us to understand why the latter became so popular on the American frontier as long as that frontier remained in the eastern woodlands. Held has written that:

> A frontiersman who often trekked through the wilderness for weeks could hardly be expected to carry along a thirteen- to twenty-pound gun, a hammer /for driving the ball down the barrel7·, the enormous quantity of powder required for .65- to .75-calibre barrels, a false muzzle and a pouch of bullets so large that a month's supply--say 150--weighed between eight and twelve pounds; and if the supplies had to be carried not only for a month, but as was often the case, for half a year, the weight would have come to the utterly impossible total of sixty-five to ninety pounds. Wheellocks were of course by far too complicated for American conditions, where a broken part often had to be heated, fused and retempered in campfires and reforged on rocks and tree. stumps instead of anvils.[45]

Held goes on to point out that European hunters could return empty-handed to their warm homes. They did not have to worry about Indian attacks as they rested in preparation for the next day's hunt.

> In America, hit-or-miss spelled life or death, and frontiersmen could not rely on rifles whose slow, lumbering bullets and high-curving trajectories required careful estimating whether the target was 100, 150, 200, 250 or 300 yards distant, and setting the rear sight accordingly.
> What the Americans demanded of their gunsmiths seemed impossible: a rifle which would weigh no more than ten pounds, shoot such small bullets that a month's supply would weigh no more than three pounds at the most and preferably only one, with proportionately small quantities of powder, be easy to load, and which would shoot with such velocity and flat trajectories that one fixed rear sight would serve as well at fifty yards as at three hundred, the

necessary but slight difference in elevation being supplied by the shooter's experience.[46]

By the middle of the 18th century, such a rifle had taken shape--the muzzleloading, flintlock Pennsylvania or Kentucky long rifle of Daniel Boone and other legendary frontiersmen. In caliber it was sometimes under .40, seldom as large as .60.[47] Greased patches, which were carried in patch boxes inletted into the right side of the stock, made ramming the bullet down the rifled barrel less time-and energy-consuming, though the long-rifle could still not be loaded as quickly as the smoothbore musket. The Pennsylvania-Kentucky rifle was powerful enough to stop the deer, bear, and mountain lions of the eastern woodlands, and accurate enough to enable the skilled marksman to hit sitting birds and other small game such as squirrels. It was both powerful and accurate enough to enable the frontiersman to cope with his human enemies, red or white, but the rifle's slow loading kept it from being an effective tool of war when the orthodox military tactics of the 18th century were being used. This shortcoming was to be discovered during the American Revolution.

Though originating with the German-speaking settlers of Pennsylvania, the weapon that has come to be popularly known as the Kentucky rifle acquired its fame in the hands of those pioneers--mostly of Scotch-Irish stock--who pushed the frontier ever westward as they moved through the Cumberland Gap into Kentucky and Tennessee.[48] It was a weapon fashioned to enable its users to cope with the eastern woodland wilderness, but, as Held has written, it "would have been of as little use in Bavaria and Switzerland as the Bavarian and Swiss rifles had been in America."[49] The Kentucky would not stop the fierce European wild boar in its tracks, and the craggy Alpine terrain which made tracking difficult called for a rifle that would stop even the timid deer and antelope in their tracks. Neither was the Kentucky particularly suited to the American frontier, once that frontier moved out of the woodlands. Arms historian Charles E. Hanson, Jr. tells of the Kentucky's transformation and why it was transformed.

> The thing to remember here is that the rifle was developed as a useful tool for a restless and ambitious people. Like every subsequent product of our ever-growing

227

productive capacity, it was conceived and
produced to fill an unsatisfied and insistent public need.

The Old Kentucky rifle "fit the forest." Its long barrel gave the ample
sighting radius needed for small targets.
Its stock was slender and dropping for
stand-up shooting. The slender barrel
and small caliber were adapted to the
light load that a far-reaching foot traveler needed.

Change, though ever-present, is usually a slow process. As the tide of immigration and exploration poured over the
Appalachians the frontiersman's path
crossed more level prairies. He rode a
horse; he shot bison and elk. Gradually
new demands filtered back to the smiths
of Lancaster and were met with newer products. Calibers began to decrease for the
local trade and began to increase for the
man from the West. Barrels became heavier
and shorter. Sun-catching ornaments and
figured wood were less popular. The man
on the prairie wanted more of the purchase
price put into range and power and less of
it into thin patch boxes and curly wood
which couldn't survive a fall from a pitching mustang.[50]

In this fashion, the Kentucky rifle, itself the offspring
of the long, smoothbore English fowling piece and the
short German Jaeger rifle, evolved into the "Hawkin"
rifle of the western plains on the one hand and the
squirrel rifle of the south-eastern backwoods on the
other.

While these variations and modifications of the
Kentucky were effective weapons whose shooting qualities
can still be appreciated today, they still left something to be desired in the eyes of those who depended on
them for hunting or protection. They still had to be
loaded from the muzzle with powder and ball, and since
most were single-barreled, single-shots, their rate of
fire was rather low. The Indians whom the frontiersmen
faced were well aware of this slow rate of fire, and
whether the whites were equipped with muzzleloading rifles or smoothbores, a favorite tactic of the redmen was
to draw the fire of their opponents and then charge them

with lance and bow and arrow before they could reload.
Not only the Indian fighter, but the hunter often enough
needed a second or third quick shot that his rifle could
not deliver. If his first shot had just wounded a griz-
zly bear, the hunter was in trouble. Samuel Colt's revolving rifle, which came into use in the late 1830's,
did much to increase the rifleman's fire-power; consequently, though such guns had some glaring faults, they
became popular even with the "mountain men" of the far
reaches of the frontier. The shooter's hand and arm extended in front of the cylinder to support a revolving
rifle could be burned by hot gases escaping from the cylinder, or even shot if, as sometimes happened, two or
more chambers fired simultaneously.[51] But the revolving
rifle's fire power, which could be increased by carrying
extra loaded cylinders, made it attractive to frontiersmen in spite of the risks associated with its use.

The Colt, though a repeater, still had to have each
of the chambers of its cylinder loaded from the front
with powder and ball. But, as noted in Chapter IV,
cartridges and breechloading were being perfected in
Europe and the United States around the middle of the
19th century. By the early 1860's such cartridge-firing,
breechloading repeaters as the Spencer and the Henry
were being produced in the United States.[52] The latter
was the forerunner of the famous Winchester lever action, the first version of which was produced in 1866.
Quick firing lever-action rifles produced by Winchester,
Marlin, Colt, and other companies became very popular
with frontiersmen and other rural folk in areas where
the rifle was a practical hunting tool. But since these
repeaters were not generally chambered for the most
powerful cartridges available, buffalo hunters and others
preferred the heavy-hitting, long-range, single-shot
breechloaders produced by such companies as Sharps and
Remington.[53] The quickest firing of the manually operated repeaters developed in the latter part of the 19th
century was the slide-action, but, possibly because such
actions could be operated accidentally while the gun was
being carried in a saddle scabbard, they did not become
very popular with those who spent much time on horseback.[54] Nevertheless, slide-action rifles, and particularly shotguns, have become popular in the United
States.

As can be seen from the above, to trace the evolution of the rifle in what is now the United States is to
be put in touch with the everchanging frontier as it was

experienced by those who gradually pushed it westward
over a period of almost 300 years. It is to be put in
touch with a recurring pioneering experience that Canadians and Australians, as noted in the previous chapter,
did not share with Americans. Americans, but not Canadians or Australians, had been called upon to modify
their firearms as they gradually moved from woodlands
out on to treeless plains and then into rugged mountains, hunting everchanging varieties of game and fighting off aboriginals all the way. Neither Canada nor
Australia produced any major firearms innovations of the
sort described above. The American rifle of the Kentucky variety may well have reached Canada before the
end of the 18th century, but it does not seem to have
been used extensively there. With the opening of the
Canadian West, the breechloaders and repeaters that had
been perfected by then became popular on the western
frontier, but the modern rifles of this sort used in
Canada were developed and manufactured in the United
States and Europe. The Canadian Northwest Mounted Police, for instance, carried Winchester Model 1876 carbines until 1914.[55] Similarly, the rifles of the Australian frontier came from the United States and Europe.

With the introduction of the rifle on the American
frontier came a practical interest in precision marksmanship of a sort that was not encouraged by the ball-
loaded smoothbore musket. On the eastern frontier of
the late 18th century, marksmanship training began at
about age twelve when boys were given rifles and assigned port-holes for fort defense.[56] Since the rifle
made precision shooting possible and marksmanship was
so important to the American frontiersman, a man on the
frontier came to be judged by his shooting ability.
According to historian Thomas D. Clark, Henry Clay, who
was standing for the Kentucky legislature at the time,
was challenged by an old backwoodsman to prove his worth
by publicly demonstrating his shooting skill.

> "Young man you want to go to the legisla-
> ture, I see. Are you a good shot?" "The
> best in the country," replied Clay. "Then
> you shall go to the legislature. But
> first you must give us a specimen of your
> skill. We must see you shoot." Clay re-
> plied "I never shoot any rifle but my own."
> "No matter, here is Old Bess; she never
> fails in the hands of a marksman. She has
> sent death through a squirrel's head at one

230

hundred yards and daylight through many
a redskin twice that distance. If you
can shoot any gun you can shoot Old Bess."
"Well, put up your mark!" said the trembl-
ing Clay. He took aim and centered the
mark! "On a chance shot!" said a bystand-
er, but the good criminal lawyer Clay
stopped all muttering by using the dodge
that when they set a better mark he would
outshoot them.[57]

Given such a preoccupation with shooting, it would
be expected that shooting matches were a popular form
of recreation on the American frontier, and they were.[58]
Shooting matches involving ball-firing weapons date back
to the militia training days of the early colonies, and
these matches could be rather impressive social events.
As many as a thousand men took part in such training
days, and the winner of the shooting competition was
presented with several yards of red ribbon to be tied to
his hatband so that the ribbon would stream down his
back as he was led away in triumph to the applause of
the crowd.[59] While sheer numbers and the ceremony involved may well have made such matches more impressive
to the spectator than were the typical frontier shooting
matches, the marksmanship displayed in the former could
hardly compare with that of the latter. The colonial
militiamen used smoothbore muskets, and first prize was
awarded to the person coming closest to what surely must
have been a rather large mark. Such standards would not
have impressed a self-respecting rifleman. The following
description of a popular variety of shooting match along
the woodland frontier is cited by Robert B. Weaver in
his history of American amusements and sports:

Several individuals who think themselves
gifted in the management of the rifle, are
often seen to meet for the purpose of displaying their skill; and, after betting a
trifling sum, put up a target, in the center of which, a common sized nail is hammered about two-thirds of its length. The
marksmen decide what they consider a proper
distance, which usually is about forty
paces. . . . A shot which comes very close
to the nail is considered that of an in-
different marksman; the bending of the nail
is of course somewhat better; but nothing
less than hitting it right on the head is

231

satisfactory. One out of three shots
generally hits the nail; and should the
shooters amount to half-a-dozen, two
nails are frequently needed before each
can have a shot. Those who drive the nail
have a further trial among themselves, and
the two best shots out of these generally
settled the affair. The sportsmen then
adjourn to some house,, and spend an hour
or two in friendly intercourse, deciding
before they part, upon a day for another
trial. This is technically termed,
"driving the nail."[60]

In a similar history, Foster Rhea Dulles states
that in a variation of this sort of match entrants shot
for barrels of whiskey or a beef at twenty-five cents
a shot.[61] This sort of match was the forerunner of the
shotgun "turkey shoots" described in the previous section, but it required far more shooting skill than its
modern version does. Turkeys were actually used as targets at one time in some areas, with the birds being
"placed at one hundred and ten yards, if a common musket
be used, but one hundred and sixty-five if the weapon
is a rifle."[62] Frontiersmen also sometimes engaged in
more hazardous shooting matches when they tried to shoot
a tin cup off of a man's head at some thirty paces.[63]

Marksmanship, however, was displayed in other than
formal matches. It was also displayed on the hunt, as
the practice of "barking off squirrels" indicates.
"Really good shots did not puncture the hides of squirrels; they 'barked' them by shooting into the tree just
under the squirrel's bellies, stunning them by the impact."[64] Even when such feats of marksmanship were accomplished by solitary hunters, the unpunctured hides
they brought back with them attested to their skill.
But squirrel hunting was often anything but a solitary
affair. Squirrel and other kinds of hunting in the more
settled areas on and behind the frontier often took on
a communal flavor. In his history of the midwestern and
southern frontiers, Clark writes that squirrel hunts were
often announced in early newspapers such as the Kentucky
Gazette.[65] Those who gathered for these hunts often divided into several parties, the party producing the most
"tails and scalps" at the end of the day being declared
the winner and awarded a beef or some other prize. The
newspaper that had announced the hunt then announced the
results, one such hunt resulting in a bag of 7,941.[66]

Though some of these squirrels were probably eaten by the hunters and their families and friends, the numbers taken would seem to indicate that such hunts were more recreational than practical. Their social aspects are certainly obvious.

Whether most riflemen on the woodland frontier could drive nails or bark squirrels, or whether even the best marksmen could do either reasonably consistantly, cannot be determined at this time. Those who wrote of such feats were generally travelers from the more "civilized" East or Europe, who not having been previously exposed to the rifle's inherent accuracy could be expected to be impressed easily and to exaggerate somewhat in relating what they had seen. Modern historians, in many cases knowing little of firearms and marksmanship themselves, have tended to pass these accounts on to us unquestioningly. But even making allowances for such exaggerations, passable marksmanship with the rifle must have been quite impressive to those who had known only the musket, and America came to be known as a nation of riflemen. This image, which Washington attempted to foster during the American Revolution, may have caused the British more trouble than the rifle itself. On several occasions, Washington arranged rifle shooting exhibitions to impress British spies and thereby indirectly demoralize British troops.[67]

Attempting to take advantage of the British respect for the frontiersman's weapon and his skill in its use, "early in the Revolution," according to Boorstin,

> General George Washington issued an order in which he "earnestly" encouraged "the use of Hunting Shirts, with long Breeches made of the same Cloth. . . . it is a dress justly supposed to carry no small terror to the enemy, who think every such person a complete marksman."[68]

Yet the rifle, as noted several times previously, had its shortcomings as a military weapon as long as it remained a muzzleloader. These shortcomings were soon discovered during the Revolution; consequently, the rifle was not the primary weapon of the revolutionary forces. Arms historian Warren Moore writes that:

> A study of the battles indicates that all

233

but a few engagements were fought in the
accepted European fashion, with the men
standing in close ranks and firing vol-
leys. In the early part of the war several American companies were formed en-
tirely of riflemen. These outfits enjoyed initial success because of their
marksmanship, but this ended abruptly
when the British began charging them with
bayonets fixed. The riflemen were equipped with a belt ax to compensate for the
lack of a bayonet, but a belt ax was no
match for a bayonet affixed to the end
of a musket, and the Americans were
forced to scatter in hasty retreat. The
American commanders realized the weak-
ness of the rifle when used in this manner, and in subsequent encounters the
rifleman served as a flanker, or sharp-
shooter, in order to take as heavy a toll
as possible of the advancing British
troops before withdrawing. The supporting musket troops then fired a volley at
the enemy before joining in bayonet
fighting. The rifle used with the support of muskets was a very deadly and formidable weapon and, although it lacked
the bayonet and was slow to load it made
possible many American military victor-
ies.[69]

Though not the primary portable firearm of the Revolution, therefore, the rifle still seems to have been the
most impressive and, to those who faced it, frightening
firearm of the time. And the exploits of those who used
the rifle then, and later during the war of 1812,
helped to focus the new nation's attentions as well as
those of Europe on the sharp-shooting American frontiersman. Rifle shooting during Canada's and Australia's formative years received no such spectacular
boosts.

While it is not likely that the majority of American males at any given time have been riflemen, most
males, and females as well, may have been passably familiar with firearms of one kind or another during the
early days of settlement. As the frontier moved westward and the settlements behind it grew into large
cities, however, the number of civilians familiar with

firearms could be expected to grow proportionately smaller. Even in areas where practically all of the white males had at one time been riflemen, an ever smaller proportion of the population was familiar with such weapons as deer and bear populations dwindled and more people lived in cities where they were less likely to develop an interest in hunting. And the non-shooting populations of the cities were increased toward the middle of the 19th century by large-scale immigration from Ireland. While many of the immigrants may have poached in Ireland, and some of them may have even used shotguns to do so, the Irish as a people were not familiar with rifles, and those who settled in American cities, as most did, had little opportunity to maintain any taste for hunting that they may have acquired in the old country. And the preceding holds true for the majority of the Italians, Poles, and other southern and eastern Europeans who came to the United States in large numbers later in the century.

But while the proportion of American civilians interested in rifle shooting decreased considerably as the United States became ever more urban and absorbed millions of immigrants from parts of the world where civilians had seldom seen rifles, rifles and rifle shooting remained popular over much of the country even in areas where large game populations had dwindled or disappeared. As can be seen from the above, there were important social aspects to hunting and target shooting even when rifles had functioned practically in the lives of those who possessed them. And there was little reason for these functions to disappear as the Indian threat faded and hunting for food became less necessary, particularly since such changes came about so gradually. Indeed, since practical hunting had its recreational side, there is no discernible point in time at which hunting in any given area shifted from the practical to the recreational. Though other food sources were tapped, that which was taken in the field or forest still supplemented diets. Deer may have become scarce, but there were still squirrels in abundance and the Kentucky rifle was used to hunt the smaller animal as well as the larger. When the breechloader and cartridges made the Kentucky and its variations obsolete, and the absence of large game in some areas made large-caliber rifles impractical for hunting the game that was left, the perfection of the .22 rimfire cartridge during the second half of the 19th century resulted in the development of small, relatively low-powered rifles that could be used for hunting small game such as squirrels.

The low-powered .22 rifle has become extremely popular in the United States, and it has enabled rifle shooting to survive in parts of the United States that intensive farming, urbanization, and industrialization have otherwise transformed into shotgun country. According to the Harris poll cited in the previous section, more American households possess shotguns than possess rifles, but according to other polls cited by Newton and Zimring, there are some four million more rifles than there are shotguns in civilian hands in the United States. And according to a manufacturer's survey conducted in 1963 also cited by Newton and Zimring—a survey which shows more households possessing rifles than possess shotguns—the number of households possessing rifles categorized as low-power (.22?) is about twice the number of those possessing "high-power" rifles.[70] This latter survey also indicates that "low-power" rifles are particularly popular in the Midwest and South, where the shotgun is the most commonly owned weapon, as well as in the West, where the rifle is the weapon most commonly found in civilian hands.[71] These are the areas where rifle marksmanship seems to have been particularly appreciated along the moving frontier during the late 18th century and all through the 19th. The low-power rifles, according to the manufacturer's survey, are far less popular in the Northeast than they are in other areas of the United States, and they are less popular in urban areas than they are in rural and small-town areas.[72]

The popularity of the .22 rifle in the United States is undoubtedly due in part to the cheapness of its ammunition relative to that used in shotguns. But given what has been said above, the .22 rifle's popularity may also be due in part to a widespread appreciation in rural and small-town areas for precision shooting of a sort that the shotgun, as practical a hunting weapon as it is, can not deliver. After all, with rifle hunting and target shooting still carried on after the frontier was long gone, there was no reason for community appreciation for such shooting to fade in areas where the older European stock had not been inundated by newcomers unfamiliar with the rifle. Even where the older stock was so inundated, pockets of appreciation for precision shooting skills could still be expected to exist. In areas where men once acquired cherished reputations as skilled marksmen by barking squirrels or driving nails, spraying small

game with shot, though effective and appreciated in its
own way, might be less than satisfactory to many individuals. Many small game hunters, however, use both
the small-caliber rifle and the shotgun, depending on
the game they are hunting and existing conditions. Some
use combination guns having one shotgun and one .22 rifle barrel, the former for fast moving game at close
range, the latter for sitting game farther away.

But rifle shooting behind the American frontier has
not all been connected with hunting. Interest in target
shooting, though fostered by conditions experienced by
frontiersmen, did not need these conditions to survive.
As with target shooting on the frontier, however, much
if not most of the target shooting behind the frontier,
past as well as present, was probably of an informal,
impromptu variety that at its informal extreme is commonly known as "plinking." Such casual shooting at bottles and tincans, etc., is done all across the United
States in rural and small-town areas, probably encouraged in part by the cheapness of .22 caliber ammunition.
However, anyone who has done well at "plinking" by the
standards of his audience, even if that audience is only
himself, knows the social side of that pastime. If several shooters are involved, a sort of impromptu competition may develop and the person taking the least number of shots to hit a distant rock, or the one having
the fewest misses out of a specified number of shots at
a tincan, is likely to be acknowledged as the best shot
and receive the praise of his friends.

As the rifles used for modern day "plinking" are generally light .22 sporters of the sort also used for
small game and pest hunting, so the rifles used in the
more or less formal shooting matches on the frontier
were generally hunting rifles. Until about 1840, few,
if any, specialized target rifles existed in the United
States.73 But by that date, transitional rifles--hunt-
ing rifles with target refinements--as well as heavy-bar-
reled target rifles with special target sights had made
their appearances. Some of the latter had such heavy
barrels that they were fired from a bench rest. With
such rifles, gunmakers sought to achieve the maximum
amount of accuracy possible, and the matches in which
they were used were as much, if not more, a test of the
riflemakers' skills as they were a test of the shooters'
skills. Bench-rest shooting still has its devotees today, though they constitute a very small minority of
modern shooters. The best of the modern bench-rest ri-

fles and shooters can fire ten shot groups at 1000 yards that measure under seven inches between the centers of the most widely separated holes.[74]

While conditions on the frontier, social and otherwise, seem to have encouraged an appreciation for marksmanship that took root socially and survived the passing of the frontier, other factors seem to have contributed to the growth and maintenance of this appreciation and to the development of the recreational forms related to it. Though immigrants such as the Irish brought little or no interest in rifle shooting with them from the old country, other immigrants such as the Germans and Swiss, as might be expected from what has been said in Chapter VI, did bring such interests with them. Toward the middle of the 19th century, German and Swiss immigrants to the Middle West introduced the schuetzen match, "a stylized form of shooting with customized small-caliber rifles /not .22/, equipped with pronged butt plates, hand rests, elaborate sights, and heavy barrels," to the United States.[75] "Shooting was usually from the standing position at targets, out to 200 yards."[76] Though the standard target was of the concentric ring variety, more elaborate targets, some with explosive centers to be fired at last, were sometimes used.

According to the National Rifle Association, the schuetzen match was one of the oldest forms of organized

> shooting in the United States. . . . By 1890 schuetzen clubs, or schuetzenbunds, were found in almost every American community where there were more than a few citizens of Teutonic ancestry. The North American Schuetzen Bund, the oldest shooting organization in America, was organized in 1865 and conducted an annual national schuetzenfest, attended by shooters from all over America. The schuetzenfest combined a massive Bavarian-style picnic with the more serious business of punching holes in targets. The winner of the national match was crowned koenig, or king, to toasts drunk in gallons of foaming beer. Although dominated by German shooters, the national and local schuetzenbunds rarely restricted their membership to shooters of Teutonic ancestry.[77]

These German immigrants, many of whom left Germany to avoid military service, not only shot targets, but once they had reached the United States they organized volunteer military companies of the sort described in Chapter VII. The activities of these companies and of the schuetzenfests often overlapped, as might be expected, and the rifle makers of such midwestern cities as Cincinnati and Milwaukee were encouraged to fashion rifles that could be used for both military duty and target shooting. These rifles were equipped with bayonet lugs as well as with target refinements.[78]

The German volunteer companies may have been among the very few such companies during the Civil War whose members could handle rifles reasonably well.[79] During the Civil War, the rifle, for the most part still muzzleloading but occasionally breechloading and cartridge firing, came into its own as a military weapon, but few soldiers had been trained to handle it.[80] The volunteer companies had practiced at targets with their smoothbore muskets, but for the most part they had concentrated on crowd-pleasing close-order drills. Even the high command of the regular army was not convinced that the ordinary soldier should be armed with a rifle and taught to shoot accurately.[81] After the war ended, the National Guard that was replacing the old militia soon reverted to the habits of the old volunteers and devoted practically all of its time and effort to drill, much to the consternation of a few of its officers who had seen service in the Civil War. The concern of these men for marksmanship resulted in the formation of the National Rifle Association of America in 1871.

By the third quarter of the 19th century, military men of the more technologically advanced parts of the world were becoming ever more impressed with the rifle as a military arm, and had set out to train soldiers and militiamen in its use. In 1859 the British founded their National Rifle Association to train their volunteer force to shoot in case Napoleon III attempted to cross the channel. By 1870 the British marksmanship program had produced in a nation with "no tradition for skill with the rifle" several thousand shooters who could hit a three foot square target regularly at 1,000 yards.[82] By that date "the United States was one of the few, and certainly the largest of the English-speaking nations, where soldiers and militiamen were not being trained formally in marksmanship."[83] The American NRA set out to rectify this state of affairs, but it had hardly gotten its program underway when the Irish team that had won the rifle championship of the British Isles challenged any team of Americans to meet them.

As many excellent marksmen as there were in the United States, few if any of them ever fired at 1,000 yards; they were practical shooters--hunters and Indian fighters. Their rifles were not capable of accurate shooting at such a distance. But by the time that the match took place in 1874, the Americans had had time to select a team and develop long-range rifles and they were actually able to beat the Irish by three points, 934 to 931.[84] This international match received a great deal of publicity in the newspapers of the day, and being held in New York, it drew a crowd of around 8,000 ranging from New York society to Irish immigrants.[85] An even larger crowd--more than 30,000--attended the return match held in Ireland near Dublin in 1875.[86] The Americans won again, 968 to 929, and received a gala reception when they returned home, along with front page coverage by the New York newspapers.[87] Other international matches were held in later years with the United States winning some, losing others, but public interest in such matches eventually faded.[88]

Meanwhile the NRA, which had coordinated the American side of these matches, was expanding its shooting program and, with some difficulty, becoming truly national in scope. In its early years, the NRA had been essentially a New York organization. Eventually it became less National Guard-oriented and more an organization catering to the varied shooting interests of its largely civilian membership. NRA members have been able to buy surplus American military rifles and pistols at very reasonable prices from the government through the Director of Civilian Marksmanship, and NRA affiliated target shooting clubs have been able to borrow such government owned rifles and pistols as are appropriate for their use.[89] Such clubs--some of which have been organized by ordinary citizens sharing an interest in target shooting with either rifle or pistol, others of which are sponsored by industrial organizations, high schools, colleges, universities, or Reserve Officers Training Corps (ROTC) programs--have also received aging government ammunition free of charge by way of promoting civilian marksmanship training. With the clamor over gun control in recent years and the NRA's opposition to such controls, membership benefits of this sort have been criticized, and in some cases they have been cur-

240

tailed.[90] As with formal shotgun shooting, an effort
has been made to deprofessionalize rifle shooting.
Since 1917, even cash prizes have not been awarded in
NRA-sanctioned matches if for no other reason than to
keep the top shooters eligible for Olympic competition.[91] As with serious shotgun competition, serious
rifle shooting, particularly with high-powered rifles,
is quite expensive, but the relative cheapness of .22
caliber ammunition and of the less sophisticated target
rifles of that caliber put smallbore target shooting
within the economic reach of the man on the street.[92]

       Before moving on to the handgun, it should be noted
that though local and state laws vary considerably
across the country, to this date rifles can be possessed
legally with little difficulty over much of the United
States. The same is true for Canada, even since that
nations new gun laws went into effect in 1978, but the
state of rifle regulation in Australia could not be determined from the information available to the author.[93]
As noted at the end of the previous section, however,
the rifle seems to be the most common gun in civilian
hands in Australia.

HANDGUNS

       Pistols probably got to the American New World
shortly after they were invented in the early 16th century. The wheellocks that were carried to America by
some of Coronado's party in 1540 may have been pistols.[94] And some of the early 17th century colonists of
English and French North America surely brought pistols
with them. But for one hundred and fifty to two hundred
years or more after colonization began, the pistol does
not seem to have been a very important weapon in the
North American New World, and understandably so. The
colonists needed guns for hunting and for protecting
themselves against Indians and rival Europeans; therefore, the musket was likely to be seen as the most
practical weapon by men who were not able to afford more
than one gun. While the pistol had become an effective
military weapon in the hands of the European cavalry of
that day, the colonists were not cavalrymen, and even
if they had been, cavalry tactics were useless against
Indians in the wooded East. And while game could be
hunted successfully even with the pistols of that day,
or with the better ones at least, the ordinary hunter
would hardly have possessed the stalking and marksman-

ship skills to put food on the table regularly with such a weapon.

In the early days of colonization, therefore, the pistol was a secondary arm for those civilians who could afford one. Once larger communities developed behind the frontier and conditions akin to those that existed in the larger European towns and the countryside between them developed in the United States, the more prosperous Americans who lived in such places acquired pistols for the same sorts of reasons as did their European counterparts--to protect themselves in town or while traveling between towns from those who would relieve them of their property. Since little seems to have been written concerning pistol usage in either English or French colonial America, however, the preceding conclusions must be surmised from the types of pistols that have come down to us from the colonial period. These pistols are of the same type as those used in Europe of that time-- horse pistols, traveling pistols, pocket pistols--and, with the exception of the Kentucky pistol to be discussed later, they show little tampering by way of adapting them to any unique New World conditions. In fact, most colonial pistols seem to have been made in Europe.[95]

After the American Revolution brought the colonial period to an end in what is now the United States, a particular form of pistol usage common in Europe of that period began to spread across the new nation. The formal duel was brought to America by caste-conscious British, French, and German officers who carried the "chivalric traditions" of honor-vindicating private warfare with them when they came "to fight a public war."[96] Once introduced in the United States, dueling flourished during the period between the Revolutionary and Civil Wars.[97] With the exception of those remarks that obviously apply only to the United States, the following comments by Boorstin concerning dueling as it took root in the Old South also applied to dueling in Europe:

> The duel . . . was a ritual in which a gentleman submitted himself to the community's good opinion, or rather to the opinion of his equals, which was commonly called the "Code of Honor. . . ."
> It /honor/ was a name for the apparent paradox that, while Southern gentlemen

242

in the three decades before the Civil War
boasted of their high-minded indifferences
to "public opinion" or the good opinion of
the whole world, they respected nothing
more than their local reputation, or the
good opinion of their fellow Southern gentleman. "To those whose god is honor,
disgrace alone is a sin." They explained
that while the slave of public opinion took
his orders from the public press and from
the clamorous voice of his mobbish infer-
iors, the gentleman of honor obeyed the
unspoken expectations of his equals. The
rules of the Code of Honor, too, being
habitual, could not really be taught or
learned, much less comprehended in the
pages of a book: they had to be inherited,
or absorbed from the atmosphere. Such a
law was as different as possible from the
increasingly technical and professional
and written law developing in New England.
It also expressed a spirit different from
that in the transient or upstart communities, where the priority rule of the claims
clubs was made by and for recent arrivals,
or where mining camp vigilantes tried cases
in the presence of the whole assembled com-
munity.98

Dueling, incidentally, was against the law all through
the South at the time that it was widely practiced by
gentlemen.99 As mentioned earlier, this was also the
case in Europe.

It will be recalled from Chapter VI, that the pistol was becoming the favored dueling weapon in Europe
toward the end of the 18th century. It was also a popular dueling weapon in the United States, though preferences seem to have varied from one part of the country to another with the pistol being the usual weapon
in Kentucky and the sword usual in French influenced
Louisiana.100 As in Europe, the pistols used in formal
duels on this side of the Atlantic were generally of the
sort that had been especially developed with such usage
in mind, as has been described previously. "Most of
these were made in England and France, but native American firms such as the Deringer company in Philadelphia
began to specialize in them."101

What has been said so far concerning pistol usage in the New World most probably applies to Canada down to the early 19th century and to Australia of the late 18th and early 19th centuries, as well as to the British colonies that became the United States. As noted in the earlier section on shotguns, wealthy Australian travelers, in the best English tradition, carried pistols to ward off bushrangers. And pistol dueling seems to have been in vogue with Australian gentlemen at about the same time that it was popular with gentlemen in the American South, though it is probable that fewer duels were fought in Australia.[102] In the early days of settlement in the New World, therefore, pistol usage differed little from that of the Old World. Once the New World nations, particularly the United States, started to push back their frontiers, however, civilians on the frontier found the pistol useful in ways other than those already mentioned.

Down well into the 19th century, the pathfinders, trappers, traders, and pioneers who pushed back the American frontier depended on their long guns, whether rifles or muskets, to provide them with food and protect them from their animal as well as human enemies. The long gun was their primary weapon, therefore, but as long as it remained muzzleloading it could deliver only one shot, or two if double-barreled, before time-consuming reloading was necessary. Since the man in the wilderness could not always depend on the presence of friendly others, or enough friendly others, to make up for his deficiencies with respect to rate of fire, a second or third backup gun, even a small one, could prove useful in certain circumstances. He needed as many advantages as he could come by, since the American Indian tended to be less than gentle with his captives, and the wounded bear would likely be less than forgiving. Men who roamed far from settled areas sometimes carried pistols as backup weapons, therefore, though these pistols have received less attention than the rifle from those--moviemakers as well as historians--who have attempted to recreate the early frontier for us.[103] The practice of carrying pistols may have become even more prevalent once the frontier reached the prairies and the frontiersman became a horseman, since the weight the pistol added to his load could more easily be managed by a horseman than by a foot traveler. Since the pistol was often carried on the person, it not only served as an emergency arm when the long gun was empty, but as "attached protection" when the more cumbersome long gun had been set aside.[104]

The pistols that the early frontiersmen carried were, of course, muzzleloading single-shots, or double-barreled varieties of European pattern, though some English pistols having barrels that were unscrewed to allow breechloading undoubtedly reached the frontier. Even dueling pistols, once they became available in the United States, were carried by some frontiersmen, including the far-ranging mountain men of the Rockies.[105] A popular pistol with frontiersmen originated in Pennsylvania in the second half of the 18th century--the Kentucky pistol. These generally smoothbored, rifle-caliber pistols were made by riflesmiths as supplemental, close-range, defensive weapons for riflemen. Though Kentucky pistols were made in various sizes, the smaller sizes were probably most popular with frontier hunters, since bulk and weight were important to those horseless souls who "prepared for every eventuality, traveled about loaded down with personal equipment-- hunting knife, tomahawk, awl, pouch and powder horn, pipe tobacco, flint and steel, etc."[106]

The pistol added to the frontiersmen's fire power, therefore, but it was still a backup weapon, and as long as it remained muzzleloading, even if a frontiersman carried two double-barreled pistols and a double-barreled rifle or shotgun, as was seldom the case, he would still have only six quick shots at his disposal. To make matters worse, the muzzleloading rifle was no horseman's weapon. Once the frontier moved out onto the plains, though the rifle was still needed for hunting, it was of limited use in a running battle against mounted Indians. The muzzleloading rifle's accuracy could not be taken advantage of from the back of a galloping horse, a fact which also affected the usefulness of repeating rifles under such conditions, and it could not be reloaded easily from such a platform. Since bow-and-arrow-armed Indians would not come within range of that traditional horseman's weapon, the sword, once the American frontier reached the plains the frontiersman's need for repeating handguns as well as repeating rifles became ever more apparent and the incentive to perfect such weapons (they had existed in crude form for several hundred years) grew ever greater.

As mentioned earlier, Samuel Colt's revolving rifle became popular on the far reaches of the frontier not long after it was introduced. The same holds true for his revolving pistol. Kit Carson, the famous scout, the Texas Rangers, and others who faced the plains Indians toward the middle of the 19th century accepted the revolver with great enthusiasm.[107] Such men were relatively few in number during the late 1830's and 1840's, however, since "the frontier line of settlement had not yet moved far west of the Mississippi."[108] And since conservative military men were reluctant to accept the new weapon, enough orders were not forthcoming to keep Colt's company solvent. At least these are the reasons given by historian of the Great Plains Walter Prescott Webb for the company's bankruptcy. Webb goes on to imply that once the frontier line of settlement left the timber, more frontiersmen became aware of the need for such a horseman's weapon.[109] Certainly it was not long before Sam Colt made his come back, and the Civil War enabled the revolver to establish itself as the primary horseman's weapon of that time.[110] By the second half of the 19th century, the pistol, or at least its repeating variety, had become more than a secondary or backup weapon to those individuals—relatively few in number—whose occupations increased the likelyhood of their coming into contact with hostile Indians or whites.

Mention in the preceding paragraph of the military's reluctance to accept Colt's revolver serves to point out something that may have been overlooked to this point: much of the encouragement to produce an effective horseman's weapon came originally from civilians or irregular military units such as the Texas Rangers.[111] To mention this civilian enouragement of weapons development, is to remind us again of the blurred distinction between soldier and civilian on the American frontier that has been discussed in the preceding chapter. It also serves to remind us of the "no-holds-barred" nature of the conflict between red man and white on the American frontier. The American frontiersman, though technically a civilian, needed the most effective personal weapons he could find if he desired to survive in his chosen environment. The Englishman confronted by a highwayman, or even the Australian confronted by a bushranger, might, if he desired to avoid bodily harm, find it prudent not to resist even if he were armed. The American frontiersman, confronted by a hostile Indian, if he desired to survive, often had to fight.

From the above, therefore, it can be seen that on

the American frontier civilian uses of the pistol other than those known in Europe and in the settled areas behind the frontier in the New World--self-defense and dueling--developed. In the hands of the frontiersman, the pistol acquired a quasi-military usage either as a backup weapon for his long gun, or if he were a horseman, as a primary offensive as well as defensive weapon. As it became a primary weapon, the pistol, which when carried for self-defense in settled areas was generally kept concealed in a greatcoat pocket or some such place, came into the open and became a prominent part of the frontiersman's costume, though smaller "hideout" guns might still be kept concealed.[112] Where long guns were routinely carried in the open (and they could hardly be carried ready for use any other way) it made little sense to carry pistols hidden. Of course, the smaller weapon was also more easily accessible when carried under the belt or in a holster attached to the belt than it was when carried out of sight. Actually, therefore, while the long gun was carried--in the hand, cradled in the arm, slung over the shoulder--the handgun was worn much as a hat, a pair of boots, or mocassins, or a personal ornament was worn. While the long gun could serve as a status symbol, it was too cumbersome to carry everywhere. The pistol, on the other hand, could readily be worn inside as well as outside, even while the person wearing it was involved in some non-shooting activity such as punching cattle, panning for gold, or playing poker. Displayed on one's person, therefore, the pistol could readily serve as a badge, as the sword had for the European aristocracy and the Japanese samurai. And the pistol evidently did serve as a badge on the frontier.

From the time that the American frontier started pushing westward in earnest toward the end of the 18th century to the beginning of the 20th century, many of the more adventuresome souls on the raw edge of that frontier had occasion to wear handguns openly--frontier hunters, trappers, traders, pathfinders, 49ers on their way to and in the gold fields, cowboys as they routinely punched cattle or drove them thousands of miles. While the rifle and shotgun were more practical weapons to the settler, given what has been said previously about the American frontier in this and the preceding chapter, it is not surprising that many footloose and adventerous men felt the need to wear sidearms. But there are strong indications that such weapons functioned symbolically as well as practically for those who wore them.

247

For instance firearms are not only frequently present but prominently displayed in posed photographs of frontier types of the late 19th century--not only lawmen, outlaws, and Indian scouts, but ordinary cowboys, miners, and other civilians as well. Revolvers are held in the hand, or they are partially drawn from holsters, or they awkwardly but prominently protrude from belts, waistbands, or pockets.[113] Therefore, the gun, particularly the handgun, seems to have been more than a tool or just another part of the westerner's costume. The gun often appears to have been regarded as the central feature of the westerner's costume. The photographers themselves were obviously aware of the gun's symbolic importance, since there is reason to believe that they often supplied the guns that their customers carried in the photographs.[114] This courtesy on the part of the photographers may have been necessary in towns where local ordinances against carrying handguns within the city limits were strictly enforced.[115] It may also have been necessary because significant numbers of customers desiring to look like tough frontiersmen did not own guns.[116]

If the perspective upon which this study is based is valid, the obvious symbolic function of handguns described above could have easily derived from the practical function of such tools within the symbolic setting of various frontier communities with no assistance from the outside. But as the frontier moved ever westward and the 19th century progressed, the symbolic significance of handguns and guns in general on the frontier received encouragement from the outside. From the earliest days of the frontier, travelers from back East and from Europe had written romanticized accounts of what they had witnessed.

By 1870, dime novels and Wild West shows were adding to this idealized, glamorized, romanticized picture of the west as such writers presented the largely, or in most cases, wholly fictional exploits of various gun-wielding Indian- and outlaw-fighting super-heroes, a number of whom were real personages with some legitimate claim to the label frontiersman. William F. (Buffalo Bill) Cody, the hero of 121 dime novels by Colonel Prentiss Ingraham, producer and star of Western melodramas, and Wild West show organizer and performer, had actually ridden for the Pony Express, scouted, fought a few Indians, and shot a great many buffalo.[117] James Butler (Wild Bill) Hickok, who had scouted for the Union Army, served as marshal in that wild cowtown, Abilene, Kansas, and who had acquired a reputation as a gunfighter, himself had a fling at Wild West shows back East in 1872.[118] The outlaw James boys, Jesse and Frank, were among the less accessible real-life favorites of the dime novelists.[119]

In these dime novels and Wild West shows, little if any distinction was made between scout, hunter, gunfighter, cowboy, and so forth. The westerner was all of these types and more rolled up in one, and he moved from one adventure to another. These adventures tested the westerner's courage, physical strength and stamina, and skill with the ever present six-shooter as well as other weapons. While many men on the frontier and elsewhere in the New World have moved from one job to another, and some westerners did serve as scouts, shift to buffalo hunting, and then shift again to punching cattle, the resemblance between these men and their dime novel and wild west show characterizations ends at that point.

Yet not only men behind the frontier but those on it often tended to take seriously the image of the westerner projected through the dime novel, and those on the frontier had the opportunity to play out that dime novel image. Robert Easton has claimed that even the toughest frontiersmen of the late 19th century avidly read dime novels or associated with those who did, and that there is reason to believe that these frontiersmen "modeled themselves after their literary counterparts."[120] He goes on to say that "certainly it was fashionable for young ranchmen and cowboys at the turn of the century to clump along board sidewalks of a western town in high-heeled boots, hats pulled low over their eyes, and guns in conspicuous evidence."[121] William H. Forbis follows up on the latter point:

> The Mayor of Dodge City, Robert Wright, observed that cowboys "delight in appearing rougher than they are." They swaggered down cattle-town streets, pistols waggling dangerously on their hips as though ready for a face-off with any man--until a reminder from the sheriff about gun ordinances caused them to meekly surrender their weapons. Some cowboys came to enjoy their swashbuckling image so much that they went to elaborate ends

> to construct incidents of phony violence
> for the benefit of gullible visitors
> from the East.[122]

Such stunts included fake shoot-outs timed to coincide
with the arrival of trains.[123] Elsewhere Forbis notes
that "cowboys were certainly aware of the aura of lethal
manliness that guns gave them, and they weighed themselves down with firearms whenever they paid a call on a
girl, confident that she would be impressed."[124] And
again, "looking back on his own broad experience on the
range, cowpuncher Jo Mora wondered why some cowboys
packed pistols during the safest roundups and the most
mundane ranching chores. He commented, 'Why we packed
guns on jobs of that kind and in that way is a mystery
to me now.'"[125]

From the preceding comments, it seems obvious that
firearms, and particularly handguns that could be worn
on one's person, were much more than tools to the cowboys and other frontier types who carried them. Yet one
should not lose sight of the fact that these weapons
could and did function practically in the lives of many
who carried them. While cowboys, for example, were generally not very proficient in the use of their revolvers,
Indians and Mexicans did constitute a menace in the
early days of the cattle industry, and later on rustlers,
range wars, and feuds were reasonably common.[126] "In
addition, a gun was useful to dispatch a pony when it
broke a leg, to turn stampeding cattle, kill a rattle-
snake or, with three stopped shots, signal for help."[127]
The revolver was particularly useful to the cowboy,
since if he hand-carried a rifle or shotgun while he was
on horseback he could do no other work. If he carried
such weapons in saddle scabbards or suspended them by
thongs from his saddlehorn, they tended to rub against
his horse producing sores or to snag his reins or lari-
at.[128] While the rifle and shotgun, for reasons that
should be obvious by now, were preferred for hunting, in
an emergency the handgun could also be pressed into service as a hunting weapon.

In the post-Civil War days of the American frontier
when men in certain lines of work regularly carried
sidearms, disputes between individuals, acting in their
official capacities or otherwise, were occasionally settled with guns. Some of these gunfights occurred when
town marshals attempted to disarm cowboys who insisted
on wearing their revolvers within the city limits.

250

Other gunfights occurred when gamblers were suspected of cheating, and still others occurred as men fought over women. Whatever the cause of such fights, most of them seem to have been spontaneous affairs with the participants simply reaching for their pistols and firing at each other. However, a few gun fights took on some of the aspects of a formal duel. Whatever form they took, most gun fights seem to have taken place in the wild saloon districts of frontier communities.

Through such close-range pistol fights and other confrontations that stopped short of shooting, some men acquired reputations as gunfighters, and much has been made of these individuals from their own day to the present. While dime novels and Wild West shows--and their successors, Hollywood and television westerns--have played their part in making Wild Bill Hickok, Wyatt Earp, Bat Masterson, and other gunfighters world famous, the glamorization of the gunfighter and exaggeration of his exploits has received a great deal of assistance from many sources. According to Paul Trachtman, the more "stable" element in the wilder cowtowns and mining towns of the frontier often did their best to get men with reputations as gunfighters to serve as their peace officers in the hope that these men could control, or at least contain, the rowdiness of the saloon districts.[129] When they found a gunfighter who did an acceptable job, even though his past might have left something to be desired, the "respectable" members of the community were inclined to brag, through their newspapers and otherwise, of his toughness and skills with the gun.[130] The gunfighter's reputation was thereby further enhanced, as was the glamor associated with gunfighting. The gunfighters themselves were not always modest and some bragged about the number of opponents they had dispatched in fair fights, "not counting Indians and Mexicans." Inflated as these "career records" were, they were generally accepted by journalists--frontier as well as eastern--and reported to their readers, reputations being further enhanced in the process.

The gunfighter's reputation often made it possible for him to face down an opponent without putting his skills to yet another test that might find them lacking. Consequently, to supplement their bragging, subtle or otherwise, gunfighters sometimes seem to have engaged in conspicuous target practice or impromptu shooting matches that had something of the exhibition about them.

251

However, it is not likely that the shooting done by such exhibitionists was as spectacular as we have been led to believe.[131] Of course, the reputations of the gunfighters may have occasionally attracted challengers in search of a reputation themselves instead of driving them away, and such shooting exhibitions might occasionally have reinforced a challenger's confidence instead of sapping it.[132] When fights occurred, and they seem to have been fewer than generally supposed, they were seldom elaborate affairs.[133] Pistols were simply produced from holsters, pockets, waistbands, sleeves, or boots, etc., as quickly as possible and fired at opponents. Some gunfighters experimented with "rigs" that enabled them to "draw" quickly, but the Hollywood quick draw and the holsters that make it possible were not part of the gunfighter's world. Some gunfighters relied on the surprise afforded them by a "hideout" gun. Due to their readiness to use their weapons, however, most successful gunfighters probably had as much advantage as they needed over their opponents.[134]

While a great deal has been written about the pistol fights and marksmanship skills of the western gunfighters--most quite exaggerated--little seems to have been written about the recreational shoots engaged in by the ordinary men who regularly carried handguns on the late 19th century American frontier. Dulles mentions that such matches were held, but he makes no effort to describe them.[135] It is possible, of course, that little interest in match-type marksmanship with the handgun developed on the frontier where these weapons were used primarily for short range defense or from the back of a horse where precision shooting could hardly be expected. Yet as one might suppose, those who regularly carried such weapons engaged in considerable impromptu "plinking." According to Forbis, "random gun play was a bunkhouse norm," and cowboys thought nothing of blasting away at pictures on the bunkhouse wall and at other targets that presented themselves.[136] And Dulles states that "the range-rider always had his six-shooter with him, and he amused himself by taking pot-shots at the jack-rabbits, prairie dogs, or occasional coyotes that crossed his trail."[137] Those individuals who acquired reputations as good pistol shots in this way surely must have tested their skills against others in a more or less formal manner on occasion, but if they did, such matches seem to have been obscured by the more colorful and exaggerated feats of the gunfighters.[138]

The pistol was also used recreationally on occasion for hunting of a less impromptu variety than that engaged in by cowboys, as mentioned above. Plainsmen such as General George Armstrong Custer and Buffalo Bill Cody hunted buffalo from horseback with the pistol, particularly when they were trying to impress visiting dignitaries such as the Russian Grand Duke Alexis.[139]

As the frontier moved on, the handgun was no longer needed as a backup for the rifle which itself had become a sporting weapon divested of its quasi-military duties--though hunters of large game sometimes still carry handguns as backups. Neither was the handgun needed as a horseman's weapon, for there were no more horse-mounted Indians or Mexicans to fight and the horse itself became obsolete as a means of transport with the invention of the automobile. But, as noted in the preceding chapter, the area behind the frontier was no more free of conflict than the frontier itself had been. In the raw boom towns of the oil or coal fields in areas that could not be considered frontier, in areas where there were labor-management conflicts, in large cities or small towns tense with racial or ethnic unrest, in the backwoods of Kentucky and West Virginia where shooting feuds continued into the 20th century, many people continued to feel that they needed the protection that a handgun could afford them. And behind the frontier, where it was less acceptable to carry firearms openly, the relatively easily-concealed handgun could be used as an offensive weapon in the wars between opposing factions, though shotguns, rifles, and, once they became available, submachine guns, were also used.

Unlike the rifle, in other words, the practical function of the handgun was not linked as completely to the open warfare with the Indian, which passed with the frontier, or to hunting, which was transformed from a primarily practical activity to a primarily recreational one as the frontier moved on. Even before the Indian threat to the invaders faded, the invaders threatened themselves--cattlemen versus sheepmen, management versus labor, old immigrant versus new, white versus black or yellow, etc. While these threats did not lead to full scale battles of the magnitude and ferocity of some of those fought between red and white, such open conflict as did, and still does, occur often resulted in loss of life. And, as was noted in the preceding chapter, it is misleading to claim that such violence is simply due to the lack of "law and order." Often violence has re-

253

sulted from the attempts by some to use "law and order" to control those with whom they disagree, when the latter have preferred to do the controlling themselves. And in a nation as overlappingly pluralistic as the United States, such factional attempts at social control have not been restricted to the raw edge of the frontier of settlement. Since the handgun has functioned as a weapon of personal defense in other parts of the modern world where people have felt that the enforcers of the law could not or would not protect them, it is not surprising that it has functioned and continues to function in this fashion in the United States where men have often lived uneasily practically next door to their enemies.

With respect to handgun carrying, therefore, areas behind the American frontier seem to have surpassed those on the frontier. Residents of a small mining boom town in the southern part of Illinois that had experienced labor and ethnic unrest down through the 1920's told sociological researchers such as the following:

> On payday you went home from the bank, another fellow with you—if you lived out by the mine—with one hand in one pocket on your pay, the other in the other pocket on a gun. That way if somebody came out of the bushes and said, "Stick 'em up," he didn't know what you would bring out of your pocket on either side.[140]

> Everybody carried guns and the people used to get tired of carrying them and would fire them at night in the sky or in the ground. Men carried guns in their pockets and would shoot electric lights out just for fun.

> I brought my wife here in '24 and we both carried pistols.

> It was pretty wild here when I came. I remember that the drunks would come down to the street at nights just shooting for all they were worth. I can remember dodging and hiding behind furniture in order to keep myself safe.[141]

In a neighboring town, ethnically diverse Herrin, Illinois, several large scale shootouts between Ku Klux Klan and anti-Klan forces occurred during the 1920's.[142] These shootouts resulted in a number of casualties, one being the gunman whom the Klan had brought in to keep southern and eastern European immigrants and a thriving American-run bootleg liquor industry from violating Prohibition. This colorful individual had made it a practice to parade around town wearing a pair of ivory-handled Colt .45 caliber semi-automatic pistols and carrying a carbine or submachine gun. The deputy sheriff who ended the gunman's career, and whose own career was ended in the same pistol fight, is supposed to have had underworld connections.

Photographs of the West Virginia based Hatfield clan taken in 1899, when that family's feud with the McCoys was still in progress, show the Hatfield men brandishing Colt and Smith and Wesson revolvers and Marlin lever-action rifles of the sort that were likely to have been found in the hip holsters and saddle scabbards of western ranchmen and cowboys of that day.[143] Though the photographer may have encouraged the Hatfields to display their weapons in such a fashion, the symbolic significance attached to their firearms seems obvious. And historians Lee Kennett and James LaVerne Anderson have claimed that "the habit of going armed" had become such a "recognized custom" in the urban East of the late 19th century that "tailors supplied men's trousers with a 'revolver pocket' placed on the right hip, whether it was used for that purpose or not."[144]

Of course, when law and order, or what passed for law and order with those factions who were able to impose their will on others, came to the settled areas on or behind the frontier, gun carrying was generally discouraged. Absentee owners of such ranches as the three-million-acre XIT Ranch in Texas officially forbade their employees to carry pistols, fighting knives, or any such personal weapons.[145] Cowtowns such as Dodge City and Abilene, Kansas posted signs at the city limits warning visitors that the carrying of firearms was prohibited within the city limits, and according to Forbis, some lawmen were feared enough that they could enforce these ordinances.[146] Visitors would leave "their weapons at a saloon, a hotel or a store" and pick them up again "only when they were ready to leave."[147] Western historian Joseph G. Rosa, however, states that laws against the wearing of firearms in frontier communities were seldom enforced.[148]

Where pistols could not be worn openly, those who felt the need for them still carried them concealed. By the early 20th century, however, to carry a concealed weapon would probably violate some state or local law. Small pocket pistols had been available in what is now the United States since colonial days, and they had been carried by some frontiersmen as "hideout" weapons as well as by Easterners.[149] Until the middle of the 19th century, these little pistols had been muzzle-loading and single-or double-barreled, as were the other firearms of the time. Once the revolver was perfected and adapted to metallic cartridges, however, small versions of these arms were produced. While the big revolvers worn openly in the hip holsters of the more publicized civilians--cowboys, ranchers, scouts, lawmen, outlaws--as well as the soldiers on the frontier were receiving most of the attention of dime novel addicts and wild west show enthusiasts, thousands of these small revolvers were being made by well known and not so well known companies. Most of the small revolvers produced by the lesser companies, many of which have long since gone out of business, were quite cheap. During the late 19th century, some revolvers could be purchased for as little as 60 cents, therefore, serviceable handguns were put well within the financial reach of the poor as well as the rich behind the frontier as well as on it during the turbulent age of large scale immigration, industrialization, and urbanization.[150] In many ways that turbulent age has yet to end.

While the earliest attempts to ban the concealed wearing of handguns by civilians in the United States were made along the western moving frontier--Kentucky in 1813, Indiana in 1819, and Arkansas and Georgia in 1837--and all western states had such laws, whether enforced or not, by 1850, attempts to restrict the possession of handguns originated in the 1870's well behind the frontier, and they can be directly linked to the racial, ethnic, class, and labor conflicts discussed in the previous chapter.[151] Given these various overlapping conflicts, it should not be surprising that the period between 1870 and 1934 was, as Don B. Kates, Jr. has noted, "the most xenophobic period of American history." And it was during this period that many of the dominant factions in the United States and even Canada "felt themselves threatened by a number of forces they associated with the handgun: blacks who wouldn't keep their place; radicals, labor agitators, assassins, robbers, and by a process of further association, the foreign-born."[153] White supremacists in control of the Tennessee legislature established the first ban on the sale of what would now be called "Saturday Night Specials" back in 1870, in a blatant attempt to keep blacks and poorer whites from acquiring the only revolvers that were cheap enough for them to afford, and Arkansas enacted a similar ban in 1881.[154] Other states of the Deep South simply forbade blacks to possess firearms. New York State's Sullivan Law, passed in 1911, was the first of many laws that required police permits for the legal possession of handguns, and while it was a serious crime control effort, the immigrant was the source of crime and labor unrest in the eyes of those who framed the law and it was the immigrant who should not have a handgun.[155] With the expanding federal power that came with the New Deal of the 1930's, liberal reformers attempted to enact federal gun controls, but while they succeeded in imposing restrictions on the legal sale and possession of two weapons associated with the gangsters of the era, machine guns and sawed-off shotguns, they were unable to enact federal handgun restrictions. The National Rifle Association made its debut as a potent opponent of gun controls in the 1930's, and it played an important part in defeating the attempts to enact handgun restrictions.

World War II temporarily halted efforts to enact gun controls of any kind in the United States, but by the late 1950's the push for controls had begun to build again, and the political assassinations and disorders of the 1960's and 1970's added fuel to these control efforts. For the most part, the most restrictive laws proposed by contemporary gun control advocates at the local, state, and federal levels are aimed at restricting handgun possession, where this is not already done, as was the case prior to World War II. Such laws would require police permits for anyone wanting to acquire a handgun legally, or they would outlaw completely the civilian possession of handguns. At the very least they would outlaw the manufacture, sale, and possession of the cheapest revolvers, the so-called "Saturday Night Specials," the only handguns members of America's "dangerous classes" are likely to be able to afford. "Saturday Night Special," after all, refers to "niggertown Saturday Night."[156]

⌈While handgun ownership restrictions and gun controls in general have received overwhelming support from the media at the national level--the major urban newspapers along with many medium sized newspapers--and from the intellectual community, the extent of the American public's support for such measures is not clear. Public opinion polls on the gun control issue have taken on an adversarial coloration, with the supposedly neutral but pro-control, media-commissioned Gallup and Harris pollsters invariably reporting broad public support for gun controls, and the less publicized NRA-commissioned Decision Making Information (DMI) pollsters invariably reporting little support for controls.[157] But even if the findings and interpretations of the polls commissioned by the pro-controllers are taken at face value, it appears that any public support for outlawing handgun possession that may have once existed in the United States has dwindled considerably. According to a 1959 Gallup poll, 59 percent of the respondents supported the outlawing of handguns, but in 1975 a Gallup poll found that only 41 percent supported such measures, and Harris and Caddell polls found even less support for them--37 percent and 32 percent, respectively.[158] And in 1976 when the people of Massachusetts, a state generally considered to be the most politically liberal in the union, were presented via referendum with the opportunity to ban handgun possession in their state, they defeated that proposition 1,662,216 to 733,418 (2.27 to 1).[159] Seventy-seven percent of the states eligible voters voted on the issue, and though supporters of the ban claimed that it was defeated because voters were concerned about the cost of its implementation; a poll commissioned by the ban supporters to find out why they had lost reported that those who voted against it did so because they believed that the ban would leave the law-abiding defenseless without reducing crime.[160]

Even where they have been enacted in the United States, strict handgun controls and gun controls in general have not generated much compliance. Authorities have estimated that residents of New York City alone possess as many as 2,000,000 handguns in violation of the vaunted Sullivan Law.[161] The gun control battle continues to rage, however, and several observers have come to view it "as a skirmish in the larger battle over the nation's cultural values."[162] The hard core of the pro-control force is composed of social change-oriented cosmopolitans--urban, upper-middle class, college "educated," liberal, not likely to be familiar with fire-

258

arms--who have seen several of their most influential leaders assassinated by gunmen. The hard core of the anti-control force is composed of tradition-oriented bedrockers--small town/rural, lower-middle/working class, less likely to be college educated, conservative, familiar with firearms.

As it had on the frontier, the handgun functioned other than practically after the frontier was gone as well as behind the frontier while it lasted. Of course, where it could not be carried openly, the handgun could not as easily serve as a badge of masculinity or toughness. Others could be made aware of the handgun's presence, however, through horseplay of the sort carried on in the Illinois coal town described above. Where such impromptu gunplay resulted in an informal shooting match, a link with the recreational was forged--a link which, as with the rifle, may have been encouraged by the development of the .22 rimfire cartridge. While those individuals on the frontier or behind it who have regularly carried handguns have engaged in impromptu "plinking" with such weapons, ammunition for the larger caliber weapons has generally been expensive enough to limit such antics. But with the .22 came handguns that were relatively inexpensive to shoot. Though some handguns of this caliber have been carried as hideout guns by women as well as by men on both sides of the law--some private soldiers even purchased .22 revolvers to carry as personal sidearms during the Civil War--over the years the .22 handgun has become a "plinking" or informal target gun in the United States. Though some small, easily-concealed .22 handguns are currently produced, most of these weapons differ little in size, weight, and general appearance from the larger-caliber revolvers and semi-automatics made for military and police as well as civilian use. These regular sized .22 handguns are quite popular with hunters, fishermen, campers, hikers, and other outdoorsmen.

Little seems to have been written concerning the grass-roots interests in formal pistol shooting in the United States; consequently, it is difficult to link such competition to things more broadly sociocultural. But as can be seen from what has been written so far in this section, by the latter part of the 19th century formal target shooting with the handgun in the United States had a rather broad-based, grass-roots familiarity with the handgun to build on; consequently, reasonably formal as well as impromptu matches with the handgun have long

been part of the American scene. Increased formaliza-
tion, however, may have been fostered in several ways.
Though only gentlemen, or those who aspired to be
classified as gentlemen, were interested in dueling, the
duel and the practice that prepared one for it may have
helped to prepare the way for a more recreational but
nevertheless formal type of pistol shooting. Certainly
the orthodox duelist's stance, or a modification thereof, is still utilized in standard formal handgun competitions, and single - shot target pistols remained popular in the United States long after cartridges and the
revolver had been perfected.

The late 19th century interest in fostering military preparedness, shared by many powerful nations including the United States, also may have encouraged the
formal organization of competitive pistol shooting, however, since at that time the pistol was still an offensive weapon of the cavalryman. Matches for the standard
service revolver were incorporated into the activities
of the still National Guard-oriented NRA as early as
1882. Traces of the linkage between these matches and
the military and a latter NRA encouragement of police
marksmanship training are still evident in American
handgun competitions today.[163] Organized handgun target
shooting of the traditional variety as well as rifle
competition in the United States is regulated by the
NRA, and standard handgun matches are conducted in such
a way that those who wish to compete for top honors must
be proficient with weapons of various calibers. In some
matches, only pistols chambered for the .45 automatic
cartridge (used by the American military since 1911) are
allowed. Handguns chambered for any centerfire cartridge above .32 caliber are used in other matches, and
in those matches the .38 Special, standard with many
police departments, is quite popular. And still other
matches are limited to guns chambered for the .22 rim-
fire so popular with civilians.

Extremely sophisticated target revolvers and semi-
automatic pistols chambering these various cartridges
are used in the standard handgun matches. Revolvers
with special target refinements, but otherwise almost
identical to the large military and civilian holster
pistols of the time, were produced by such companies
as Colt and Smith and Wesson by the early 1880's.[164]
The exhibition shooters of the day, who through their
activities may have themselves done much to promote target shooting of all kinds, seem to have helped bring

260

about these early refinements. But while dueling practice, attempts to foster military and police preparedness, and exhibition shooters may have each in their
own way, and in combination with each other, encouraged
the development of formal competitive handgun shooting
in the United States, it should not be forgotten that
these activities did not create the grass-roots familiarity with the handgun and the informal interest in
handgun shooting that served as a base for the sport.
It might be pointed out that, according to the various
estimates cited in Chapter I, more than a quarter of the
guns possessed by households in all parts of the United
States, urban as well as rural, are handguns.

During the past decade or so, two notable devia-
tions from the standard duelist's stance target competitions for the handgun have evolved, one deriving from
the handgun's use as a hunting weapon in the United
States and the other from its use as a defensive weapon.
While rifles and shotguns have distinct advantages over
handguns as hunting weapons, handguns have undoubtedly
been pressed into emergency service as hunting weapons
since these small guns were invented, and many modern
outdoorsmen have used handguns to provide themselves
with camp meat. But the very fact that bagging game with
a handgun is more difficult than bagging game with a rifle or shotgun seems to have made hunting with the handgun a challenging activity to sports hunters who can accept such a challenge since their survival and that of
their dependents does not depend on the meat provided by
a successful hunt. At any rate, hunting with the handgun is becoming increasingly popular in the United
States, and guns and equipment designed especially for
this type of hunting have been devised. These developments include telescopic sights for handguns and even
handguns that are nothing more than short high-powered
rifles with pistol grips instead of shoulder stocks.[165]
And with the development of such equipment has come organized target competition in the form of silhouette
shoots. Silhouette shooting originated in Mexico as a
rifle competition and came to the United States as such.
For handgun silhouette shooting, the targets, which are
heavy steel silhouettes of various game birds and animals,
are placed at distances ranging from 50 meters to 200 meters, and to score a hit the target must not only be hit
but knocked over.[166] The knock-over requirement means
that only handguns chambered for the most powerful handgun cartridges, such as the .357, .41, and .44 Magnums,
or even for such rifle cartridges as the .30-30, .35

Remington, or .375 Winchester are likely to be effective for such matches. No telescopes are allowed in some competitions, and the closer targets are shot from the standing position using a two-hand grip, while the distant targets are shot lying down--back or stomach. And the sport has become formalized to the extent that there are two classes of competition, one for production guns--those that are commercially available in a standard form--and one for unlimited guns--custom creations limited primarily by maximum weight and barrel length requirements of 4½ pounds and 15 inches respectively.[167] It should be noted, however, that though silhouette shooting has extended handgun competitions out to ranges normally associated with rifle competitions, at such ranges the rifle still has a distinct advantage over a silhouette handgun of equal quality.

While long-range silhouette shooting with the handgun is linked to hunting with the handgun, combat matches for the handgun grew out of attempts to improve the combat proficiency of handgun-armed police and combat military personnel. However, disturbed by the black and student riots of the 1960's and 70's, and by an ever-rising and widely-publicized violent crime rate, enough Americans, female as well as male, have shown an interest in learning to defend themselves with a handgun that the proprietors of pistol ranges all across the nation have found it profitable to teach the rudiments of combat or practical pistol shooting to civilians. While most of these courses are designed to familiarize their students with handguns and teach them to hit the vital areas of stationary man-sized targets at a common defensive range of a few yards, some courses set up by ex-military men, a few of whom have served as mercenaries, are at least as sophisticated as the courses set up to train military special forces and police.[168] These sophisticated courses are set up to teach students to draw their weapons quickly, shoot effectively with both hands and either hand, reload quickly, hit moving targets, shoot from behind barricades, and to decide quickly whether to fire or not, among other skills. What began as a practical training effort soon spawned combat or practical shooting competitions, and by 1980 practical shooting competitors had already split off into two warring factions--the "martial artists" and the "gamesmen."[169] Practical shooters of both orientations fire large-caliber handguns suitable for military or police use. However, the martial artists insist that the handguns used, the holsters from which they are

262

drawn, and the match conditions be kept as close as possible to the needs and the likely combat experiences of the policeman, soldier, or civilian called upon to defend himself, while the gamesmen, for instance, see nothing wrong with using tied-down, quick-draw holsters that allow fast draws but would be impractical for the policeman, soldier, or civilian who regularly carries a handgun as he goes about his everyday affairs.

Both silhouette and combat, or practical, handgun competitions are getting considerable coverage in such gun periodicals as Guns and Combat Handguns during the fourth quarter of the 20th century, but the more orthodox and established bullseye competition utilizing the traditional duelist's stance still seems to be the dominant form of competitive handgun shooting at this time. And while silhouette competition with the handgun seems not to have caught on outside of North America to this point, practical competitions have become popular in parts of the world where whites have come to consider themselves to be members of a threatened minority. South African and Rhodesian teams regularly win or place high in the annual world championships, and the best shooters on South Africa's government subsidized practical pistol team are considered to be national heroes.[170]

It was noted earlier in this section that as of the early part of the 19th century pistol usage in Canada and Australia seemed to differ little from that in the United States. But as the handgun became an ever more popular weapon with Americans attempting to cope with their ethnic, racial, political, and class enemies behind, as well as on, their frontier, the pistol seems not to have gained in popularity with Canadians and Australians who experienced fewer threats of this sort from one another. Of course, handguns were used on the Canadian and Australian frontiers. However, in the Canadian West the Mounted Police discouraged the wearing of sidearms and the transplanted easterners who settled the area seem not to have made an issue of the prohibition. Given what has been said in this and the previous chapter, it is not surprising that Canadians are not particularly interested in handguns. In Australia, sidearms seem to have been reasonably common in the "backblocks," or back country, during the latter half of the 19th century, but the impression is that the populace as a whole has never become familiar with such weapons.[171] According to estimates cited in an Australian study, there are .272 handguns per person in civilian hands in the United States, while the corresponding figures for Canada and Australia are .013 and .006 respectively.[172] A Canadian survey also reports that few Canadians own handguns, but goes on to point out that most Canadian handgun owners live in metropolitan areas.[173]

Canadians and Australians have placed more restrictions on handgun ownership than they have on the ownership of ordinary sporting rifles and shotguns. In 1978 Canada enacted a new gun law at the national level that kept handguns in a restricted category along with "centerfire semi-auto rifles (carbines) with barrel lengths of less than 18.5 inches or over-all lengths of less than 26 inches."[174] Such weapons can be legally possessed by Canadians, but the red tape associated with their acquisition and possession has increased. In Australia, with the exceptions of the federally-controlled Australian Capitol Territory and the Northern Territory, the various states have enacted their own gun laws, and since the 1920's these laws have placed heavy restrictions on the private possession and use of handguns. Persons handling large sums of money, security officers, farmers, and graziers can generally acquire licenses to carry as well as possess handguns, but until 1956 (the year of the Melbourne Olympics) target shooting was not considered to be an acceptable reason for pistol ownership in Australia.[175] Now Australians can legally acquire handguns for target shooting, but to do so they must belong to registered pistol clubs and complete much bureaucratic paperwork. One Australian observer has noted, however, that unlicensed handguns are used in most Australian armed crime, while an Australian police association official claims that "sawn-off rifles and shotguns" have become increasingly popular with the Australian armed criminal and now constitute "the Australian version of the U.S. 'Saturday night special.'"[176] And in Canada, the Royal Canadian Mounted Police "estimated that in 1975 there were around 50,000 unregistered restricted weapons /including handguns/ in private hands," a figure that other authorities claimed was too low.[177] It should also be noted that those handguns that have been used in Australia and Canada have been manufactured in the United States and Europe.

SUMMARY

As with Chapter VI, a brief summary of the major points that have been made in placing firearms in social historical context in this chapter seems called for. These are as follows:

1. Portable firearms came to what are now the United States and Canada before the middle of the 16th century, and to Australia by the early 17th century, in the hands of those explorers and soldiers who opened these new lands to European expansion. By the early 17th century, however, civilians were using firearms in the parts of the North American New World mentioned. In Australia, which began as a penal colony, the civilian use of firearms seems not to have become widespread until the free population began to increase in number during the first half of the 19th century.

2. In the North American and Australian New Worlds, particularly that part of the former which was to become the United States, firearms in civilian hands served as tools of war as well as tools of the hunt. In those parts of the Old World covered by this study, civilians did not use firearms as tools of war, although such arms were widely used as tools of the hunt.

3. Since the early explorers and the later colonists in these areas came from parts of Europe where rifles had hardly been known, the long guns they brought with them were smoothbores capable of firing either ball or shot. Civilian colonists used such weapons to hunt both large and small game where both types of game could be found, as in North America, and to fight hostile aboriginals. As the shotgun evolved from the unspecialized smoothbore in Europe and large game and hostile aboriginals faded from the New World scene, it became the hunting gun of the common man in the New World as it had in the Old. The shotgun has taken second place to the rifle in the New World, however, and this was not the case in most parts of the Old World.

4. The rifle was introduced into the New World in what is now the United States during the early 18th century by German and Swiss immigrants. Here it found favor with the pathfinding frontiersmen who eventually filtered through the Cumberland Gap and began to move the frontier ever westward. During the American Revolution and the War of 1812, such men impressed their coun-

trymen, their allies, and their enemies with their marksmanship skills, skills that were greatly admired on the frontier and remained so behind it. Rifles got to Canada and Australia later than they did to the United States, and rifle shooting in those nations received no spectacular boosts during their formative years.

5. Though the pistol probably reached the New World shortly after that weapon was invented in the early 16th century, it remained of limited use for some time. Once the American frontier began to move westward the pistol became the backup gun of the frontiersman, and later, in its repeating version, it became the primary offensive arm of the frontier horsemen, civilian as well as military, of the Great Plains. In the urban areas behind the frontier it served as a defensive arm for those at all socioeconomic levels, once cheap versions became available after the middle of the 19th century. For a number of reasons, the pistol seems to have been much more popular in the United States than in either Canada or Australia.

6. In the United States formal shooting competition with ball-loaded smoothbores dates back to the militia training sessions of the early 17th century. Rifle matches date from the 18th century, shotgun matches from at least the first half of the 19th century, and pistol matches from the second half.

7. Firearms in general and handguns in particular seem to have been incorporated into the costume of those civilians who regularly carried them on the American frontier, and thereby seem to have served as badges of status.

FOOTNOTES

1. Carl P. Russell, <u>Guns on the Early Frontier: A History of Firearms from Colonial Times Through the Years of the Western Fur Trade</u> (Berkeley and Los Angeles: University of California Press, 1962), p. 4.

2. Ibid.

3. Ibid., 5.

4. Ibid.

5. Russell, 10.

6. Ibid., 9.

7. Ibid.

8. Manning Clark, <u>A Short History of Australia</u> (New York: A Mentor Book from New American Library, 1969), pp. 13-27.

9. Ibid., 37.

10. Warren Moore, <u>Weapons of the American Revolution-- and Accouterments</u> (New York: Funk & Wagnalls, 1967), p. 59.

11. Russell, 232.

12. Ibid., 68.

13. Ibid., 232-233.

14. Henry J. Kauffman, <u>The Pennsylvania-Kentucky Rifle</u> (Harrisburg, Pennsylvania: Stackpole Books, 1960, p. 102.

15. Herbert Manchester, <u>Four Centuries of Sport in America 1490-1890</u> (New York: Benjamin Bloom, 1931), p. 63.

16. Ibid., 91-92.

17. Ibid.

18. Jaroslav Lugs, A History of Shooting: Marksman-ship, Duelling and Exhibition Shooting (The Centre, Feltham, Middlesex: Spring Books, 1968), p. 120.

19. Ibid., 123.

20. Ibid.

21. Allen Hatch, Remington Arms: In American History (New York: Rinehart & Company, Inc., 1956), p. 232.

22. Harold F. Williamson, Winchester: The Gun that Won the West (Washington, D.C.: A Sportsman's Press Book Published by the Combat Forces Press, 1952), pp. 6-8.

23. Just how vigorous this competition was can be seen from the following letter sent by Sam Colt to his agent in Arizona in 1860:

> I am noticing in the newspapers oc-
> casionally complimentary notices of
> the Sharps & Burnside Rifles & Car-
> bines, anecdotes of their use upon
> Grisly Bears, Indians, Mexicans & c.
> & c. Now this is all wrong--it
> should be published Colts Rifles,
> Carbines & c. When there is or can
> be made a good Story of the use of
> a Colt's Revolving Rifle, Carbine,
> Shotgun or Pistol, for publication
> in the Arizonian the opportunity
> should not be lost, and in the event
> of such notices being published you
> must always send me one hundred cop-
> ies. If there is a chance to do a
> few good things in this way, give
> the editor--Pistol or Rifle compli-
> ment, in the way it will tell--.
> You know how to do this & Do not for-
> get to have his Columnist report all
> the accidents that occur to the Sharps
> & other humbug arms. I hope soon to
> see the evidence of your usefulness
> in this line of business.

   William B. Edwards, "Shootin' Irons," in This is the West, ed. by Robert West Howard (New York:

Signet Books, 1957), p. 166.

24. Williamson, 182-183.

25. Lugs, 124.

26. Bill R. Davidson, <u>To Keep and Bear Arms</u> (New Ro-
    chelle, New York: Arlington House, 1969), p. 172.

27. Ned Polsky, "Of Pool Playing and Poolrooms," <u>Games,
    Sport and Power</u>, ed. Gregory P. Stone (New Bruns-
    wick, New Jersey: Transaction Books, 1972), p. 37.

28. George D. Newton and Franklin E. Zimring, <u>Firearms
    & Violence in American Life</u> (Washington, D.C.:
    U.S. Government Printing Office, 1969), p. 10.

29. Michael Brander, <u>Hunting & Shooting: From Earliest
    Times to the Present Day</u> (New York: G.D. Putnam's
    Sons, 1971), pp. 166-169.

30. Davidson, 160.

31. Ibid.

32. <u>Guns & Ammo 1973 Annual</u> (Los Angeles: Peterson
    Publishing Co., 1972), p. 113.

33. Newton and Zimring, 10. It should be remembered
    that since many firearms owners are concerned
    about restrictive firearms legislation, they are of-
    ten reluctant to talk to other than close friends
    about their weapons. Surveys of firearms owner-
    ship, therefore, cannot be taken at face value.

34. Ibid., 11.

35. Ibid., 10.

36. Philip C. Stenning and Sharon Moyer, <u>Firearms
    Ownership and Use in Canada: A Report of Survey
    Findings, 1976</u> (Toronto: Centre of Criminology,
    University of Toronto, 1981), pp. 33, 36, 55. The
    author acquired this material after the first chap-
    ter had been prepared for publication.

37. Held, 151.

38. Russel Ward and John Robertson, ed., _Such Was Life_:
    Select Documents in Australian Social History 1788-
    _1850_ (Sydney & London: Ure Smith, 1969), pp. 230-
    233, 253, 279, 282. Though the muskets referred
    to by these early 19th century Australians were
    probably actually smoothbores since those who
    brought them came from England, musket and rifle
    were not always distinguished from one another by
    the writers of the period. See Hank Wieand Bowman,
    Antique Guns (Greenwich, Connecticut: Fawcett
    Books, 1953), p. 15.

39. Brander, 187.

40. Edgar Waters, "Recreation," in _The Pattern of_
    Australian Culture, ed. by A. L. McLeod (Ithaca,
    New York: Cornell University Press, 1963), p. 426.

41. Newton and Zimring, 120.

42. Richard Harding, _Firearms and Violence in Austral-_
    ian Life (University of Western Australia Press,
    1980), p. 54.

43. Kauffman, 8; and Roger Burlingame, _March of the_
    Iron Men (New York and London: Charles Scribner's
    Sons and Charles Scribner's Sons Ltd., 1938), p.123.

44. Burlingame, 124. Also see Hatch, 13.

45. Held, 142.

46. Ibid., 142-143.

47. Kauffman, 19.

48. Robert Easton, "Guns of the American West," in _The_
    Book of the American West, ed. by Jay Monaghan
    (New York: Julian Messner, Inc., 1963), pp. 381-
    382).

49. Held, 144.

50. Charles E. Hanson, _The Plains Rifle_ (Harrisburg,
    Pennsylvania: The Stackpole Company, 1960), pp.
    1-2.

51. Russell, 76-77.

52. Easton, 387-388.

53. Ibid., 414-418.

54. Ibid., 423.

55. Ibid., 418; and James E. Serven, Conquering the
    Frontiers: Stories of American Pioneers and the
    Guns Which Helped Them Establish a New Life (La
    Habra, California: Foundation Press, 1974), pp.
    165-179.

56. Daniel J. Boorstin, The Americans: The Colonial
    Experience (Vintage Books New York: Random
    House, 1958), p. 350.

57. Thomas D. Clark, The Rampaging Frontier: Manners
    and Humors of Pioneer Days in the South and the
    Middle West (New York and Indianapolis: The Bobbs-
    Merrill Company, 1939), pp. 31-32.

58. Foster Rhea Dulles, A History of Recreation: Amer-
    ica Learns to Play (New York: Appleton-Century-
    Crofts, 1965), p. 71.

59. Ibid., 29; and Manchester, 27.

60. Robert B. Weaver, Amusements and Sports in American
    Life (New York: Greenwood Press, Publishers,
    1939), p. 43.

61. Dulles, 71.

62. Weaver, 49.

63. Dulles, 72. Obviously more than marksmanship was
    being displayed when such feats were attempted.

64. Clark, 31; Weaver, 43-44.

65. Clark, 30-31.

66. Ibid., 31.

67. Boorstin, 351. Also see Burlingame 127-128 and
    Warren Moore, 60-61.

68. Boostin, 351.

69. Warren Moore, 59.

70. Newton and Zimring, 10.

71. Ibid.

72. Ibid., 11.

73. N. H. Roberts, The Muzzle-Loading Cap Lock Rifle (Harrisburg, Pennsylvania: The Stackpole Company, 1958), p. 29.

74. The American Rifleman, Vol. 122 (December, 1974), 14.

75. James B. Trefethen and James E. Serven, Americans and Their Guns: The National Rifle Association Story Through Nearly a Century of Service to the Nation (Harrisburg, Pennsylvania: Stackpole Company, 1967), pp. 111.

76. Ibid.

77. Ibid., 111-112.

78. William B. Edwards, Civil War Guns (Harrisburg, Pennsylvania: The Stackpole Company, 1962), p. 8.

79. Ibid., 13.

80. Hatch, 160.

81. James B. Trefethen and James E. Serven, Americans and Their Guns: The National Rifle Association Story Through Nearly a Century of Service to the Nation (Harrisburg, Pennsylvania: Stackpole Company, 1967), pp. 22-27.

82. Ibid., 33.

83. Ibid.

84. Ibid., 66.

85. Ibid., 62.

86. Ibid., 67.

87. Ibid., 73.

88. Such matches are still held in conjunction with the International Shooting Union, the Pan-American Games and the Olympic Games. See Trefethen and Serven's history of the NRA, Americans and Their Guns, for a detailed history of these international matches.

89. Robert J. Kukla, Gun Control (Harrisburg, Pennsylvania: Stackpole Books, 1973), pp. 84-119.

90. Ibid.

91. Trefethen and Serven, 182.

92. Davidson claims that NRA subsidies have helped make rifle and pistol target shooting middle-class sports in the United States, 172.

93. G. N. Dentay, "Gun Control Canada . . . and the Visitor," in Guns Illustrated: 1980, ed. by Harold A. Murtz and the editors of Gun Digest (Northfield, Illinois: DBI Books, Inc., 1980), pp. 61-62.

94. Easton, 400.

95. Warren Moore, 7; and Kauffman, 93.

96. Daniel J. Boorstin, The Americans: The National Experience (Vintage Books, New York: Random House, 1965), p. 207.

97. Ibid.

98. Ibid., 211.

99. Ibid., 207.

100. Ibid., 209.

101. Easton, 400.

102. Ward and Robertson.

103. Hanson, 153-154.

104. Ibid., 153.

105. Easton, 400.

106. Hanson, 154.

107. Russell, 94-95.

108. Walter Prescott Webb, The Great Plains (Boston, New York, Chicago, London, Atlanta, Dallas, Columbus, San Francisco: Ginn and Company, 1931), p. 176.

109. Ibid.

110. John E. Parsons, The Peacemaker and its Rivals: An Account of the Single Action Colt (New York: William Morrow and Company, 1950), p. 171.

111. Russell, 62.

112. See Paul Trachtman, The Gunfighters (New York: Time-Life Books, 1974), pp. 48-49.

113. See William H. Forbis, The Cowboys (New York: Time-Life Books, 1973), pp. 16, 28, 178-179, 194-195, 202, 211, 216, 224-233 for example. Also Trachtman, 52-53, 57, 83, 92, 94-95, 98-99, 154, 159, 161, 168.

114. Forbis, 224.

115. Ibid., 202-203.

116. Don B. Kates, Jr., "Toward a History of Handgun Prohibition in the United States," in Restricting Handguns: The Liberal Skeptics Speak Out, ed. by Don B. Kates, Jr. (North River Press, Inc. 1979), pp. 10-12.

117. Forbis, 220. Kennett and Anderson claim that a total of more than 1,700 novels were written about Buffalo Bill between 1869 and 1933. Lee Kennett and James LaVerne Anderson, The Gun in America: The Origins of a National Dilemma (Westport, Connecticut & London, England: Greenwood Press, 1975), p. 125.

118. Forbis, 203-220.

119. Ibid., 218.

120. Easton, 409.

121. Ibid., 409-410.

122. Forbis, 220.

123. Ibid.

124. Ibid., 29.

125. Ibid., 217.

126. Ibid., 214 & 217.

127. Ramon F. Adams, "Cowboys and Horses of the American West," in The Book of the American West, ed. by Jay Monaghan (New York: Julian Messner, Inc., 1963), p. 333.

128. Forbis, 22 & 26.

129. Trachtman, 113.

130. Ibid., 113, 115.

131. Bat Masterson, among others, evidently engaged in such exhibitions. Trachtman, 124. Movie, TV and pulp westerns have such characters drawing their weapons from their holsters with lightening speed and hitting coins and other small objects that have been tossed into the air. Often they are shown "fanning" their single-actions, slapping back the hammer with the palm of the hand not holding the gun, for rapid fire and doing fantastically accurate shooting in this manner. Even historians, popular and otherwise, have helped perpetuate this image--see Alistair Cooke, Alistair Cooke's America (New York: Alfred A. Knoph, 1973), p. 233. They are not taken seriously by modern shooting authorities, however. Only the very best modern exhibition shooters have approached such feats, with the help of modern equipment--see Ed McGivern, Fast and Fancy Revolver Shooting and Police Training (Chicago: Follett Publishing Company, 1962). Old-time exhibition shooters sometimes resorted to trickery or shot shells to give the impression that they were better than they were. See Lugs, 169-173.

132. Trachtman, 125.

133. Forbis, 217; Trachtman, 38-39; Joseph G. Rosa, The Gunfighter: Man or Myth (Norman, Oklahoma: University of Oklahoma Press, 1969), pp. 124-154; and W. Eugene Hollon, Frontier Violence: Another Look (London, Oxford, New York: Oxford University Press, 1974), pp. 200-203.

134. Jeff Cooper, Fighting Handguns (Los Angeles: Trend Books, 1958), p. 41.

135. Dulles, 171.

136. Forbis, 82.

137. Dulles, 174.

138. The cowboy who was to become known as Butch Cassidy the outlaw, is said to have been known for his shooting skills. As an outlaw, however, he seems to have been reluctant to use these skills. Trachtman, 91, and Forbis, 65.

139. Whit Collins and Garry James, "The Custer Few People Know," in Guns & Ammo 1973 Annual (Los Angeles: Peterson Publishing Company, 1972), 52-53.

140. Herman Lantz with the assistance of J. S. McCrary, People of Coal Town (Carbondale and Edwardsville, Illinois: Southern Illinois University Press, 1971), p. 98.

141. Ibid., 99.

142. Paul Angle, Bloody Williamson: A Chapter in American Lawlessness (New York: Alfred Knopf, 1962), pp. 132-205.

143. Graham and Gurr photograph section.

144. Kennett and Anderson, 156-157.

145. Forbis, 82.

146. Ibid., 186 & 203.

147. Ibid., 203.

148. Rosa, 62-63.

149. Trachtman, 48-49.

150. Martin Rywell, Fell's Collector's Guide to American Antique Firearms (New York: Frederick Fell, Inc., 1963), p. 181.

151. Kates, 11-12.

152. Ibid., 16.

153. Ibid., 21.

154. Ibid., 14.

155. Ibid.; Kennett and Anderson, 177-178.

156. Kates, 25.

157. David J. Bordua, "Gun Control and Opinion Measurement: Adversary Polling and the Construction of Social Meaning," as yet unpublished paper read at the Annual Meetings of the American Sociological Association, New York, August 27-31, 1980.

158. Kates, 28.

159. Bordua, 14.

160. Ibid., 16.

161. David T. Hardy and Kenneth L. Chotiner, "The Potential for Civil Liberties Violations in the Enforcement of Handgun Prohibition," in Restricting Handguns: The Liberal Skeptics Speak Out, ed. by Don B. Kates, Jr. (North River Press, Inc., 1979), pp. 200-201.

162. Kennett and Anderson, 254.

163. Trefethen and Serven, 202-227.

164. Parson, 100-110.

165. Bob Milek, "Hunting Handguns," in Special Purpose Handguns (Los Angeles: Petersen Publishing Company, 1981), pp. 22-27.

166. Payton Miller, "Metallic Silhouette Handguns," in Special Purpose Handguns (Los Angeles: Petersen

Publishing Company, 1981), 2. Also see Hal Swig-
gett, "This Silhouette Game--Where Its Been and
Where Its Headed," in Guns Illustrated: 1980
(Northfield, Illinois: DBI Books, Inc., 1980),
4-11, for a discussion of the evolution of this
gun sport.

167. Miller, 3.

168. See Peter A. Lake, "Shooting to Kill," Esquire,
Vol. 96 (February, 1981), 70-75. This article,
one of an increasing number of (but still rare)
pro-gun articles to appear in general interest
periodicals in the late 1970's and early 1980's,
describes the authors experiences in a combat program run by one of the founding fathers of combat
match shooting, retired Marine lieutenant colonel,
Jeff Cooper.

169. See Greg Moats, "Combat Pistolcraft: Martial Arts
or Gamesmanship," Guns, Vol. XXVI (April, 1980),
30-31+; and Richard Nichols, "Tougher Leather:
New Rules on Match Holsters Shake Up Competitors,"
Combat Handguns, Vol. 2 (April, 1981), 36-39.

170. Stuart M. Williams, "Portrait of a Champion," Combat Handguns, Vol. 2 (April, 1981), 65.

171. Jeff Carter, In the Tracks of the Cattle (Sydney,
Melbourne, London: Argus and Robertson, 1968),
pp. 183 & 105.

172. "Firearms: Laws and Use," a report presented at
the First Australian National Conference, Perth,
Western Australia, June 25-27, 1981, by University Extension, University of Western Australia
in Association with The Australian Institute of
Criminology and The Postgraduate Legal Education
Committee, University of Western Australia, p. 17.

173. Stenning and Moyer, 49-53.

174. Dentay, 62.

175. John Robinson, "Handgunning in Australia," The
American Handgunner, Vol. 3 (January/February,
1978), 24.

176. From an address by R. W. Page of the New South

Wales Police Association at The Australian Institute of Criminology Conference, June 30, 1981, p. 3.

177. Stenning and Moyer, 50.

CHAPTER IX

MISCELLANY--RECREATIONAL AND SYMBOLIC

GUNS AS BADGES

In the preceding chapter it was noted that the handgun became part of the American frontiersman's costume, and evidence to the effect that it came to serve as a badge-like status symbol of the westerner was presented. Nothing that was said, however, should be taken to imply that firearms, handguns or otherwise, have served as symbols of status only on the American frontier of the 19th century. While only on the American frontier, <u>of those parts of the world being considered in this study</u>, did a gun of any kind become an article of apparel, a central feature of the costume of a significant number of ordinary, though well-publicized, civilians, there is reason to believe that firearms have served as status symbols in all circles where they have been used regularly for practical or recreational purposes.[1] The fowling piece, it will be recalled from Chapter VI, was an important status symbol among European aristocrats, once shooting became a popular pastime with them, though the gun was not carried at all times. The matchlocks of the samurai nobility of Tokugawa Japan also appear to have served as symbols of rank. Surely the Kentucky rifle, the dueling pistol, and the target rifle, etc., have served as status symbols to those who regularly used them. The writer's firsthand association with the modern shooting fraternity leads him to expect that this was the case.

Those who know and appreciate firearms never tire of talking about them, and their talk often concerns the types and special features of the firearms used by themselves or others--well-known personalities past as well as present, fictional as well as real. Whole books and many articles in firearms periodicals have been devoted to a description of the guns carried by historical personages, and even to those guns carried by the Hollywood cowboy stars.[2] While possession of a firearm marks one off as someone with whom others who have an interest in firearms may have something in common, the type possessed enables others to make preliminary judgements concerning how seriously the possessor should be taken with respect to a number of things. The individual who shows up at a smallbore rifle match with a light sporting rifle has not marked himself off as a target shooter in the eyes of the others there assembled. He has much to learn before he can be one of them. On the other hand, the individual who goes hunting with a custom-made English shotgun has marked himself off as a man of means whether he can shoot or not. Russell, commenting on one of a pair of dueling pistols that were carried as sidearms by Jedediah Smith, states, "Smith was a prominent man in the fur brigades, and this pistol would indicate that he armed himself in a manner befitting his station."[3]

Since the badge function of firearms has already been illustrated in several cultural and historical contexts in the preceding chapters, the remainder of this chapter will explore related but more subtle recreational and symbolic aspects of firearms usage that have yet to be touched upon. In order best to accomplish this task, the format used so far will be abandoned, since it will not be necessary to treat the three basic types of firearms under discussion separately. Also, the United States will take over center stage though reference will occasionally be made to other parts of the world that have been touched on previously.

THE COLLECTING GAME

The first phenomenon to be considered is collecting, an activity through which firearms can function recreationally in the lives of those who possess them even though they may never be fired. There is no clear-cut line marking off those who possess more than one firearm from those who consider themselves to be collectors. To those who see themselves as collectors and are so defined by others who think of themselves as such, however, there is a rather clear-cut distinction to be made between an arsenal and a collection, even when the collection consists of late model firearms rather than those likely to be defined as obsolete. While those who collect may also hunt, target shoot, or keep firearms for personal protection--some do none of these--they will readily acknowledge that they have more guns than they need for these purposes. In fact, those firearms that form the collection proper may seldom, if ever, be fired. A man considered to be one of America's all-time great firearms collectors never fired the Pennsylvania-Kentucky rifles in which he specialized.[4] A member of "an old Pennsylvania German sect dedicated to peace," he "never shot anything more than a few .22 rim-fire rounds as a youngster during his 72 years."[5] To members of the collecting fraternity, therefore, their collections are other than sources of firepower.

Another difference between an arsenal and a collection, or a "serious" modern collection at least, is that the latter is likely to be built around some theme or be oriented toward some goal. Some collections, for instance, may consist of firearms associated with the American frontier of the last half of the 19th century. Others may consist of the various models produced by one specific company, Colt for example. Yet other collections may consist of variations of one specific model of Colt that have been produced over the years. And still others may consist of pocket pistols regardless of make or date of manufacture. There are obviously endless possibilities for collection themes. The guns in these collections, however, may be extremely ornate or very plain, the one-of-a-kind products of individual gunsmiths or of industrial experimentation or samples of models that have been produced by the hundreds of thousands, ancient or contemporary, associated with historical personages or events or straight off of the production line, precisionally fitted or shoddily tossed together. In fact, examples of all of the above and more might be brought together in the same collection. Though ornate or historical pieces may constitute the pride and joy of a collector, the "success" of his collection as judged by others depends on how the various pieces are seen to relate to each other.[6] "Serious" collecting, then, is not haphazard collecting.

It has been estimated that anywhere from 250,000 to 1,000,000 Americans are engaged in the sort of systematic collecting described above.[7] Many of these collectors belong to collectors' associations of which there are at least one hundred in the United States, with every state having at least one.[8] One of the largest of these associations had over 7,000 members as of 1974.[9] According to Hank Wieand Bowman, collector and author of several books on antique firearms,

> nearly all of these groups, either as individual collectors associations or in co-operation with one or more fellow associations, hold conventions at which many of the finer privately owned firearms are displayed and often offered for sale or

sold at auction.[10]

While all serious collectors may not belong to such associations, they can hardly get along without other collectors for without interacting with others who share
their interests individual collectors would not know
what firearms were considered to be worth collecting.
Even if they did know what guns were considered desirable, they would have no contacts to help them locate
and authenticate such pieces. And even if they found
the guns anyway, there would be no one to provide them
with recognition for the worth of some choice items and
the more subtle collection themes are likely to be lost
on the non-collecting public.[11]

Collectors have a world of their own, therefore, a
"status community" with a web of formal as well as informal contacts at least as widespread as that of target
shooters and probably greater than that of hunters. And
in this world, collectors' items are created as collectors trying to anticipate trends sometimes, through self-
fulfilling prophecies, create them. In 1948, for example, a Henry rifle was simply an old gun. Yes, it was
the forerunner of the Winchester line of lever-actions
and it had been used in the Civil War and on the frontier, but if it had most of its original finish, it
could be had for $28, according to collector Payton
Autry. In 1974 that same rifle, according to Autry,
could have brought $2,800 on the collectors' market.[12]
And that was the 1974 value of a plain production model
Henry, not of the ornate, custom built gun of an emper-
or. The record price paid for a firearm of the latter
sort as of 1974, was $300,000 paid by a museum for a
fowling piece made in 1615 for Louis VIII.[13] But the
Henry is not the only ordinary gun that collector interest has transformed into a gold mine. Consequently,
collectors often advise those of modest means who wish
to join their fraternity to spend as little as possible
now on items that, though of little present interest,
have the potential to increase in interest and value in
the future.[14]

Yet there is obviously more to collecting than making money. If money were the prime concern, a Henry
could still be had for $28, or even less. The collection
of Pennsylvania-Kentucky rifles owned by the Pennsylvania
pacifist mentioned above was undoubtedly worth a great
deal of money to collectors, but the collection rather
than its monetary value seems to have been what made him

one of the "greatest American firearms collectors of all time" in the eyes of those who shared his interests.[15] This is not to say, however, that money-related matters have nothing to do with one's acquiring recognition as a collector. The moneyed collector is obviously in a better position to acquire the pieces most admired by others, and even if he fails, his efforts may gain him recognition. The author of the article on the $300,000 gun felt it worthy of note that a private collector, whose name he reported, made a losing bid of $268,000.[16] On the other hand, the collector who seems adept at acquiring collectors' items at a fraction of the going price from uninformed pawnshop owners, etc., may also acquire a reputation as a sophisticate who knows where to look. His ethics, however, may be questioned by some of his fellow collectors if he makes a practice of taking what might be considered undue advantage of the uninformed. At any rate, as can be seen from the above, there is much more to serious collecting than acquiring a number of guns, and that more has to do with others and what they are likely to think of one's acquisitions, and even of one's means of acquisition.

Collecting of the sort described above seems to have developed in the early 20th century, and it is still limited to those parts of the world that have the highest standards of living and to the moneyed elites of the so-called underdeveloped parts of the world.[17] This is not surprising, since when and where people have lived barely above the subsistence level, they have seldom accumulated tools that would not earn their keep. For centuries, kings, emperors, and well-to-do aristocrats have maintained armories composed of their own fighting and hunting weapons, the weapons of their ancestors, presentation weapons, and weapons acquired from their enemies on the battlefield, but few if any of these individuals seem to have systematically attempted to build collections as do modern collectors. Yet firearms acquired in such a haphazard fashion have formed the basis of more formal collections and interests in serious collecting on the part of individuals of modest means in parts of the world, such as the United States, where firearms have been used for centuries by common people. In the United States, in some circles at least, firearms have long been considered appropriate gifts for young men who have come of age, and given what has been said in this and the previous chapter, one can certainly understand why.[18] Many Americans have acquired their first gun in this fashion. Of course, others have bought guns

for their personal use. Still others have brought guns
back from wars as souvenirs. And since guns are made
of metal and other such relatively durable materials as
wood, once in circulation, unless lost, rusted out, or
otherwise destroyed, they are passed from one generation to the next. There is no telling how many Americans still have guns that one of their own ancestors
carried on the frontier or in the Civil or even the
Revolutionary War, though those individuals already in
the collecting game have ferreted out many of these
antique weapons in recent years. Many Americans, then,
have accumulated a number of guns, old as well as new,
without intending to become collectors. Nevertheless,
in doing so they have acquired something more than a
working arsenal. With their guns they have acquired
links to the past, etc., that given encouragement, have
often enough expanded into an interest in formal collecting. And as shall be seen, the necessary encouragement can easily be had.

THE GUN AS SYMBOLIC LINK

The advice that **veteran** collectors give to those
interested in becoming collectors concerning the types
of guns that the latter should collect, would seem to
indicate that collectors see their avocation to be a
worthwhile activity in and of itself. The potential
collector's problem is not how to acquire the type of
firearms that he already has decided to collect; rather
his problem is to select a type that is readily available so that he can get involved in the game. Yet there
is another side to collecting which has to do more with
that which is collected than with collecting as an activity, and in considering this other side we move to
the final phenomenon to be explored in this chapter.

In attempting to explain why firearms are collected,
collector Frederick Wilkinson, an Englishman, has written:

> What, then, is it that arouses such inter-
> est in these lethal weapons? First of
> all, it must be stressed that for the
> great majority of collectors the purpose
> of the weapon is of very minor importance.
> Many say that this is an escapist ap-
> proach, as indeed it probably is, but very
> **few** collectors see these items as being

intended to maim or kill. They are viewed
purely, almost exclusively, as artistic
objects in their own right; they are valued for their mechanical design and for
their aesthetic appeal. Interest in a
firearm may be aroused by many things, but
most of the collectors, if they are honest,
would admit that there is in them an element of romance. A flintlock pistol may
never have left the workshop where it was
made, but it could equally have travelled
across America with Lewis and Clark or
have seen action on the battlefield of
Waterloo; it may have been used to hold up
or defend a coach, or any one of a dozen
or more exciting events may have befallen
it.[19]

Another Englishman, Macdonald Hastings, who spe-
cializes in collecting English sporting guns and their
accessories, has put it this way:

The lesson, it applies to all old things,
is that if you keep them long enough posterity will give them the recognition of
what may be called romantic disuse. The
powder flasks and the shot pouches I have
shown on these pages might well have been
thrown away, as most of them were, when
their time was done. Some survived in
attics; so some are here to remind us of
an earlier generation. The luck in history is always what somebody was too lazy
to destroy. The charm of it is the recol-
lection that the people who belonged--in
this context, those pot hatted characters
with their muzzleloaders--were just like
us, the sort of chaps it would have been
fun to swap pints of beer with.
     With an old gun in your hands, with
the imagination to recreate the people
who used it, you are in effect extending
a lifetime far beyond your own.[20]

And American firearms enthusiast and shooter Jeff
Cooper has written of one specific gun, the Colt Model
"P": "Just to hold one in your hand produces a feeling
of kinship with our western heritage--an appreciation of
things like courage and honor and chivalry and the sanc-

tity of a man's word."[21]

A different sort of symbolic linkage, a less historical one, is expressed by a gun fancier who has made it
a practice over the years to trade off the weapons he
has used for a while so that he can acquire and try out
different models. In explaining why he would not consider trading off his first rifle, a .22, in this fashion, he relates how he still takes it out hunting and
plinking when his freelance writing bogs down.

> I could always take a better gun for such
> occasions, of course. But I don't. For
> some reason, the old .22 seems to fit those
> hours when a man is trying to recreate him-
> self mentally. It is a link with the past,
> used not as a means to withdrawal but more
> like a medium by which one remembers the
> dreams and aspirations of his youth. In-
> deed, sighting down the barrel of one's
> boyhood .22 helps him see again the future
> toward which he has always been pointing,
> but which may have been obscured by out-
> side forces.
>   So my boyhood .22 will not be traded.
> It is filled with fond memories of the
> past. It has taught me things about shoot-
> ing, about life, and about myself. It was
> my first rifle and it will also be my
> last.[22]

Themes of this sort linking firearms to phenomena
transcending by far narrow matters of weapon usage are
common, if not ubiquitous, in the works of those, collectors or otherwise, who have attempted to explain
their interests in firearms in general or in certain
types of firearms in particular. But such a linkage is
manifested not only through what many gun enthusiasts,
collectors and otherwise, say, but through what they do.
An examination of the demand for replicas of old firearms and of guns incorporating the latest developments
but patterned after the old, as indicated by the market
for such weapons that has been expanding since World
War II, should illustrate this point.

Over the centuries, as the advances in firearms technology touched upon in the preceding pages have been
made, they have not completely stripped earlier weapons
of their effectiveness. A 16th century matchlock, or

even a 14th century hand cannon, is no less a weapon today than it was in its own day even though modern cartridge-firing repeaters can be loaded more quickly and
fired more quickly and accurately. Yet the matchlock and
the hand cannon are not likely to be taken seriously as
weapons by moderns who have access to modern guns and
need them to cope with their enemies, or to hunt for
their food, or for that matter, to produce the best possible score on the target range. Given such goals, the
new tools are much more effective than the ancient
tools; consequently, the old guns have passed from use
and been defined as obsolete. This is not to imply, of
course, that the earlier patterns have generally passed
from the scene quickly as firearms improvements have
appeared.

It has generally taken some time to perfect new developments; therefore, many prospective users over the
years have hesitated to replace proven weapons with new
weapons that might fail them during an emergency. As
we have seen, the matchlock remained in use even in the
more technologically advanced parts of the world long
after not only the wheellock but the flintlock had been
perfected. Economic considerations evidently kept nation states as well as many individual hunters from replacing the old ignition system with the new as long as
the former was felt to be able to do the job it was
called upon to do on the battlefield or in the forest.
Similarly, though the transition from muzzleloader to
cartridge-firing breechloaders took only fifty years or
so in the "modern" parts of the world, some individuals
continued to use the former well after the latter were
in common use. For those persons who settled far back
in the wilderness, powder and lead might be more easily
acquired than cartridges of a specific caliber. Kentucky type rifles seem to have been regularly used in
some of the more isolated areas of Appalachia well into
the 20th century. But moderns who acquire replicas of
old guns, or modern guns patterned after the old, apparently do not have such practical considerations in mind.
Perhaps the most effective way to make this point, is
through a case history of an American revolver that most
who know guns would consider to be obsolescent rather
than obsolete.

The Colt Model "P", which Jeff Cooper has claimed
links him symbolically with "our western heritage," was
in continuous production from 1873 until 1941 when Colt
stopped production of its commercial line to focus its

attention on the war effort. During those sixty-eight
years, nearly 360,000 of these revolvers, also known in
one version or other as the Single Action Army, the
Peacemaker, or the Frontier Six Shooter, were produced.[23]
The Model "P" in .45 caliber was used by the United
States Army from 1873 until 1892, and it remained limited standard until 1909. Of the total number produced,
however, the Army purchased only 37,000 or so and most
of the rest went to civilians on the western frontier.
There the gun was extremely popular in various calibers
from the mid-1870's through the first decade or two of
the 20th century. During this period, it was the revolver most likely to be found in the hip holsters of cowboys and other westerners, and practically all of the
best known frontier characters carried a Model "P" at
one time or other during their careers--Wyatt Earp,
Bat Masterson, Buffalo Bill, Jesse James, Billy the
Kid, and rancher Theodore Roosevelt among them.[24]

For various reasons, many gun experts have found
fault with the Model "P" from practically the moment it
was introduced to this day. Cavalrymen found it difficult to reload the gun from the back of a galloping
horse, since each empty cartridge had to be manually
punched from its cylinder one at a time and each new
cartridge had to be inserted one at a time.[25] As a
single-action, its hammer had to be pulled back manually
before the trigger could be pulled to fire a shot. Since
the double-action principle had been in use for about
twenty years at the time that the Model "P" was introduced, and revolvers combining single-and double-action
principles had been available for fifteen years, some
authorities considered the Model "P" obsolescent in this
respect.[26] And yet other authorities have found the internal construction of the gun to be overly fragile.[27]
On the plus side, however, the gun could still function
with several of its parts out of order, and possibly
most important, there is almost unanimous agreement
among those who have handled the Model "P" that it is
superbly balanced.[28]

As double-action revolvers that could also be fired
single-action were improved and semi-automatic pistols
were perfected, the Model "P"'s popularity gradually
faded, though it continued to have its admirers--one of
World War II general George S. Patton's ivory-handled
pistols was a Model "P". The market for the gun dwindled considerably during the 1930's, however, and once
Colt resumed commerical production after World War II,

the Model "P" was dropped from its line.[29] But at about
the same time that it was becoming merely an old none
too rare gun to those who used handguns for practical or
recreational purposes, the Model "P" began to receive a
great deal of publicity in other circles. The Colt six-
shooter had long been the standard sidearm of the pulp
western successors of the dime novel heroes, and with
the coming of the moving picture western, countless numbers of Americans, even those not familiar with firearms, were exposed to it in the hands of Hollywood idols
from William S. Hart through singing cowboys Gene Autry
and Roy Rogers to "adult western" stars such as Gary
Cooper and John Wayne. Other revolvers actually used
on the frontier seldom were to be seen in the western
movies of the 1930's through the 1960's, even when the
story being depicted was supposed to have taken place
long before 1873 when the Model "P" first made its appearance.[30]

One side effect of this Model "P" western movie
exposure is that the cap pistols patterned after the
sidearms carried by matinee idols Autry, Rogers, and
Hopalong Cassidy, etc., toys that millions of American
boys (and girls) have owned, all are reasonable fac-
similes of this Colt. After World War II, the Single
Action Colt's exposure was increased even more with the
advent of widespread television ownership and the TV
"adult western." TV's Matt Dillon, the Mavericks, the
Cartwrights and all of their friends as well as the vil-
lains they faced, carried the Colt six-shooter, as did
the movie "cowboys" making their reappearance on TV.

Colt's announcement after World War II that the
Model "P" would no longer be produced, therefore, coin-
cided with, and may have helped to stimulate, a renewed
interest in that revolver. Though not rare, the Colt
six-shooter became a collector's item literally overnight during a period of economic boom when many ordinary people were acquiring the means to develop and in-
dulge their interests in collecting. The five hundred
revolvers assembled after the war from parts produced
before the war were immediately snapped up, and second-
hand guns in reasonable condition that could be had for
$10 or less before the announcement that production
would be discontinued sold for $75 afterwards. The
price continued to increase sharply.

Not only collectors, dedicated and otherwise, but
adherents of the new sport of fast draw, which was based

on the highly artificial TV and movie versions of the
western gunfight, wanted single-action Colt six-shooters.
The fast draw had been emphasized so much in the TV and
movie westerns of the postwar era that special belt holster combinations had been developed to enable actors,
doubles, and stuntmen to draw ever more quickly, though
such "rigs" were of little practical use to those who
actually had to depend on their handguns.[31] So much
emphasis was placed on speed of draw, that elaborate
electric timers were developed to measure the split sec-
onds it took for an individual to pull his six-shooter
from his holster and fire a blank or a wax bullet. From
actors and exhibition shooters, interest in fast draw
spread to the populace at large and competitions
evolved, the competitors themselves being attired as
western gunmen--or Hollywood-TV versions thereof--and
armed with single-action Colts--or copies thereof.

With the demand for this 1873 model revolver running high, the Great Western Arms Company of Hollywood,
California, began producing almost exact-copies of them
equipped with imitation staghorn grips--genuine staghorn
gripped six-shooters having been the favorites of many
movie heroes. In 1953 another new company, Sturm, Ruger, introduced a .22 caliber single-action revolver
that, though scaled down in size and incorporating many
internal improvements, externally resembled the Colt
rather closely. Within a few years, Ruger was producing
larger-caliber revolvers of the same pattern. Since
that time, some companies have followed Great Western's
lead and produced almost exact duplicates of the Colt,
some of these revolvers being manufactured in Europe,
while other companys have followed Ruger and produced
revolvers bearing some resemblance to the original, in
some cases going to great lengths to do so. High-Stan-
dard, for example, has gone to great lengths to make its
double-action, swing-out-cylinder, nine-shot, .22 caliber revolver look like a single-action, fixed cylinder,
Colt six-shooter. The hammer has the Colt's graceful
curve, which is useful for thumb cocking but is not
generally to be found on other revolvers that can be
fired double-as well as single-action. The cylinder is
released to swing out for loading by a device contained
in a housing under the barrel. This housing resembles
the ejector housing on the Colt--the rod used to punch
the empties from its fixed-cylinder--but the device it
contains would not be needed if the housing itself was
not there. If it was not there, however, the appearance of a "western six-shooter" would be lost. The

names of newer versions of this revolver, which in its original form is still called the "Double-Nine," are the "Longhorn" and the "Durango." Harrington and Richardson and Iver Johnson also produce double-action-single-action .22s of western pattern, but the ejector rods are necessary on these guns since their cylinders do not swing out, ease of loading having been sacrificed for that "western look." The former is called the "Forty-Niner," the latter the "Sidewinder." Savage Arms Company went so far as to produce a single-shot .22 caliber pistol with a dummy cylinder and ejector rod, etc., that gave it the appearance of a "western"--i.e., Colt revolver.

Though any or all of these modern non-Colt, "western pattern," revolvers and imitation revolvers may be transformed into collectors' items someday, they are not so defined presently. Rather, they compete with each other and with other revolvers and semi-automatics possessing more modern features, but priced within the same range, for the attention of those who wish to acquire handguns for practical or recreational purposes.[32] The very fact that many of these "western" revolvers-- notably the various Ruger models--have more than held their own on the market, would seem to indicate that guns are more than just guns to many who acquire them. For those individuals who acquire guns for recreational use, or for such low-risk practical purposes as pest control, appearances that link these weapons to a frontier past glamorously socially reconstructed in the present with the help of TV and the movies can compete on equal terms with modern features that make for easier loading and quicker firing. Colt eventually came to this conclusion, at any rate, and reintroduced its ancient Model "P" in 1955.[33] Two years later Colt introduced a scaled-down .22 caliber version of the Model "P" called the 'Frontier Scout." And in advertising these weapons, the company has focused on their links to the frontier and to the Colt heritage rather than on more practical matters of performance.

An advertisement for the old Colt, for example, shows a photograph of one of these revolvers with a 7½ inch cavalry-length barrel under a color drawing of the lower extremities of galloping horses and the legs of their uniformed riders flashing past a feathered Indian spear imbedded in the ground. Printed on the drawing is: "A COLT says: distant drums, hoof beats, pursuit, confidence." Under the photograph of the revolver at the bottom of the full page ad is:

> "Boots and Saddles" once was a thrilling
> sound accompanying a Colt's Single Action
> Army revolver in battle. Today the bugles
> are still, the sabres sheathed. But the
> classic lines of Colt's most famous single-
> action revolver still live, recreated in
> Colt's Single Action Army "Peacemaker."
> Superbly detailed in the Colt tradition
> of fine craftsmanship, it not only reflects
> its famous heritage but Colt's advance-
> ments in design and metallurgy, as well.
> Heft it, sight it. Give your imagination
> a whirl. You might even hear the strains
> of "Gary Owen" as the burgees of the 7th
> cavalry whip by. . . .[34]

Advertisements for the new .22 also have linked it
to the past, a past in which it played no part. Two
ads each pictured a "Frontier Scout" equipped with imitation staghorn grips under color drawings of western
scenes, one of a tiny horse and rider lost in the vastness of a western landscape, the other of a westerner
seated by a campfire contemplating the Colt six-shooter
he holds in his hand. On the former: "A COLT says:
lone vigil, coyote call, sundown, confidence." On the
latter: "A COLT says: embers, shadows, snapped twig,
confidence." Under the former: "Out there, surrounded
by the haunting stillness of the trail, many a man has
conquered loneliness with the feel of a Colt at his side.
Colt's Frontier Scout is that kind of gun."[35] Under the
latter:

> A Colt says a lot of things. Little Big
> Horn, Dodge City, and Cripple Creek.
> Frontier marshal and Wyatt Earp. For a
> Colt is no ordinary handgun.
> Rich in heritage, uncompromising in
> quality, Colt's revolvers made today still
> reflect Colt's 131-year-tradition of su-
> perb craftsmanship . . . plus all the re-
> finements and design improvements that
> modern metallurgy and precision manufac-
> turing techniques make possible.
> Isn't it time you had a better grip
> on American History? Visit your nearby
> Colt's Registered Dealer today.[36]

The Colt Model "P," one of the best known guns among those who know little about guns as well as those who know much about them, as a result of its TV and movie exposure outside of the United States as well as inside, may well have been the first gun of a pattern generally considered to be obsolescent to have been resurrected. For this reason, its renewed popularity has been used to make the point that those acquiring firearms often see them as links with phenomena transcending by far narrow matters of weapon usage. But other old patterns have also been resurrected. Copies of the tiny double-barreled derringer produced by Remington from 1865 until 1930, the hideout weapon of gamblers, saloon girls, and others in the movie-TV as well as the real West, have been made by Great Western as well as by a number of lesser European manufacturers. Colt has offered a .22 caliber version of its .41 caliber single-shot derringer of the 1870's. Navy Arms offers an Italian made copy of the Remington Model 1875 revolver that once was a rival of the Colt Model "P," but that has had very little movie or TV exposure. Harrington and Richardson has produced a replica of the Model 1873 "trapdoor" Springfield single-shot rifles carried by the Indian fighting Army of the 1870's and 80's, and by some National Guard units in the Spanish American War. Savage-Stevens introduced a near copy of a tiny .22 caliber single-shot rifle that had little to do with "winning the West," but that introduced many boys to shooting around the turn of the century. Ruger has created several technologically modern single-shot rifles that bear a striking resemblance to single-shot carbines and target rifles of the late 19th and early 20th centuries. Even foreign guns have been resurrected, as the "Luger," used by the German Army as well as by many other armies from the very early 20th century through World War II, is now being produced commercially again by Mauser. This pistol has had a great deal of war and spy movie exposure, and was considered a choice souvenir by American GIs during both world wars.

Many more examples could be listed, but these should suffice to show that new guns are being bought for reasons not wholly linked to the practical or to the recreational. Yet few if any of the guns mentioned above would be considered completely obsolete, since they are all cartridge-firing breechloaders. Most of these weapons could still be used for the purposes for which they were originally created--hunting, self-protection, etc.--without unduly handicapping or incon-

veniencing the user. General Douglas MacArthur carried
a Remington 1865 double-barreled derringer through World
War II. Even older powder-and-ball weapons are making
a comeback, however, and their slow-loading, tedious
cleaning requirements, and in some cases, power and accuracy deficiencies do handicap and inconvenience their
shooters.

In a certain sense, muzzleloading guns have never
departed the scene in the modern world. Some European
companies continued to make cheap muzzleloaders for the
African, South American, and Southeast Asian trade well
into the 20th century, and these guns were also sold to
such muzzleloading enthusiasts that were interested in
them in the United States and elsewhere.[37] In the
United States, some folk craftsmen have, through the
years, continued painstakingly to fashion handmade rifles of the Kentucky pattern. Such weapons were still
in use in some isolated parts of the country well into
the 20th century. And, of course, many Americans have,
over the years, acquired old muzzleloaders through
inheritance or some such fashion.

In 1931, 67 muzzleloading enthusiasts gathered at
Friendship, Indiana to test their skills with these old
weapons against each other, and the National Muzzle
Loading Rifle Association, which numbered 18,000 members
by 1974, had its start.[38] Since these matches were
initiated some 20 years or so before the interest in
firearms collecting started to spread in the United
States, most of the rifles, shotguns, and handguns used
in them were originals. Even as late as 1950, when the
first match of the North-South Skirmish Association--a
Civil War-oriented group--was fired at Berwyn, Maryland,
the Union and Confederate teams that competed against
one another were able to acquire unissued Civil War rifle muskets from Francis Bannerman Sons at $25 apiece.[39]
Once prices began to skyrocket, however, original weapons were put out of the reach of the man on the street.
Originals, consequently, have gradually faded from the
firing line at Friendship and Berwyn and other places
where muzzleloading enthusiasts compete against one
another. Some shooters have resorted to making their
own guns from modern factory-made parts while others
have them custom built.[40] The latter alternative can
be rather expensive, however.[41] For those powder-and-
ball shooters interested in the repeating arms of the
Civil War--and the Civil War Centenial seems to have
stimulated such an interest--neither using original guns

296

nor making their own copies of such weapons is likely to be seen as practical. Enter the powder-and-ball replica.

The author of an article appearing in the 1973 annual edition of a gun periodical wrote that

> as recently as ten years ago, it would have been easy to write a survey of black powder guns and accessories. There were only about a half-dozen major firms in the business. Today, there are so many makers and importers of black powder replicas that space won't allow complete coverage of them all.[42]

In the catalog following his article, no fewer than 51 different factory made powder-and-ball rifles, shotguns, and handguns are pictured along with several replicas of cartridge-firing breechloaders.[43] Some of these guns are merely muzzleloaders, little or no attempt having been made to make them look like any particular antique weapon. Such is the case with Harrington and Richardson's "Huntsman" rifle and Ruger's "Old Army" cap-and-ball revolver. Other guns range from reasonably close to faithful replicas of Kentucky rifles, various models of Colt and Remington revolvers, and Brown Bess muskets of the Revolutionary period. One revolver, in fact, is something more than a replica. Colt has resumed production of its 1851 Navy revolver of Civil War and pre-Model "P" frontier fame. A 1971 advertisement for this weapon centers around a black and white photograph of one lying on what appears to be a saddle bag. Arranged around the revolver, but less emphasized, are a broad-brimmed hat, the hilt of a cavalry sabre, spurs, and six pistol balls. At the top of the page, "The Age of the Colt" in a fancy scroll is followed by:

> The most famous of all cap-and-ball revolvers is back. After 98 years, Colt's resumes production of the original 1851 Navy. The same gun "Wild Bill" Hickok used to carve a niche for himself in American history. Go back with him to desolate Rock Creek Station where he single handedly out-fought the McCanles gang with a brace of Navys. Heft one at your Colt's Registered Dealer.[44]

297

Since bringing back the Navy in the early 1970's, Colt
has reintroduced practically its whole line of pre-
Civil War cap-and-ball revolvers, which like the Navy
and the Model "P," have also been replicated by other
companies. Many of these non-Colt replicas of Colts,
it might be noted, have been produced in Europe for
sale in the United States.[45]

As the very name of the North-South Skirmish Association implies, there is often much more to the organized shooting of old weapons than shooting competition.
A member of this association has written that

> shooting is not the only skirmishing
> activity, nor are men the only partici-
> pants. The Association has a fife and
> drum corps made up of volunteer musicians
> from the Association's membership. Bands-
> men, many of whom play century-old in-
> struments, parade on the evening before
> each skirmish, performing songs well known
> to troops of both sides. The band also
> provides music for all skirmish ceremon-
> ies.
>   In addition to shooting matches, con-
> tests are held to select the best looking
> uniform and ladies compete for awards for
> the reproduction of Civil War-era dresses.
> Synthetic fibers are not acceptable. Sew-
> ing machines may be used for straight
> stitching, but all decorations and em-
> broidery must be hand sewn. Likewise, zip-
> pers are forbidden and contestants may
> use only buttons or hook-and-eye fasten-
> ers--sewn in place by hand. Contestants
> are graded on the completeness, original-
> ity and authenticity of their costumes.
> Competition is keen and prizes are hard
> won.[46]

Even at Friendship where the matches are not linked to
any particular historical event

> primitive matches were initiated . . .
> in 1967. The objective was to recreate
> the American frontier of the period 1770-
> 1840. Costume and prowess in skills that
> were practiced by the pioneers, as well
> as marksmanship, are judged. Primitive

matches use targets similar to those described in journals of the trappers' ren-
dezvous of the 1820's. Ability to hit a
mark with knife or tomahawk, or to start
a fire with flint and steel, rank equally
with ability to shoot a rifle.[47]

Along with the replica firearms, then, have come replicas of period costumes.[48]

To date, such elaborate recreations of the past
have been connected only with the organized use of powder-and-ball guns in the United States, though breechloaders and cartridge guns of the period can also be
used in Civil War-related events. With the exception
of "fast draw" competitions of dubious historical au-
thenticity that have been related to the renewed interest in the Colt Model "P," the shooting of old breechloaders and cartridge guns and their modern replicas,
guns not marked off as clearly as the powder-and-ball
weapons from modern weapons, has yet to result in anything comparable to the powder-and-ball competitions.
However, organizations such as the Second U.S. Reacti-
vated Cavalry have attempted to recreate for recreational purposes the military life of the late frontier, and
several companies are producing replicas of the clothing
and shooting accouterments of that period.[49] The broadly symbolic aspects of not only the weapons used but of
these various historical recreations seems obvious, as
do the recreational aspects of these activities. The
interest in firing antique firearms, or replicas thereof, though possibly more widespread in the United States
than elsewhere, is not limited to this country. Though
information on this phenomenon as it is manifested in
other parts of the world is scarce, there are indications that it does exist elsewhere. The Japanese have
acquired an interest in shooting replicas of their ancient matchlocks, and Japanese matchlockmen have become
regular participants, along with American, English, German, Spanish, and many other shooters in the matches
sponsored by the Muzzle Loaders International Committees.[50]

Europeans shoot replicas of the Colt six-shooter
with which they became familiar through American movies
and TV, but their interest in these revolvers may often
be more recreationally or even practically rooted than
symbolic. In France, for instance, current firearms
laws classify firearms designed before the invention of

smokeless powder in 1885 as collectors' items; and consequently, such guns and the black powder ammunition used with them can be purchased without restriction.[51] Therefore, the Model "P," or a replica thereof, is a logical choice for Frenchmen who wish to possess a serviceable handgun legally but avoid what Josserand has called "the cumbersome and arbitrary machinery of the police licensing bureau."[52] When we turn to other types of obsolete or obsolescent personal arms, of course, the sword, bow and arrow, and crossbow, for example, recreational and symbolic interests of the sort manifested through the various muzzleloading groups and their activities can be found in all of the technologically advanced parts of the world.[53]

Before bringing this chapter to a close, it should be noted that some advanced collectors have felt threatened by the flood of replicas that has hit the market in recent years. With a few alterations, some of these guns conceivably could be passed off as the real thing, thus making the collector's task of authenticating desirable items even more difficult and risky than it already is. To acquire such a weapon only to have it identified later as a fake, would not only be costly but embarrassing to a person whose very reputation rests on his supposed expertise as a collector. Even Colt's 1851 Navy, which after all is the real thing reintroduced after 98 years, could conceivably detract from the value of the originals in collections if enough of these new guns were to be produced. Consequently, some influential collectors have attempted in one way or another to bring pressure to bear on the producers of replicas.[54] To avoid such problems, most producers avoid making exact duplicates of the originals, though the differences between the replicas and the originals may be so small that only an "expert" can detect them. Colt has even slightly altered its own 1851 Navy to make it somewhat different from the original.

Not all collectors have felt threatened by replicas, however. As might be expected, some collect replicas, though so far such collecting has been limited mostly to "commemorative" guns produced expressly to be collected. The American Bicentennial Company commemorated the American Revolution with a faithful replica of the British Brown Bess musket used on both sides during that war. The gun was handmade in England.[55] Only 811 were made, one for each man who served with the Royal Welch Fusiliers, the regiment that held Fusilier's Redoubt at

Yorktown until Cornwallis' surrender in 1781. Each musket had the owner's name inscribed on an engraved Fusilier's badge, a tradition of that regiment. The price, $585, was high by 1976 standards, and put the gun out of the reach of ordinary gun fanciers. The replicas of George Washington's pistols produced for the Bicentennial were also out of reach of the latter, but not all commemoratives are. Neither are all commemoratives based on obsolescent or obsolete guns. Colt, which seems to have lead the way with such guns, used its .45 semi-automatic pistol, which has been the standard pistol of the armed forces of the United States since 1911, to commemorate various World War I battles. Winchester, Remington, Marlin, Savage, and other companies have used current production models to commemorate all sorts of prominent persons, organizations, and events in some way or other related even remotely to firearms.[56] Since all commemoratives are limited editions planned as such, their collectors' values have increased tremendously in a short period of time. For example, 104 Colt .22 caliber replicas of their .41 caliber derringer of the 1870's, produced for Geneseo, Illinois' 125th anniversary, cost under $30 when first marketed, $325 fourteen years later.[57]

SUMMARY

While the symbolic link between firearms and historical events manifested through the appearance on the market of commemorative arms might seem somewhat contrived, that manifested through collecting and the appearance of replicas and resurrected old guns, as can be seen from what has been said in this chapter, seems to have developed of its own accord through interaction at the grass-roots level. Taken together, however, these phenomena seem to offer convincing evidence to the effect that to many of those who possess them firearms are much more than tools or even pieces of sporting equipment. Recreationally they can tie even the non-shooting collector into a status community that provides him with recognition. Symbolically they can tie their possessors, collectors or otherwise, to phenomena far transcending the simple use of a tool. While links with the grandiosely historical have been emphasized for effect, the remarks of the gun trader concerning his feelings for his first rifle suggest that there are other kinds of links.

FOOTNOTES

1. As mentioned in Chapter VI, Scottish lords wore pistols openly to the end of the 18th century or so, and Montenegrin commoners, on the periphery of the area being considered, wore them well into the 20th century. In other parts of the world the badge nature of firearms is obvious. In modern Brazil's Rio Branco region, for example,

> as many people as can afford them carry revolvers, usually a .22 caliber, but occasionally a .32, .38, or even a .45. The smaller caliber is more popular because of the price and the weight of the ammunition. Marksmanship with these guns is of a low order and they are very rarely used. Sometimes as a result of boredom an old tin is used as a target, but the only times I observed a revolver practically employed were an unsuccessful attempt to hunt a deer from horseback and the successful slaughter of a cow from point-blank range. Even if they are of little practical value, there is considerable etiquette surrounding the wearing of sidearms. No one will sit down to eat wearing a gun, nor would one enter another's house with one, the normal practice being to leave it in the bunkhouse or near the door of the house. In the small cowtown of Murusu, the delegadeo (sheriff) has decreed that all visitors are to hand in their arms at the police post on arrival in town and can collect them there again on departure. The small bar and general store in which I lived for some months had a notice to this effect on the wall and this, together with the other behavior surrounding sidearms, seem to reflect an almost conscious attempt to emulate the 'Wild West' in certain areas of their lives.

Peter Riviera, The Forgotten Frontier: Ranches of

Northern Brazil (New York, Chicago, San Francisco, Atlanta, Dallas, Montreal, Toronto, London, Sydney: Holt, Rinehart and Winston, Inc., 1972), p. 35. And in modern Pakistan's Independent Tribal Territory, "men and boys carry rifles and pistols wherever they go and never remove them except when entering some restaurants which post signs prohibiting weapons being worn while dining and providing a check room for them." Jack Lott, "The People of the Gun," Guns and Ammo 1973 Annual (Los Angeles: Peterson Publishing Company, 1972), p. 259.

2. See, for example, George E. Virgines, Saga of the Colt Six-Shooter and the Famous Men Who Used It (New York: Frederick Fell, Inc., 1969), and Guns and Ammo Guide to Guns of the Gunfighters (Los Angeles: Petersen Publishing Co., 1975).

3. Carl P. Russell, Guns on the Early Frontier: A History of Firearms from Colonial Times Through the Years of the Western Fur Trade (Berkeley and Los Angeles: University of California Press, 1962), p. 90.

4. Editorial, "Gun Collecting as A Fine Art," The American Rifleman, Vol. 121 (July, 1973), 20.

5. Ibid.

6. James E. Serven, "Some Thoughts on Assembling a Gun Collection," The American Rifleman, Vol. 122 (March, 1974), 30.

7. Editorial, "Gun Collecting As A Fine Art," 20. For an interesting list of well-known Americans, past and present, who have collected guns, see Leonid Tarassuk and R. L. Wilson, "Gun Collecting's Stately Pedigree," The American Rifleman, Vol. 129 (July, 1981), 22-25+.

8. Serven, and Hank Wieand Bowman, Famous Guns from Famous Collections (Greenwich, Connecticut: Fawcett Publications, 1957), p. 5.

9. Serven, 30.

10. Bowman, 5.

11. See Ashley Halsey, Jr., "The Best Kentuckies--Old

or New?" <u>The American Rifleman</u>, Vol. 122 (May, 1974), 47.

12. Peyton Autry, "Collectors: Spendthrifts or Investors?" <u>The American Rifleman</u>, Vol. 122 (August, 1974), 27.

13. Elliot L. Minor, "The World's Costliest Gun," <u>The American Rifleman</u>, Vol. 121 (April, 1973), 24. Even more, $325,000, was paid in 1975 for a Scottish-made 17th century flintlock sporting gun, one of only two known to exist. It belonged to no one particularly famous. Sidney du Broff, "Antique Guns Are Where You Find Them," <u>The American Rifleman</u>, Vol. 123 (February, 1975), 29.

14. Robert Abels, "Great Guns Never Die," <u>The World of Guns</u>, presented by the Shooting Industry (Skokie, Illinois: Publishers Development Corporation, 1964), p. 53.

15. Halsey, 47.

16. Minor, 24.

17. Frederick Wilkinson, <u>Antique Guns and Gun Collecting</u> (London, New York, Sydney, Toronto: Hamlyn, 1974), p. 6.

18. For those who wish to see something Freudian in this, it might be noted that watches and pen and pencil sets are also used for such occasions now.

19. Wilkinson, 6, 18.

20. Macdonald Hastings, <u>English Sporting Guns and Accessories</u> (London and Sydney: Ward Lock & Company Limited, 1969), p. 40.

21. Jeff Cooper, <u>Fighting Handguns</u> (Los Angeles: Trend Books, 1958), p. 31.

22. Don Zutz, "First Rifle, Last Rifle," <u>The American Rifleman</u>, Vol. 122 (July, 1974), p. 35.

23. John E. Parsons, <u>The Peacemaker and Its Rivals: An Account of the Single Action Colt</u> (New York: William Morrow and Company, 1950), p. 87.

24. Michel H. Josserand and Jan Stevenson, <u>Pistols,</u>
<u>Revolvers, and Ammunition</u> (New York: Crown Pub-
lishers, Inc., 1972), p. 174.

25. Parsons, 31.

26. Josserand and Stevenson, 171.

27. Ibid., 175.

28. Ibid.; and Cooper, 29.

29. Parsons, 87.

30. Sometimes more modern revolvers that can be fired
double-or single-action are altered to look more
or less like the Model "P" by welding fake ejector
housings under their barrels. Guns so modified
are then substituted for the real thing in scenes
that call for actors to do rapid shooting. Model
"P"s themselves have been altered in Hollywood so
that in silhouette they look something like earlier
cap-and-ball Colts and Remingtons. These guns are
sometimes used in movies that depict events taking
place before 1873. See Charley MacDonald Heard,
"Hollywood Gunmen," <u>Gun Digest, Thirteenth Annual</u>
<u>Edition 1959</u>, ed. John T. Amber (Chicago: The
Gun Digest Company, 1958), p. 189, photograph.

31. Ibid., 192.

32. Colt's Model "P" with a 7½ inch barrel cost $374.50
in 1980, slightly more than that company's match-
grade .45 semi-automatic pistol, and approximately
$170 more than Ruger's single-actions of more ad-
vanced design. <u>Guns Illustrated: 1980</u>, ed. by
Harold A. Murtz and the editors of Gun Digest
(Northfield, Illinois: DBI Books, Inc., 1980),
pp. 131, 154, 157.

33. Colt discontinued the Model "P" again in 1974,
started again in 1976, and as of this writing has
decided to discontinue production again in late
1981 due to "current market and economic conditions." See Skeeter Skelton, "Is Colt's SAA At
the End Of the Trail?," <u>Shooting Times</u> (September,
1981), 32-35.

34. See <u>The American Rifleman</u>, Vol. 117 (August, 1969)

inside back cover.

35. See The American Rifleman, Vol. 117 (February, 1969), p. 9.

36. See The American Rifleman, Vol. 116 (July, 1968), p. 11.

37. The Shooter's Bible: 1940 Edition (New York: Stoegers Arms Corporation, 1940), pp. 117-121.

38. Joseph B. Roberts, "Muzzle-loading at Friendship," The American Rifleman, Vol. 122 (November, 1974), 23.

39. Joseph B. Roberts, "Still 'Fighting' the Civil War," The American Rifleman, Vol. 122 (July, 1974), 29.

40. Robert's,"Muzzle-loading at Friendship," 23.

41. Robert F. Jones, "Putting Some Fun Back Into the Gun," Sports Illustrated, Vol. 42 (February 10, 1975), 49; and Halsey, 47.

42. John Lachuk, "So What's Old?," Guns and Ammo 1973 Annual (Los Angeles: Peterson Publishing Company, 1972), 232.

43. Guns and Ammo 1973 Annual, 240-247.

44. See The American Riflemen, Vol. 119 (August, 1971), 12.

45. Guns and Ammo 1973 Annual, 232; and William B. Edwards, Civil War Guns (Harrisburg,Pennsylvania: The Stackpole Company, 1962), pp. 421-428.

46. Roberts, "Still 'Fighting' the Civil War," 29.

47. Roberts, "Muzzle-loading at Friendship," 23.

48. Lachuk, 237.

49. Ernest L. Reedstrom, Bugles, Banners and War Bonnets (Caldwell, Idaho: The Caxton Printers, Ltd., 1977), pp. xx, 198-203, 206.

50. Hastings, 24; and J. B. Roberts, Jr., "Museum at

the Range," The American Rifleman, Vol. 128 (November, 1980), 28-31.

51. Josserand and Stevenson, 289-291.

52. Ibid., 289.

53. Charles Chenevix Trench, A History of Marksmanship (Norwich, Great Britain: Harrold & Sons Ltd., 1972), pp. 77-101.

54. Edwards, 421.

55. See The American Rifleman, Vol. 119 (November, 1971), 6.

56. Wallace Beinfeld, "Collecting Commemoratives," Guns and Ammo 1973 Annual (Los Angeles: Peterson Publishing Company, 1972), 34-35.

57. Ibid., 35.

CHAPTER X

SUMMARY AND CONCLUSION

By the late 1960's there were at least 90 million firearms in civilian hands in the United States, if not considerably more, and the number has steadily increased. To some Americans, politicians, reformers, and intellectuals, considered by themselves and others to be philosophically as well as politically "liberal," this state of affairs is not "natural" for the "modern" parts of the 20th century world. No other modern nations, these social critics claim, have what one of them, historian Richard Hofstadter, called a "gun culture," as evidenced by the lower rates of firearms crime in other modern nations relative to the American rate. Since these other nations are assumed to have once had "gun cultures" of their own, it is further assumed that they no longer have them because they have rationally legislated their "gun cultures" out of existence. It then follows that the reason that the American "gun culture," considered to be the legacy of a frontier past, still exists is that vested interests have taken advantage of the weaknesses inherent in a federal form of government to keep our "gun culture" from being legislated out of existence like the others—the cultural lag-vested interest explanation of a state of affairs considered to be troublesome as well as unnatural.

Of course, firearms enthusiasts, philosophical and political "conservatives" and "libertarians," and others see the widespread civilian possession of firearms in the United States as neither troublesome nor unnatural, nor do they accept the cultural lag-vested interest explanation of widespread firearms possession, arguing instead that firearms are still around in numbers simply because they are still of use in a threatening world— the utilitarian explanation. However, the cultural lag-vested interest explanation has received much more media exposure and acceptance in intellectual, scholarly, and scientific circles than has the utilitarian explanation. In fact it seems to have been taken quite seriously as something more than a value-laden justification for reform in those very circles supposedly dedicated to promoting "objective" research into the workings of man and society, and as a result, little if any light has been shed on the phenomenon in question.

The cultural lag-vested interest explanation as
articulated by Hofstadter, is based on several questionable assumptions. One of these assumptions, indicated
by the use of the "gun culture" concept, is that firearms are somehow central to some overall American way
of life. Another assumption is that firearms once figured just as prominently in the ways of life common to
other now modern nations such as Canada, Australia, and
Japan. And still another assumption is that firearms
no longer figure prominently in the ways of life common
to these or any other modern urban industrial nations,
since their "gun cultures" have been legislated out of
existence. By accepting these assumptions, Hofstadter
could write of an American "gun culture" without giving
much attention at all to such grass-roots attachments
to firearms as their widespread possession in the United
States would seem to suggest actually exist. Since such
attachments, indeed even "culture," can be overcome by
legislation, as other countries have shown, the lack
of legislation rather than any popular attachment to
firearms accounts for the continued presence of firearms
in the United States according to him.

But Hofstadter's basic assumptions have all been
called into question in the first two chapters of this
book, and in the process, the differences between the
United States and other modern urban industrial nations
with respect to firearms possession by civilians has
been blurred to the point that the very uniqueness of
the American phenomenon has been challenged. While
there may be more firearms per person in civilian hands
in the United States than there are in other parts of
the modern world, and differences in usage exist from
area to area, we have seen that there is reason to believe that firearms possession is more widespread in at
least some parts of the urban industrial world outside
of the United States than Hofstadter and others have
taken for granted. This being the case, the widespread
possession of firearms in the United States, and elsewhere, for that matter, if still considered to be worthy
of special attention, can hardly be accounted for by a
lack of restrictive legislation. If this phenomenon is
to be understood, its social and existential roots can
not be ignored as those subscribing to the cultural lag-
vested interest explanation have done. In considering
these roots, however, the popular attachment to firearms, wherever it is to be found, is divested of any
special standing assigned it as a phenomenon by those
who consider it to be troublesome. It simply becomes a

popular interest an exploration of which can help us to
understand how men's interests evolve and are maintained through their interaction with others and through
their attempts to cope with their "objective" environ-
ments--"the world out there" as experienced by them--
which includes these others but is not restricted to
them.

While Hofstadter himself alluded to the practical,
recreational, and symbolic uses to which people have
put firearms, he failed to examine why guns are able to
function in these various ways or to explore the re-
lationships between these functions. Since these are
key issues, given the concerns of this study, much of
Chapter II was devoted to explaining how, in theory,
the recreational and symbolic functions of firearms
could derive from the practical function which itself
develops as men attempt to cope with "the world out
there." These theoretical considerations were then
linked to the phenomenon being explored--the American
popular attachment to firearms--through the six propositions of the thesis statement. Since this phenomenon,
as we have seen, is neither uniquely American nor minimally social as it has been treated with few exceptions,
these propositions called for cross-cultural and historical support. Consequently, in Chapters IV through
IX, firearms and their development and use have been
fitted into social-historical context in those parts of
the world, including the United States, referred to in
the West as "modern" and "free." It remains to relate
this material to the six thesis propositions by way of
attempting to support these propositions.

PROPOSITION I   Firearms are basically tools developed
by men to enable them to cope with objective conditions
as these conditions are socially defined and subjectively experienced.

The point being made here concerning the basic
tool nature of firearms, is not that they are objectively tools apart from the meanings attached to them by
people. To claim that guns are objectively tools would
not be consistent with the perspective upon which this
study is based, which has it that all meaning is socially constructed. The point being made is that firearms
in general and in their basic varieties were apparently
developed by men with clear-cut practical goals in mind--
enabling themselves and others to cope with their enemies or to put food on their tables--and that guns were

311

initially put to such practical uses where they originated and wherever they were introduced. The practical function came first, in other words, providing the starting point for all to be considered here. This none too controversial claim can easily be supported.

As we have seen, in Europe, where portable firearms seem to have originated, they were apparently used by men to cope with their enemies on the field of battle as soon as firearms had been perfected to the point where they could fire a projectile with enough force to do damage. This degree of perfection evidently was reached around the middle of the 14th century. No sooner had firearms been introduced into Japan during the 16th century by shipwrecked Portuguese merchant seamen who used them to cope with enemies themselves, than guns were adopted by the Japanese for military purposes. Firearms first came to the New World, Australian as well as American, in the hands of the explorers and the soldiers and sailors who accompanied them. Later the Europeans and their descendants who settled these lands used firearms not only to cope with their enemies but to put food on the table, the latter usage having originated in Europe by the early 16th century, if not well before then. And when we consider that however the 14th century handcannon or the most extremely specialized modern target rifle functions in the life of its modern owner, the former was designed as a tool of war, the latter evolved from a hunting and military tool, and both could still be used as weapons, it can be seen that the tool function of firearms remains, in a sense, basic to the other functions.

As can be seen from their design characteristics and the uses to which they were originally put, not only the first unspecialized portable firearms but the three basic types that have evolved from them--shotguns, rifles, and handguns--came into existence as men attempted to develop more effective aids to the accomplishment of specific tasks presented them by the "world out there" as men saw that world. The ancient handcannons were inaccurate and temperamental, but if used in numbers large enough to insure that something would be hit, they enabled soldiers recruited from the non-warrior classes to cope effectively with armored opponents. And handcannons evidently were first used by such people for such purposes, the warrior aristocracy looking on such weapons with contempt for almost two hundred years after they became available. Shot

fired from smoothbore barrels enabled hunters to increase the probability of hitting small animals and
birds at short range, and it was evidently first used
for such purposes by peasants and other commoners interested in putting food on their tables at a time when the
aristocracy was interested only in the recreational
hunts for larger animals and still disapproved of firearms. Rifling enabled marksmen to hit larger animals
and men at several hundred yards distance with projectiles large enough and fired with enough force to down
large animals or men in their tracks. While rifles may
have been used for target shooting as early as the latter part of the 15th century, these matches were evidently between men who ordinarily used such weapons to
hunt for food or to cope with enemies. Since the muzzleloading smoothbore could be loaded much more quickly
than the muzzleloading rifle, however, the smoothbore
rather than the rifle remained the primary military
small arm until the very end of the muzzleloading era,
since given the tactics of the day, volume of fire was
considered much more important than accuracy. The handgun adapted firearms to military use by horsemen and
provided any who felt the need for one--women as well
as men, weak as well as strong--with an effective defensive weapon that could be carried in readiness on the
person. The handgun may have first been used by cavalry, but the propertied classes eventually adopted it as
a defensive weapon.

The transformation of these three basic types of
civilian small arms from muzzleloading single-shots to
breechloading, cartridge-firing repeaters also shows much
evidence to the effect that men were attempting to develop more effective tools, but the distinction between
the practical and the recreational eventually becomes
blurred. As we have seen, the shotgun, as distinct from
the unspecialized smoothbore capable of firing shot, was
developed as such for the recreational uses of the elites
and then in its cheaper versions filtered back down to
the common folk for practical and later recreational
use.

If we consider that while men, animals, and material things may exist in some objective sense out there
apart from the categories to which symbol-using men have
assigned them, enemies to be eradicated, game to be
hunted, and property to be protected at the risk of
one's life have no existence apart from socially constructed frames of reference, it is obvious that the

313

conditions with which men have attempted to cope through the creation and use of firearms or any other tools have not been simply objective. From what has been said in Chapters V through VIII, it can be seen that in fashioning and using tools or anything else, men have not responded directly to conditions in the "world out there" as they "really were," but rather to those conditions as they have been socially defined and subjectively experienced--those conditions, in other words, as men have collectively come to see them. This point becomes particularly obvious when we consider that at a time when European peasants and other commoners hunted and trapped all sorts of birds and small animals to supplement their generally meager food supplies, aristocrats, or the wealthier ones at least, who saw themselves as hunters but who hunted as much for recreational as for practical purposes, considered birds and small animals to be unworthy of aristocratic attention. While birds and small animals existed as part of the "world out there" for both commoners and aristocrats, then, such creatures were viewed differently by those in one camp than they were by those in the other camp. Only commoners who depended on such creatures for food evidently received much encouragement from their peers to accept more efficient methods of acquiring small game. Aristocrats, on the other hand, were not only encouraged through their interaction with their own kind to ignore small game, but to continue to use older less efficient weapons and methods in hunting those animals collectively defined as acceptable game. Similarly, when we consider that among "gentlemen" of certain areas a mere word or a glance that would have likely gone unnoticed in other circles of the same time and place could get one involved in a duel, it becomes rather obvious that enemies to be dealt with in a given fashion are created as people interact with each other in terms of socially acquired frames of reference that they may or may not share with those by whom they feel threatened.

PROPOSITION II Due to the ramifications of man's social shaping through symbolic interaction, recreational and symbolic functions tend to derive almost automatically from the practical uses to which firearms have been put, the derivative functions beginning to develop almost simultaneously with the practical.

In Chapter II it was argued that the recreational function of firearms derives from the practical as a result of man's ability to use symbols, and the concerns

314

for self-images and the expectations of others, etc., that come with this ability. If anything should stand out in the preceding chapters, particularly Chapters VI, VIII, and IX, it is that firearms have neither been created nor used in a social vacuum. While few, if any, of those who have attempted to explain man's weapons-using activities have completely neglected social factors, no one seems to have considered the implications of their intimate, ongoing, interactive nature.

As we have seen, wherever firearms use has been common, those who have used guns well by whatever standards have come to be generally accepted have received a great deal of recognition from other users as well as those non-users who, for one reason or another, have acquired an appreciation for marksmanship skills. We have also seen that users have not only welcomed but eagerly sought after such recognition, and that they have not limited their efforts to the target range. Even as men have coped with their enemies or hunted for their food, they have done so as others, often others with a stake in the outcome, have observed them. Therefore, more than the shooter's mere survival has been at stake. Dime novelists, newsmen, and "the man on the street" eagerly followed the careers of the gunfighters of the American West, measuring the prowess of these gunmen by the number of opponents--"not counting Mexicans or Indians"--they had allegedly shot down and passing the score on to others and posterity. Far from having been upset by such attention on the part of their detractors as well as their admirers, many, if not most, gunfighters encouraged it, as can be seen from their willingness to inflate their career records for the benefit of the gullible. And what was true with respect to the gunfighters was in large part true with respect to those, in the New World as well as the Old, who acquired reputations as duelists. Among those obsessed with honor, the duelist's reputation was in large part based on the number of times he had successfully defended his, therefore, little attempt was made to keep the record secret.

So far as serious hunting goes, on the early American frontier where men had to hunt much of their food and others often depended on them, there was a very practical basis for concern over bag size. But that prowess was also judged by the number of animals of various types that hunters brought in seems indicated by the fact that they made something of a competitive

315

sport out of their practical food acquiring efforts long before hunting became more a recreational than a practical activity. Squirrel hunts that resulted in many more of these animals being shot than were needed for food were advertised in frontier newspapers and their results reported there. Team competitions were even conducted, and eventually hunters in some areas organized clubs and competed for championships based on the number of points they had accrued for shooting various types of animals over a given period of time. Later, on the western American frontier of the second half of the 19th century, men such as Buffalo Bill Cody built reputations on the number of buffaloes they had slaughtered for their meat and hide. In Australia, attempts to exterminate rabbits and kangaroos may have enabled those who used firearms on them to engage in this sort of reputation-building also, but since the sources used for this study provide no description of the interactional contexts of such hunts, such reputation-building has not been verified. For similar reasons, we cannot be sure that those European peasants, Australians, and Canadians who have found it necessary to hunt more for practical than for recreational reasons have generally been rewarded socially through the recognition of significant others for having done well at it. Given what has been said about the overall sociocultural contexts within which such hunts took place, however, it is difficult to believe that these hunters have not been so recognized, since after all, others have been dependent upon their success. This point will be elaborated upon further as PROPOSITION III is discussed.

But it seems obvious that marksmanship displays apart from those directly involved in the accomplishment of practical objectives, displays most often involving the use of inanimate targets in fact, have also provided practical shooters with an ongoing means of proving themselves to themselves as well as others. As gunfighters and duelists practiced to acquire and perfect the skills they would need to outshoot future opponents who might well be skilled marksmen themselves, they impressed their friends and admirers, shooters as well as nonshooters, and their prospective opponents if the marksmanship they displayed was particularly remarkable.

Hunters on the American woodland frontier shot more squirrels than they needed, "barking them off" if possible, to show off their hunting skills as much as their marksmanship, but when they drove nails or engaged in turkey shoots in competition with others, pure marksmanship was not only being displayed but compared as well. Since others depended on these frontier marksmen for food and protection, the marksmen received a great deal of encouragement from their communities to develop their shooting skills to the fullest. Those who came to be known as superior marksmen, therefore, received a great deal of flattering attention from family, friends, fellow shooters, and the community at large. In fact, as long as an American frontier existed, it seems to have been a common practice to judge the whole man on the basis of his ability to shoot.

In central Europe, extravagant festivals involving whole communities and lasting several days accompanied shooting matches arranged to encourage practical shooters to perfect their marksmanship skills in case they were needed to defend their communities. Those who won such matches not only received prizes of various sorts, some quite valuable, but were feted as heroes at the matches themselves as well as back in their home areas. In the early American colonies, militia training days pitted marksmen against each other and provided a large and appreciative audience to applaud the winner.

From what has been said so far, it would seem that hunters have proven themselves to themselves and others through their bags when and where men still hunted a large part of their food, and that marksmen have proven themselves to themselves and others by outshooting their opponents on targets when and where men still used their firearms primarily to hunt food or to cope with their enemies. It would seem safe to conclude, therefore, particularly in the light of further circumstantial support to be touched upon as PROPOSITION III is considered, that as practical shooters have interacted with others, shooters as well as nonshooters, in terms of their own self-images and the expectations of these others, the utilitarian uses to which firearms have been put have taken on added significance. The utilitarian uses have acquired an essentially recreational aspect that, as shall be seen later, can be maintained through interaction and continue to exist as the utilitarian gradually fades away or is absorbed by the recreational.

With respect to the symbolic function of firearms, it was argued in Chapter II that it derives from the practical as a result of man's ability to attach meaning

317

to things and socially construct reality through symbolic interaction with others. Particularly when carried openly on the person, firearms serve as badges that enable those individuals displaying them to mark themselves off as being worthy of special attention without even firing a shot. The gun "tells something" about the person carrying it, or at least someone assumes that it does. That objects can come to serve as status symbols goes unquestioned in sociological circles, but the claim here is that firearms have come to serve as status symbols wherever numbers of people have taken them up to cope with conditions in the "world out there." The most convincing support for this claim comes from the western American frontier of the last half of the 19th century where the handguns that a well-publicized segment of the citizenry regularly wore, as well as other guns, were obviously as much badges of the frontiersman and "tough customer" as tools to their owners. The comments of many of those who have written of the western American frontier attest to this, and they are supported by many photographs of frontiersmen displaying their weapons, or those provided by the photographers, as prominently as possible as if it were very important that the guns be noticed by future viewers.

Additional support for the claim that firearms come to function as status symbols wherever they have seen widespread practical use is largely circumstantial, however, except for a few brief comments by various writers and a few examples drawn from outside of the geographic areas being considered. It has been noted that portraits indicate that well into the 18th century Scottish noblemen carried ornately engraved all-metal flintlock pistols clipped prominently to their waistbands as badges of rank and warrior status. One writer has implied that fine pistols served to indicate that those who carried them were prominent men in the fur brigades of the early 19th century American frontier. Several other examples were cited in footnotes because they were in one way or another peripheral to the civilian use of firearms in the modern, urban, industrial world. In one of these, a historian claimed that there was a certain amount of prestige attached to carrying a musket in the English army of the late 16th century, while in another it was noted that Pathan tribesmen still regularly carry all sorts of firearms as badges of manhood as well as for practical purposes. It has also been mentioned that northern Brazilian ranchmen still wear revolvers openly and routinely as much, if not more, for symbolic

as practical purposes, and that Montenegrins wore huge
revolvers as part of their national costumes as late as
the 1920's. The circumstantial support for stated
claims concerning the relationship between the practical and the badge functions of firearms will be presented later. However, patchy and uneven though it may
be, taken as a whole the evidence that has been offered
above would seem to suggest strongly that when and where
guns have been widely used for practical purposes they
have also served symbolically to mark off those who
used them.

But the preceding chapters have also provided some
indication that firearms have served symbolically as other than mere status symbols to those who have used them
to accomplish practical goals. As we have seen in
Chapters V and VI, the weapons usage of the aristocracy,
recreational as well as practical, was bound up with
tradition and notions of honor which for some time made
members of this class contemptuous of weapons that allowed their users to avoid hand-to-hand combat. Eventually, however, firearms were not only accepted but
used to settle personal quarrels on the field of honor
itself, and thereby also came to be linked to tradition
and honor. We have also seen that in a feudal world
where the aristocracy attempted to monopolize the arms-
bearing privilege, arms possession and usage was also
a jealously guarded privilege to non-aristocrats such
as the townsmen of central Europe. To the latter, arms,
and particularly firearms, were symbolic of a certain
freedom from feudal control, a symbolic linkage that
European peasants also made and which eventually came
to be enshrined in the Second Amendment of the Consti-
tution of the United States. Though brief, these examples serve to point out that firearms have often symbolically linked even their practical users to phenomena transcending by far mere weapons usage.

PROPOSITION III Where objective environmental and
sociocultural conditions, as they have been socially defined and subjectively experienced, foster widespread
practical use of firearms, firearms will thereby tend
to acquire widespread recreational and symbolic significance which, in terms of the type of firearms involved,
their designs, and the form which the sports and hobbies involving them take, bear the stamp of the practical.

As was seen in Chapter V, European peasants well

into the 19th century were seldom blessed with an over abundance of food, the poorer peasants sometimes starving and even the wealthier ones feeling deprivation if the harvest was bad. Consequently, though they were primarily agriculturists, peasants often hunted or trapped the wild creatures that inhabited the countryside around their villages to add to their food supply even in areas where there was a nobility that attempted to keep them from doing so. When they were first introduced to the peasantry, firearms were probably seen as instruments of the devil, but eventually their usefulness as hunting tools obviously came to be rather widely appreciated and those peasants who could acquire firearms in one way or another did so. Since the European countryside into the 19th century could be a rather threatening place, peasants may also have recognized the defensive potential of firearms. But since few peasants traveled any distance at all or possessed much worth stealing, and most of them lived in close-knit villages which offered them security, the usefulness of firearms for hunting seems to have impressed them most.

In most parts of Europe, the guns the peasants managed to acquire were smoothbores whether they had been made for hunters or soldiers. This was an advantage rather than a disadvantage, however, since smoothbores could be loaded with shot to be used on the small game to which most peasants had access, or ball where there was large game to be hunted--or poached. Since little has been written regarding the use of firearms by European peasants, we cannot be sure whether or not there were recreational aspects to their use of firearms for hunting. And yet the relish with which poaching was carried on, regardless of the techniques used, and the probability that any game brought back to hungry dependents earned the hunter a great deal of flattering attention from them and envy from others, suggests that firearms did function recreationally as well as practically in the lives of those peasants who hunted with them. Whether this recreational side of hunting resulted in a scaled-down version of the competitive hunts of the American frontiersmen, we do not know, but surely bags were at least compared. Similarly, while we do not know that firearms functioned as status symbols for those peasants who possessed them, it is difficult to believe that they did not since only the wealthier peasants could afford to purchase firearms and others had to acquire them as best they could. In some areas firearms may also have served as symbols of re-

sistance to the attempts of the aristocracy to monopolize arms-bearing.

As was also seen in Chapter V, as firearms were
being transformed into ever more efficient fighting
tools during the 14th, 15th, and 16th centuries, the
towns and cities in which this transformation was taking place were attempting to free themselves from feudal obligations at the same time that many of them were
vying with each other over the development of trading
spheres. Burghers had reason to be concerned about
community defense, therefore; consequently, in central
Europe at least, they took it upon themselves to become
proficient in the use of firearms and other missile
weapons that could be used from the walls of their
cities. Since a premium was placed on accurate shooting, the rifle was perfected in this area and it soon
became popular with villagers who hunted large animals
in rugged terrain as well as with the town defenders.
With this practical interest in precision marksmanship
came the colorful and extravagant central European
shooting festivals, and though the rifles used in them
were evidently the same as those used for hunting and
war, their use in such matches obviously had much more
of the recreational than the practical about it. And
given the great interest in marksmanship that existed
at the time and the way that the marksmen themselves
were honored, rifles must also have served as status
symbols, though this cannot be supported through the
sources used. As noted earlier, however, rifles do
seem to have been symbols of a certain freedom from
feudal controls, a freedom cherished by townsmen.

Again from Chapter V, we have seen that the European countryside down into the 19th century was infested
by brigands and highwaymen, and that as peasants were
forced off of the land to swell the populations of the
cities, city streets and alleys became infested with
footpads. For the most part, only the wealthy who
traveled cross city and cross country and who possessed
something likely to be coveted by others had reason to
be concerned about robbers; consequently, it was the
wealthy who armed themselves against robbers. Once
stage travel replaced travel by horse, the pistol replaced the sword as the defensive weapon of the traveler, and since personal weapons were also used by gentlemen to settle personal quarrels at that time, pistols
also came to be commonly used for dueling. The prospect of becoming involved in a pistol duel, as much if

321

not more than the prospect of having to fend off robbers, seems to have encouraged gentlemen to sharpen
their pistol marksmanship through practice. At least
the exclusive use of the duelist's stance during practice sessions would lead one to believe that it was the
duel for which the shooters were preparing.

Of course, practice sessions also afforded gentlemen the opportunity to impress others and to earn themselves reputations in their own circles. But while
such target sessions were surely often accompanied by
informal competitions and wagering, they did not blos-
som into anything approaching the community sponsored
formal rifle matches of central Europe. This relative
lack of community interest in pistol matches may have
been due to the fact that only those at the upper social
levels were interested in pistol marksmanship which prepared one for a very personal and stylized form of combat of little use in the defense of a community. However, though formal pistol matches were not to take
place until the practice of dueling had nearly faded
away, special target pistols patterned after dueling
pistols came into being quite early. These target pistols had rifled barrels, while dueling pistols, in England and America at least, were smoothbored, therefore,
target pistols seem to have been made and used for recreational rather than practical shooting. Since the
traveling pistols and the dueling pistols used by gentlemen were generally finely finished, such pistols
must have been taken to reflect the social standing of
their owners. However, since traveling pistols were not
carried openly on the person and dueling pistols were
not routinely carried on the person at all, the badge
function of the pistols of 18th and 19th century Europe
was limited. However, dueling pistols seem to have
served as symbols of the honor that so obsessed gentlemen.

When Europeans came to settle the northeastern part
of what is now the United States toward the beginning
of the 17th century, they found large numbers of wild-
life--large as well as small--and the American Indian.
If the settlers were to survive, they had to hunt or
trap the former for food, and often enough, they had to
protect themselves from the latter. Since the descendants of these settlers along the fringes of the frontier were to face the same problem, dealing with white
enemies of one sort or another as well, until the late
19th or early 20th centuries, the distinction between

private citizen, soldier, and policeman was often blurred in America. The gun, therefore, was a very important tool to the American frontiersman as well as to the early settlers. The smoothbores the settlers brought with them from parts of Europe where the rifle was seldom seen, could be used with either ball or shot, therefore, they could be used for fighting as well as for hunting small or large game. Once the rifle was introduced by immigrants from central Europe, it became, in modified form, the favorite hunting and fighting weapon of the far-ranging American frontiersmen. Such men needed accurate weapons, since they could not carry much lead with them and had to make every shot count. The pistol also came into use early on the frontier as a backup weapon for the muzzleloading, single-shot rifles and muskets. And once the pistol became a repeater and the frontiersmen became a plains horseman, these small guns came into their own as offensive weapons.

But these various weapons functioned recreationally as well as practically in the lives of those who used them. Frontier hunters often made a competitive sport of food gathering, and from the earliest colonial days marksmanship was encouraged through militia training. Once the rifle made really precision shooting possible, however, shooting skill became the measure of the man on the frontier and was demonstrated and compared at every opportunity on the hunt and on targets in impromptu as well as organized matches. Recreational shooting with the pistol seems to have taken the form of "plinking" for the most part, though occasionally competitions based on the duelist's stance evidently were held. The guns used in these various competitions were ordinary work guns at first, but rifles and pistols with target refinements made their appearance toward the middle of the 19th century. Toward the last quarter of the 19th century, it is obvious that guns, particularly pistols worn openly, had become, probably with some assistance from dime novelists, journalists, and Wild West showmen, badge-like status symbols of the westerners. That guns of various sorts had served as badges of status on the frontier long before the late 19th century, seems likely but lacks such convincing support.

We have also seen that the sorts of threats from other human beings with which Americans had to contend on the frontier did not disappear with the frontier. In a little over three hundred and fifty years, that part of North America that is now the United States has been transformed from a colonial foothold in a sparsely populated wilderness into a powerful, independent, urban, industrial, socially and culturally pluralistic nation of over two hundred million people. As this transformation has taken place, people have often been pitted against each other on a day to day basis over many issues--revolutionists vs. Tories, northern industrialists vs. southern slave-owning agriculturists, blacks or yellows or browns vs. whites, new immigrants vs. old, management vs. labor, poor vs. rich, etc. Since such law and order as has existed at any given time has, understandably enough, favored those on one side of any given conflict over those on the other side, and since even the most effective law enforcement agencies have been unable to cope with the ever-present nature of the threat experienced by many private citizens, many Americans down through the years have kept firearms in their homes for defensive purposes.

The shotguns or rifles used for practical as well as recreational hunting have often served as home defense weapons as well. However, small pocket pistols that could be kept in a bureau drawer or carried concealed on the person have been reasonably popular as defensive weapons with all social classes, particularly since cheap revolvers of this sort became available toward the middle of the 19th century. Since these small relatively inaccurate pistols have been acquired for close-range defensive purposes, they have not fostered much of an interest in precision target shooting with the handgun, but they have added to the American grass-roots familiarity with handguns that has kept such weapons popular as informal target or "plinking" guns. Though these small pistols have not been worn openly, if carried on the person at all, they seem to have benefitted from and added to the glamor associated with handguns fostered by the more publicized usage of such weapons on the frontier.

When the French began to settle Canada, the conditions with which they had to cope were similar to those facing the English and others to the south. The French, therefore, used their smoothbore long guns in the same manner as did their neighbors. But the Indian threat that the French experienced in Canada had faded considerably by the late 18th century, and by the time the West of English Canada began to be settled in the late 19th century, relations between white and red were generally far more peaceful than they were south of the border. Similarly, a centrally-controlled police force and, relative to the United States, an orderly influx of settlers straight from the East made law enforcement less of a problem in the Canadian West. Consequently, the distinction between civilian, soldier, and policeman was not blurred in Canada as it was on the American frontier. Canadians, therefore, used their muskets, and later shotguns and rifles, far more for hunting than they did for fighting, and they seldom used the handgun at all. There is no reason to believe that practical hunting in Canada has not had its recreational side as such hunting has had in the United States and elsewhere, and recreational hunting and shooting competitions with rifle and shotgun seem to be as popular in Canada as such sports are in the United States.

As was seen in Chapter VII, a large part of the English speaking peoples who first "settled" Australia in the late 18th and early 19th centuries were convicts, and these people were not as free to look after themselves as were the first Europeans to settle in North America. But the free settlers and the convicts, once the latter were emancipated, had to cope with problems similar to those their North American counterparts had to face. The Australians had to provide themselves with food, and this encouraged them to hunt the wildlife which was plentiful in the coastal regions, but limited mostly to relatively small creatures. The Australians also had to provide themselves with protection from the Aborigines as well as from bushrangers. However, the Aborigines, with neither the horse nor the gun, were no match for the whites, and the bushrangers, combated by a strong but widely hated centrally-controlled police force, were worshipped rather than feared by much of the populace--working class and convict related as much of that populace was. Free Australians, therefore, used the smoothbore muskets and shotguns that were still the standard long guns of the English speaking world outside of the United States to hunt Australian animals that were generally classifiable as small game.

Since over the years Australian hunting has often been carried out to control pests as well as to acquire food, it would seem likely that bag comparisons have been made from the earliest days. Australians have also used smoothbores and pistols--and later rifles--to fend off Aborigines and bushrangers. But while Australian frontiersmen had to defend themselves occasionally, they were called upon to do little of their own soldiering and little of their own policing through vigilante movements. As in Canada, therefore, the distinction between soldier, policeman, and civilian was not blurred on the Australian frontier. Practical shooting by civilians has generally been limited to hunting by country dwellers in the past, then, and recreational hunting with rifle and shotgun still seems to be popular in rural Australia today. Hunting guns must have symbolized a new freedom for emancipated convicts, particularly those who had been transported for poaching, however, such symbolic linkages have not been supported in the preceding chapters. The handgun's use as a horseman's weapon was limited on the Australian frontier, and its use as a defensive weapon seems to have been even more limited in a nation that has been less transformed by urbanization, industrialization, and immigration than the United States has been.

PROPOSITION IV This tendency will insure that the widespread interest in and attachment to firearms will survive the fading of their practical function, or, if certain objective conditions continue to exist and be defined as threatening, support the continuation of the practical function.

When those European peasants who could acquire them began using smoothbores capable of firing shot to add to their food supplies, most Europeans were peasants, but most Europeans no longer are peasants. Now most Europeans live in larger towns and cities rather than in peasant villages. Most modern Europeans, therefore, not only do not have easy access to wild life, but with other food sources available and convenient, they no longer must rely on hunting and trapping to provide themselves with food. Even the country folk of modern Europe, however, being generally more prosperous than they were in the past and also having access to other food sources, have been forced to hunt for food only in times of the greatest scarcity--war, economic depression, etc. Yet as we saw in Chapter VI, shotgun ownership is apparently widespread in Europe. In countries such as France, small game hunting is so popular with urbanites who flock to the countryside to engage in it, as well as with country folk, that game has to be imported to meet the demand. While the game that these hunters shoot still ends up being eaten, the great commotion raised by the successful hunter's companions would seem to indicate that hunters are rewarded in other ways, ways in which successful peasant food hunters of the past must have been rewarded by those depending on them. Shotguns, therefore, are the instruments through which hunters acquire these social rewards. And when we consider that the European aristocracy once attempted to reserve the right to hunt for itself and that in England hunting is still largely monopolized by the upper classes, the activity itself as well as the weapons used for it would also be expected to have great symbolic significance for ordinary folk.

Long before firearms became available, European aristocrats had come to consider hunting prowess to be an aristocratic trait and hunts had become occasions through which skill with the horse and the fighting weapons of the time--swords and spears--or modified versions thereof, were developed and displayed before others. While the poorer nobility and country gentry may have used firearms for food hunting at an early date, by the time that the use of firearms in battle had helped to foster a more widespread appreciation for these weapons among a somewhat transformed aristocracy, the wealthy were hunting to impress themselves and others rather than for practical purposes. Once the gun became an aristocratic hunting weapon, the chief means the fashionably attired hunters had of impressing others with their hunting prowess was to shoot as much game as possible. This concern for numbers is indicated by the aristocratic mania for record keeping and by the publicity their records received. There was never any intention of consuming most of the game that was shot, on the large hunts at least, or of using it to feed others. Animals were preserved simply so that they would be there to hunt. In areas where deforestation left only small game, aristocrats became interested in bird shooting and encouraged gunsmiths to make the changes that gradually tranformed the unspecialized smoothbore capable of using ball as well as shot into the shotgun capable of hitting birds on the wing. Wing shooting was particularly challenging and eventually led to formal competitions using live pigeons as targets. As opposition to pigeon shooting under these controlled conditions increased, clay pigeons were often substituted for live birds. But the matches remained grand social occasions for the wealthy, titled or otherwise--occasions that offered shooters the opportunity to prove themselves to themselves and an appreciative audience. The shotguns they used not only enabled gentlemen to impress others; they also served as status symbols of the gentleman.

In Switzerland, where every able bodied male within a certain age range is in the militia and keeps his weapon at home with him, the rifle still figures practically in the lives of civilians as it did in the lives of European townsmen down into the 17th century. But for the most part, privately owned rifles in Switzerland, as well as other parts of Europe where such weapons are popular, are used for non-practical purposes such as recreational hunting and recreational target shooting. And the grass roots interest in target shooting in central Europe, though certainly affected by militia membership in Switzerland and by government sponsored marksmanship training programs elsewhere, seems to have originated with practical concerns that not only predate these government efforts but which faded long ago. As we have seen, the central Europeans shooting festivals survived by several centuries the concerns for city defense which spawned them. By the early 19th century, special target rifles that were eventually to become much too fragile and intricate for use on the field of battle were being used by target shooters to win trophies. The shooters also won the acclaim of others who still appreciated marksmanship and who made the marksmen aware of their appreciation through elaborate award ceremonies and much publicity. Such festivals were carried on as late as the 1930's in Germany, and though World War II may have put an end to them, target matches involving the use of extremely specialized rifles, even air rifles, are still popular across central Europe. These matches still allow exceptional marksmen to make names for themselves, even at the international level.

By the middle of the 19th century, though there was still considerable political unrest and class conflict in England and on the Continent, reasonably effective police forces had been established to maintain order and to look out for the interests of the propertied, and the countryside and city streets had been pretty well cleared of robbers. Of course, crime was not completely wiped out. The wealthy still carried, or at least owned, pistols, and once cheap mass-produced pistols became available, pistol ownership may have become more common at the lower levels of the middle class. Pistol ownership from the middle-socioeconomic levels on up may still be reasonably common over much of Europe today in spite of attempts that have been made to regulate handgun possession. But such interest in pistol shooting as has existed in Europe seems to have been fostered less by the practice of carrying or keeping pistols for personal defense than by a gentlemanly predilection (which is no longer indulged in) for settling personal quarrels through the duel. Even after dueling went out of style, target shooting with pistols that had retained some of the features of dueling pistols, as well as with revolvers, remained a gentlemanly pastime and afforded those who engaged in it an opportunity to earn themselves reputations as crack shots. Past ties to dueling may have made such reputations desirable. Eventually formal matches--based on the upright, arm extended, duelist's stance--were held and they are still held today, but appreciation for pistol marksmanship seems to have remained class specific in Europe.

As the American frontier moved westward, those who stayed behind no longer had to worry about Indian attacks, and as other food sources gradually became available, those behind the frontier no longer had to hunt to eat. With the passing of the frontier toward the end of the 19th century, therefore, American civilians no longer had to use their rifles or their shotguns for either fighting or the procurement of food. But as we have seen, hunting and target shooting--casual as well as formal--had become a widely accepted ongoing means of proving one's worth on the frontier itself. And since these activities were rooted in the recreational as well as the practical, there was no reason for interest in them to cease after only the practical had faded--and gradually at that. Consequently, in some circles at least, it still means something to be a hunter in the United States and hunters still prove themselves by bagging game, though they can no longer shoot as many animals as they once could without risking running afoul of the law. As in Europe, and with some European influence, formal target shooting with the shotgun as well as the rifle has developed in the United States, and more practical firearms have gradually been transformed into specialized target guns for use in these matches. Shooting champions are awarded trophies, medals, or firearms, and the best get the chance to compete internationally. The best shooters are quite celebrated in target shooting circles, but the major matches no longer receive the media coverage at the national level that they once received. Many more Americans engage in casual target shooting or plinking, how-

329

ever, than ever involve themselves in formal competition. Though no medals or trophies are given for such
informal competitions, cherished reputations as the
best shot in town, or even as the best shot in one's
circle of friends, are acquired in this manner.

Unlike the rifle and the shotgun, the handgun did
not cease to function practically in the lives of American civilians with the passing of the frontier. While
the handgun was no longer used as a horseman's weapon
once the horse and those who used it as a weapon's
platform disappeared from the scene with the frontier,
conditions that existed behind the frontier in the past,
and that still exist in many parts of the United States,
have encouraged many private citizens to keep such weapons for defensive purposes. As in the past, many Americans caught up in racial, ethnic, class, or other conflicts have found the law and its enforcers in the enemy camp or unwilling or unable to provide them with the
protection they felt they needed. Therefore, many Americans have resorted to the traditional and widely accepted American means of coping with threats from
others: they have acquired a handgun. But while the
handgun still functions practically in the lives of many
Americans, it also functions recreationally and what has
been said above concerning the rifle and the shotgun
also applies to it.

The mere fact that so many of the firearms that
have played such a prominent part in the shaping of the
United States are still around has given Americans the
opportunity to collect something that others consider
to be of some significance and to thereby impress these
others in the process. But the interest in collecting,
and particularly the replica phenomenon in its various
manifestations, seems to indicate that many Americans
are linked symbolically to their past and their traditions through firearms--a past and traditions that blur
the distinction between civilian, policeman, and soldier, and supports the civilian possession of firearms.
Interest in collecting and even interest in replicas,
as we have seen, is not limited to the United States.
Elsewhere, however, the linkages afforded through collecting and replicas are with different histories and
different traditions, as indicated by the interest in
matchlock replicas in Japan and the Englishman's interest in collecting sporting guns.

Most Canadians and Australians, like most Americans

and Europeans, now live in urban areas rather than in small villages or in the country, and neither they nor their country cousins have to hunt to eat. Yet Canadians and Australians, or at least some of them, still use rifles and shotguns to hunt as did their ancestors. In Australia, where rabbits and kangaroos are very numerous in some areas and are viewed as pests, the hunting of these creatures still retains its link with the practical. But though little seems to have been written about the interactional context of modern Canadian and Australian hunting, it would seem safe to assume that, as appears to be the case elsewhere, such hunting provides those who engage in it an ongoing means to prove themselves, a means passed down by their ancestors.

PROPOSITION V Objective environmental and sociocultural conditions in the United States, as they have been socially defined and subjectively experienced, have fostered the widespread practical use of shotguns, rifles, and handguns, while conditions, as they have been socially defined and subjectively experienced, that have prevailed in other parts of the urban industrial world have fostered the use of none or only one or two of these types of firearms.

This point should be obvious from the discussion of PROPOSITION III, but a summary of the main points still seems called for. In Europe the conditions with which firearms were used to cope were rather class- or region-specific; consequently, the weapons used were also class- or region-specific. Peasants had use for the shot- or ball-firing smoothbore which allowed them to hunt either small game, which was common all over Europe, or large game where it existed. Only in central Europe, with its rugged terrain and large game, did country folk have much use for the rifle, and the handgun was a luxury all but the wealthy could do without. The mountain folk of Switzerland and other central European areas had use for the rifle, therefore, as did the townsmen of that region who needed accurate weapons with which to defend their cities. The smoothbore could still be used on small game in that region, however, and loaded with several large-sized balls, it could even be used defensively. But whether shot-firing guns were used for city defense or not cannot be discerned from the sources used. The wealthy, titled or otherwise, of all parts of Europe had use for the handgun if they wished to protect their property, but for the most part, they used the smoothbore and the rifle for recreational rather than practical purposes such as food hunting and fighting. Gentlemen over much of Europe, of course, also may have felt the need to be familiar with the handgun due to the fact that it was used in duels.

In the early New World settlements, all classes had use for the musket since it could be used for hunting as well as the fighting that was necessary on occasion, and the rifle was so used once it was introduced. The use of the rifle or the musket for fighting, however, was much more widespread on the American frontier as it gradually moved westward than it was on the other two frontiers. Since they had to look out for themselves, ordinary as well as wealthy Americans behind as well as on the frontier also had use for handguns. In Australia and Canada, by way of contrast, handgun usage seems to have been much less widespread.

It will be noted that Japan was not touched upon at all as PROPOSITION III was discussed, the reason being that, as can be seen from Chapters V and VI, it seems that the practical use of firearms of any type by Japanese civilians has never been widespread. Indeed the rifle seems not to have been introduced into Japan until Perry's arrival, and handguns remained matchlocks, much more suitable as symbols of rank than as defensive weapons, until that time.

PROPOSITION VI Differences in, and for that matter, similarities between the United States and other urban industrial nations with respect to the civilian possession of firearms and related phenomena, can thereby be adequately accounted for in terms of the preceding.

This point should also be obvious from the discussion of previous propositions, III, IV, and V to be exact. The pattern of firearms possession in various parts of the modern world would seem to have been established in the past as men created and used guns to cope with conditions in the world around them as they saw those conditions. These patterns seem to have been maintained to this day, where the perceived conditions that produced them have continued to exist. The patterns have also been maintained where the recreational and symbolic usages which derived from the practical usages of firearms in the past have been maintained through the ongoing interaction of symbol-using men after the practical function has faded. All over Europe where the shotgun was once used by commoners for practical hunting or poaching, and for recreational hunting by the aristocracy and upper classes, shotgun possession is evidently still quite widespread. In fact, shotgun ownership may be more widespread now than it was in the past. In central Europe the rifle was once a practical hunting weapon as well as the quasi-military weapon of the townsmen, and it evidently is still commonly found there. Rifle possession in Switzerland is not only widespread, but government-supported. The handgun as the traditional weapon of the propertied evidently is still possessed, legally or illegally, by the propertied all across Europe. The shotgun and rifle used for hunting, and sometimes for fighting, in Australia and Canada are still commonly possessed in both nations, at least by town and country dwellers. In the United States where not only the shotgun or the rifle or the handgun, but all of these weapons have at one time or other been put to practical use by people at various social levels, all of these weapons are still commonly possessed. In Japan where the civilian use of firearms has evidently never been widespread, possession of firearms by civilians is still not widespread.

As can be seen from the partial treatment that some points have received as the preceding propositions have been dealt with, the cross-cultural picture of firearms use over the centuries that has been pieced together from various sources in the preceding five chapters contains some rather glaring gaps. So little has been written on firearms usage by ordinary Europeans, Canadians, Australians, and Japanese, present as well as past, that at best only a glimpse of the interactional contexts of such usage can be gotten through secondary sources. And we not only have no way of knowing with any degree of certainty how many firearms are in civilian hands in the United States, but in spite of the strict registration and licensing systems existing in other countries, we have no way of knowing how many firearms are in circulation elsewhere. Neither do we have any way of knowing with any degree of certainty, how widespread firearms possession is in the United States or elsewhere. For those interested in understanding civilian attachments to weapons of various sorts rather than polemicizing for or against such attachments, there are obviously many aspects of the phenomenon badly in need of investigation. But gaps notwithstanding, the picture painted in the preceding chapters does seem to provide some tentative support for the six propositions probing the social and existen-

333

tial roots of the American attachment to firearms.

BIBLIOGRAPHY

Abels, Robert. "Great Guns Never Die." The World of Guns. Presented by the Shooting Industry. Skokie, Illinois: Publishers Development Corporation, 1964.

Adams, Ramon F. "Cowboys and Horses of the American West." The Book of the American West. Edited by Jay Monaghan. New York: Julian Messner, Inc. 1963.

Allen, H.C. Bush and Backwoods: A Comparison of the Frontier in Australia and the United States. Sydney, London, Wellington, Melbourne: Angus & Robertson and Michigan State University Press, 1959.

Allen, William Sheridan. The Nazi Seizure of Power: The Experience of a Single German Town, 1930-1935. Chicago: Quadrangle Books, 1965.

Anderson, David D., ed. Sunshine and Smoke: American Writers and the American Environment. Philadelphia, New York, Toronto: J.B. Lippincott Company, 1971.

Andrzejewski, Stanislaw. Military Organization and Society. London: Routledge and Kegan Paul Ltd., 1964.

Angle, Paul. Bloody Williamson: A Chapter in American Lawlessness. New York: Alfred A. Knopf, 1962.

"Australia." The New Encyclopaedia Britannica, Micropaedia. 15th ed., I.

Autry, Peyton. "Collectors: Spendthrifts or Investors?" The American Rifleman, 122 (August, 1974), 26-27.

Bakal, Carl. The Right to Bear Arms. New York, Toronto, London: McGraw Hill Book Company, 1966.

Banfield, Edward C. The Unheavenly City: The Nature and the Future of Our Urban Crisis. Boston & Toronto: Little, Brown and Company, 1968.

Banton, Michael. "The Fragility of Simple Role Systems." The Sociological Perspective. Edited by Scott G. McNall. Boston: Little, Brown and Company, 1971.

Bates, E.S. Touring in 1600: A Study in the Development of Travel as a Means of Education. Boston and New York: Houghton Mifflin Company, 1911.

Bauer, Erwin A. Big Game Animals. New York, Evanston, San Francisco, London: Harper & Row/Outdoor Life, 1972.

Bayne-Powell, Rasomond. Travellers in Eighteenth-Century England. London: John Murray, Albemarle Street W., 1951.

Beinfeld, Wallace. "Collecting Commemoratives." Guns & Ammo 1973 Annual. Edited by Jack Lott. Los Angeles: Peterson Publishing Company, 1972.

Bensman, Joseph. "Classical Music and the Status Game." Games, Sport and Power. Edited by Gregory P. Stone. New Brunswick, New Jersey: Transaction Books, 1972.

Berger, Peter L. and Luckmann, Thomas. The Social Construction of Reality: A Treatise in the Sociology of Knowledge. Anchor Books. New York: Doubleday & Company, Inc., 1966.

Bierstedt, Robert. The Social Order. 3rd ed. New York: McGraw-Hill Book Company, 1970.

Billington, Ray Allen. "Frontiers." The Comparative Approach to American History. Edited by C. Vann Woodward. New York and London: Basic Books, Inc., Publishers, 1968.

Blackmore, Howard L. Guns and Rifles of the World. New York: The Viking Press, 1965.

_____. Hunting Weapons. London: Barrie & Jenkins, 1971.

Blair, Claude. Pistols of the World. New York: The Viking Press, 1968.

Boorstin, Daniel J. The Americans: The Colonial Experience. New York: Vintage Books, A Division of Random House, 1958.

_____. The Americans: The National Experience. New York: Vintage Books, A Division of Random House, 1965.

Bordua, David J. "Gun Control and Opinion Measurement: Adversary Polling and the Construction of Social Meaning." Paper read at the Annual Meetings of the American Sociological Association, New York, August 27-31, 1980.

Boston, Noel. Old Guns and Pistols. London: Ernest Benn Limited, 1958.

Bowman, Hank Wieand. Antique Guns. Greenwich, Connecticut: Fawcett Books, 1953.

_____. Famous Guns from Famous Collections. Greenwich, Connecticut: Fawcett Publications, 1957.

Boynton, Lindsay. The Elizabethan Militia 1558-1638. London: Routledge & Kegan Paul: Toronto: University of Toronto Press, 1967.

Brander, Michael. The Hunting Instinct: The Development of Field Sports Over the Ages. Edinburgh & London: Oliver & Bond, 1964.

_____. Hunting & Shooting: From Earliest Times to the Present Day. New York: G.P. Putnam's Sons, 1971.

Brown, Ina Corinne. Understanding Race Relations. Englewood Cliffs, New Jersey: Prentice-Hall, Inc., 1973.

Brown, Richard Maxwell. "The American Vigilante Tradition." The History of Violence in America. Edited by David Graham and Ted Gurr. New York, Toronto, London: Bantam Books, 1969.

Brusewitz, Gunnar. Hunting: Hunters, Game, Weapons and Hunting Methods from the Remote Past to the Present Day. New York: Stein and Day, Publishers, 1969.

337

Burch, William R., Jr. <u>Daydreams and Nightmares: A Sociological Essay on the American Environment</u>. New York: Harper & Row, 1971.

Burlingame, Roger. <u>March of the Iron Men</u>. New York and London: Charles Scribner's Sons and Charles Scribner's Sons Ltd., 1938.

Campbell, Mildred. <u>The English Yeoman: Under Elizabeth and the Early Stuarts</u>. New York: Augustus M. Kelley Publishers, 1968.

"Canada." <u>The New Encyclopaedia Britannica, Micropaedia</u> 15th ed., II.

Carr, Philip. <u>The French at Home: In the Country and in Town</u>. New York: The Dual Press, 1930's?

Carroll, Joseph T. <u>The French: How They Live and Work</u>. Newton Abbot: David & Charles, 1968.

Chater, Melville. "Dalmatian Days: Coasting Along Debatable Shores Where Latin and Slav Meet." <u>The National Geographic Magazine</u>, LIII (January, 1928), 47-90.

Clark, Manning. <u>A Short History of Australia</u>. New York and Scarborough, Ontario: A Mentor Book, New American Library, 1963.

Clark, Thomas D. <u>The Rampaging Frontier: Manners and Humors of Pioneer Days in the South and Middle West</u>. New York and Indianapolis: The Bobbs-Merrill Company, 1939.

Cole, G.D.H. and Postgate, Raymond. <u>The British People, 1746-1946</u>. New York: Alfred A. Knopf, 1947.

Collins, Whit and James, Garry. "The Custer Few People Know." <u>Guns and Ammo 1973 Annual</u>. Los Angeles: Peterson Publishing Company, 1972.

Cooke, Alistair. <u>Alistair Cooke's America</u>. New York: Alfred A. Knopf, 1973.

Cooper, Jeff. <u>Fighting Handguns</u>. Los Angeles: Trend Books, 1958.

Cruichshank, C.G. <u>Elizabeth's Army</u>. 2nd ed. Oxford:
    At the Claredon Press, 1966.

Cunliffe, Marcus. <u>Soldiers & Civilians: The Martial</u>
    <u>Spirit in America 1775-1865</u>. Boston and Toronto:
    Little, Brown and Company, 1968.

Daniels, Roger and Kitano, Harry H.L. <u>American Racism</u>:
    <u>Explorations of the Nature of Prejudice</u>. Engle-
    wood Cliffs, New Jersey: Prentice-Hall, Inc.,
    1970.

Davidson, Bill R. <u>To Keep and Bear Arms</u>. New York:
    Arlington House, 1969.

Dawson, William Harbutt. <u>German Life in Town and Coun-</u>
    <u>try</u>. New York & London: G.P. Putnam's Sons, The
    Knickerbocker Press, 1903.

Dentay, G.N. "Gun Control Canada . . . and the Visi-
    tors." <u>Guns Illustrated: 1980</u>. Edited by
    Harold A. Murtz. Northfield, Illinois: DBI
    Books, Inc., 1980.

Deutscher, Irwin. <u>What We Say/What We Do</u>. Glenview,
    Illinois and Brighton, England: Scott, Foresman
    and Company, 1973.

Diesel, Eugen. <u>Germany and the Germans</u>. New York:
    The Macmillan Company, 1931.

Dixon, Norman. <u>Georgian Pistols</u>. York, Pennsylvania:
    George Shumway, Publishers, 1971.

Douglas, Jack D. <u>American Social Order</u>. New York:
    The Free Press and London: Collier-Macmillan,
    Ltd., 1971.

DuBroff, Sidney. "Antique Guns Are Where You Find
    Them." <u>The American Rifleman</u>, 123 (February,
    1975), 28-29.

Dulles, Foster Rhea. <u>A History of Recreation: America</u>
    <u>Learns to Play</u>. New York: Appleton-Century-
    Crofts, 1965.

Dunbar, John Telfur. <u>History of Highland Dress</u>. Edin-
    burgh & London: Oliver & Boyd, 1962.

Duncan, Hugh Dalziel. _Symbols in Society_. New York: Oxford University Press, 1968.

Easton, Robert. "Guns of the American West." _The Book of the American West_. Edited by Jay Monaghan. New York: Julian Messner, Inc., 1963.

Edwards, William B. _Civil War Guns_. Harrisburg, Pennsylvania: The Stackpole Company, 1962.

_____. "Shootin' Irons." _This is the West_. Edited by Robert West Howard. New York: Signet Books, 1957.

Finnemore, John. _Social Life in England: From the Nineteenth Century to the Present Day_. London: A & C Black Ltd., 1956.

"Firearms: Laws and Use." A report presented at the First Australian National Conference, Perth, Western Australia, June 25-27, 1981, by University Extension, University of Western Australia in Association with The Australian Institute of Criminology and the Postgraduate Legal Education Committee, University of Western Australia.

Firth, C.H. _Cromwell's Army: A History of the English Soldier during the Civil Wars, the Commonwealth and the Protectorate_. London: Methuen & Co., Ltd.; New York: Barnes & Noble, Inc., 1962.

Forbis, William H. _The Cowboys_. New York: Time-Life Books, 1973.

Frantz, Joe B. "The Frontier Tradition: An Invitation to Violence." _The History of Violence in America: A Report to the National Commission on the Causes and Prevention of Violence_. Edited by David Graham and Ted Gurr. New York, Toronto, London: Bantam Books, 1969.

Funck-Brentano, Frantz. _The Old Regime in France_. New York: Longman's, Green & Co. and London: Edward Arnold & Co., 1929.

George, John Nigel. _English Pistols and Revolvers_. London: The Holland Press, 1938.

Glazer, Nathan. "Ethnic Groups in America: From National Culture to Ideology." _Minority Responses_. Edited by Minako Kurokawa. New York: Random House, 1970.

Greenwood, Collin. "British Gun Controls Don't Work." _Guns & Ammo_, (December, 1972), 33+.

_____. _Firearms Control: A Study of Armed Crime and Firearms Control in England and Wales_. London: Routledge & Kegan Paul, 1972.

"Gun Collecting As a Fine Art." _The American Rifleman_. Editorial, Vol. 121 (July, 1972), 20.

Guns & Ammo 1973 Annual. Edited by Jack Lott. Los Angeles: Peterson Publishing Company, 1972.

Guns and Ammo Guide to the Guns of the Gunfighters. Los Angeles: Peterson Publishing Co., 1975.

Guns Illustrated: 1980. Edited by Harold A. Murtz. Northfield, Illinois: DBI Books, Inc., 1980.

Halsey, Ashley, Jr. "The Best Kentuckies--Old or New?" _The American Rifleman_, 122 (May, 1974), 46-50.

"Hands Up!" _Newsweek_, (February 18, 1974), 57.

Hannon, Leslie E. _Canada at War_. Toronto: McClelland and Stewart, 1968.

Hanson, Charles E. _The Plains Rifle_. Harrisburg, Pennsylvania: The Stackpole Company, 1960.

Harbison, E. Harris. _The Age of Reformation_. Ithaca, New York: Cornell University Press, 1955.

Harding, Richard. _Firearms and Violence in Australian Life_. University of Western Australia Press, 1980.

Hardy, David and Chotiner, Kenneth L. "The Potential for Civil Liberties Violations in the Enforcement of Handgun Prohibition." _Restricting Handguns: The Liberal Skeptics Speak Out_. Edited by Don B. Kates, Jr. North River Press, Inc., 1979.

Hastings, Macdonald. <u>English Sporting Guns and Acces-</u><u>sories</u>. London and Sydney: Ward Lock & Company Limited, 1969.

Hatch, Allen. <u>Remington Arms: In American History</u>. New York: Rinehart & Company, Inc., 1956.

Heard, Charley MacDonald. "Hollywood Gunmen." <u>Gun Di-</u><u>gest, Thirteenth Annual Edition 1959</u>. Edited by John T. Amber. Chicago: The Gun Digest Company, 1958.

Heath, Richard. <u>The English Peasant; Studies: Histori-</u><u>cal, Local, and Biographic</u>. London: T. Fisher Urwin, Paternoster Square, 1893.

Held, Robert. <u>The Age of Firearms: A Pictorial His-</u><u>tory</u>. Northfield, Illinois: Gun Digest Company, 1970.

Higham, John. "Immigration." <u>The Comparative Approach</u> <u>to American History</u>. Edited by C. Vann Woodward. New York and London: Basic Books, Inc. Publishers, 1968.

_____. <u>Strangers in the Land: Patterns of Amer-</u><u>ican Nativism</u>. New York: Atheneum, 1970.

Hills, Stuart L. <u>Crime, Power and Morality: The Crim-</u><u>inal Law Process in the United States</u>. Scranton, London, Toronto: Chandler Publishing Company, 1971.

Hobsbawm, Eric. <u>Bandits</u>. New York: Dell Publishing Co., Inc., 1969.

Hofstadter, Richard. "America as a Gun Culture." <u>Amer-</u><u>ican Heritage</u>, (October, 1970), 4-11+.

_____ and Wallace, Michael, ed. <u>American</u> <u>Violence: A Documentary History</u>. Vintage Books. New York: Random House, 1971.

Hole, Christina. <u>English Home-Life 1500-1800</u>, 2nd ed. London, New York, Toronto, Sydney: B.T. Batsford Ltd., 1949.

Hollon, Eugene W. <u>Frontier Violence: Another Look</u>. Lon-don, Oxford, New York: Oxford University Press, 1974.

Hugon, Cecille. Social France in the XVII Century. London: Methuen & Co., Ltd., 1911.

Hunt, Chester L. and Walker, Lewis. Ethnic Dynamics: Patterns of Intergroup Relations in Various Societies. Homewood, Illinois: The Dorsey Press, 1974.

Johnson, Clifton. Along French Byways. New York: The Macmillan Company, 1900.

_____. Among English Hedgerows. New York: The Macmillan Company, 1899.

Jones, Robert F. "Putting Some Fun Back Into the Gun." Sports Illustrated, (February 10, 1975), 48-53.

Josserand, Michel H. and Stevenson, Jan. Pistols, Revolvers, and Ammunition. New York: Crown Publishers, Inc., 1972.

Kates, Don B., Jr. "Against Civil Disarmament." Harper's, (September, 1978), 28-33.

_____. "Handgun Control: Prohibition Revisited." Inquiry, (December 5, 1977), 20-23.

_____. Restricting Handguns: The Liberal Skeptics Speak Out. North River Press, Inc., 1979.

_____. "Toward a History of Handgun Prohibition in the United States." Restricting Handguns: The Liberal Skeptics Speak Out. Edited by Don B. Kates, Jr. North River Press, Inc., 1979.

_____. "Why Gun Control Won't Work." Commonweal, (March 13, 1981), 136-138.

Kauffman, Henry J. The Pennsylvania Kentucky Rifle. Harrisburg, Pennsylvania: Stackpole Books, 1960.

Keiser, R. Lincoln. The Vice Lords: Warriors of the Streets. New York, Chicago, San Francisco, Atlanta, Dallas, Montreal, Toronto, London, Sydney: Holt, Rinehart and Winston, 1969.

Kennett, Lee and Anderson, James LaVerne. The Gun in America: The Origins of a National Dilemma.

Westport, Connecticut and London, England: Greenwood Press, 1975.

Kiernan, V.G. "Foreign Mercenaries and Absolute Monarchy." Crisis in Europe 1560-1660. Edited by Trevor Aston. New York: Basic Books, Inc., 1956.

Klapp, Orrin E. Collective Search for Identity. New York: Holt, Rinehart and Winston, Inc., 1968.

Kluckhon, Clyde. Mirror for Man. A Premier Book. Greenwich, Connecticut: Fawcett Publications, 1963.

Kram, Mark. "Of Arms and Men They Sing." Sports Illustrated, (May 7, 1973), 60-62+.

Kukla, Robert J. Gun Control. Harrisburg, Pennsylvania: Stackpole Books, 1973.

Kvale, Nils. "Gun Laws in Scandinavia." The American Rifleman, 114 (July, 1966), 17-20.

Lachuk, John. "So What's Old?" Guns & Ammo 1973 Annual. Edited by Jack Lott. Los Angeles: Peterson Publishing Company, 1972.

Lake, Peter A. "Shooting to Kill." Esquire, 96 (February, 1981), 70-75.

Lang, Kurt and Lang, Gladys Engel. Collective Dynamics. New York: Thomas Y. Crowell Company, 1961.

Lantz, Herman R. with the assistance of McCrary, J.S. People of Coal Town. Carbondale, Illinois: Southern Illinois University Press and London & Amsterdam: Feffer & Simon, Inc., 1971.

Lipset, Seymour Martin. "The 'Newness' of the New Nations." The Comparative Approach to American History. Edited by C. Vann Woodward. New York and London: Basic Books Inc., Publishers, 1968.

Lopreato, Joseph. Italian Americans. New York: Random House, Inc., 1970.

Lott, Jack. "The People of the Gun." Guns and Ammo 1973 Annual. Edited by Jack Lott. Los Angeles:

Peterson Publishing Company, 1972.

Lugs, Jaroslav. A History of Shooting: Marksmanship, Duelling and Exhibition Shooting. The Centre, Feltham, Middlesex: Spring Books, 1968.

Manchester, Herbert. Four Centuries of Sport in America 1490-1890. New York: Benjamin Bloom, 1931.

Mannheim, Karl. Ideology and Utopia: An Introduction to the Sociology of Knowledge. Translated by Louis Wirth. A Harvest Book. New York: Harcourt, Brace & World, Inc., 1955.

Manning, Peter K. "The Police: Mandate, Strategies, and Appearances." Criminal Justice in America: A Critical Understanding. Edited by Richard Quinney. Boston: Little, Brown and Company, 1974.

Mantoux, Paul. The Industrial Revolution in the Eighteenth Century: An Outline of the Beginnings of the Modern Factory System in England. Harper Torchbooks, The Academy Library. New York and Evanston: Harper & Row Publishers, 1961.

Margetson, Stella. Leisure and Pleasure in the Eighteenth Century. London: Caswell & Company, Ltd., 1970.

Marshall, Jock and Drysdale, Russell. Journey Among Men. Hodder & Stoughton, 1962.

Matza, David. Becoming Deviant. Englewood Cliffs, New Jersey: Prentice-Hall, Inc., 1969.

McGivern, Ed. Fast and Fancy Revolver Shooting and Police Training. Chicago: Follett Publishing Company, 1962.

McGregor, Craig. Profile of Australia. London: Hodder and Stoughton, 1966.

McGuire, Frank G. "How Swiss Gun Laws Work." The American Rifleman, 114 (December, 1966), 44-45.

McKelvey, Blake. American Urbanization: A Comparative History. Glenview, Illinois and Brighton, England: Scott, Foresman and Company, 1973.

345

Meyers, F.S. "Right of the People to Bear Arms." National Review. (July 2, 1968), 657.

Milek, Bob. "Hunting Handguns." Special Purpose Handguns. Los Angeles: Peterson Publishing Company, 1981.

Miller, Payton. "Metallic Silhouette Handguns." Special Purpose Handguns. Los Angeles: Peterson Publishing Company, 1981.

Minor, Elliot L. "The World's Costliest Gun." The American Rifleman, 121 (April, 1973), 24-28.

Moars, Greg. "Combat Pistolcraft: Martial Arts or Gamesmanship." Guns XXVI (April, 1980), 30-31+.

Moore, Barrington, Jr. Social Origins of Dictatorship and Democracy: Lord and Peasant in the Making of the Modern World. Boston: Beacon Press, 1966.

Moore, Warren. Weapons of the American Revolution--and Accoutrements. New York: Funk & Wagnalls, 1967.

Moses, George Higgins. "Greece and Montenegro," The National Geographic Magazine, XXIV (March, 1913), 281-310.

Nelson, Robert, et al. A Pictorial History of Australians at War. London, Sydney, New York, Toronto: H.G. Paul Hamlin, 1970.

Newton, George D., Jr. and Zimring, Franklin E. (Directors). Firearms & Violence in American Life. A Staff Report Submitted to the National Commission on the Causes and Prevention of Violence. Washington, D.C.: U.S. Government Printing Office, 1969.

Nichols, Richard. "Tougher Leather: New Rules on Match Holsters Shake Up Competitors." Combat Handguns 2 (April, 1981), 36-39.

Nieburg, H.L. "Uses of Violence." Civil Strife in America: A Historical Approach to the Study of Riots in America. Edited by Norman S. Cohen. Hinsdale, Illinois: The Dryden Press, Inc., 1972.

Norman, A.V.B. and Pottinger, Don. Warrior to Soldier
    449 to 1660: A Brief Introduction to the History
    of English Warfare. London: Weidenfeld & Nicol-
    son, Limited, 1964.

Norman, E. Herbert. Soldier and Peasant in Japan: The
    Origins of Conscription. New York: Internation-
    al Secretariat Institute of Pacific Relations,
    1943.

Oakley, Kenneth Page. Man the Tool-Maker. Phoenix
    Books. Chicago: The University of Chicago Press,
    1958.

Oelkers, John S. "Track and Field." Motivation in
    Play, Games and Sports. Edited by Ralf Slovenko
    and James A. Knight. Springfield, Illinois:
    Charles C. Thomas Publishers, 1967.

Oman, Charles. A History of the Art of War in the Mid-
    dle Ages Vol. II 1278-1485. New York: Burt
    Franklin, 1924.

Page, R.W. Address at the Australian Institute of
    Criminology Conference, June 30, 1981.

Park, Joan. Travel in England: In the Seventeenth
    Century. London: Humphrey Milford: Oxford Uni-
    versity Press, 1925.

Parsons, John E. The Peacemaker and Its Rivals: An
    Account of the Single Action Colt. New York:
    William Morrow and Company, 1950.

_____. and du Mont, John S. Firearms in the
    Custer Battle. Harrisburg, Pennsylvania: The
    Stackpole Company, 1958.

Paxton, John, ed. The Statesman's Year Book 1980-1981.
    New York: St. Martin's Press, 1980.

Pear, T.H. English Social Differences. London: George
    Allen & Unwin Ltd., 1955.

Perrin, Noel. Giving Up the Gun: Japan's Reversion to
    the Sword, 1543-1879. Boston: David R. Godine,
    1979.

Polsky, Ned. "Of Pool Playing and Poolrooms." Games, Sport and Power. Edited by Gregory P. Stone. New Brunswick, New Jersey: Transaction Books, 1972.

Preston, Richard A. and Wise, Sydney F. Men in Arms: A History of Warfare and Its Interrelationships with Western Society. New York & Washington: Praeger Publishers, 1970.

Reason, Charles E. and Kaykendall, Jack L., ed. Race, Crime and Justice. Pacific Palisades, California. Goodyear Publishing Company, Inc., 1972.

Reedstrom, Ernest L. Bugles, Banners and War Bonnets. Caldwell, Idaho: The Caxton Printers, Ltd., 1977.

Richardson, A.E. Georgian England: A Survey of Social Life, Trades, Industries & Arts from 1700 to 1820. Freeport, New York: Books for Libraries Press, Inc., 1931.

Riviere, Peter. The Forgotten Frontier: Ranches of Northern Brazil. New York, Chicago, San Francisco, Atlanta, Dallas, Montreal, Toronto, London, Sydney: Holt, Rinehart and Winston, Inc., 1972.

Roberts, Joseph B. "Muzzle-Loading at Friendship." The American Rifleman, 122 (November, 1974), 22-23.

_____. "Still 'Fighting' the Civil War." The American Rifleman, 122 (July, 1974), 26-27.

Roberts, N.H. The Muzzle-Loading Cap Lock Rifle. Harrisburg, Pennsylvania: The Stackpole Company, 1938.

Robinson, John. "Handgunning in Australia." The American Handgunner, 3 (January/February, 1978), 24-27.

Rosa, Joseph G. The Gunfighter: Man or Myth. Norman, Oklahoma: University of Oklahoma Press, 1969.

Rubenstein, Richard E. "Rebels in Eden: The Structure of Mass Political Violence in America." The New American Revolution. Edited by Roderick Aya and Norman Miller. New York: The Free Press and London: Collier-Macmillan Limited, 1971.

Russell, Carl P. Guns on the Early Frontier: A History
of Firearms from Colonial Times Through the Years
of the Western Fur Trade. Berkeley and Los Angeles: University of California Press, 1962.

Rywell, Martin. Fell's Collector's Guide to American
Antique Firearms. New York: Frederick Fell,
Inc., 1963.

Sansom, George. A History of Japan 1334-1615 Vol. II.
Stanford, California: Stanford University Press,
1961.

_____. A History of Japan 1615-1867 Vol. III.
Stanford, California: Stanford University Press,
1963

_____. Japan: A Short Cultural History. New
York: D. Appleton-Century Company, Inc., 1936.

Schapiro, Jacob Salwyn. "Social Reform and the Refor-
mation." Studies in History, Economics and Public
Law. Vol. XXXIV No. 2. Edited by the faculty of
Political Science of Columbia University. New
York: Columbia University, 1909.

Schutz, Alfred. Alfred Schutz: On Phenomenology and
Social Relations. Edited by Helmut R. Wagner.
Chicago and London: The University of Chicago
Press, 1970.

Serven, James E. Conquering the Frontiers: Stories of
American Pioneers and the Guns Which Helped Them
Establish a New Life. La Habra, California: The
Foundation Press, 1974.

_____. "Some Thoughts on Assembling a Gun
Collection." The American Rifleman, 122 (March,
1974), 30-32.

_____, ed. and Trefethen, James B., compilor.
Americans and Their Guns: The National Rifle Association Story Through Nearly a Century of Service to the Nation. Harrisburg, Pennsylvania:
Stackpole Company, 1967.

Sharp, Paul F. Whoop-Up Country: The Canadian American
West, 1865-1885. Minneapolis: University of Min-
nesota Press, 1955.

Shibutani, Tamotsu and Kwan, Kian M.   Ethnic Stratifica-
     tion: A Comparative Approach. New York: Mac-
     millan Company and London: Collier-Macmillan
     Limited, 1965.

The Shooter's Bible: 1940 Edition. New York: Stoeger
     Arms Corporation, 1940.

Sieburg, Friedrich. Who Are These French. New York:
     The Macmillan Company, 1938.

Silver, Alan. "The Demand for Order in Civil Society:
     A Review of Some Themes in the History of Urban
     Crime, Police, and Riots." Criminal Justice in
     America: A Critical Understanding. Edited b y
     Richard Quinney. Boston: Little, Brown and Com-
     pany, 1974.

Sjoberg, Gideon. The Preindustrial City: Past and Pre-
     sent. New York: The Free Press and London:
     Collier-Macmillan Ltd., 1960.

Skelton, Skeeter. "Is Colt's SAA At the End of the
     Trail?" Shooting Times (September, 1981). 32-35.

Stearns, Peter N. European Society in Upheaval: Social
     History Since 1800. New York. The Macmillan Com-
     pany and London: Collier-Macmillan Limited, 1967.

Stenning, Philip C., and Mayer, Sharon. Firearms Owner-
     ship and Use in Canada: A Report of Survey Find-
     ings, 1976. Toronto: Centre of Criminology, Uni-
     versity of Toronto, 1981.

Stone, Gregory P. "Wrestling--The Great American Pas-
     sion Play." Sport: Readings from a Sociological
     Perspective. Edited by Eric Dunning. Toronto:
     University of Toronto Press, 1972.

Sutherland, Edwin H. and Cressey, Donald R. "Learning
     to be Deviant." The Study of Social Problems: 5
     Perspectives. Edited by Earl Rubington and Martin
     S. Weinberg. New York, London and Toronto: Ox-
     ford University Press, 1971.

"Switzerland." The New Encyclopaedia Britannica. 15th
     ed., XVII.

Tarassuk, Leonid and Wilson, R.L. "Gun Collecting's
    Stately Pedigree." The American Rifleman, 129
    (July, 1981), 22-25+

Taylorson, A.W.F. The Revolver 1889-1914. New York:
    Crown Publishers, Inc., 1971.

Thompson, F.M.L. English Landed Society in the Nine-
    teenth Century. London: Routledge & Kegan Paul;
    Toronto: University of Toronto Press, 1963.

Tilly, Charles. "Collective Violence in European Per-
    spective." The History of Violence in America.
    Edited by David Graham and Ted Gurr. New York,
    Toronto, London: Bantam Books, 1969.

Trachtman, Paul. The Gunfighters. New York: Time-
    Life Books, 1974.

Trench, Charles Chenevix. A History of Marksmanship.
    Norwich, Great Britain: Harrold & Sons Ltd.,
    1972.

"The United States." The New Encyclopaedia Britannica,
    Micropaedia. X.

Vagts, Alfred. A History of Militarism: Romance and
    Realities of a Profession. New York: W.W. Nor-
    ton & Company, Inc., 1937.

Varley, H. Paul with Morris, Ivan and Morris, Nobuka.
    Samurai. New York: Dell Publishing Co., Inc.,
    1970.

Vernon, Glenn M. Human Interaction: An Introduction to
    Sociology. 2nd ed. New York: The Ronald Press
    Co., 1972.

Virgines, George E. Saga of the Colt Six-Shooter and
    the Famous Men Who Used It. New York: Frederick
    Fell, Inc., 1969.

Ward, Russel. The Australian Legend. Melbourne, Lon-
    don, Wellington, New York: Oxford University
    Press, 1958.

_____, and Robertson, John, ed. Such Was Life:
    Selected Documents in Australian Social History
    1788-1850. Sydney and London: Ure Smith, 1969.

Waters, Edgar. "Recreation." The Pattern of Australian
    Culture. Edited by A.L. McLeod. Ithaca, New
    York: Cornell University Press, 1963.

Watt, Richard. Kings Depart: The Tragedy of Germany,
    Versailles and the German Revolution. New York:
    Simon and Schuster, 1968.

Wax, Murray L. Indian Americans: Unity and Diversity.
    Englewood Cliffs, New Jersey: Prentice-Hall,
    Inc., 1971.

Weaver, Robert B. Amusements and Sports in American
    Life. New York: Greenwood Press, Publishers,
    1939.

Webb, Walter Prescott. The Great Plains. Boston, New
    York, Chicago, London, Atlanta, Dallas, Columbus,
    San Francisco: Ginn and Company, 1931.

Weber, Max. The Theory of Social and Economic Organi-
    zation. Translated by A.M. Henderson and Talcott
    Parsons. New York: The Free Press and London:
    Collier Macmillan Ltd., 1964.

Weir, L.H. Europe at Play. New York: A.S. Barnes &
    Company, 1937.

Weller, Jack. "Hunting in France." The American Rifle-
    man, 112 (February, 1964), 24-27.

Whisker, James B. Our Vanishing Freedom. McLean, Vir-
    ginia: Heritage House Publishers, 1972.

Whiteley, J.H. Wesley's England: A Survey of XVIIIth
    Century Social and Cultural Conditions. London:
    The Epworth Press, 1938.

Wilke, Paul. "As the Blacks Move In, The Ethnics Move
    Out: It's not much fun to go home again." New
    York Times Magazine, January 24, 1971.

Wilkinson, Frederick. Antique Guns and Gun Collecting.
    London, New York, Sydney, Toronto: Hamlyn, 1974.

Williams, Stuart M. "Portrait of a Champion." Combat
    Handguns, 2 (April, 1981). 60-65.

Williamson, Harold F. Winchester: The Gun that Won the West. Washington, D.C.: A Sportsman's Press Book Published by the Combat Forces Press, 1952.

Wolfe, Tom. The Kandy-Kolored Tangerine-Flake Streamline Baby. New York: Farrar, Straus & Girous, 1965.

Wrong, Dennis H. "The Oversocialized Conception of Man." American Sociological Review, 26 (April, 1961), 183-193.

Yin, Robert K., ed. Race, Creed, Color, or National Origin: A Reader on Racial and Ethnic Identities in American Society. Itasca, Illinois: F.E. Peacock Publishers, Inc., 1973.

Zutz, Don. "First Rifle, Last Rifle." The American Rifleman, 122 (July, 1974), 35.

INDEX

absolute monarchs, 78, 81-82,
    102, 104-105, 166
air rifles, 123, n156, 328
Alexis, Grand Duke, 253
Alfonso, King of Spain, 115
Allen, H.C., 182
Allen, William, 6
amateur shooters, 217-218
"America as a Gun Culture," 3
American Revolution, 170, 178,
    185, 187, 222, 233-234,
    242, 265, 286, 297, 300
American Rifleman, 19, 24-25,
    33
American Violence: A Documen-
    tary History, 3
Anderson, James LaVerne, 255
Andrzejewski, Stanislaw, 74-
    75, 82
anomie, 34
anti-horsethief societies, 178
aristocracy, characteristics
    of, 82-84
"Armed Citizen," 24
automatic characteristics, 68
Autry, Gene, 291
Autry, Payton, 284

badge function, 36, 142-143,
    145, 149, 247-248, 259,
    266, 281-282, n302-303,
    318-319, 323
Bakal, Carl, 18
"barking off squirrels," 232,
    316
Bates, E.S., 131
Bell, Daniel, 195
bench-rest shooting, 237-238
Bierstedt, Robert, 4
Billington, Ray Allen, 167,
    179
Billy the Kid, 180, 290
Blackmore, Howard, 63, 119,
    133, 145
Black Panthers, 196
Blair, Claude, 66

blunderbuss characteristics,
    66
Boone, Daniel, 38, 227
Boorstin, Daniel, 170, 242
Bourbon, House of, 83
Bowman, Hank Wieand, 283
Boynton, Lindsay, 106
Brander, Michael, 107, 114
breechloader characteristics,
    67-68
British Home Guard, 125
Brown, Richard Maxwell, 175-176
Brusewitz, Gunnar, 110, 115,
    126
burghers, characteristics of,
    77-79
Burlingame, Roger, 225
bushido, 91

Caddell poll, 258
Cagoule Plot, 142
Canadian Northwest Mounted Po-
    lice, 178-181, 230, 263-
    264
carabine characteristics, 66
caracole, 131
carriage travel, 134-135
Carson, Kit, 246
cartridges, characteristics of,
    67
Cassidy, Hopalong, 291
castle towns, 90
Chesterfield, Lord, 218
Cincinnati Independent Shooting
    Club, 215-216
Civil War, 38, 185-186, 188,
    194, 216, 239, 242-243,
    246, 250, 259, 284, 286,
    296-299
Clark, Thomas D., 230, 232
Clay, Henry, 230-231
clay pigeons, 115, 216
Cody, William F. (Buffalo
    Bill), 248, 253, 290, 316
Coke of Holkham, 114
collectivism (Japan), 91-92,
    94

355

357

361